A HISTORY OF
HORROR
FEAR & THE
UNCANNY

A HISTORY OF HORROR FEAR & THE UNCANNY

CONTENTS

Before 500
ANCIENT FEARS

- 14 — Prehistoric Death Rituals and Burial Practices
- 16 — The Role of Fear in Hunter-Gatherer Societies
- 18 — Mesopotamian Demons
- 20 — Gilgamesh and the Underworld
- 22 — The Judgement of Souls
- 24 — Ancient Egyptian Ghosts and Demons
- 26 — Evil Beings in Hinduism
- 28 — The Goddess Kali
- 30 — Gods and Monsters of Greek Myth
- 34 — Fate and Revenge in Greek Drama
- 36 — Medusa
- 38 — Tales of the Pacific
- 40 — Buddhist Realms of Hell
- 42 — The Morrígan and Celtic Death Omens
- 44 — Roman Lemures or Larvae
- 46 — Senecan Tragedy
- 48 — Changelings in European Folklore
- 50 — Creatures of Slavic Folklore
- 52 — Monsters of the Maya
- 54 — Evil Beings in Chinese Tradition
- 56 — African Mythologies

500–1500
THE MONSTROUS MEDIEVAL

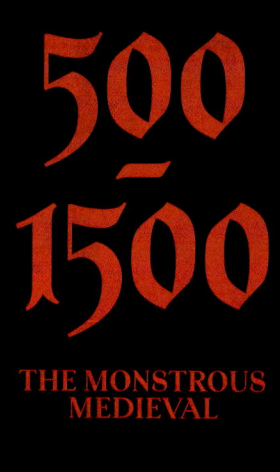

- 60 — Hell and Eternal Damnation
- 62 — The Last Judgement
- 64 — Spirits of the Silk Road
- 68 — Islamic Jinn and Shayatin
- 70 — Monsters and Demons of Heian Japan
- 74 — Gods and Realms in Norse Mythology
- 76 — The Wild Hunt
- 78 — The Ride of Asgard
- 80 — Beowulf's Foes
- 82 — Creatures of Indigenous Folklore
- 84 — Demonic Possession and Christian Exorcism
- 86 — Medieval Mysteries
- 88 — Horror in Arthurian Legends
- 90 — Monsters in Medieval Bestiaries
- 94 — Chaos and Evil in Kabbalah
- 96 — Dante's Journey Through Hell
- 98 — Into the Inferno
- 100 — The Dance of Death (Danse Macabre)
- 102 — Aztec and Inca Death Gods
- 104 — The Malleus Maleficarum and Fear of Witchcraft

1500–1700

EARLY MODERN ENCOUNTERS

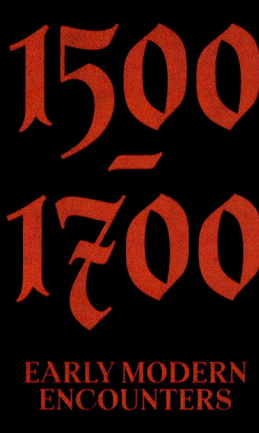

- 110 Latin American Ghosts
- 112 Renaissance Scepticism
- 114 Bosch's Hellish Visions
- 116 European Werewolf Trials
- 118 The Golem of Prague
- 120 Demonic Hierarchies
- 122 The Faustian Bargain
- 124 The Terrors of the Night
- 126 Supernatural Fears in Colonial America
- 130 Revenge Tragedies
- 132 The Weird Sisters
- 134 The Loudun Possessions
- 136 The Great Witch Hysteria
- 138 Vodou and Zombies

1700–1900

THE GOTHIC ERA

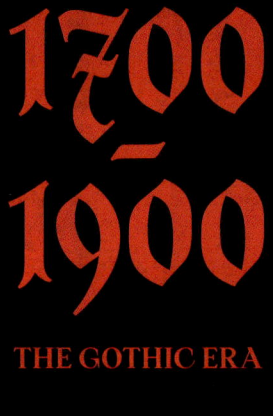

- 142 Vampire Panics
- 144 Cathedrals of Fear
- 146 Horror in Romantic Art
- 148 The Birth of British Gothic Literature
- 152 American Gothic
- 156 Edgar Allan Poe
- 158 Frankenstein and Science Fiction
- 162 Penny Dreadfuls and the New Newgate Calendar
- 164 Victorian Gothic
- 168 Gothic Opera
- 170 Ghosts and Bloody Pictures
- 172 Edo Ghost Art
- 174 Celebrating Halloween
- 176 Australian Horror
- 178 Vampire Fiction
- 180 Latin American Gothic
- 182 The Science of Fear
- 186 The Allure of Horror
- 188 The Grand Guignol Theatre

1500–1700
EARLY MODERN ENCOUNTERS

- **110** Latin American Ghosts
- **112** Renaissance Scepticism
- **114** Bosch's Hellish Visions
- **116** European Werewolf Trials
- **118** The Golem of Prague
- **120** Demonic Hierarchies
- **122** The Faustian Bargain
- **124** The Terrors of the Night
- **126** Supernatural Fears in Colonial America
- **130** Revenge Tragedies
- **132** The Weird Sisters
- **134** The Loudun Possessions
- **136** The Great Witch Hysteria
- **138** Vodou and Zombies

1700–1900
THE GOTHIC ERA

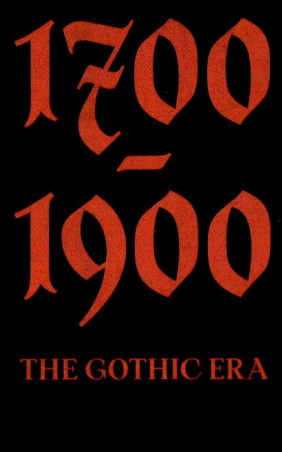

- **142** Vampire Panics
- **144** Cathedrals of Fear
- **146** Horror in Romantic Art
- **148** The Birth of British Gothic Literature
- **152** American Gothic
- **156** Edgar Allan Poe
- **158** Frankenstein and Science Fiction
- **162** Penny Dreadfuls and the New Newgate Calendar
- **164** Victorian Gothic
- **168** Gothic Opera
- **170** Ghosts and Bloody Pictures
- **172** Edo Ghost Art
- **174** Celebrating Halloween
- **176** Australian Horror
- **178** Vampire Fiction
- **180** Latin American Gothic
- **182** The Science of Fear
- **186** The Allure of Horror
- **188** The Grand Guignol Theatre

1900–1969

THE DAWN OF MODERN HORROR

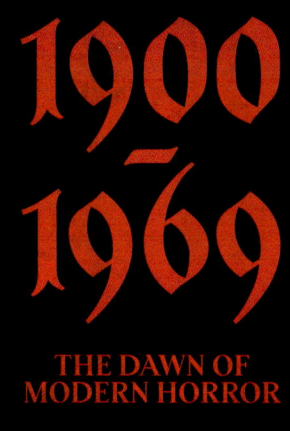

- 92   M.R. James
- 94   Cosmic Horror
- 96   The Phantom of the Opera
- 98   Dark Fantasy and Horror
- 200   Sigmund Freud and the Uncanny
- 202   The Cabinet of Dr Caligari
- 204   Nosferatu and Dracula Films
- 206   H.P. Lovecraft
- 208   Universal Monsters
- 210   Live Horror Radio
- 212   Disability in Horror
- 214   The Golden Age of Horror Comics
- 216   Horror in Modern Art
- 218   Horror in Surrealist Art
- 220   Comedic Horror
- 222   Hammer Horror
- 224   Godzilla, Kaiju, and Nuclear Fears
- 226   The Haunting of Hill House
- 228   Horror on Television
- 230   Psychological Horror
- 232   Giallo
- 234   Neo-Giallo
- 236   Zombies on Film
- 238   Youth Horror

1969–

PRESENT HORRORS

- 242   Stephen King
- 244   Body Horror
- 246   Feminist Body Horror
- 248   Blacula, Blaxploitation, and Beyond
- 250   The Rise of Feminist Horror
- 254   Occult Cinema
- 256   Jaws and Natural Horror
- 258   Suspiria
- 260   Slasher Films
- 264   Alien
- 266   New Wave Horror
- 268   The Asian Horror Renaissance
- 272   Twin Peaks
- 274   Diversifying the Horror Landscape
- 278   Horror Games and Entertainment
- 282   Found Footage
- 284   "Torture Porn"
- 286   New French Extremity
- 288   Horror on Stage
- 290   The Folk Horror Revival
- 292   A24 and "Elevated Horror"
- 296   Contemporary Black Horror
- 298   Eco-Horror

- 300   Ones to Read
- 302   Ones to Watch
- 304   Glossary
- 308   Index and Acknowledgments

University Press, 2023) and, as co-editor, *Folk Horror: New Global Pathways* (University of Wales Press, 2023). She has published more than 25 scholarly articles on horror and Gothic film, fiction, and television, and writes regularly for her *Horror Homeroom* website.

Katy Soar is senior lecturer in classical archaeology at the University of Winchester, UK. She is interested in the way archaeology and the ancient world are represented in popular culture, particularly as they relate to horror, folk horror, and folklore, and has published academic articles on these subjects. She is also a frequent contributor to *Hellebore* magazine and writes a column on horror for the British Fantasy Society's *BFS Journal*.

Hispanic studies at the University of Edinburgh, UK, and has a special interest in Gothic literature.

Daniel Cook is a professor of English at the University of Dundee, UK, where he teaches Gothic and horror fiction.

Johannes Dillinger is professor of early modern history at Oxford Brookes University, UK. His research interests include witchcraft, magic, folk religion, ghosts, and alternative history.

Ben Gazur is a freelance writer with an interest in history, folklore, and the cultural origins of horror.

Richard J. Hand is a professor at the University of East Anglia, UK, and a leading scholar in horror and performance studies.

Roger Luckhurst is a professor at Birkbeck, University of London, UK, where he specializes in Gothic literature.

Abigail Mitchell is a postgraduate researcher at the University of Southampton, UK, and a historian of early modern witchcraft.

Aditi Sen is an associate professor at Queen's University, Canada, jointly appointed in the Department of History and School of Religion. Her research includes extensive work on horror in South Asia.

Adam Smith is a UK-based film journalist and critic and a contributing editor to *Empire* magazine.

Andrew Szudek is a writer and editor with a long-standing love of horror.

Charity Urbanski is a teaching professor in history at the University of Washington, US.

Willow Winsham is an author and historian specializing in folklore and the history of the English witch trials.

Francis Young is a historian of supernatural belief. He teaches at Oxford University's Department for Continuing Education.

INTRODUCTION

The most basic definition of horror is something that inspires feelings of fear, unease, shock, or dread. Horror explores the grotesque, the macabre and the supernatural, but it also exploits psychological fears and the uncanny – familiar things that are somehow unfamiliar at the same time, and therefore deeply unsettling. The etymology of the word "horror" links it to the physical effects of fear on the human body: the Latin verb *horrere* means "to bristle, shudder, or be terrified".

Ancient narratives

Since prehistoric times, horror evolved from fears relating to survival – whether real or imagined. Folktales, and the beliefs they expressed, helped our ancient ancestors come to terms with the terrors that surrounded them, from predators lurking just out of sight and human enemies, to the threat of natural disaster, disease, and death. These stories may have inspired practical responses to fear, as societies developed rituals and religious practices around protecting themselves from powerful external forces, both in life and death.

The rise of modern religions around 3,000 years ago provided a new language of horror. Foundational works, such as early Buddhist scriptures, gave fear a moral dimension by describing horrors related to transgression and judgement. Concepts of hell, the punishment of misdeeds after death, and a host of tormenting devils fed worries about what might lie ahead in an afterlife. Christian writers and artists honed these notions into a rich iconography during the medieval era, with images of a fiery pit of Hell controlled by a monstrous devil – Satan – as a deterrent against sin.

Living fears

While scholars debated hypothetical horrors – such as the type of torture that awaited different kinds of sinners after death – plague, famine, and war made the macabre a part of daily life. By the late 15th century, anxieties stoked by these crises, combined with religious fervour, led to the terror of widespread witch hunts. During the late 17th and 18th centuries, Enlightenment thinkers challenged fears based on superstition – but the era of rapid scientific progress and industrial innovation also created its own horrors.

The expansion of human knowledge hinted at the vastness of what remained unknown. The resulting mix of awe and unease, along with fears that the traditional order of society was in peril, gave rise to Gothic horror and the birth of science fiction in seminal works such as Mary Shelley's *Frankenstein* (1818). Gothic horror explored grotesque bodily transformation and the terrors that plague the mind – inner torment, feelings of isolation, crises of identity, and hidden desires – laying the foundation for the later genres of body and psychological horror.

In the 19th century, a surging interest in the field of psychology prompted a deeper interest in the uncanny, with recognition that horror lies

Christian horrors
The Last Judgement (1440–41), by Flemish painter Jan van Eyck, depicts the terrible fate of sinners in Hell.

> "The oldest and strongest emotion of mankind is fear, and the oldest and strongest kind of fear is fear of the unknown."
>
> H.P. LOVECRAFT, "SUPERNATURAL HORROR IN LITERATURE", 1927

> "Monsters are real; ghosts are real too. They live inside us, and sometimes, they win."
>
> STEPHEN KING, INTRODUCTION TO THE 2001 EDITION OF *THE SHINING*

within us — whether the product of an inherently disturbed mind, or through the pressure of external forces. Malevolent entities were no longer restricted to dark forests or remote, crumbling castles, but were present in the everyday — within ordinary homes and on urban streets. Unsettling tales such as Charlotte Perkins Gilman's "The Yellow Wallpaper" (1892), a short story about mental illness and patriarchal control, showed that locking the front door was no longer a way to keep fears at bay.

Old and new threats

While scary stories had long been part of popular culture, the term "horror" was first used to describe the emerging film genre in the 1920s and '30s. Many consider this era to be the Golden Age of Horror, giving birth to Universal Studios' monster films and other influential classics, such as *The Cabinet of Dr Caligari* (1920) and *Nosferatu* (1922). Hammer Films was also founded during this period.

Over time, horror has developed myriad subgenres with their own tropes, and revivals of those genres that interrogate those tropes. The monster-heavy films of the 1930s gave way to more psychological takes on horror, while different schools of horror prioritized gore, special effects, or atmosphere. Many films have also straddled genres, bringing other influences into horror — from science fiction and fantasy to comedy. Much modern horror is self-conscious, commenting on its own origins and archetypes, as well as critiquing wider society.

Ever-evolving and seeking ways to reinvent itself, horror pushes at boundaries to test beliefs, fears, and expectations. The monsters and cautionary fables of the distant past may no longer be a source of genuine fear, but even these ideas have been reinterpreted, most notably in Folk Horror. This subgenre is characterized by remote settings, isolated communities with traditional, often pagan beliefs, and the idea of landscape and nature as a sentient power — old ideas and beliefs made new.

In recent years, horror has diversified to address issues of the modern world that scare us, including climate change and social injustice.

Philosophical questions

The horror genre engages with philosophical concepts, exploring existential fear, nihilistic violence, and the matter of free will. While characters notoriously make irrational decisions in horror films, they also embody the idea that humans have no true agency to control their lives. In the *Saw* franchise, the antagonist sets up game after unwinnable game, giving the involuntary players the illusion of choice. Horror narratives often present life in this way — as an unchosen and impossible contest.

Horror also questions our very perception of reality. In the film *The Cabin in the Woods* (2011), one character declares "We are not who we are". This idea is the very basis of horror: that we are not who we think we are — and that reality is not what it appears to be. Something darker lurks beneath, appearing in the cracks, defying everything we thought we knew. This book invites you to peer into that darkness — if you dare.

Rogues' gallery
Terrifying portrayals in horror include (top left to bottom right): Bela Lugosi in *Dracula* (1931); Boris Karloff in *Bride of Frankenstein* (1935); Herbert Lom in *The Phantom of the Opera* (1962); Vincent Price in *The Haunted Palace* (1963); Barbara Steele in *Black Sunday* (1960); Anthony Perkins in *Psycho* (1960); Sissy Spacek in *Carrie* (1976); Anthony Hopkins in *The Silence of the Lambs* (1991); and Lupita Nyong'o in *Us* (2019).

Before 500

ANCIENT FEARS

PREHISTORIC DEATH RITUALS AND BURIAL PRACTICES

THE WAYS IN WHICH OUR EARLIEST ANCESTORS TREATED THEIR DEAD AND DEPICTED THEIR SPIRITS SHEDS LIGHT ON SOME OF THEIR DEEPEST FEARS AND BELIEFS.

Understanding the beliefs of prehistoric people can be difficult, as we have no written records. Only their sometimes unsettling art, often featuring part-human and part-animal figures, and their archaeology can give insights into their thinking. These material remains suggest our ancestors developed complex notions about death and its role as a transition to an afterlife. They also show fear and reverence towards the spirits and supernatural entities associated with this realm.

Two human skeletons dating from around 160,000 years ago in Ethiopia show clear cut marks on the bones where flesh was stripped from the bodies before burial. Evidence of excarnation, as this is called, is also found in later burials around the world and has led some to think that our ancestors were routinely cannibalistic. Consumption of the dead may have been a ritual to link the deceased with the living – perhaps a means of harnessing their spirit or power. Others think it likely that the skeletons were simply being cleaned before burial and the flesh discarded. Exposing a corpse to the elements or to animals in an open site, or allowing it to decompose naturally in a cave, were other common forms of excarnation.

Cult of the dead

Once clean, the bones of the deceased might be collected for further rituals to manage the passage to the afterlife, or taken for burial elsewhere. A 33,000-year-old skeleton found in Wales named the Red Lady of Paviland (although the remains are now known to be those of a young man) has bones

Prehistoric spirit guide
Found in Brno, Czech Republic, in the grave of a man believed to be a shaman, this 26,000-year-old puppet may have been used in rituals to channel or contact spirits. It is made from mammoth ivory.

Ancient Fears

Harnessing ancestral powers
First Australians decorated caves and rock shelters that served as burial sites with images of powerful spirits such as Wandjina, ancestral rain spirits.

that have been dyed a vivid crimson with red ochre. This pigment may have symbolized rebirth and regeneration and was also used on skeletons unearthed in the ancient city of Çatalhöyük, a large Neolithic settlement in modern-day Türkiye. These bodies were buried around 9,000 years ago under the floors of homes that people continued to occupy. The dead therefore continued to "live" on in their family homes surrounded by their relatives.

Mediating with spirits

The importance of ancestor spirits and connecting with the dead is reflected in a series of 9,000-year-old skulls excavated in Jericho in the Jordan Valley. These skulls were covered in plaster that had been shaped to resemble a living face. Shells had been pressed into the eye sockets to give the appearance of staring eyes and the remains of paint suggested decoration to make the skulls more lifelike.

Grave goods, such as beads, tools, and pottery, buried alongside the dead from around 13,000 years ago, also show concern for the afterlife. Some appear to aid transition to the next world, others are offerings to spirits. The serious nature of dealing with these supernatural entities is evidenced by 9,000-year-old remains found at Bad Dürrenberg, Germany. Here a woman, believed to be a shaman, was buried with a set of deer antlers — most likely part of a headdress — and a rich array of animal teeth, shells, and tools. Analysis of her skeleton has revealed abnormalities that could have caused involuntary eye or body movements, which were perhaps taken as evidence of the woman's special powers. The burial suggests the high status of shamans in their unique role as spirit mediators between the realms of the living and the dead.

> "Some bodies were buried and years later exhumed, with certain bones removed, perhaps as ancestral relics."
>
> DR RICHARD MADGWICK, CARDIFF UNIVERSITY, ON IRON AGE BURIAL PRACTICES, 2016

THE ROLE OF FEAR IN HUNTER-GATHERER SOCIETIES

HORROR NARRATIVES MIGHT BE AS OLD AS HUMANITY. THE ART LEFT BEHIND BY PREHISTORIC PEOPLES SUGGESTS THEY EXPERIENCED REAL AND IMAGINED FEARS THAT SHAPED THEIR LIVES.

Lion man
Found in a German cave, this 35,000–40,000-year-old ivory figure with a lion's head is one of the oldest known pieces of therianthropic art.

Humans are religious animals. Every culture has some belief in the supernatural, suggesting that such thinking was an early evolutionary development. Emerging around 2 million years ago, the earliest known human communities were hunter-gatherer societies who lived by foraging, hunting, and fishing. They formed groups for survival in the face of dangers — animals, other humans, and natural forces.

Fearsome forces

Belief in gods and spirits may have been the only way for early humans to understand the dangerous and unpredictable world around them. These entities might help a person but could, if not respected, strike them down at will. Beliefs about supernatural punishment for transgressions may also have been a way for hunter-gatherer groups to maintain social cohesion. Those who were murdered or experienced traumatic deaths, for example, might return to the land of the living as ferocious spirits to wreak revenge by inflicting disease or madness.

> "[S]tories served as ways in which humans coped with their fears and dealt with uncertainty."
>
> STEPHEN ORTEGA, "FEAR AND AMBIVALENCE IN ANCIENT STORIES", *WORLD HISTORY CONNECTED*, 2017

Spirit art
Therianthropes, such as this creature drawn in Lesotho's Drakensberg Caves, may represent shamans fusing with animal spirits.

Archaeological evidence, including burial remains and grave goods, suggests that ritual activity helped to unite human groups in driving off threats and managing fears. Some items (such as the ivory beads found in a burial site in Brno, Czech Republic) are thought to have belonged to shamans – individuals believed to have special abilities to communicate and mediate with the spirit world.

Many myths and legends reflect ancient fears. It is thought that common modern fears – of the dark, of heights, of animals such as spiders and snakes, of isolation and the unknown, including death – also have their roots in ancestral threats. They are kept alive by storytelling, itself both a practical warning about dangers and a psychological aid to help people cope with fear.

Sacred and feared

Hunter-gatherers had complex relationships with animals, in which both were prey and predators simultaneously. In this context, animals were feared but also revered, fulfilling functional, symbolic, and spiritual roles. Much hunter-gatherer art (such as the rock paintings of Lascaux Cave, France, and the "Lion man" discovered in Hohlenstein-Stadel, Germany) includes images of therianthropes – animal-human hybrids. These may represent spirits inhabiting the natural world who were able to both aid and harm ancient humans. They may also symbolize the interconnectedness of the human and spirit worlds and those, such as shamans, who could pass between them.

The ability to feel fear was an evolutionary advantage. Evolutionary biologist Charles Darwin identified fear as a useful defence mechanism for mammals. Early humans who did not fear predators or outsiders were more at risk of being killed than their more cautious neighbours. Anthropologists studying some of the last societies to continue hunter-gatherer practices, such as the San people of southern Africa, often find that outsiders are regarded as both a physical and spiritual danger. Several groups fear specific neighbours for their supposed shamanistic and magical powers. This fear of others may lead to conflict, or to groups concealing themselves – perhaps explaining beliefs in the existence of hidden spirits inhabiting the landscape.

Eerie handprints
These paintings from Argentina's Cave of the Hands are 9,500–13,000 years old. They may be part of a hunting ritual.

MESOPOTAMIAN DEMONS

TO ANCIENT MESOPOTAMIANS, THE WORLD WAS FILLED WITH MALEVOLENT DEMONS WAITING TO AMBUSH THE UNSUSPECTING AND INTENT ON CAUSING DISEASE AND CHAOS.

Diverse civilizations, including the Sumerians, Akkadians, Babylonians, and Assyrians, occupied the region of ancient Mesopotamia – now centred on Iraq – between 4000 and 539 BCE. Despite cultural differences, all believed that the world was governed by supernatural beings, including demons. Capable of causing many misfortunes, from sickness to crop failure, demons were seen as a threat to both individuals and wider society.

Mesopotamian creation myths describe the birth of the first demons. An Assyro-Babylonian text, the *Enūma Eliš* ("When on High"), probably written between 1900 and 1500 BCE, states that the world was created when the sea, personified as the goddess Tiamat, joined with freshwater, the god Apsû. Their union produced a pantheon of younger gods whose behaviour was so rowdy that Tiamat conjured up legions of demons to drive them out. These included Uridimmu, a monstrous hound with the head of a human, and Ušumgallu, a terrifying three-horned snake.

One of the most notorious demons created by the gods, Lamashtu, was said to have the body of a donkey, the head of a lion, and bloody claws. Feared by pregnant women, she was believed to cause miscarriages, kill babies, and feed on the flesh of infants. Lamashtu was one of many demons believed to live in the Underworld, a hideous cavern deep underground. Among these, *galla* were particularly feared, as they were said to travel up to Earth to haul mortals down into the abyss.

Several demons were believed to exist as forces of nature capable of wreaking devastation. Anzû, the spirit of the southern wind, took the form of a

Overcoming evil
This carving from southern Mesopotamia, c. 2600 BCE, shows the god Ninurta confronting a fierce, seven-headed mythical beast. He has already severed one of its heads.

Demonic battle
In this drawing of a relief from the Assyrian city of Nineveh, c. 865 BCE, the god Ninurta wields thunderbolts as he chases down the demon Anzû.

vast bird with a lion's head and was associated with violent thunderstorms. Another wind demon, Pazuzu, is depicted as a monstrous figure with talons on his feet, a scorpion's tail, and spreading wings. Texts describe him as a destructive "king of the demons", but he also seems to have had a protective role in that he could break the wings of other demons to prevent them from harming others.

Escaping evil

Protection from demons was a major concern. Amulets bearing images of Lamashtu and Pazuzu, and clay cuneiform tablets recording prayers, spells, and incantations show the many ways people tried to ward off malevolent spirits. On a grander scale, the entrances to large buildings, such as palaces and temples, were often flanked by vast sculptures of winged, human-headed bulls or lions — beasts designed to scare demons away. If these measures failed, and demonic interference or possession was suspected, a priest called an *ašipu* could be called. A specialist in exorcism, he would drive out an evil spirit using incense, chants, effigies, and even knots tied in string, which were intended to trap the demon.

PAZUZU IN HORROR

The demon Pazuzu has gained notoriety in modern times as the deeply evil spirit who possesses a 12-year-old girl, Regan MacNeil, in the 1973 horror classic *The Exorcist*. Enacting a battle between faith and evil, the film follows two priests tasked with attempting to rescue the girl by exorcising the demon.

In this famous exorcism scene from *The Exorcist*, Catholic priest Father Karras struggles with Pazuzu.

> "Begone Evil, evil angel, evil demon, evil poltergeist, evil ghost /evil devil, evil god, evil spirit, Lamashtu."
>
> BABYLONIAN EXORCISM INCANTATION, c. 9TH CENTURY BCE

GILGAMESH AND THE UNDERWORLD

THE ANCIENT MESOPOTAMIAN *EPIC OF GILGAMESH* PROVIDES ONE OF THE EARLIEST ACCOUNTS OF THE HORRORS OF DEATH AND THE DISMAL GLOOM OF THE AFTERLIFE.

The *Epic of Gilgamesh* is one of the oldest surviving written stories and contains many of the tropes that shaped later legends of divine horrors and dreadful monsters. It also reveals ancient fears and beliefs about the nature of death, the afterlife, and the power of the gods. Based on Sumerian poems circulating around 2000 BCE, the tale recounts the adventures of Gilgamesh, a king of the city of Uruk, who becomes overly proud of his achievements and has to be chastened by the gods.

In their first attempt to subdue Gilgamesh, the gods send Enkidu, a ferociously strong man covered in hair. The two wrestle, but Gilgamesh brings Enkidu down and they become friends (or lovers, in some interpretations). Gilgamesh leads Enkidu to steal timber from a cedar forest guarded by a demon, Humbaba. They decapitate Humbaba, taking his head as a prize. Later Mesopotamians decorated buildings with images of this grotesque head as an apotropaic motif – a design to ward off evil.

Legendary strength
This alabaster statue of Gilgamesh, dating from 8th-century BCE Iraq, shows the hero overpowering a lion.

> "Seizing me, he led me down to the House of Darkness… along the road of no return."
>
> ENKIDU'S DREAM, *EPIC OF GILGAMESH*, TABLET VII

Powerful display
A relief from a 10th–9th-century BCE Syrian palace shows Gilgamesh between two demonic bull-men.

In the next instalment of the story, Gilgamesh spurns the advances of the goddess Ishtar (or Inanna, her Akkadian equivalent), ruler of love and war. Enraged, Ishtar reveals the horrors she can summon up as punishment. She says that she will smash open the gates of the Underworld and release the dead to walk the Earth where they will consume the flesh of the living. This may be the first mention of zombies in literature.

Cavern of death

Visions of the Underworld are fleshed out in a dream sent to Enkidu. The gods have decided Enkidu must die, and he is shown how the dead are sent to a House of Darkness under the Earth. Here, even the greatest kings are no more than servants and are forced to lay aside their crowns. The dead eat only dust and clay and must sit in the dark forever. This reflects ancient Mesopotamian beliefs that the Underworld was a real place – a gloomy cavern beneath the ground where the deceased met with Ereshkigal, the goddess of death. Unlike other mythologies, this god did not judge the dead. There were no rewards for those who had lived a good life or punishment for evil acts – the dead were plunged into a uniformly dismal afterlife.

When Enkidu becomes sick, Gilgamesh begins to understand the meaning of mortality for the first time. He is overcome with grief when Enkidu dies, only accepting that his friend is gone when Enkidu's corpse begins to rot. Humanity's greatest fear – death – is made clear. Gilgamesh spends the rest of his epic on a quest to find immortality but, in the end, death is the one foe he cannot defeat.

THE JUDGEMENT OF SOULS

THE CULTURES OF ANCIENT EGYPT AND ANCIENT GREECE QUESTIONED WHAT IT TOOK FOR PEOPLE TO AVOID HORRIFYING FATES AFTER DEATH.

Heart and feather
This ancient Egyptian stone carving from Deir el Medina depicts the gods Horus and Anubis weighing a man's heart against a feather.

Few people have been as focused on death as the ancient Egyptians, who are known for their towering pyramids, gorgeously decorated tombs, and complex mummification procedures. The Egyptians believed people had a life essence (*ka*) and spirit, or personality (*ba*). When an Egyptian died, the *ba* would traverse the Underworld and pass through a series of gates that were guarded by various spirits. Those who knew the correct prayers would be allowed to pass; those who did not would face the wrath of a variety of monstrous creatures. Once the *ba* crossed the Underworld, it faced a test of purity and, finally, judgement.

Egyptian judgement
In the Hall of Maat, the Egyptian soul faced jackal-headed Anubis, god of mummification and the afterlife, who weighed its heart against a feather, representing truth. If the heart was lighter than the feather, then the soul was ushered into the Land of Reeds, a heavenly paradise ruled by the god Osiris, and the *ka* and *ba* united to form the *akh*, or eternal spirit. If the heart was heavier, due to the immoral life led by the deceased, then the soul was immediately devoured by the goddess Ammit (or Ammut), whose name means "swallower of the dead". Ammit was depicted as having the head of a crocodile, the body of a lion, and the back legs of a hippopotamus – the three animals the Egyptians most feared. Once a soul was consumed by Ammit's ravenous jaws, it ceased to exist forever.

Greek tortures
Homer's epic poems *The Iliad* and *The Odyssey*, composed in the late 8th or early 7th century BCE, suggest that the ancient Greeks believed most people ended up in the same featureless afterlife, which contained none of life's joys. According to broader Greek mythology, however, those who truly offended the gods were doomed to eternal torment in a pit known as Tartarus. The judges of Greek souls were Minos, Aeacus, and Rhadamanthus, the mortal sons of Zeus, king of the gods.

The punishments meted out by these ruthless judges were inventive, based on the culprit's deeds. For example, King Tantalus attempted to trick the gods by murdering his own son and serving him as a meal to his divine guests. When the gods discovered this, they placed Tantalus in a pool overhung by branches laden with tempting fruit. Whenever he attempted to eat, the branches moved out of reach, and whenever he tried to drink, the pool's waters receded, leaving him eternally hungry and thirsty. Likewise, Sisyphus, king of Corinth, was guilty of many deceptions. He was sentenced to push a boulder up a hill for eternity – before its summit, the rock always rolled back down to the bottom. Another wicked ruler, Ixion, king of the Lapiths, was strapped to an ever-turning wheel of fire after murdering his father-in-law and lusting after Zeus's wife, Hera.

Fiery punishment
A painting on an ancient Greek amphora from the late 4th century BCE illustrates the myth of King Ixion, who was tied to an endlessly spinning fiery wheel to punish his crimes.

Preserved pharaoh
This mummy of Ramses II (1297-1213 BCE) reflects ancient Egyptian beliefs that the deceased needed a body in the afterlife.

ANCIENT EGYPTIAN GHOSTS AND DEMONS

WHETHER CREATING CHAOS OR FIGHTING IT, TERRIFYING SPIRITS WERE BELIEVED TO PLAY A VITAL ROLE IN THE DAY-TO-DAY LIFE OF ANCIENT EGYPTIANS.

The ancient Egyptians held deep spiritual beliefs, and their greatest fears were closely tied to their understanding of religion, the afterlife, and cosmic order. Above all, they feared chaos, or *isfet*, which represented disorder, darkness, and destruction. It stood in direct opposition to *ma'at*, the principle of truth, balance, and harmony that maintained the Universe. The loss of *ma'at*, through events such as war, natural disasters, or moral decay, was seen as a threat to both society and the cosmos itself. Supernatural entities such as gods, demons, and ghosts were believed to play an important role in maintaining this delicate cosmic balance: malevolent demons might disrupt *ma'at* by sowing chaos and discord, while benevolent spirits upheld *ma'at* through help, guidance, and support.

Demonic disruptors

In view of the value placed on harmony, Set (or Seth) was one of the most feared Egyptian gods. The god of chaos, storms, deserts, and violence, he was infamous for murdering his brother Osiris in a foundational myth that symbolized the disruption of *ma'at*. The lion-headed goddess Sekhmet also inspired great fear. Rumoured to drink the blood of humans, she was associated with war, destruction, and plagues. A myth describes her brutally attacking humanity for disobeying the Sun god Ra.

A host of unruly demons could also disrupt the natural order. One of these, the serpent demon Apophis (also called Apep), represented pure chaos and evil. He sought to destroy the Sun each night by attacking Ra's solar barque as it travelled through the Underworld. Ancient Egyptians believed that if Apophis succeeded, the Sun would not rise the next morning, plunging the world into eternal darkness.

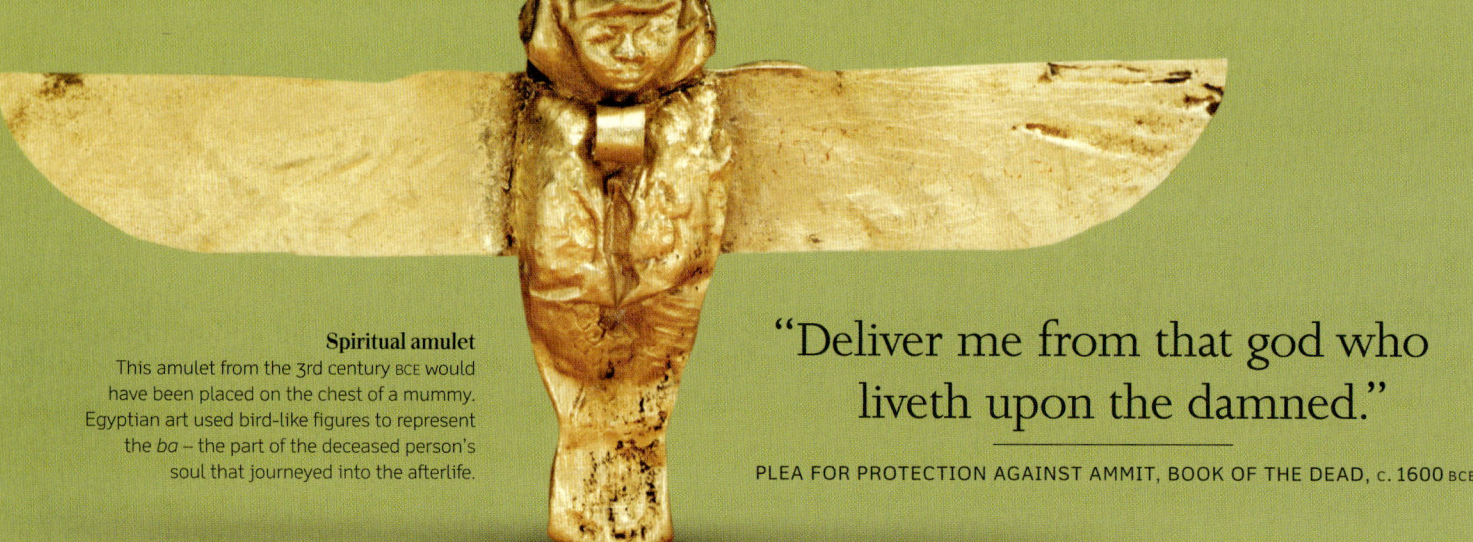

Spiritual amulet
This amulet from the 3rd century BCE would have been placed on the chest of a mummy. Egyptian art used bird-like figures to represent the *ba* – the part of the deceased person's soul that journeyed into the afterlife.

> "Deliver me from that god who liveth upon the damned."
>
> PLEA FOR PROTECTION AGAINST AMMIT, BOOK OF THE DEAD, c. 1600 BCE

Restoring order
The Sun god Ra, in the form of a cat, slays the serpent demon Apophis under a sacred sycamore tree in this wall painting representing the cosmic battle between order and chaos from the Tomb of Inherkau, Thebes, constructed c.1186–1149 BCE.

Ammit (or Ammut) was another demonic resident of the Underworld. A terrifying crocodile-lion-hippopotamus hybrid, Ammit devoured the hearts of those deemed unworthy of entering the afterlife. Condemning souls to oblivion, she represented the loss of eternal life and extinction from the cosmos.

Spirits of the dead
Fears of disorder extended beyond life into death and the afterlife. The story of Khonsuemheb and the ghost from the Ramesside Period (c.1292–c.1077 BCE), sometimes called the first recorded ghost story, shows how failure to follow correct protocol after death might lead to restless spirits disturbing the living. In the tale, the ghost of a Middle Kingdom official, Nebusemekh, haunts a priest, Khonsuemheb, because his tomb is in need of repair. While Nebusemekh is portrayed as a benign ghost, there is evidence of belief in more malicious ones. The 3rd-century CE *Demotic Magical Papyrus of London and Leiden* contains spells for conjuring damned spirits, but warns practitioners to take care: evil spirits were thought to be able to reanimate corpses, and summoning the dead risked invoking the wrath of the god Osiris.

CURSED MUMMIES IN HORROR FILMS

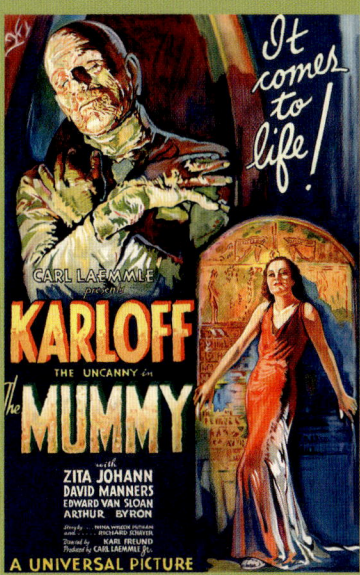

Ancient Egyptian beliefs have provided fiction writers and filmmakers with an irresistible cast of monsters, ghosts, and demons. One of the most famous is the cursed mummy, popularized by the 1932 film, *The Mummy*. Telling the story of an ancient Egyptian prince, Imhotep (played by Boris Karloff), who is resurrected as a mummy, the film blended ancient myths with early 20th-century fears of the supernatural, creating a lasting archetype of the undead mummy within the horror genre.

EVIL BEINGS IN HINDUISM

DESTRUCTIVE SPIRITS IN HINDU BELIEFS ARE NOT ALWAYS LINKED TO VIOLENCE, HARM, AND DARKNESS. THEY HAVE MANY FUNCTIONS, REPRESENTING THE COMPLEX NATURE OF RIGHT AND WRONG.

Hinduism does not have a binary worldview of good and evil, and this is reflected in its portrayal of evil beings, many of which serve a dual purpose or have both good and evil characteristics. However, they may still be feared for the violence and chaos they inflict. Common ways to ward off evil spirits include chanting holy mantras, wearing a protective amulet, and avoiding spaces where they lurk.

Chaos and destruction

The earliest Hindu texts, composed around 1500–1200 BCE, describe some gods as *asuras* – powerful, and sometimes ruthless, rulers. Over time, however, this term acquired more negative connotations and by 1000 BCE was being used to denote malevolent beings or demons who opposed benevolent deities (the *devas*). In one ancient tale, Mahishasura, the famous buffalo *asura*, is slain by the goddess Durga after a 10-day battle. Although not all *asuras* are destructive, they often represent forces that challenge the existing order.

Other agents of chaos include *rakshasas* and their female counterparts, *rakshasis* – supernatural beings believed to dwell in forests. The two major Indian epics, the *Mahabharata* and the *Ramayana*, contain many tales about these demons, who are frequently portrayed as violent, ruthless, man-eating creatures. Like *asuras*, they are not purely evil, and are often simply defending their forests from human encroachment. Some *rakshasas* are also depicted as wise and opposed to violence.

Facing a tyrant
The *asura* Surapadma rises from the sea to fight the warrior god Kartikeya (or Murugan). Ancient Hindu texts describe how this *asura* and his siblings oppressed humankind.

Ancient Fears

Pishachas are ghouls who live in cremation grounds, graveyards, deep forests, and dark caverns. They are the only group of spirits who are totally evil, with the sole objective of causing harm. Usually intent on killing, they also shapeshift to torment people. The *Mahabharata* describes *pishachas* as cannibalistic demons. They are blamed for madness, possession, and nightmares, and feared for their insatiable hunger for human flesh.

Vetalas are vampires, and sometimes seen as a sub-group of *pishachas*. Associated with bats, they are often accused of slowly draining people of their life force. Yet the *Vetala Panchavimshati* ("Twenty-Five Tales of the Vetala"), from around the 11th century, relates the adventures of King Vikram and a *vetala* who tells him moral stories to test his knowledge of justice and righteousness. This *vetala* is depicted as knowledgeable, not evil.

Bhutas are ghosts of the departed who linger on Earth to sort out unsettled issues. The character of a *bhuta* depends on the nature of their unresolved problem and their cause of death. They can possess the living, inflict curses, and seek vengeance on those who have wronged them. Many evil spirits in Hinduism, such as *bhutas* and *pishachas*, can also be found in Buddhism, as the two religions share deep historical and cultural roots.

Demon-slayer
This detail of a painting from c. 1585 depicts Narakasura, the king of the *asuras*, split in two by a missile thrown by Lord Krishna.

> "I shall (today) drink… human blood, hot and fresh and frothy…"
>
> THE *RAKSHASA* HIDIMVA IN THE *MAHABHARATA*, BOOK I, SECTION 154

THE GODDESS KALI

A terrifying warrior goddess, Kali is usually pictured with her tongue hanging from her mouth, a necklace of skulls or decapitated heads around her neck, and a selection of bloodied weapons in her multiple hands. In this guise, she is a destroyer of evil, a fierce protector of those who worship her, and a force of nature. Her black or blue skin symbolizes her divine connection to the infinite nature of the Universe and time.

The 6th-century philosophical Hindu text the *Devi Mahatmya* ("Glory of the Goddess") is one of the first sources to describe Kali's birth and powers. It tells how Kali sprang from the forehead of the warrior mother goddess Durga – a personification of Durga's rage and power – during a battle with two demons. Quickly slaying the demons, Kali showed herself to be a powerful manifestation of divine feminine energy (*Shakti*), a power referenced in images of her standing over her husband, the deity Shiva. In another tale, Kali defeats Raktabija ("Blood-seed"), a demon who can replicate himself through drops of his own blood. As they fight, Kali laps up the blood flowing from Raktabija's wounds, preventing his replication and leading to his defeat.

While Kali is feared for her bloodlust and links with death and destruction, these aspects are also believed to be necessary to the cycle of creation and rebirth. Spiritual renewal is part of this pattern, with the stories of Kali's battles serving as allegories for the need to embrace chaos or face inner demons in a bid to achieve enlightenment. Existing outside of the usual limitations of good and evil, Kali presents a complex view of the Universe in which horror can be a positive catalyst for change and transformation.

Hindu homage
This early 18th-century watercolour shows, from left, the Hindu gods Shiva, Vishnu, and Brahma paying tribute to Kali, the goddess of time, death, and destruction.

GODS AND MONSTERS OF GREEK MYTH

DEPICTIONS OF GODS AND MONSTERS IN THE TALES OF ANCIENT GREECE REVEAL HOW IMPORTANT THEY WERE IN UNDERSTANDING THE WORLD.

Monsters in Greek mythology serve many purposes. They can personify the elements or reflect the dangers of a specific terrain – the poisonous nine-headed Hydra of Lerna lives in a swampy, uninhabitable region – but they also serve as a warning to respect and honour the gods. Curiously, many of the most formidable monsters in Greek mythology are female. Scholars have suggested that this reflects a patriarchal unease with the power that women could potentially wield over men, whether through sexual attraction, cunning, or supernatural force. In this context, the myths act both as cautionary tales and as symbolic expressions of anxiety in a society that was built on male authority.

A fearful sight
The beast gives off a menacing aura in the 2008 production of *The Minotaur* at London's Royal Opera House. The work was hailed as one of the classical greats of the 21st century.

SEA MONSTERS

The seas around the Greek islands were believed to be filled with monsters. The sorceress Circe warned Odysseus of two that he would encounter on his voyage. Scylla, with six heads and 12 feet, lurked in a sea cave waiting for ships to pass, and Charybdis summoned whirlpools to sink them. Meanwhile, the beautiful sirens mesmerized sailors with their singing, only to drag them into the watery depths.

Dating from c.450 BCE, this terracotta plaque depicts Scylla. Two of her six heads, at the front, are clearly recognizable as those of dogs.

Monsters populate Greek creation myths. According to Hesiod's *Theogony*, Gaia, the goddess and personification of Earth, is mother to the giants, including the one-eyed cyclopes (though not Polyphemus) and the hecatoncheires, also known as the hundred-handed ones.

Divine punishments

Some of the most horrifying creatures that terrorize mortal souls are offspring of the gods; others are the result of brief human encounters with deities. Another group are those who become monsters – the products of transformation by vengeful gods. While born a Gorgon to the sea gods Phorcys and Ceto, Medusa, unlike her sisters, originally looks human and is considered beautiful by mortals and immortals alike. However, after she is raped by Poseidon in one of Athena's temples, the goddess of war exacts revenge by turning Medusa's hair into a nest of snakes.

The Minotaur is another victim of divine punishment. The sea god Poseidon gives a white Cretan bull to King Minos as a sign of his favour towards the ruler; in return, Minos is supposed to sacrifice the beast in tribute to Poseidon. However, captivated by its beauty and strength, the king keeps it, failing the test of obedience. In retaliation, Poseidon conspires with Aphrodite, the goddess of desire and sexual attraction, to curse Minos's wife, Pasiphaë, and make her fall in love with the bull. The ensuing union produces the Minotaur, a half-man, half-bull creature so ferocious that it is imprisoned in a labyrinth beneath the Cretan palace. To keep the monster at bay, every nine years Minos must send seven young men and seven young women into the maze, where they inevitably face and are devoured by the creature.

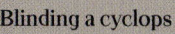

Blinding a cyclops
The painting at the top of this 7th-century-BCE amphora depicts Odysseus blinding the one-eyed giant Polyphemus. This enabled Odysseus and his surviving men to escape.

Both unfairly punished by the gods for the actions of others, Medusa and the Minotaur show how monstrous beings were cast as outsiders and became the subject of fear and disdain.

Hybrid beasts

Several other composite creatures reinforce the terrifying power of the gods, such as the harpies: winged creatures with beautiful faces and sharp talons that can tear apart human flesh. One of the most powerful hybrid beasts is Echidna. A serpentine being with a human head, she is the progenitor of multiple horrifying monsters.

After mating with Typhon, Echidna gives birth to the Hydra of Lerna, the two-headed dog Orthus, the multiheaded guard dog of the Underworld known as Cerberus, the Colchian Dragon that guarded the famous Golden Fleece, the sea monster Scylla, and the fire-breathing Chimaera. Through a later relationship with Orthus, Echidna also gives birth to the Nemean Lion and the Sphinx encountered by Oedipus on his return to Thebes. In order to keep many of these monsters at bay, mortals must rely on the benevolence of the gods, offering gifts and sacrifices in exchange for their safety.

A cunning plan
In this 16th-century painting, Heracles and his nephew are cauterizing the necks of the Hydra to prevent regrowth of its heads.

Ancient Fears

> "No ship ever yet got past [Scylla] without losing some men, for she… carries off a man in each mouth."
>
> HOMER, *THE ODYSSEY* BOOK XII

Some mortals and demigods in Greek mythology prove their heroism by confronting formidable foes such as the Nemean Lion, the Sphinx, and Medusa. Many of these beings must be overcome through strength, cunning, or courage. Heracles, the demigod son of Zeus, is celebrated for completing his "12 Labours", six of which involve slaying or capturing dangerous beasts. To atone for killing his wife and children, Heracles must defeat the Hydra of Lerna, the lion of Nemea, and the Stymphalian birds. His final task requires him to bring Cerberus from Hades, the god of the underworld, to the mortal realm.

Divine fears

While monsters are often a source of terror, the Olympian gods also inflict cruelty, upon both mortals and their own kin. After gifting humans the power of fire, the Titan Prometheus is sentenced to eternal punishment by the other gods. Strapped to a rock, he is left to have his liver eaten by the Caucasian Eagle, only for the organ to regenerate the next day. Zeus also commits monstrous acts that often have devastating consequences for the human world. His rape of Leda leads to the birth of Helena and Clytemnestra, two mortal woman who contribute to the fall of Troy and ruin of the House of Atreus.

The goddesses also have a formidable reputation. The daughters of Gaia and Ouranos, the Furies – Alecto, Megaera and Tisiphone – are the goddesses of vengeance who seek retribution for mortal sins, particularly crimes against familial members (blood crimes). These unforgiving sisters torture their victims, often driving them to madness.

The gods themselves have their own monsters to fear. The first and most fearsome of all monsters in Greek mythology is Typhon, the son of Gaia and Tartarus. Some accounts describe him as having a dragon-like appearance with hundreds of fire-breathing snakes sprawling from his shoulders. When Typhon attacks Olympus, threatening the lives of both mortal and immortal beings, only Zeus is strong enough to defeat him, his thunderbolts opening up Earth and sending Typhon within. His name lives on today in the word "typhoon": these strong winds were said to be the result of his fury.

DIONYSUS AND THE MAENADS

Of the many Greek tragedies that have survived, Euripides's *The Bacchae* stands out. In it, Pentheus, the new king of Thebes, denounces Dionysus as a false god and his female followers, the maenads, as a cult. Despite being witness to various miracles, Pentheus refuses to change his mind, so Dionysus has the maenads, including Pentheus's own mother, tear him limb from limb.

Even in the 21st century, Greek mythology continues to enthral. Director Peter Hall's adaptation of *The Bacchae* was a box-office hit in London in 2002.

FATE AND REVENGE IN GREEK DRAMA

ANCIENT GREEK TRAGEDIES EXPOSED THE HORRORS OF THE HUMAN CONDITION BY EXPLORING CYCLES OF VIOLENCE AND THE IRRESISTIBLE FORCES OF FATE.

From the 6th century BCE, the great playwrights of ancient Athens entered their work into annual competitions honouring Dionysus, the god of theatre. Based on tales from Greek mythology, these dramas, or tragedies, explored interactions between the mortal and immortal worlds and their consequences. Of the plays that have survived, most grapple with weighty themes such as the tension between fate and free will, the destructive power of revenge, and divine punishment of human misdeeds.

Terrible fates

First performed around 430 BCE, Sophocles's *Oedipus Rex* explores the folly of trying to escape a predetermined destiny. The play follows Oedipus, King of Thebes, as he seeks the murderer of his

> "I fear the beating storm of bloody rain that shakes the house."
>
> AESCHYLUS, *AGAMEMNON*

Murder most foul
This 1st-century CE painting from Pompeii, Italy, shows Alcmaeon killing his mother, a popular story used in plays by Sophocles and Euripides.

predecessor, King Laius, to end a plague – a divine punishment for the unsolved murder. Oedipus's investigation uncovers terrible truths: he is the murderer and Laius was his father. In marrying Laius's widow, Jocasta, Oedipus has also wed his own mother. Unaware that he was abandoned at birth to avoid a prophecy he would kill his father and marry his mother, Oedipus had believed his adoptive parents, the king and queen of Corinth, to be his real parents. The revelations culminate in a gruesome finale in which Jocasta takes her own life and Oedipus blinds himself with her dress pins.

Wreaking revenge

Aeschylus's *Oresteia* trilogy, from 458 BCE, centres on a family trapped in a cycle of revenge following King Agamemnon's sacrificial killing of his daughter, Iphigenia, to appease the goddess Artemis. In the first play, *Agamemnon*, the king is murdered by his wife Clytemnestra to avenge the killing of their daughter. In *The Choephori* (also known as *The Libation Bearers*), the second play, Agamemnon's surviving children, Orestes and Electra, seek revenge for their father's death, and Orestes kills his mother Clytemnestra and her lover, Aegisthus. In the final play, *Eumenides*, Orestes is pursued by the Furies, three goddesses of vengeance, for his actions. His fate is decided by a trial in which the goddess Athena acquits him of blame, ending the pattern of violence.

Extreme vengeance and familial conflict are also key themes in Euripides's play *Medea*, dating from 431 BCE. In this tale, Medea seeks revenge on her husband Jason after he abandons her and their two children for a Corinthian princess. Embarking on a trail of destruction, Medea punishes Jason by killing his new wife, father-in-law, and children by Jason before fleeing to Athens.

These studies in vengeance and suffering would have resonated with ancient Greek audiences. Regardless of their hopes for justice, happiness, or advancement, the dramas showed that their best attempts might be thwarted by predestination, divine meddling, and their own flawed personalities and decision-making. They also served as sobering reminders that feuds, cycles of vengeance, and savage brutality could afflict any family – given the right circumstances, anyone could be a victim or a perpetrator of terrible violence.

Victims of vengeance
The desperate tragedy of Medea's decision to kill her children as an act of revenge is evoked in a 1947 photoshoot for *American Vogue* featuring Australian actor Judith Anderson.

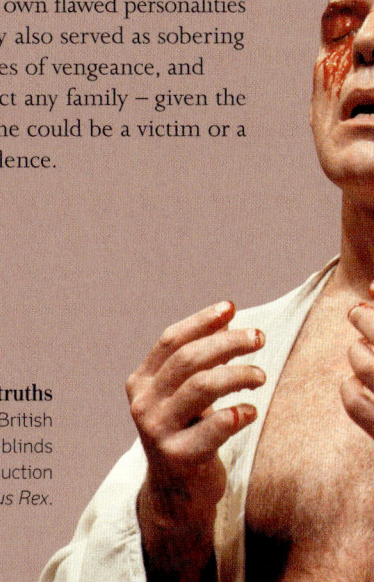

Terrible truths
Oedipus, played by British actor John Shrapnel, blinds himself in a 1988 production of Sophocles's *Oedipus Rex*.

MEDUSA

In the ancient Greek world, few faces were more familiar, or more feared, than that of the hideous Medusa, her tongue projecting from a mouth full of fangs and her head crowned by a tangle of serpents. Believed to keep evil away, her image could be seen on armour, vases, and buildings. In Greek mythology, Medusa was one of three terrifying sisters known as the Gorgons, who could turn anyone who looked at them into stone. However, while Stheno and Euryale were immortal, their sister Medusa was not.

Perseus, a son of Zeus, the king of the gods, was challenged by King Polydectes of Seriphos to slay Medusa and return with her head. Various gods gave him winged sandals, a cloak of invisibility, and a polished shield to help him in his task. When the time came, Perseus walked backwards into Medusa's cave, looking only at the reflection in his shield, to avoid meeting her petrifying gaze. With a single slash he cut off her head and placed it safely in a sack. When he presented the head to Polydectes, the king was turned to stone. Athena, goddess of wisdom and war, then took the head and mounted it on her shield to terrify her enemies in battle.

According to the Roman poet Ovid, Medusa was raped by Poseidon, god of the sea, while serving in Athena's temple. He claimed Athena turned Medusa into a gorgon as a punishment for desecrating her site, or possibly so that she could protect herself in future. Some modern scholars see Medusa as an icon of female empowerment rather than a monster.

The head of Medusa
Medusa's terrifying gaze is captured in this work by 17th-century Flemish painter Peter Paul Rubens. She is both a living curse on whoever looks at her and a force against evil itself.

TALES OF THE PACIFIC

THE SUPERNATURAL CREATURES OF PACIFIC ISLAND MYTHOLOGIES INSPIRE BOTH FEAR AND REVERENCE, REFLECTING A DEEP RESPECT FOR THE NATURAL WORLD THEY INHABIT AND COMMAND.

Traditional taniwha
Usually shown with blazing eyes and a serpent's tail, as here, the *taniwha* can also shape-shift, taking a whale- or shark-like form.

Fiery goddess
This 17th–18th-century statue depicts the Hawaiian fire goddess Pele, said to live in a crater at the summit of the Kīlauea volcano.

Traditional Polynesian belief systems include a large pantheon of gods, monsters, and spirits, many of them linked to the ocean. Ancient stories, passed down over thousands of years through chant, song, ritual, and performance, describe how these supernatural beings influence seafaring and navigation as well as natural phenomena, such as wind and volcanic activity. These tales probably originated 2,000–3,000 years ago, during the Austronesian expansion that carried seafaring cultures from Taiwan through the islands of Southeast Asia and on to the open Pacific.

Protectors and enforcers

Gods and spirits often reflect the island geography of their associated Pacific culture. They may take the form of animals, plants, humans, or natural features, and are frequently both revered and feared. Pele, for example, the Hawaiian goddess of fire and volcanoes, is renowned for her violent temper. It is said that who disrespect her or her land by taking rocks or sand may be cursed or destroyed in a volcanic eruption. Similarly, Tangaroa, the

> "Kaumariki at once recognized these monsters as the dreaded *patupaiarehe*, man-eating demons…"
>
> MĀORI FOLKTALE

Polynesian god of the sea, can be invoked for protection, but is also believed to send storms and to drown the unworthy. Some Pacific cultures have myriad lesser gods or spirits called *aitu*, who can be cruel and bring misfortune. In Samoa, *aitu* are evil, fanged spirits said to bite people and make them unwell.

According to traditional beliefs, the violation of sacred taboos, or *tapu*, incurs serious consequences from gods and spirits, such as illness, madness, bad luck, or death. Taboos include touching a dead person, or entering a space where someone has died before a set amount of time has passed. Entering sacred fishing zones or protected forests, or eating food meant for chiefs or gods are also proscribed. Acting as a form of social control, these prohibitions help regulate behaviour, protect sacred sites, and are believed to maintain cosmic harmony between spirits, ancestors, and gods. To avoid supernatural retribution, ritual specialists or elders may be called in to cleanse or protect those who break taboos.

Lurking in the deep

Sea monsters are common in the mythologies of the Pacific region, reflecting the islanders' complex relationship with the sea, which is a source of sustenance but also unpredictable and dangerous. Many of these creatures share similarities with Nangananga, the Fijian goddess of death, who can capsize canoes, steal children, and curse fishermen. The Māori of Aotearoa (New Zealand) revere the *taniwha*, large, serpent-like sea creatures thought to be the spirits of dead ancestors. Sometimes benevolent, at other times malevolent, they guard locations and punish those who break taboos. Stories from Vanuatu describe the Qasavara, a cannibalistic sea ogre who drowns or devours victims, while Samoan legends feature the Pa'itele, a large, fish-like monster that lives in the Apolima Strait. In all their forms, these fearsome beasts teach a strong respect for the ocean and its mysteries.

Power of the ocean
This mural featuring Tangaroa, the god of the sea, on the Cook Islands Library and Museum Society, Rarotonga, shows the continuing importance of ancient mythologies for Pacific islanders.

BUDDHIST REALMS OF HELL

THE FIERY AND FROZEN REALMS OF BUDDHIST *NARAKA* ENTAIL A LIFETIME OF TORMENT FOR BAD KARMA, WITH PUNISHMENT TO FIT EVERY CRIME.

The word *naraka* means hell in Hinduism and in Buddhism, reflecting their shared roots. In both religions, it is a place of condemnation and punishment. While Buddhists do not generally fear death, which brings reincarnation within a cycle called *samsara*, they do fear rebirth in *naraka*. Buddhist reincarnation is directly linked to the doctrine of karma – defined as the sum total of an individual's good and bad intentions and actions, carried over many lifetimes. A person with negative karma might be reborn into *naraka* to face the suffering they have earned.

Hot and cold

Buddhist scriptures describe *naraka* as a place of many realms. It is broadly divided into two types, hot and cold, which punish actions and intent respectively. There are eight major hot realms. These include *Sanjiva* ("reviving hell"), which is for people who harm innocents without remorse. In this hell, culprits are stabbed, then revived, only to be stabbed again. Deception is punished in *Kala Sutra* ("black thread hell"), where bodies are burned and dismembered. In *Samagatha* ("crushing hell"),

Karmic punishments
Top: This scene from a fresco in Hong Kong's Tiger Balm Gardens shows the punishment meted out to adulterers by the wardens of hell.
Bottom: This Cambodian mural depicts the punishment for cockfighting – people are reborn as a cock-human hybrid and forced to beat each other.

> "The wardens of hell prise open his mouth with red-hot iron tongs, burning, blazing, and glowing."
>
> DEVADUTA SUTTA, BUDDHIST SCRIPTURE, C. 600–200 BCE

Boiling hell
This Burmese temple painting depicts individuals in a hot *naraka* realm. Trapped in a flaming cauldron, they are stabbed by the wardens of hell for their bad karma.

people are crushed between mountains for oppressing others. In *Tapana* ("heating hell"), people are skewered and roasted for sexually manipulating others and lying with intent to harm. Murder is punished in *Avici* ("uninterrupted hell"), which contains various forms of unending torment.

Ill intent is punished in cold *naraka* realms, regardless of whether the intent leads to actual harm. Echoing their coldness and lack of empathy, the culprits in cold *naraka* are condemned to shiver and suffer without warmth or kindness. Crimes such as mocking the weak, bullying, indifference to suffering, or neglecting duties all incur retribution. Like hot *naraka*, cold *naraka* has eight realms, but punishments are less harsh. The realms include *Arbuda* ("hell of blisters"), *Nirarbuda* ("hell of bursting blisters") and *Atata* ("hell of shivering and chattering teeth"). The cold *naraka* realms are characterized by progressively colder temperatures, which cause increasingly severe torment to their inhabitants. In *Mahapadma* ("the great crimson lotus hell"), the coldest realm, the freezing temperatures cause skin to break open, with the wounds resembling a crimson lotus flower.

Mental anguish

Naraka can also be understood as a person's state of mind. The hell of *Sanjiva*, for example, may be the persistent memory of a traumatic experience. Some scholars argue that people feeling existential despair, suffering from self-hate, or depression experience different kinds of hell, and that the concept of *naraka* actually reflects the torture of mental struggle.

THE MORRÍGAN AND CELTIC DEATH OMENS

AMONG THE POWERFUL SPIRITS BELIEVED TO GOVERN ALL ASPECTS OF CELTIC LIFE AND DEATH, THE MORRÍGAN WAS THE MOST FEARED. OVERSEEING BATTLES AND DECIDING FATES, HER SINISTER PRESENCE WAS A HARBINGER OF DOOM AND DESTRUCTION.

The Celts were a loose grouping of tribes with similar languages and cultural traditions who originated in Iron Age Europe around 1200 BCE. These clan-based societies cultivated a deep respect for ancestry, the supernatural, and omens but each Celtic group held distinct beliefs. The Bretons, living on the northwestern French coast, feared the ghostly ship of the Bag an Noz, used by a Grim Reaper figure named Ankou to transport souls to an afterlife on the so-called Blessed Isle, a mythical paradise. Cornish myths also feature Ankou, but depict him in a large black stagecoach, driven by two horses. Despite such differences, most Celtic cultures believed in an afterlife, or Otherworld, and in the possibility of communication between the two realms. During the Celtic festival of Samhain (which influenced the later celebration of Halloween), evil spirits and supernatural creatures were believed to escape from the Otherworld. People wore masks during this period to protect themselves from harm.

Irish traditions

Celtic settlers arrived in Ireland around 500 BCE, and by the coming of Christianity in 500 CE had developed a rich mythology that included a cosmos of gods and spirits. The Morrígan was a prominent figure in this tradition, often depicted as a goddess of war, fate, and death. She is one of the Tuatha Dé Danann, a race of supernatural beings who live in the Otherworld but influence human affairs.

The Morrígan is sometimes described as a triple goddess, appearing as a trio of sisters — Badb, Macha, and Nemain — each representing different aspects of warfare and death. She is known for shapeshifting, especially into a crow or raven, and her appearance often foretells doom or the death of a warrior. In some legends, however, she also brings guidance to those she supports. In the Irish epic *Táin Bó Cúailnge* (*The Cattle Raid of Cooley*), she confronts the hero Cú Chulainn, both helping and opposing him, and eventually prophesies his death. As with many gods of war and death, the Morrígan was regarded with both dread and awe.

BANSHEES IN IRISH FOLKLORE

The banshee (*bean sí* in Irish) is a female spirit whose terrible wailing signals imminent death in a family — most often in families with old Irish noble bloodlines (those with O' or Mac surnames, such as O'Neill, O'Brien, or MacCarthy). The Banshee may appear as a cloaked old crone or as a beautiful young woman, and is often depicted combing her hair while keening.

> "I do not see a world of the living / Summer will be without flowers / Cows will be without milk…"
>
> A VISION OF THE MORRÍGAN, *CATH MAIGE TUIRED* (*THE BATTLE OF MOYTURA*), C. 12TH CENTURY CE

Several ancient Irish legends include other figures associated with death. One of these, the monstrous giant Balor, had a deadly eye that could kill or destroy anything it looked upon. His eye had to be held shut by his own warriors until battle, when they would prise it open to unleash devastation. Another terrifying figure was the Dullahan, a headless rider on a black horse who carried his own head. He was said to call out the name of a person whose death was near and was sometimes depicted driving a coach made of bones (the *cóiste bodhar*).

Similar to other European Celtic beliefs in the Wild Hunt – a ghostly horde of huntsmen – Irish mythology included a host of restless spirits of the dead, the *Sluagh Sidhe*. These spectres were thought to fly in dark flocks across the sky, snatching the souls of the dying to carry them away.

Shape-shifter
Transforming into a crow, the goddess Morrígan was believed to circle battlefields. Her cries were interpreted as an omen of death.

ROMAN LEMURES OR LARVAE

FRIGHTENING SPECTRES CALLED *LEMURES* OR *LARVAE* WERE A MAJOR CONCERN FOR ANCIENT ROMANS WORRIED ABOUT DEATH.

Ancient Romans were no strangers to thoughts of death. *Memento mori* ("remember you must die") was a common motif in Roman philosophy, art, and literature. Overcoming the fear of death was, according to Plato, the key reason to practise philosophy. Stoic and Epicurean thinkers sometimes saw death as a release or a return to nature, but dread of imminent death remained common. Reflecting this anxiety – and the proximity of the realm of spirits – a line in Virgil's *Aeneid* states, "Night and day the door of dark Dis [the legendary Underworld] stands open".

Restless spirits

Guests at Roman parties were often given the figure of a skeleton, called a *larva convivalis* ("banquet ghost"), to remind them of their own mortality even as they feasted. The belief that spirits could interfere in the world of the living also reminded them that death lurked just around the corner. According to Roman mythology, *larvae* were restless ghosts – the spirits of people who had died violently, or carried guilt for misdeeds in life. Horrifying spectres, they were thought to cause madness in those they haunted.

Sometimes *larvae* were also called *lemures* – a name also given to a festival to appease them celebrated on 9, 11, and 13 May. On these days, spirits were thought to roam the streets. Temples were closed and the head of each Roman household performed protective rites, such as spitting out nine black beans, banging copper objects together, and chanting spells.

Beyond the grave

Ancient Romans' attitude to death was influenced by religion, tradition, and philosophy. Most believed the soul (*anima*) journeyed to an Underworld ruled by the god Pluto, as long as burial rites were properly followed. Pluto was greatly feared and people avoided speaking his name in case they attracted his attention. Failure to follow correct burial procedures, such as anointing the corpse, might result in a person becoming a *lemure*.

Romans greatly feared dying without rites, heirs, or remembrance – being forgotten was worse than death itself. Once the spirit of the deceased had passed into the realm of the dead, it was important that it was properly venerated. Ancestor worship was a vital part of Romans' relationship with death and festivals such as Parentalia (held annually between 13 and 21 February) honoured good spirits (*manes*). To this end, the Romans built tombs and inscribed names on monuments to preserve the legacy of the dead and ensure their continuing influence from the afterlife. One of the most extreme forms of punishment was to eradicate the memory of a person, consigning them to oblivion.

Stark reminder
Small bronze skeletons, like this one, were given to revellers at banquets as a *memento mori* object – a reminder to enjoy life, because it is fleeting.

Funerary ceremonies
Public rites involving dances and processions, as in this 4th-century CE fresco, aimed to ensure the safe passage of the dead to the afterlife.

Shrine to the dead
Many Roman households had shrines to invoke the protection of guardian spirits. This example from Pompeii shows the head of the household making a sacrifice flanked by two spirits.

> "A spectre appeared in the form of an old man... with long beard and dishevelled hair, rattling the chains on his feet and hands."
>
> LETTER FROM PLINY THE YOUNGER, c.100–09 CE

Roman Lemures or Larvae

45

Murderous intent
The dark theme of this fresco, painted on a house wall in Pompeii, Italy, around 62–79 CE, shows Medea planning the murder of her children.

SENECAN TRAGEDY

FILLED WITH BETRAYAL, RAGE, AND HORRIFIC ACTS, SENECA'S BLOOD-SOAKED TRAGEDIES CREATED A TEMPLATE FOR LATER REVENGE NARRATIVES.

The Roman philosopher and statesman Seneca served under the murderous Emperor Nero in the 1st century CE and so probably knew about violent terrors first-hand. Among the writings attributed to Seneca are 10 tragedies that, centuries later, helped shape Renaissance theatre and European notions of horror. In these tragedies, which were probably meant to be read rather than performed on stage, the terrible things that happen to the characters are recounted in grim detail. These were not gratuitous descriptions – as a Stoic philosopher, Seneca believed that destructive emotions and their catastrophic consequences resulted from errors of judgement, making his tragedies cautionary tales.

> "With hooked fingers, he greedily searches out his eyes, and torn from their very roots, he drags both eyeballs out."
>
> SENECA, *OEDIPUS*, 1ST CENTURY CE

In Seneca's *Medea*, the title character is the lover of Jason, heroic leader of the Argonauts. She has given birth to two of his sons but finds herself cast aside so that Jason can marry the daughter of a king. Seeking revenge, Medea calls on the spirits of dreaded goddesses and vicious serpents to devour her enemies. She invokes the goddess of witchcraft, Hecate, and poisons a gown that she sends to Jason's new bride. As soon as the girl puts on the dress, she bursts into flames, as does her father when he tries to extinguish the blaze. This vengeful rampage does not satisfy Medea, as Jason is left unharmed. To strike at him, Medea takes their children to the roof of her home and slays them before dumping their bodies in front of their grieving father.

A bloody trail

The play *Thyestes* recounts the hideous fate of two brothers, Atreus and Thyestes, who, locked in a cycle of jealousy and betrayal, seek vengeance on each other. Feigning reconciliation while really plotting revenge, Atreus convinces Thyestes to visit him. Before his arrival, Atreus murders Thyestes's sons, stabbing one brutally in the throat and the other through the chest. He then butchers the boys and roasts their flesh to create a meal. Thyestes arrives and shares a splendid dinner with his brother, thinking all is forgiven. In a final flourish, Atreus uncovers a platter bearing the decapitated heads of the sons. As the cannibalistic nature of the feast is revealed, Thyestes calls on the gods to destroy Atreus.

Seneca's retelling of the ancient Greek myth of Oedipus is another tale of family horror featuring bloody vengeance. Seneca uses the classic plotline, in which Oedipus inadvertently murders his father and marries his own mother, but introduces a new level of graphic violence. On discovering he has performed patricide and incest, Oedipus digs out his own eyes and rakes at the empty sockets with his bloody fingernails. The text features gruesome details, such as how the shredded eyes flap against Oedipus's cheeks.

The vivid language and violent themes of Seneca's tragedies directly influenced Renaissance writers, such as Shakespeare, who rediscovered the works in the 16th century. Seneca's life had an aptly bloody end when he was accused of treason and ordered by Emperor Nero to die by suicide. When Seneca tried to cut open his own veins, he bled so slowly that he suffered a prolonged, painful demise.

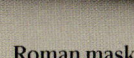

Roman mask
This 1st-century CE carving from the roof of a building in Pompeii, Italy, represents the type of mask used by actors in ancient Roman tragedy plays.

Divine driving force
In Seneca's *Thyestes*, the goddess Furia (shown here in a 1994 production of the tragedy) exacerbates the family conflict, inciting hatred and Atreus's vengeful actions against his brother.

CHANGELINGS IN EUROPEAN FOLKLORE

TALES OF BABIES OR YOUNG CHILDREN REPLACED WITH EVIL SUBSTITUTES REVEAL DARK FEARS AND SUPERSTITIONS.

Devilish exchange
Infant abductions began to be blamed on the Devil rather than fairies during the medieval period, as in this 14th-century altarpiece.

Ongoing enchantment
Arthur Rackham's *The Changeling* (1905) reflects the enduring appeal of tales of fairy abduction, which lasted into the modern era.

The story of a child stolen from its cradle and substituted with a supernatural being, called a changeling, is a common theme in pre-Christian folktales from across Europe. In Scandinavia, trolls or elves were blamed for the infant kidnappings; other cultures also accused demons. The most common malefactor, particularly in Celtic myths, was the fairy (also faerie, faierie or fae), deriving from the Old French term *faie*, meaning "to enchant" or "to bewitch". While sometimes benign, fairies were generally feared as evil, dangerous, or mischievous beings who should not be crossed.

Many Irish folktales feature changelings (known as *Iarlaisí*). Most commonly, a fairy replaces an infant so that it can benefit from the food or love bestowed by the child's parents, or in order for the stolen child to become a servant in the fairy realm, or out of revenge or malice. Occasionally, an elderly fairy replaces the child, hoping to live out its old age in comfort. While initially taken in, the parents of the child begin to notice unusual behaviour – perhaps a precocious talent for talking or playing an instrument, or conversely, incessant crying, or a general failure to thrive. Alerted to supernatural foul play, the parents conduct a test to expose the imposter and drive it out, hoping their own child will be returned.

Fears and superstitions

The wide range of traits that might identify a changeling reveals much about ancient anxieties around illness and disability. In a time of high mortality and little medical knowledge, fairy substitution was a way of explaining birth defects, delays in development, paralysis, weight loss, or any other characteristics considered "abnormal". The troll changelings in Scandinavian tales, for example, are often described as large, slow-moving, or malformed in some way. Substitution stories also reflect fears that malign spirits could cross from the fairy kingdom or from untamed wilderness areas to meddle in human affairs.

Folktales revel in the extreme measures taken to expel fairy imposters. Irish tales recommend beating children or throwing them onto a fire to test their authenticity, while a tale from Wales maintains that the "real" child would return if the changeling was buried alive. Unfortunately, such measures were not confined to fictional accounts. Many innocent children became victims of abuse, torture, or abandonment, as their parents attempted to restore their "true" offspring. The changeling folktales may therefore reflect a dark truth – that some turned to infanticide rather than caring for a sick or disabled child in times of uncertainty and scarce resources.

> "It had the face of an old man, drank like a wolf, and could never be satisfied."
>
> NORWEGIAN FOLKTALE DESCRIBING A CHANGELING

CREATURES OF SLAVIC FOLKLORE

THE TALES OF SLAVIC FOLKLORE ARE FILLED WITH TERRIFYING ENTITIES — EVEN THOUGH THE ROOTS OF MANY ARE OF A LESS MALEVOLENT NATURE.

An unusual steed
In this 19th-century Russian print, the witch Baba Yaga sits astride a pig while doing battle with what the accompanying text describes as a crocodile.

After Christianity was introduced to Slavic lands from around the 9th century CE, some local folk creatures previously regarded as benevolent were recast as ill-meaning, a revision aimed at quashing ancient pagan beliefs. One example, the *leshy* (sometimes *leszy* or *leshi*), common to several Slavic countries, originated as a benign forest spirit protecting trees and animals before it was reimagined as a sinister character akin to a devil.

Believed to be a satyr-like mix of man and beast, with claws, horns, and a beard, the *leshy* is said to be covered in moss and live in the woods. It can shape-shift and mimic voices, sometimes using these skills to lead travellers astray. Under the influence of Christian demonology, the *leshy*'s mischievous nature becomes darker — no longer a simple trickster, it is portrayed as abducting people (especially women and children) who wander in the woods. Its appearance also alters, with devilish traits such as cloven feet or a lack of eyelashes or eyebrows reinforcing its more evil identity.

Dark and vengeful

Some Slavic creatures were seen as malevolent from the outset, as was Poland's *boruta*. This creature – essentially a more wicked iteration of the *leshy* – became associated with the Devil in Polish Christianity. The forest-dwelling *bies* is another example; historically seen as evil spirits, *biesy* were more explicitly linked with devils or demons, in both deed and appearance, once Christianity took hold. The *bies* also came to be identified with the *chort*, or *czort* – the names were increasingly used interchangeably despite the creatures originally being distinct from each other.

Described in its natural state as looking like a small man covered in hair, a *čert* also has a tail, horns, and hooves in keeping with the portrayal of such creatures as some sort of demon. This shape-shifting character of Czech and Slovak folklore is a variation of the Slavic *chort* but also associated with tests of moral strength in which it lures people to part with their souls. While not inherently evil, *čerti* act in ways that are often less than benign and are sometimes said to drag malefactors into Hell. In other tales, however, a *čert* may assist a human protagonist, albeit only to gain something in return.

Baba Yaga is an iconic witch of eastern Slavic folklore, most commonly that of Russia, Ukraine, and Belarus. Depicted as a vengeful forest hag, she lives in a hut on chicken-leg stilts that is surrounded by a fence of bones topped with human skulls. The earliest written record of Baba Yaga comes from the mid-18th century, but her origins are believed to be considerably earlier: one popular theory suggests that she may have roots in nature goddesses or nature spirits.

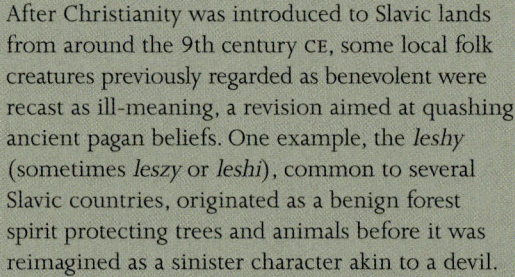

> "Baba Yaga… was a wicked hag who… ate men like chickens."
>
> "VASILISA THE BEAUTY", RUSSIAN FOLKTALE

Moss beast
The *leshy* is a mysterious forest spirit. Tall and humanoid, it is often depicted, as in this artwork, with bark-like skin sprouting moss and animal-like horns.

LIKHO

Likho is a one-eyed ogress from Slavic fairy tales, seen as the embodiment of misfortune and the negative side of fate. Linked with grief, sickness, and death, Likho has a great aptitude for mischief and is not easy to outwit: tales abound of those who believe they have outsmarted her, only to become her next victim. Known for luring desperate or unwary travellers into her home, Likho is fast on her feet; she chases her victims, before leaping on them and strangling them to death. She then proceeds to feed on their life force, draining their luck, as well as their spirit.

MONSTERS OF THE MAYA

THE ART OF THE MAYA DEPICTS A FEARSOME BESTIARY, CREATURES DESIGNED TO INSTIL AWE, EXPLAIN NATURAL PHENOMENA, OR GUIDE SPIRITS THROUGH THE UNDERWORLD.

Scholars have gathered many insights into the beliefs of the Maya – the ancient civilization of Mesoamerica – from the fantastical beasts that adorn their architecture and artefacts. Excavations in Mexico, Guatemala, Belize, Honduras, and El Salvador have uncovered representations of many creatures. Whether these were seen as gods, monsters, or even dreams is not wholly clear. The Spanish who colonized Maya lands in the 16th century CE either sought to interpret Indigenous beliefs through a Christian lens or simply dismissed them as barbaric or backwards.

Several creatures have been characterized by historians and anthropologists as "monsters" within Maya culture. One of the best known is

Serpent bowl
A male figure and a waterlily serpent appear on this bowl from 700–900 CE. The intricate carvings are typical of the Chocholá style of Mexico's Northern Yucatán area.

Ancient Fears

> "There were many places of torture in Xibalba [the Underworld]."
>
> *POPOL VUH*, PART II, 16TH CENTURY

the *cauac*, a beast whose head was often carved into the facades of buildings. A personification of the earth and its fertility, the *cauac* did not have one specific appearance and so could be represented by various animals, particularly those connected to both land and water, such as frogs, crocodiles, and turtles. The creature was often identified by the "cauac" glyph, or symbol, that accompanied its image.

Creation and creations

Like other Mesoamerican peoples, the Maya had various myths that linked Earth's creation to crocodilian creatures. In the *Books of Chilam Balam* from Yucatán – sacred Maya texts that blend history, prophecy, medicine, and mythology – a sky-ascending crocodilian named Itzam Kab' Ayin wreaked havoc by attempting to flood the world. When Bolon Ti' K'uh (the nine gods) defeated him, his scaly back became Earth's surface, and his spilled blood nourished the newly formed land.

One supernatural being that was regarded more as a deity is the waterlily serpent, which in modern academic writings is often referred to as the imix monster. A jawless snake-like creature adorned with water lilies, it is associated with bodies of water above and below ground (including within caves), as well as the Moon and wind. Occasionally represented with a skull-like face, the waterlily serpent has also been linked to the Underworld.

A number of the monsters depicted in Maya sculpture and ceramics are composite creatures, with anatomical parts from various animals. Beasts referred to as "celestial monsters" or "cosmic serpents" often have a crocodile's face combined with other non-crocodile features. One of these hybrids has a crocodile head and scaly body, along with deer ears and hooves; later given the modern name starry deer crocodile, it is associated with

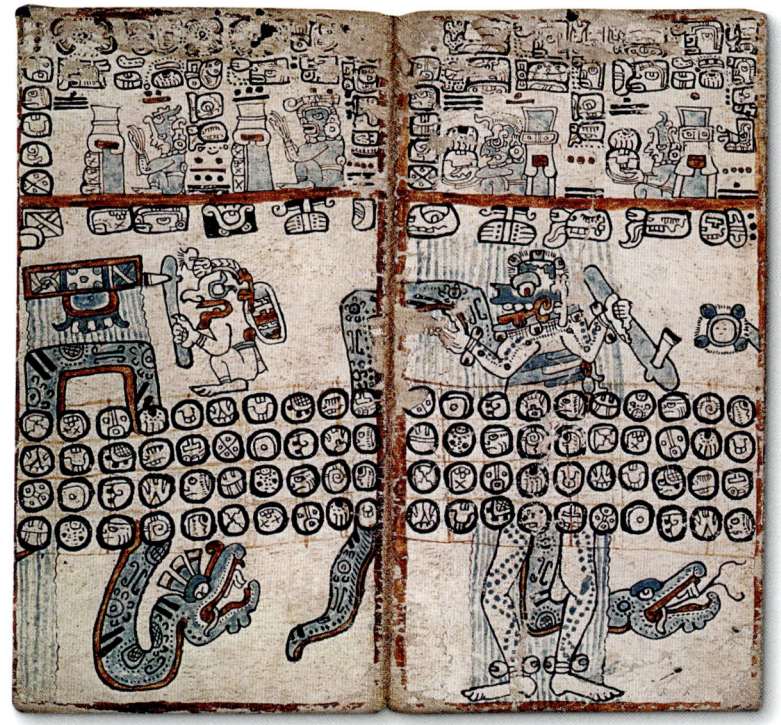

Symbolic serpents
In this illustration from the *Madrid Codex*, rattlesnakes – often associated with the deity K'awiil – may represent vision serpents, symbolic beings that serve as conduits between the human and divine realms.

the nocturnal sky, particularly the stars and the cycles of the planet Venus. Some scholars believe this creature to be the one slain by Bolon Ti' K'uh in the *Books of Chilam Balam*.

Among real animals, one of the most highly esteemed in Maya mythology is the shark, or *xook*. Although most Maya cities were inland, encounters with sharks along the coast – and rare sightings in rivers – led to it being seen as a powerful creature, sometimes linked to danger or the Underworld, though not directly connected to creation myths like the *Popol Vuh* ("Book of the Community").

Life after death

The otherworldly beasts of Maya culture were not limited to immortal beings. Maya dynasties believed that, in death, their rulers could be reborn as supernatural figures linked to the cosmos – as a Sun god, for example. Additionally, bicephalic serpent-monsters – with a human face at the front and an animal's face at the rear – often appear in royal imagery, as at Yaxchilán, where they represent dynastic power and the divine authority of kings.

EVIL BEINGS IN CHINESE TRADITION

IN CHINA'S OLDEST STORIES, SUPERNATURAL THREATS WERE LINKED TO THE MISDEEDS OF THE LIVING — AND THEIR FAILURE TO APPEASE THE RESTLESS DEAD.

Ghostly hero
This 18th-century painting depicts Zhong Kui, a figure famed in Chinese mythology for his ability to vanquish demons and evil spirits.

China was one of the cradles of civilization and its written history dates back to at least 1250 BCE, when questions were inscribed on oracle bones by those seeking the guidance of spirits. The ancient Chinese world (from around 6000 BCE until the end of the Han dynasty in 220 CE) was heavily influenced by belief in the supernatural. One of the most basic tenets of Chinese culture was reverence for the dead and the veneration of ancestors. If the spirits of the dead were not cared for, it was thought they could return from the grave and inflict harm on the living.

Terrifying tales

One story of a vengeful ghost dates from the 8th century BCE. According to legend, King Xuan of Zhou ordered a large number of women to be slaughtered, after receiving a prophecy that one would endanger the town of Jiangshan. When his chief minister Du Bo (the Duke of Tangdu) rebuked him for this cruel act, the king had Du Bo executed as well. Du Bo's spirit was unable to rest and returned to haunt the king. Soon after, the king fell ill

Fierce figures
This *zhenmushou*, or tomb guardian, dates from the Han dynasty. Such creatures were believed to protect the dead from evil spirits.

Festive flames
Hungry ghost festivals, like this one in Kuala Lumpur in 2014, still take place to appease restless spirits by burning offerings.

and claimed he had seen Du Bo shooting spectral arrows at him. King Xuan died of his illness, after which Du Bo's ghost was presumably able to rest.

Ancient Chinese texts – such as the *Shen Yi Jing* ("The Classic of Gods and Aberrations"), written during the Han dynasty – contain references to supernatural beings, many of them fearsome. As in other cultures, the Chinese found security in their settlements and believed the wilderness harboured strange beings or other humans with monstrous aspects. A Han dynasty text from the 2nd century CE refers to men over 3 m (10 ft) tall who crept from the mountains and invaded villages to steal food; getting too close to them risked catching a fatal illness. Other mountain creatures, called Xiao, were described as ape-like beings with long arms capable of hurling objects over great distances. Some mythological beasts could bring deadly natural disasters such as drought and typhoons.

Mixing traditions

When Buddhism was introduced to China in the 1st century CE, traditional beliefs and the new religion merged. An afterlife was envisaged in which those who committed theft or murder would be reborn as "hungry ghosts" – spirits ravaged by unquenchable thirst and insatiable hunger. These were said to return to Earth and torment the living at times of the year when the barriers between life and death were thinnest.

JIANGSHI

A Chinese legend from the Qing dynasty (1644–1911) is that of the *jiangshi* – literally "stiff corpse", though also called hopping vampires due to how they move. They are depicted with outstretched arms, rigid bodies, and wearing the uniform of a Qing official. Believed to steal the *qi*, or life force, of their victims, *jiangshi* became popular antagonists in Hong Kong horror films in the 1980s.

A man dresses as a *jiangshi* in Qing uniform.

> "... respect spiritual beings but keep them at a distance."
>
> CONFUCIUS, *THE ANALECTS*, COLLECTED IN THE 5TH–3RD CENTURY BCE

AFRICAN MYTHOLOGIES

TRADITIONAL AFRICAN FOLKLORE IS RICH WITH STORIES OF MONSTERS, REFLECTING THE SPIRITUAL BELIEFS, NATURAL ENVIRONMENTS, AND SOCIAL VALUES OF THE CULTURES THAT CREATED THEM.

For many centuries, the Ewe people (from the West African countries of Togo, Ghana, and Benin) have told stories of the *adze*, a vampiric spirit that feeds on blood. Generation after generation has passed down stories about this firefly-like creature able to shape-shift into a human being and often taking on the form of a beautiful woman or man to deceive its victims. The *adze* is often said to attack people while they sleep, sucking the blood of children or weak adults and causing illness and death. In some stories, the *adze* is linked to witchcraft and can be used as a spirit weapon by witches to cause harm to others.

Cursed creatures

The many monstrous beings in African mythologies typically embody the fears and taboos of the societies in which they exist. They range from benevolent supernatural spirits to malevolent forces. Like the *adze*, some of these creatures are associated with witchcraft, or the use of magic for harmful purposes. Belief in witchcraft plays a significant role in many African cultures, and the monsters it is said to invoke typically serve as agents of vengeance or spiritual punishment, or as enforcers of taboos.

The Zulu people, primarily in South Africa's KwaZulu-Natal province, believe in a witch's familiar called an *impundulu*, or lightning bird, said to bring death and destruction through lightning strikes. In Nigeria, Benin, and Togo, the Yoruba people's folktales include the *abiku*, a spirit responsible for infant death. Some traditions suggest that the *abiku* is a curse placed on a family; it takes the form of a spirit child that is sent to torment parents by repeatedly causing the deaths of their children.

Ritual statuette
Some African rituals to track or remove evil spirits include the use of amulets or statuettes, like this West African example.

Ancient Fears

Healing of Abiku Children
In this 1973 painting, Nigerian artist Twins Seven Seven – once considered an *abiku* child himself – portrays a Yoruba ritual to break the cycle of spirit-child deaths.

> "The warriors found the monster… and were swallowed up."

ALICE WERNER, "THE SWALLOWING MONSTER", *MYTHS AND LEGENDS OF THE BANTU*, 1933

Some monsters in African mythologies are similar to wild animals. The *nanabolele*, for example, is an alligator-like creature in the folklore of the Basotho people; this reptilian monster emits light in the dark and eats people. Many African cultures have myths and legends featuring snake monsters, usually tied to supernatural, evil, or chaotic forces. Legends of the Bantu people of sub-Saharan Africa tell of the *nyoka*, a multi-headed serpent that guards treasure and causes earthquakes, while the *ninki nanka* of Gambia is a harbinger of death that devours those who come too close. Snakes have deep symbolic significance in African mythologies, often representing both danger and spiritual power.

Combined beliefs

The spread of Christianity and Islam through Africa had a significant impact on traditional African beliefs, including those regarding monsters and the supernatural. With their basis in a singular, all-powerful god, these religions often clashed with or altered pre-existing African belief systems, many of which were polytheistic and deeply intertwined with the worship of nature, spirits, and ancestors.

Many traditional African monsters became associated with Satan, demons, or evil entities in Christian teachings. Snake-like creatures or ancestral spirits revered in traditional beliefs were now seen as demonic, just as serpents symbolize Satan in Christian theology. Today, these traditional stories are being revisited, especially in the horror genre, with creatures from African folklore at the centre of films such as *The Tokoloshe* (2018), which features a Zulu trickster demon terrorizing the protagonists – a young woman and a girl.

500–1500

THE MONSTROUS MEDIEVAL

HELL AND ETERNAL DAMNATION

DURING THE MEDIEVAL PERIOD, NOTIONS OF HELL GREW MORE DISTINCT, LEAVING CHRISTIAN SINNERS IN NO DOUBT ABOUT THE TORMENTS THAT AWAITED THEM.

The ancient Greeks and Romans generally imagined the afterlife as a fairly dull and monotonous place, where souls existed as pale shadows devoid of happiness but without too much suffering either. The emergence of Christianity led to widespread belief in a Day of Judgement that determined entry to a Heaven of eternal joy or to Hell, where sinners are tortured in gruesome ways for all eternity. The concept of Hell would come to dominate Christian fears for most of the medieval era.

Early Christianity had little to say about the nature of Hell. The New Testament, written sometime between 50 and 100 CE, includes the words Hades and Gehenna – usually translated as "Hell" in English versions of the Bible – but they are not explicitly described as places of eternal torment. There is mention, however, of burning lakes and the unrighteous being plunged into unquenchable fire. It is from these descriptions that many of the most popular images of Hell derive.

Hellish visions

A widely circulated work known as the *Apocalypse of Peter* shows that notions of Hell were forming by the 2nd century CE. The unknown author describes sinners hanging by their tongues over pits of fire, being held in a pit of snakes, or blinded with red-hot pokers. Many of the punishments have an ironic twist: people who have habitually lied, for example, are doomed to spend eternity with their tongues on fire. The penalties are not meant to improve the souls of the damned – Hell is a place of vindictive justice with no escape.

By the 7th century, scholars were producing popular texts that offered readers guided tours of Heaven and Hell, painting gruesome pictures of hellish suffering. In the 12th-century work *The Visions of Tundale*, written by an Irish monk, the souls of the damned fly up from a stinking pit, like sparks, only to fall back down, in an endless cycle of torment. Vivid accounts of the damned being torn apart by wild beasts, boiled in huge cauldrons, and chained to flaming chairs proved a great spur to the faithful. Other texts described fiery demons who inflicted excruciating pain on their victims. Satan became the Lord of Hell and was often shown as both chief tormentor of sinners and as a recipient of the worst punishments.

The ultimate inferno

Dante Alighieri's 14th-century *Divine Comedy* is the most famous medieval account of Hell. Here, Hell is a pit with nine circles where sinners are punished in a variety of ways, such as being flayed, thrown into pitch, or frozen in ice. Literary depictions of

Dire warnings
An example of a "doom" painting, used as an aid to religious teaching, this 12th-century fresco on the wall of an English church shows monstrous demons torturing the souls of the damned after the Day of Judgement.

Realm of fire
This 15th-century Dutch painting emphasizes the notion of Hell as a fiery abyss from which there is no return.

Hell and Eternal Damnation

61

Hell greatly influenced artists and theologians and, through them, the wider public. Literacy in medieval Europe was far from universal, so most Christian worshippers learned about Hell from priests, who spoke at length about the eternal punishments awaiting wrongdoers. These sermons were reinforced by terrifying visual aids – church paintings and stained-glass windows showing sinners being dragged into Hell by hideous demons.

"Of that fyr com more stynk
Then any erthely mon myght thynk
… in that stynke dvd thei brenne
And wer molten as wax…"

DESCRIPTION OF HELL FROM *THE VISIONS OF TUNDALE*, c. 1149

THE LAST JUDGEMENT

In Fra Angelico's *Last Judgement*, Christ, illuminated by celestial light and attended by saints and angels, decides whether souls will enter Heaven or Hell. Heaven, to his right, is a verdant paradise, and Hell, on his left, a place of torment, where demons with pitchforks thrust the damned into dark, rocky caverns filled with gruesome punishments appropriate to their sins. Gluttons stare at a table of food they cannot eat, money-grabbers are force-fed gold, and the wrathful bite each other. In a pit at the bottom, a terrifying, three-headed Satan munches on those who have committed the worst crimes.

Produced between 1425 and 1430 and displayed in the church of Santa Maria degli Angeli in Florence, Fra Angelico's work is testament to the popularity of "doom paintings". Powerful renditions of the Last Judgement, such images were designed to remind people of the consequences of sin and the need to adhere to Church doctrine. As in Fra Angelico's painting, Hell is usually shown as a horrific place of torment, filled with malicious demons. The sharp division between those saved and those damned creates a strong moral message: there is no middle ground, and Christ – at the top of the hierarchy – sees all.

As the medieval period progressed, the tone and structure of Last Judgement images began to change. Rather than focusing on physical tortures and the gulf between Heaven and Hell, paintings of the 16th century emphasized the emotional agony and psychological cost of sin. Michelangelo's *Last Judgement* – painted on the altar wall of the Vatican's Sistine Chapel between 1536 and 1541 – typifies this trend. In this work, all the horror lies in the faces of the damned: fear, anxiety, doubt, and dashed hopes expressing the worst outcomes for humanity.

The pit of Hell
This detail from Fra Angelico's *Last Judgement* shows the worst punishments of Hell: demons push sinners into an icy lake, while Satan stuffs victims into his three mouths.

SPIRITS OF THE SILK ROAD

ALONG WITH PRECIOUS SILKS, TEA, AND PORCELAIN, THE FAMOUS SILK ROAD TRADE ROUTE CARRIED RELIGIOUS BELIEFS AND STORIES RICH IN TERRIFYING GHOSTS, MONSTERS, AND DEMONS.

Yaksha demon
A nature spirit figuring in both Buddhist and Hindu legends, this *yaksha* dating from the Tang dynasty guards a Buddhist cave temple in Dunhuang, China.

Silk road spirits
A supernatural figure flies along the wall of a Buddhist cave temple carved into a cliff near the ancient oasis town of Dunhuang, China.

From around 130 BCE to 1453 CE, an ancient network of trade routes known as the Silk Road connected China to the Mediterranean region, transporting goods such as textiles, spices, and precious metals across Asia. The merchants and travellers who plied this route also took their culture with them, leading to a lively exchange of knowledge and ideas, including about religion and the afterlife. Buddhism, which emerged in India around the 6th century BCE, and Daoism, which evolved soon after in China, were two of the most influential religions transmitted along the Silk Road. These spiritual systems shaped how people across Asia understood the unseen world, establishing beliefs that blended Indian, Central Asian, and Chinese traditions. They also offered explanations for supernatural phenomena and set out detailed rituals for interacting with or repelling hostile spirits.

Buddhist influences

According to Buddhist belief, death is part of a cycle of rebirth whereby individuals are reborn into one of six realms depending on their actions and intentions (karma) in past lifetimes. These realms include a heavenly plane, hellish domains, and the realm of the *pretas* or hungry ghosts – those who have exhibited greed, jealousy, or insatiable desire during their lives. Condemned to suffer extreme hunger and thirst, these restless spirits are not always malicious, but they may cause disturbances or misfortune among the living in their attempts to satisfy their needs. Spreading from India along the Silk Road, Buddhism brought the concept of the hungry ghost to Central Asia,

Back from the dead
A hungry ghost haunts a family – a warning to venerate the dead – in this painting dating from China's Song dynasty (960–1279 CE).

China, Korea, and Japan. In China, these Buddhist notions about spirits melded with Daoist teaching about ghosts and the afterlife. Daoism already contained a rich tradition of beliefs related to ghosts, including fear of demons thought to cause illness or misfortune and the need for proper burial ceremonies to prevent wandering spirits.

Spirits of Daoism

Daoist cosmology describes a spirit hierarchy that mirrors the administrative structure of the imperial Chinese state – a "heavenly bureaucracy" with celestial officials, judges, and spirit police. Priests were valued intermediaries in this system, negotiating between the human and spirit realms through ritual practices such as incantations, offerings, and the use of talismans. In cases of suspected haunting, priests conducted ceremonies to pacify restless ghosts, exorcise malign spirits, and guide lost souls to their proper place in the afterlife.

Conducting appropriate funerary and burial rites was one of the most important ways of preventing unwanted visitations from the spirit world. Daoists believe that the soul consists of two parts, the *hun* and the *po*. The *hun* – the ethereal part – ascends to a heavenly realm after death, while the *po* – the corporeal element – remains in the body of the deceased. If the two parts are not correctly balanced in a state of spiritual harmony at the time of death, if proper burial rites are not performed, or if the dead are not venerated, one or both of these souls may become a restless ghost and torment the living.

When Daoist beliefs spread across East Asia, they merged with local traditions and other religious systems and philosophies, including Buddhism, Confucianism, and Indigenous animist practices. In Japan, for example, belief in ghosts known as *yūrei* were shaped in part by Daoist cosmology, but they developed uniquely Japanese forms. Korean and Vietnamese traditions similarly absorbed Daoist ideas, especially in their approaches to ancestor worship and ritual healing.

Painted temples

At Silk Road hubs such as the town of Dunhuang (on the edge of the Gobi Desert, now in China's Gansu Province), archaeological and textual evidence testifies to the exchange of ideas about the supernatural. Paintings of Buddhist hells adorn caves and temples; house scrolls describe rituals to rescue souls; and inscriptions combine Buddhist and Daoist thought.

Members of other religious communities, including Nestorian Christians and followers of Manichaeism (a Persian dualistic religion focused

> "[The] Yaksha… had eyes like the red of lightning sparks and a mouth as red as blood."
>
> TANG DYNASTY STORY

on the struggle between good and evil), also adopted local beliefs about demons and spirits as they travelled the Silk Road, sometimes reframing them to fit their own belief systems. These spiritual exchanges were not always cordial – sometimes religions competed to explain diseases, dreams, or disasters in terms of supernatural influences – but they led to a rich syncretism, especially when it came to folk beliefs. Villagers might consult both a Buddhist monk and a Daoist priest to deal with a haunting, and some supernatural entities such as *pishachas* – flesh-eating demons – were common to both Hindu and Buddhist legends.

Shared fears

Across Asian traditions, ghosts are often categorized according to the way the person died, their funerary rites, and the degree to which they were venerated after death. Many ghost types are presented as moral or cautionary figures, reflecting cultural anxieties around family, honour, gender roles, and karmic justice. The *churel*, for example, is a terrifying and vengeful female ghost described in tales from North India, Pakistan, and Bangladesh. She is believed to be the spirit of a woman who has died during pregnancy or childbirth, or who was wronged or mistreated in life by her family.

Similar ghosts are said to exist in other Asian cultures. While the *churel* is native to South Asia, *ubume* are the ghosts of would-be mothers in Japan; the *pontianak* is found in Malaysian stories and the *kuntilanak* in Indonesian legends – perhaps reflecting universal fears about maternal mortality.

Navigating the afterlife
A 10th-century painting at Dunhuang depicts the Buddhist afterlife, filled with spirits and presided over by Ti Tsang P'usa, a figure revered in China, Korea, and Japan.

One of Thailand's most famous ghosts, Mae Nak Phra Khanong (Mother Nak of Phra Khanong), is that of a woman who died in childbirth while her husband was away at war. When he returns, he lives with her ghost, unaware she is dead.

Ghostly texts

Under China's Tang dynasty (618–907 CE), trade along the Silk Road soared, making China a central hub of commercial activity, religion, and culture. This golden age produced a boom in literature, with stories related to the supernatural becoming especially popular. A new genre known as *zhiguai xiaoshuo* ("stories of the strange" or "records of anomalies") about gods, ghosts, and demons emerged.

Many of these Tang texts were preserved in the *Taiping Guangji* ("Extensive Records of the Taiping Era") of 978 CE. Circulated widely, this 500-volume anthology became a sourcebook for later writers, providing a wealth of material that was continually adapted, incorporated, and reinterpreted in literary works across East Asia. The popularity of tales of the uncanny and supernatural in the literature and drama of countries such as Korea, Vietnam, Japan, and China can be traced back to the trade networks of the Silk Road.

Wrathful spirit
This image of a *ubume*, from an 18th-century Japanese demonology, shows the bloodied and desperate spirit carrying her baby.

Spirits of the Silk Road

67

ISLAMIC JINN AND SHAYATIN

DISPLAYING VARIOUS TRAITS AND DEGREES OF MORALITY, THESE QUR'ANIC BEINGS — SOME MALEVOLENT — PLAY A KEY PART IN THE ISLAMIC BELIEF SYSTEM.

Mind whisperers
Appearing frequently in the Qur'an, the *shayatin* encourage humans to carry out their evil deeds by whispering into their victim's minds.

According to the Qur'an, Allah created the *jinn*, a species of spirit-beings, from "smokeless fire" before he created human beings from clay. The *jinn* can shift in and out of visibility, as well as change their form; they also possess impressive supernatural powers. However, like humans, they can have relationships, families, and children; and they also have free will. They can choose to be good or evil and whether to submit to Allah. Some *jinn* are Muslims, while others do not follow Allah's message.

The Islamic concept of *jinn* makes it possible for an almost limitless range of folkloric beings to coexist with humankind, since Islam allows for an entire unseen parallel society of good, bad, and indifferent *jinn*. *Jinn* are said to

JINN EXORCISM

In Islamic belief, *jinn* and *shayatin* can possess a person, taking over their personality. In such instances, a practitioner of *ruqyah* – a form of spiritual healing through prayer and recitation of the Qur'an – may try to exorcise the *jinni* or *shaytan* by asking the possessed person to recite the Shahada, the Islamic statement of faith. If the spirit is made to profess Islam via the mouth of the possessed person, the *jinni* will be converted to Islam and have to submit to Allah. It will then leave its host's body.

"As for the *jinn*, We created them earlier from smokeless fire."

QUR'AN 15:27

range from the benevolent, to the morally neutral, to the malign, and humans who unwittingly disturb or deliberately summon *jinn* can be persecuted or even possessed by them. However, *jinn* sometimes want contact — and occasionally sexual relationships — with humans.

When Islam spread to South Asia and Southeast Asia, *jinn* and local spirits merged. In Bengal, for example, the Nishi Dak is a *jinni* that mesmerizes its victim by calling their name, leading them to become lost forever in the jungle. In Java, Wewe Gombel, a monster in the form of a woman with pendulous breasts, stalks and kidnaps children, while the *langsuyar* of Malaysia is a flying vampire-like creature who sucks their blood.

The shayatin

According to the Qur'an, when Allah created Adam from clay, he commanded the *jinn* to bow before Adam. However, a *jinni* called Iblis and his family refused to pay tribute in this way and so became the *shayatin* ("adversaries"), a group of *jinn* who

Three-headed jinni
With his demonic middle head and two that have a more human appearance, Huma is the *jinni* of fever, bringing heat and disease to human bodies.

are overtly hostile to humans and try to cause them harm. The *shayatin* are the demons of Islam, responsible for different kinds of temptation. For example, Iblis's daughter Bidhukh haunts graveyards and offers people magical powers in exchange for sex with her. Iblis also has several sons, among them Awar, who encourages adultery, and Dasim, who sows domestic discord.

While *shayatin* tend to harm rather than kill humans in Islamic tradition, in some stories they do kill. For example, a type of *shaytan* called a *ghul* (the origin of the English word "ghoul") lives in the desert and drags people there to feed on their flesh.

A rude awakening
In the Persian epic *Shahnameh* ("Book of Kings", written c. 977–1010 CE) the *shaytan* Akvan carries a sleeping Rustam, son of the warrior Zaal, on a clump of earth. He attempts to kill Rustam by throwing him into the sea.

MONSTERS AND DEMONS OF HEIAN JAPAN

IN THE HEIAN PERIOD, JAPAN WAS BELIEVED TO BE A HOTBED OF SUPERNATURAL ACTIVITY, STALKED BY SHAPE-SHIFTING SPIRITS AND UNSEEN FORCES.

Although the Edo period (1603–1868) was a golden age for Japanese art and literature about *yōkai* (supernatural spirits or monsters), several of Japan's best-known otherworldly beings have their origins in or just before the earlier Heian period (794–1185). During this time, accounts of strange occurrences flourished, paving the way for the later surge of interest in the supernatural. Creatures that are seen as fun and comical today were originally viewed quite differently.

Completed in 720 CE, the *Nihon Shoki* ("Chronicles of Japan") is the second-oldest extant record of Japanese history. A mix of historical fact and mythology, it includes several fearsome beings from folklore, many of which appear there for the first time.

Ravenous beast

One of the most terrifying figures in Japanese mythology is the *oni*. Described as blue-, red-, yellow-, or black-skinned, usually naked except for

Defeating the demon
In an ancient Japanese tale, the courageous warrior Raikō and his loyal retainers overcome the fearsome ogre Shuten-dōji and his minions, rescuing the captive women held in his lair.

a tiger-skin loincloth, and armed with claw-like fingernails and an iron club, *oni* are brutal ogres. In one of the earliest known references, an *oni* attacks a man working in a field, then devours him while his horrified parents watch helplessly from a nearby bamboo thicket. The idea of *oni* feasting on human flesh became so widespread that it gave rise to the phrase *oni hitokuchi* to describe an instantaneous and grisly action, an allusion to the beast consuming its victim in a single gulp.

People often blamed *oni* for deaths or disappearances that were otherwise unexplained, such as in tales of people vanishing mysteriously from the imperial court. These occurrences were sometimes attributed to Shuten-dōji, the head of the *oni*, who was said to abduct and eat young women in Kyoto. *Oni* were also believed to have the power to shape-shift. Although typically male, they could appear as either sex and were thought to be able to switch between genders to deceive or seduce their prey.

Some sources claim that *oni* are the souls of the dead, but others describe them as corporeal creatures in their own right. It has been suggested that belief in *oni* may have stemmed from fear

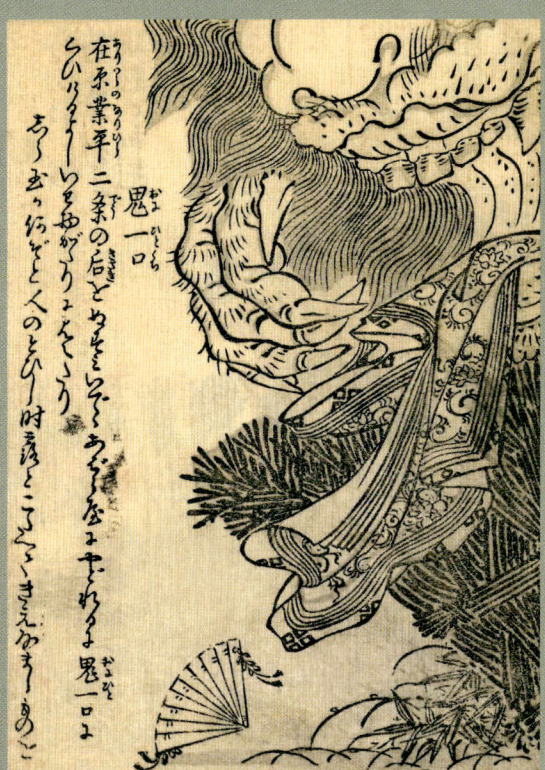

Fearsome claws
An *oni* devours its victim in this late 18th-century scroll painting by Sekien Toriyama, who specialized in illustrating folktales.

Monsters and Demons of Heian Japan

71

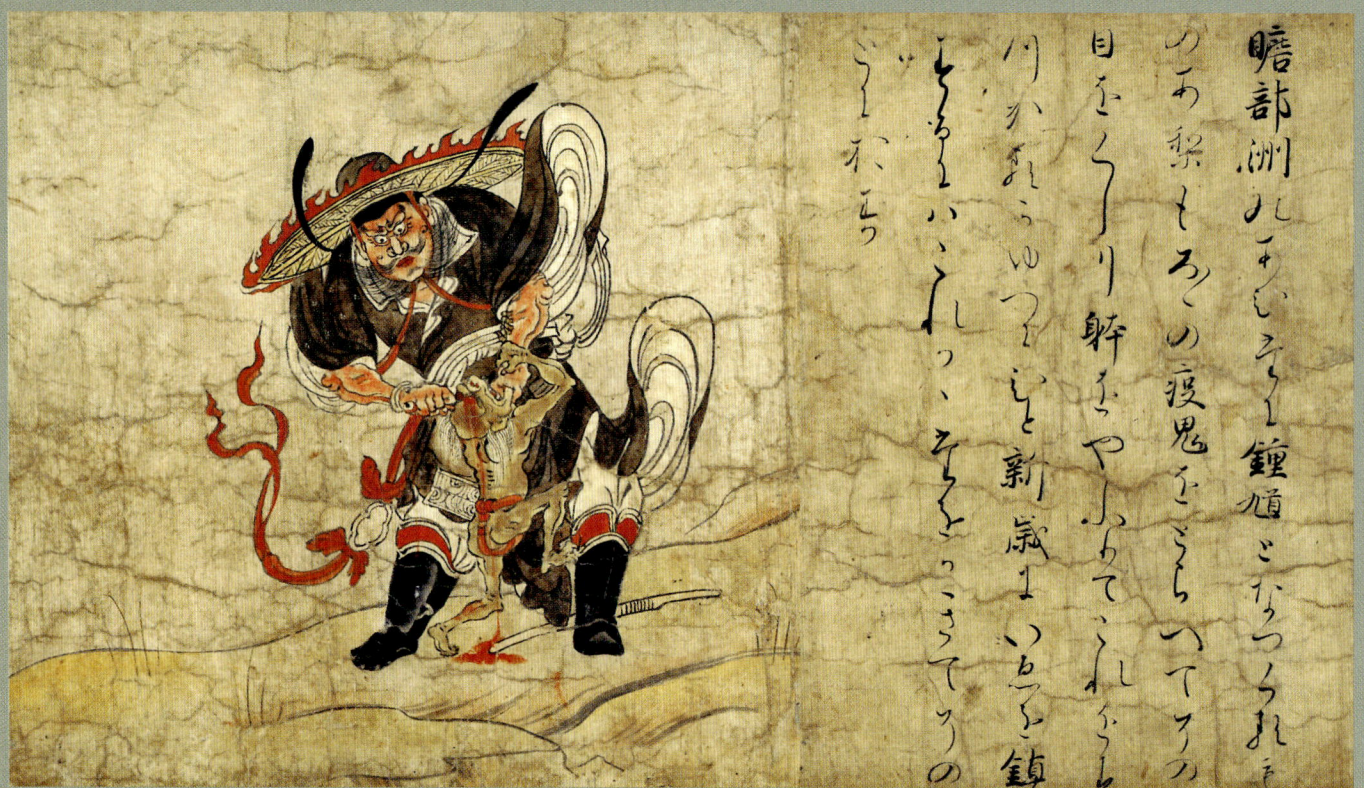

Extermination of evil
In this 12th-century painting, Shōki – a deity imported from Chinese mythology for his skill in demon-slaying – strikes a malevolent spirit.

and misunderstanding of natural phenomena such as lightning. Despite the many tales of evil *oni*, they were not always considered malevolent; indeed, they were sometimes presented in a neutral, if not necessarily positive, way.

Ominous dog

Another creature dating back to the Heian period, or possibly earlier, is the *tengu* – "heavenly dog". A *tengu* is often described as a *yōkai* but sometimes as a Shinto *kami* – a spirit or god. Traditionally, *tengu* have a mix of human, monkey, and bird features and are said to be able to fly.

Some argue that the *tengu* actually originated in China. While notable differences exist between the earlier Chinese *tengu* and the Japanese creature sharing its name, many similarities between the *tengu* and the Chinese celestial fox suggest a historical connection.

In the *Nihon Shoki*, there is a record of "a great star" passing swiftly across the sky, accompanied by the ominous sound of thunder. While some believed the noise was that of the star falling, a Buddhist priest suggested it was the barking of the celestial dog – the *tengu* – whose sudden appearance was a sign of impending tragedy and great misfortune.

The *Konjaku Monogatarishū* ("Anthology of Tales Old and New"), published in the late Heian period, contains some of the earliest tales of *tengu*. Here, *tengu* are generally meddlesome. Aiming to thwart those who would lead pious lives, they

> "*Kappa* subsisted on cucumbers and small river creatures yet also… showed interest in wrestling, sumo, and other martial disciplines."
>
> MAHER ASAAD BAKER, *TALES OF JAPANESE FOLKLORE*, 2024

impersonate nuns and priests, attempt to seduce their victims morally or physically, and bestow supernatural powers on those who worship them.

According to legend, 12th-century Emperor Sutoku became a *tengu* after his failed attempt to reclaim the throne. Consumed by rage, he is said to have cursed the imperial court, and his vengeful spirit was blamed for the subsequent civil war and the death of the new emperor.

A hollow head

More *kami* than *yōkai*, the water-dwelling *kappa* was considered a malevolent, mischievous spirit. Said to be the size of a child, highly intelligent, and a menace near the rivers and ponds where it lived, a *kappa* would pull its unwary prey to a watery grave.

Over time, the notion developed that *kappa* had a shallow indentation, or dish, on their head. This dish was filled with water, which was the source of the *kappa's* power. However, it was also the key to controlling the creature: if the water spilled from the dish, the *kappa* was unable to move or do anything until it was refilled, leaving it indebted for life to whoever replenished the liquid.

Like many such creatures, the *kappa* served a cautionary purpose to deter children and others from straying too close to bodies of water, and also as an explanation for the deaths of humans and livestock by drowning. A later legend maintained that the *kappa* killed their human victims in order to extract a mythical ball-shaped organ through the anus. This *shirikodama* was said to contain the human soul, which the *kappa* prized, feeding on it for strength or stealing it for power.

Fox forms

The concept of *kitsunetsuki* – possession by a fox – also has roots in the Heian period, though it gained greater popularity during the Edo era. *Kitsune* (shape-shifting foxes or fox spirits) were often blamed for unexplained illnesses and erratic behaviour due to their association with bad omens and supernatural powers. In addition to changing their form, these intelligent and cunning creatures were said to be capable of bewitching humans.

Belief in such supernatural interactions shows how the boundary between the human and spirit worlds was thought to be thin in Heian-era Japan. Tales of ghosts, shape-shifters, and vengeful forces were a means of giving near-tangible form to the unknown and uncanny.

Bow down to win
It was thought that although devious, *kappa* could be tricked into spilling water from their head dish. One way was to bow respectfully – a gesture the *kappa* would return out of politeness.

GODS AND REALMS IN NORSE MYTHOLOGY

> "He shall be filled with the flesh of all those men that die, and he shall swallow the Moon, and sprinkle with blood the heavens."
>
> SNORRI STURLUSON ON THE MIDGARD SERPENT AT RAGNARÖK, IN *GYLFAGINNING* ("THE BEGUILING OF GYLFI"), THE *PROSE EDDA*, C.1222–23

DESPITE THE STEREOTYPICAL VIEW OF VIKINGS AS VICIOUS FIGHTERS WHO TERRORIZED AND PILLAGED, THE NORSE PEOPLE HAD MANY OF THEIR OWN FEARS AND SUPERSTITIONS.

Between the 8th and 11th centuries, before the people of Scandinavia converted to Christianity, fear of their own gods was deeply woven into everyday life. They saw the divine as both awe-inspiring and dangerously unpredictable. The god Odin was not only the *Alföðr* ("Allfather"), the god of wisdom, war, and poetry, but also a figure associated with deceit, sacrifice, and the occult. He was revered for his power and knowledge, yet feared for the lengths he would go to attain them – famously sacrificing an eye for wisdom.

Norse gods are often portrayed as powerful but fallible beings who demand respect, offerings, and loyalty, lest they bring misfortune or withhold protection. Fear of this divine retribution was reinforced by a belief in fate (*wyrd*). To avoid peril, Vikings sought guidance from seers – mostly female figures thought to hold supernatural powers, who induced reverence and apprehension.

Realms of terror

The Norse cosmos was divided into nine realms, connected by Yggdrasil, the "world tree". These realms were home to a range of fearsome beings that inspired both awe and dread. Giants (*jötnar*)

Hammer time
Thor, the Norse god of thunder, raises his hammer, Mjölnir, above his head and prepares to deliver a fatal blow to the Midgard serpent.

A new beginning
In Norse mythology, the Universe will be consumed by fire during Ragnarök. Surviving gods will rule during a new golden age.

from Jotunheim were ancient, powerful enemies of the gods, often associated with chaos and destruction. Svartalfheim was the realm of dark elves skilled in sorcery and craftsmanship but also capable of curses and deceit.

Even in Midgard, the realm of humans, the Norse people feared monsters – such as Jörmungandr, also called the Midgard serpent, a figure of immense evil. An enormous sea snake biting its own tail, it was thought to encircle the whole world. People also feared undead creatures such as the *draugar* – restless corpses said to return from the grave to guard their treasure, haunt the living, or seek revenge. They were typically found in burial mounds and often had grotesquely decayed bodies. Described as bloated, blackened, and foul-smelling, they were also attributed with supernatural powers such as shape-shifting, controlling the weather, and the ability to pass through solid rock.

Warriors' fears

Vikings took advantage of the fear they instilled in others. The Norse sagas record tales of berserkers, elite Norse warriors famed for entering a trance-like, frenzied state during battle, channelling the spirits of powerful beasts such as bears or wolves. Their rage, known as *berserkergang*, made them terrifying to both enemies and allies: they could howl, bite their shields, and exhibit wild, uncontrollable behaviour.

More than pain or death, Vikings feared the ignominy of dying ingloriously. Helheim, the land of the dead, was ruled by the goddess Hel and filled with the spirits of those who had died in shame. Those who died in battle, on the other hand, were said to feast in Valhalla, the great drinking hall of the afterlife. The ultimate destiny for all, however, was believed to be Ragnarök, the Norse apocalypse, an inescapable future doomsday when even the gods would perish.

FENRIR

Norse myths include the prophesy that a monstrous giant wolf, Fenrir, will bring destruction during Ragnarök, the end of the world. Born to the god Loki and a giantess, Fenrir grows so powerful that the gods bind him with a magical chain. Despite their efforts, he is fated to break free and kill Odin, the chief god in the Norse pantheon, and then bring chaos. A fearsome figure in mythology, Fenrir symbolizes uncontrollable destruction and the inevitable fate that even gods cannot escape.

In this 1680 Icelandic artwork, Fenrir is depicted alongside the mythical "world tree" Yggdrasil.

THE WILD HUNT

WITH THEIR SPECTRAL RIDERS, ODD BEASTS, AND ABDUCTED SOULS, TALES OF THE WILD HUNT REFLECT DEEP FEARS OF DEATH AND FORCES THAT ARE BEYOND HUMAN CONTROL.

Dark and evocative
In his 1889 painting *The Wild Hunt*, Franz von Stuck uses a sombre palette to suggest dark energy and a sense of impending chaos.

An unholy parade
This alternative take on the Wild Hunt by 16th-century artist Agostino Veneziano depicts humans marching alongside skeletal beasts.

An enduring theme in northern European folklore, the Wild Hunt is said to be a spectral and terrifying procession of the dead riding through the skies. The legend was popularized in the mid- to late 19th century through *Deutsche Mythologie* (*Teutonic Mythology*) by German writer Jacob Grimm, who suggested that the Wild Hunt, or *Wilde Jagd*, originated from pre-Christian ideas of a more benevolent procession led by a pagan god or goddess. Over time, it was reinvented as a malevolent, demonic horde linked with portents and bad omens – a shift that was reflected in the later tales told of the hunt.

Although many of Grimm's theories have been disputed, three similar but ultimately differing notions of spectral huntsmen and their activities have been identified in medieval sources. The first is that of a demonic figure hunting down the sinful; the second takes the form of a demon-hunting wild man; and the third is that of a man condemned to roam Earth as penance for his terrible crimes. Each of them was said to operate alone, without an attending host of either the living or the dead; the myth that hordes of the malevolent dead roamed Earth together in large numbers was not widespread until the 11th century.

There is potential overlap with what became the Wild Hunt in beliefs – from the 9th century onwards – of a nocturnal spirit procession led by a single female figure. Identified variously as the Alpine pagan goddess Perchta, the Roman goddess Diana, or a mythical witch queen called Herodias, she was attended by spirits and, in some reports, the souls of unbaptized children. Some living humans also claimed to have joined the throng according to medieval sources, in either a physical sense or spirit form.

Varying traditions

One of the earliest written references to the Wild Hunt comes from English monks at Peterborough Abbey, who in 1127 recorded witnessing 20 to 30 demonic hunters, accompanied by black dogs and the call of hunting horns. According to the *Peterborough Chronicle*, an Old English manuscript, "The hunters were black and large and hideous and their hounds all black and broad-eyed and hideous, and they rode on black horses and on black bucks." The baying of hunting dogs became a bad omen synonymous with death in several Wild Hunt mythologies.

While Grimm recorded the Wild Hunt as Germanic folklore, similar tales also appear in other traditions. In Ireland, there is a procession of figures known as the *Sluagh Sidhe*, a fairy horde that takes to the night sky and wreaks havoc on any humans they encounter. In Scandinavia, the term *Oskoreia* refers to a cavalcade of warriors led by the high-god Odin, among them his trusty Valkyries, who race across the heavens in a great hunt. However, this is not always a literal hunt; often it is simply a riotous ceremonial ride.

"Children dying unbaptized come into the furious host."

JACOB GRIMM, *TEUTONIC MYTHOLOGY, VOL. III*, 1883

THE RIDE OF ASGARD

Scandinavia has its own version of Germany's Wild Hunt – *Asgardsreien*, or the ride of Asgard (the Norse realm of the gods ruled by Odin), also known as *Oskoreia*. During *Asgardsreien*, Odin is said to lead dead souls in a great hunt across the skies, accompanied by ravens, wolves, and valkyries – his female servants who determined who would die in battle.

This idea reflects 19th-century folktales rather than Old Norse legends. Stories of a diabolical night ride emerged in different parts of Europe after the publication of Jacob Grimm's *Deutsche Mythologie* (*Teutonic Mythology*; 1835), which asserted that the hunt was an ancient folk belief. Norwegian folklorist Peter Christen Asbjørnsen included themes related to the hunt in his folktale collections produced between 1842 and 1871, while in 1896 Scottish scholar Sir William Alexander Craigie printed some hunt stories he had collected in Denmark. The publication of such stories by respected folklorists inspired writers and artists, who continued to add to the Wild Hunt mythos.

For some neopagan communities – among them people who worship versions of the Old Norse gods – *Asgardsreien* is a living folk belief. Modern pagans believe that it takes place from 31 October to 30 April. The sounds of wind and thunder are linked to the cacophony of Odin's chariot crossing the sky. Some neopagans associate *Asgardsreien* with Yule – and, by extension, with tales of Santa Claus and his sleigh – due to Odin's own association with that time of year. Even today, some claim that *Asgardsreien* is an authentic old Norse belief, supposedly twisted by the advent of Christianity into a portent of doom.

Gods in the sky
The Wild Hunt of Odin (1872) painted by Norwegian artist Peter Nicolai Arbo is a dramatic interpretation of the Norse myth. Based on a poem by fellow Norwegian Johan Sebastian Welhaven, it reflects the revival of interest in Scandinavian folklore in the 19th century.

BEOWULF'S FOES

THE MONSTERS IN *BEOWULF* HAVE HELPED SHAPE THE EPIC POEM'S ENDURING POWER. BETWEEN THEM, GRENDEL, HIS MOTHER, AND THE DRAGON TEST THE HERO'S STRENGTH, HONOUR, AND MORTALITY.

In the classic Old English tale *Beowulf* (c. 700–1000 CE), the title character battles natural and supernatural forces that menace civilization and threaten to destroy humanity. The monsters of *Beowulf* provide the hero with the opportunity to prove his valour. They embody negative human qualities and personify the things that humans most fear. These supernatural beings may also be the reason *Beowulf* has survived. The poem exists in a single manuscript that contains several other stories, all of which feature monsters.

Monstrous race

Beowulf's most infamous foe is Grendel. This fiend lives in the wilderness of the moors and fens, a savage space inhabited only by beasts. Preternaturally large and strong, Grendel kills his victims with his bare hands, sometimes drinking the blood and eating the bodies of his victims. Grendel's nocturnal attacks inflict so much terror

> "There woke from [Cain] / such fate-sent ghosts as Grendel."
>
> BEOWULF, LINES 1265–66

Body bag
In this artwork by Joseph Ratcliffe Skelton, Grendel carries his victims' remains back to his lair in what the poem calls a "rare patchwork of devilishly fitted dragon-skins".

Fearsome lake creature
This 21st-century artwork of Grendel's monstrous mother captures how she is described in the poem – as a powerful warrior woman.

that the mead hall Heorot, a symbol of human civilization, eventually sits empty and devoid of life. The horror that Grendel inspires is compounded by the anguish he causes. He removes the remains of his victims, preventing their burial, and vanishes into the moors, leaving the warriors unable to avenge the deaths of their friends.

Grendel's mother is also associated with savage wastelands. She lives at the bottom of a mysterious lake teeming with ravenous sea monsters; her underwater den is so forbidding that no human has ever seen it. She also happens to possess supernatural powers. Finding that his weapons are completely useless against her, Beowulf must use a magical sword forged by giants to cut off her head. Even then, the charmed blade disintegrates after contact with her poisonous blood.

The poem's unknown author explicitly links both Grendels to demons. The poet also describes them as descendants of Cain, the Bible's first murderer (in Genesis 4:8), and as members of a cursed race, associating them with the monsters that were believed to inhabit the untamed edges of the world. These monstrous races were physically aberrant creations that embodied barbarism, engaged in taboo behaviour such as cannibalism, and were often aggressive. They feature in a number of ancient and medieval works, including the *Liber Monstrorum* ("Book of Monsters"), a 7th- or 8th-century English encyclopedia that may have influenced the *Beowulf* author.

Enter the dragon

The dragon that Beowulf faces is even more menacing and destructive than the Grendels. Associated with Satan in the Christian tradition, dragons were usually portrayed as almost invincible agents of unimaginable slaughter, and this one is no exception. It flies over Beowulf's kingdom in a deadly rage, decimating his people and devastating their property with its fiery breath. It ultimately kills Beowulf with its poison.

CREATURES OF INDIGENOUS FOLKLORE

PASSED DOWN THROUGH GENERATIONS, INDIGENOUS AMERICAN TALES OFTEN EXPLORE BOUNDARIES BETWEEN LIFE AND DEATH, OR HUMAN AND NON-HUMAN — LIMINAL SPACES CONNECTED WITH THE SUPERNATURAL.

Many Indigenous folktales contain supernatural elements, both reflecting real beliefs in monsters and spirits and imparting important cultural commentary or lessons. Among the most famous monsters in Indigenous myth is the *wendigo* (also called the *windigo* or *wetigo*), a malevolent beast that was once human. This creature features in the traditional beliefs of several Indigenous groups in North America, particularly among Algonquian-speaking peoples such as the Cree, Ojibwe, Innu, and Algonquin. *Wendigo* stories are not uniform across nations, but they share common themes.

Wendigos are associated with winter and times of famine. They traditionally appear as gaunt giants, with sunken eyes and bones pushing against their skin. Modern accounts, however, often portray them as having icy breath and the antlers of a deer. In many stories, a person becomes a *wendigo* after engaging in cannibalism, either out of desperation

"'We'll have to make him fatter before we eat him,' replied the older *wetigo*."

"THE *WETIGO* AND THE HUNTER", STORY COLLECTED BY BYRON APETAGON, 1991

A legend of long standing

Tales of *wendigos* span centuries. The earliest European record appeared in 1636, written by a Jesuit missionary reporting to his Paris superiors.

or through moral failure. In other versions, a person might be possessed by a *wendigo* spirit if they act with extreme selfishness or gluttony. Traditionally, *wendigos* were figures of fear but they also serve a cautionary purpose, helping Indigenous societies survive when resources became scarce. Today, *wendigos* often appear in tales about the destruction of Indigenous culture by white people.

Dangerous beings

Almost all Indigenous nations' monsters reflect dangers specific to their environment. For the Inuit people of the Coastal Arctic regions, for example, the *qalupalik* is a sea-dwelling humanoid monster with greenish skin, long fingernails, and flowing hair. These creatures lurk under sea ice, snatching disobedient or wandering children to live with them forever. Similarly, the Yacumama, a giant serpent in the myths of the Quechua and other cultures around the Amazon Basin, is said to swallow boats whole and control water. With a name that means "Mother of the Water", the Yacumama is believed to appear during storms or floods that affect the Amazon River.

The Kwakwaka'wakw people of British Columbia, Canada, believe in forest figures called *bakwas*, or wild men. These small, green creatures approach settlements to steal food or kidnap women and children. They might tempt humans to eat "ghost food" (empty cockle shells) so that they, too, will become spirits; or they may leave humans they like with supernatural powers.

Ceremonial costume
In this 1914 photograph, a Qagyuhl man wears a mask that represents a *bakwas*, a wild man of the woods. The hemlock branches on his shirt signify spiritual transformation.

Some beings in Indigenous tales are both feared and revered – as is the *wakinyantanka* ("thunderbird") by peoples of the Great Plains. For Cheyenne, Arapaho, and others, these sky spirits control storms, thunder, and lightning. They are often depicted as huge, powerful birds able to cause destruction with a flap of their wings or a blink of their eyes and are viewed as totemic figures – spiritual protectors. The Ho-Chunk people from the Upper Midwest of the US also hold the thunderbird in high regard. In their tradition, the Thunderbird Clan is linked to sacred fire and leadership, and a man who receives a vision of the thunderbird during a fast may become a war chief. While thunderbirds are protectors, they are also immensely powerful beings, demanding caution and respect.

Impressive decoration
This late-19th-century wooden screen features an image of a thunderbird painted by members of the Tlingit people of Canada and Alaska. The bird is seen capturing an orca

DEMONIC POSSESSION AND CHRISTIAN EXORCISM

SOME PEOPLE BELIEVE ANYTHING IN THE MATERIAL WORLD MAY BE POSSESSED BY A DEMON — FROM PEOPLE AND ANIMALS, TO ENTIRE BUILDINGS.

The typical and most feared form of demonic possession is that of a living human being, when a demon is believed to enter the victim's body and control its behaviour, movements, and even its voice and speech. The personality of the possessed person is often said to change abruptly and radically. While religions such as Vodou, Candomblé, and shamanic traditions sometimes see possession as desirable or spiritually beneficial, Christianity regards it as one of the most feared and dangerous states a person can experience. The possessed person (or demoniac) is not held responsible for their state. In contrast to a witch or a conjuror, who chooses to be in contact with demons, the demoniac is considered to be a passive victim. However, taking part in occult practices such as divination, spirit communication, or ritual magic is traditionally thought to make a person more susceptible to demonic influences.

Demoniacs are associated with a wide range of symptoms. It is said that sometimes the presence of the demon is not perceptible at all. In other cases, the demon might interfere with the senses or the muscles; it may make the victim appear mute or paralysed. Other demoniacs appear to pass through fits of rage, screaming and

A saintly exorcism
In this 15th-century painting, Antonio Vivarini shows St Peter Martyr exorcising a woman. The demon is expelled from her mouth as St Peter splashes her with holy water.

84 The Monstrous Medieval

blaspheming, and physically assaulting others. In the presence of sacramentals, such as holy water or a crucifix, they experience fear or anger.

The ecclesiastical authorities have always had difficulty establishing whether a person is really possessed or simply ill – or even faking possession. Three traditional questions are asked in a bid to be certain: Does the demoniac understand a language they have never learned? Is the demoniac significantly stronger than their bodily state would seem to allow? Does the demoniac know things they cannot possibly know – for example, details about the lives of people he or she has just met?

Ridding the demon

In order to be rid of a demon, an exorcism is undertaken. This takes the form of a ritual prayer to evict a demon from an object or being. The Bible mentions exorcism several times – for example, in Mark 3:15, Jesus grants his disciples the power to cast out devils; and in Mark 5:8, Christ himself commands an unclean spirit to leave a man's body. However, it was only in the 17th century that the Church developed exorcism prayers for trained priests authorized to carry out the procedure.

The first standardized exorcism was part of the *Rituale Romanum* (*Roman Ritual*) of 1614. This was replaced by a new text in 1999 that includes a modernization of the language used and emphasizes care in distinguishing between possession and mental illness. While the Protestant Church rejects the Catholic ritual, it still performs exorcisms.

Classic exorcism
In this powerful scene from *The Exorcist* (1973), the priests use rites invoking Christ's power adapted from the *Rituale Romanum*.

MEDIEVAL MYSTERIES

TALES OF GHOSTLY ENCOUNTERS, ENCHANTED OBJECTS, AND STRANGE HAPPENINGS REFLECT MEDIEVAL ANXIETIES ABOUT RELIGION AND DEATH, AND FEAR OF THE SUPERNATURAL.

Medieval European chronicles are steeped in ghost tales and accounts of uncanny phenomena, belief in the supernatural being deeply intertwined with religious and moral concerns. There are eerie reports of the consecrated host (bread used in the Eucharist) beginning to "bleed" when touched by a non-believer – as was said to occur in Paris in 1290 – and numerous accounts of mystics who received visions or supernatural visitors. Ermine de Reims, a woman living in France in the late 14th century, claimed to have nightly visits from demons and angels. Medieval people believed in many fearsome beings that may seem fantastical to modern minds, from ghosts and demons to vampires and werewolves.

Medieval ghosts

English writers described a broad spectrum of apparitions. In the 12th century, historian and Augustinian canon William of Newburgh wrote of revenants, bloodied corpses rising from the grave to torment the living, in tales he termed *prodigiosa* or "unnatural marvels". Similarly, Benedictine monk Orderic Vitalis described the procession of an army of wandering souls. This was a common theme for several medieval chroniclers, including German abbot Ekkehard of Aura, a Crusader, who wrote of recently killed knights appearing to him. These reports are similar to those of the Wild Hunt, a spectral horde that features in Germanic folklore.

Benedictine abbot Geoffrey of Burton's *Life and Miracles of St Modwenna* provides another 12th-century account of ghostly revenants – two men who die fighting each other, are buried, then rise up again that same night. Local villagers spot them carrying off their own coffins and transforming into various wild beasts.

> "A great rogue, having been buried, after his death sallied forth…"
>
> WILLIAM OF NEWBURGH, *THE HISTORY OF ENGLISH AFFAIRS*, 12TH CENTURY

Devilish dance
This painting by Flemish artist Pieter Brueghel the Younger depicts an outbreak of Dancing Plague in 1592 in Molenbeek, Belgium.

Risen from the grave
Symbolizing death's power over all, this 15th-century Italian fresco vividly conveys the medieval fear of supernatural entities being ever present and ready to attack the living.

Some chroniclers recorded serious reports of supernatural events in everyday life, while others incorporated stories of the supernatural for entertainment or social commentary. Walter Map's *De Nugis Curialium* ("Courtiers' Trifles"), written in the late 12th century, blended satire with the macabre, portraying undead lovers, demons, and shape-shifting spirits to expose personal grievances and societal corruption.

Earthly causes?

In 1374, a strange malady struck the people of Aachen, Germany. Thousands of sufferers danced uncontrollably for days, often until they collapsed from exhaustion or injury, in what was later termed the Dancing Plague. Another case broke out in Strasbourg, France, in 1518. The cause of these frenzies remains unclear, but theories range from mass hysteria to ergot poisoning caused by mouldy grain. To the medieval mind, they were proof of the supernatural world and its terrifying power over humanity.

THE GREEN CHILDREN OF WOOLPIT

A 13th-century chronicle records the uncanny appearance of two children in the village of Woolpit, Suffolk, in 1150. They had green-hued skin, spoke an unknown language, and refused to eat anything but raw beans. They were taken in by a local family and baptized, but the boy died soon after. The girl lost her green tint, assimilated, and learned to speak English. She claimed that the children came from "St Martin's Land", which was supposedly underground.

HORROR IN ARTHURIAN LEGENDS

Murderous beasts
This 14th-century painting shows the knight Lancelot fighting a dragon – just one of the challenges on his quest to find the Holy Grail.

FILLED WITH MONSTROUS CREATURES, MAGIC, AND PSYCHOLOGICAL THREATS, THE MEDIEVAL TALES OF KING ARTHUR EXPLORE DANGERS AND DARK THEMES.

"He raised his head and saw a very great beast coming, so deformed that no man had ever seen any form like it."

DESCRIPTION OF THE QUESTING BEAST FROM *THE CRY OF MERLIN THE WISE*, 1498

Dangerous quest
Sir Gawain agrees to the challenge (top), and the Green Knight retrieves his own severed head (bottom), in this 15th-century drawing.

The Arthurian legends, a diverse body of texts about King Arthur and his knights, span centuries, languages, and literary traditions. Early medieval Welsh sources contain the first references to Arthur, but his story gained new popularity in Geoffrey of Monmouth's widely circulated *Historia Regum Britanniae* ("History of the Kings of Britain"), written in Latin in c.1136. Towards the end of the 12th century, French poet Chrétien de Troyes reimaged Arthur's story as a chivalric romance and introduced new themes, including the quest for a Holy Grail and the love affair between Arthur's wife Guinevere and his knight Lancelot. These became established tropes when English writer Sir Thomas Malory synthesized many earlier sources into a single prose narrative, *Le Morte d'Arthur* ("The Death of Arthur") in 1485.

Dark themes
Medieval Arthurian legends were more than just light entertainment. Often dealing with complex notions of heroism, mortality, and chivalry, they contain many elements found in later horror stories, including madness, the power of magic, monsters, and betrayal. King Arthur is said to have slain giants and is depicted as a hero who fights other monstrous forces. He is also regarded as a supernatural figure – a "once and future king" who is destined to return from the dead at England's time of need.

In the course of their adventures, Arthur and his knights face threats from terrible beasts drawn from various mythologies, such as the Afanc, a lake monster originating in ancient Welsh folktales. Other creatures are uniquely Arthurian. One of these, the Questing Beast, appears in many texts as a symbol of death and danger. It is a gruesome hybrid, with a snake's head, leopard's body, lion's hindquarters, and the feet of a stag.

Gawain and the Green Knight
Horror features prominently in one of the most famous tales in the Arthurian canon, the 14th-century romance *Sir Gawain and the Green Knight*. In this poem, Gawain accepts a challenge from a mysterious Green Knight to strike him with an axe and then receive a return blow after a year and a day. When Gawain beheads the knight, the supernatural creature simply collects his head and gets back on his horse. The year's end approaches and Gawain undertakes a quest to find the knight. Filled with dread, the story builds psychological tension as Gawain faces a series of tests, including an attempted seduction, all the time journeying closer, it seems, to his own death. In a surprising ending, the knight just nicks Gawain's neck with his axe and reveals that the contest was set up as a test by a powerful sorceress, Morgan le Fay.

A FUTURE IN HORROR

The Arthurian legends have provided a rich source of material for the modern horror genre across all mediums. Released in 2021, the video game *The Hand of Merlin* shows how Arthurian characters, settings, and the plotline of a quest have been reimagined to tackle a darker cosmic threat. By contrast, internal struggles provide the danger in the 2021 film *The Green Knight*, which uses the story of Sir Gawain to explore a deep psychological journey. In a new twist, King Arthur is reframed as evil in the horror comic book series *Once & Future* (2019–22). His rampages are stopped by the real heroine, a grandmother named Bridgette.

MONSTERS IN MEDIEVAL BESTIARIES

TERRIFYING BEASTS, SUCH AS THE VICIOUS MANTICORE, SERVED AS POWERFUL SYMBOLS TO EXPLORE THEMES OF GOOD AND EVIL AND THE CONSEQUENCES OF SIN.

An illustrated compendium of creatures ranging from the everyday to the fabulous and monstrous, the bestiary was one of the most popular book genres during the medieval period. While the selection of creatures sometimes varied, the text melded myth, observed features, and allegory, accompanied by vivid illustrations. As Christians believed God had created every species of animal and communicated his intentions through them, bestiaries were a useful way of providing moral and theological guidance. A standard inclusion, descriptions of the pelican served this purpose perfectly. Believed to kill its young, then revive them with its own blood, the pelican was depicted stabbing itself with its beak to release a spray of blood. This display of self-sacrifice represented that of Christ, who suffered for humanity's sins and spiritually nourished his followers.

Spiritual guidance

The moralizing text of most medieval bestiaries was based on a 2nd-century CE Greek work called *Physiologus* ("The Naturalist"). This incredibly popular collection, which was translated into many European languages during the medieval era, was one of the first to give descriptions of beasts an explicitly Christian slant. Many monsters were specifically created to present a moral message, either warning against sinful behaviour or displaying attributes usually ascribed to the Devil.

The fox is one example of a familiar animal given a satanic twist. In the *Physiologus* and then in bestiaries, it is portrayed as a sly trickster that uses deception and stealth to snatch the unwary. Illustrations show it lying on its back, playing dead. As soon as hungry birds approach, hoping to feed on the corpse, the cunning fox jumps up and grabs one for his own dinner – like the Devil looking to capture souls.

Devilish dragons
Dragons, like this example from around 1270, were viewed as bearers of death or incarnations of the Devil.

Devilish characteristics could also take physical form. Many animals were described as having bizarre or repulsive features, believed to be outward representations of a demonic nature. Worms or worm-like beasts were often personified as demons or demonic agents that could cause disease. One, the seta, was a horrible headless worm covered in coarse hair that grew to the length of a human forearm. Near impossible to kill, even by crushing or boiling, it emitted venom that caused a torturous death. The bonnacon was another beast capable of deadly attack. A bull-like creature with incurved horns, it sprayed pursuers with a stream of dung so toxic that it could set things ablaze. This fiery emission represented the destructive power of sin.

Faraway realms

Bestiaries included some creatures that were either wholly imaginary or confected from multiple animals to create new and monstrous forms. These hybrid beasts were often said to live in remote locations at the edges of the European known world, where few had ever been. Far from

Monstrous end
The consequences of sin are vividly imagined as consumption by terrible beasts in this 13th-century illustration of Hell's mouth.

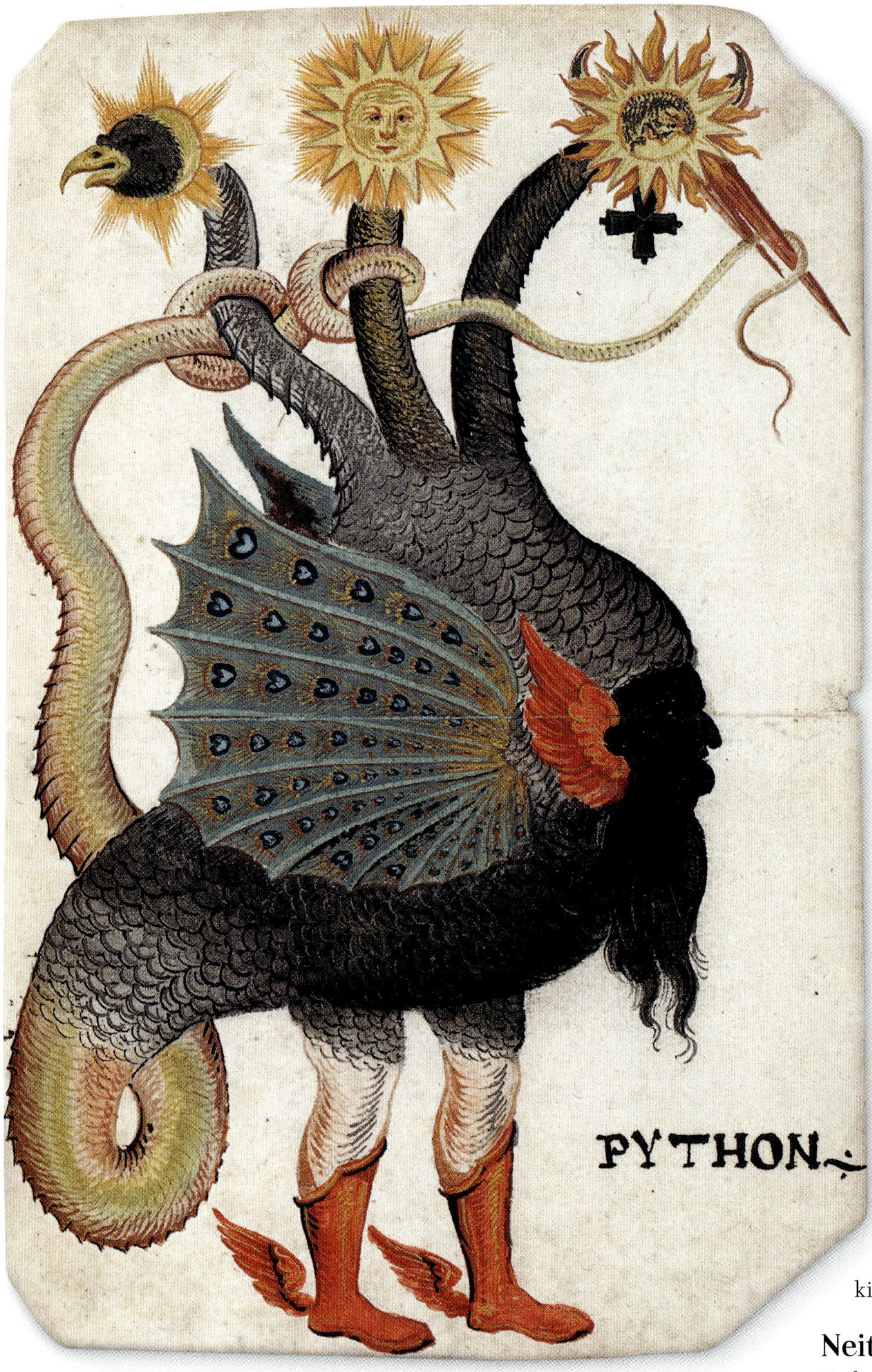

eius
Et concupierunt concupiscenciam
in deserto: et temptauerunt deum in
inaquoso
Et dedit eis peticionem ipsorum: et
misit saturitatem in animas eorū.
Et irritauerunt moysen in castris:
aaron sanctum domini
Aperta est terra et deglutiuit datan:
et operuit super congregacionē abirō.
Et exarsit ignis in sinagoga eorū:
flamma combussit peccatores
Et fecerunt uitulum in oreb: et ad
orauerunt sculptile

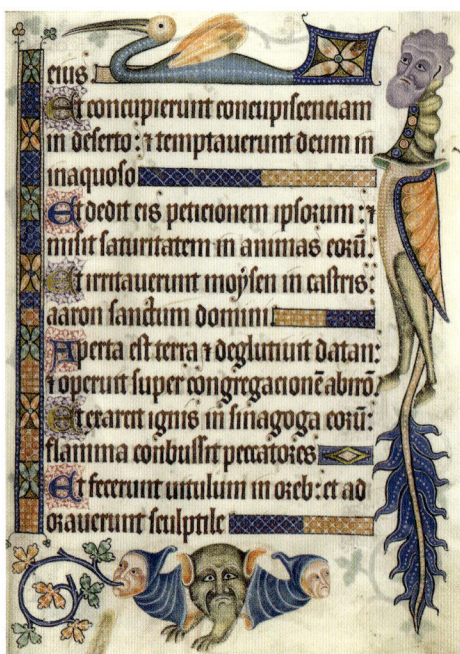

Grotesque lesson
Monsters melding human and animal parts were often used to reinforce moralizing messages, as on this page from the Luttrell Psalter (c. 1325–35).

Enduring beasts
This 18th-century image of a python shows the lasting influence of the monstrous hybrids of medieval bestiaries.

Christian civilization, these realms represented terrifying places of spiritual darkness, distanced from God's care. The leucrota was one of the beasts thought to live in these far-off lands. Believed to be the product of a hyena mated with a lioness, it had the legs of a deer, the body of a lion, and the head of a camel or a badger. Able to imitate the human voice, it had a mouth that contained a single bony ridge, instead of many teeth, and stretched from ear to ear.

Another deadly hybrid, the basilisk, was believed to inhabit deserts or other desolate regions. Thought to hatch from an egg laid by a cockerel then incubated by a toad, it was sometimes described as a fearsome crested serpent or as a vicious cockerel with a long, snake-like tail. Every part of the basilisk was deadly: its venom was lethal and just the sound of its cry could kill, as could a single glance.

Neither man nor beast

Perhaps the most alarming monsters were those that blurred the line between human and beast, suggesting that devilish nature might be hiding in plain sight. The cefusa was clearly an animal but had the feet and hands of a human, and could be identified by its distinctive footprints. Interpreted as a symbol of hypocrisy, it represented those who appeared virtuous but were truly deceitful. The great 13th-century German philosopher

"With grey eyes the colour of blood... it most greedily desires human flesh."

DESCRIPTION OF A MANTICORE, c. 1230–45

Albertus Magnus claimed to have seen a pair of cefusas captured in India – it is possible they were really apes.

Other part-human creatures were the stuff of nightmares. The draconcopedes had the tail and body of a winged dragon but the head of a maiden. It was thought by some to be the beast that had tempted Adam and Eve in the Garden of Eden. The manticore was identified even more closely with the Devil. It had the muscled body of a lion, a stinging tail covered in venom-filled barbs, and the head of a human. It had three rows of vicious teeth to tear the flesh from its victims – not even bones were left behind.

Agents of disease

Lacking the scientific understanding of modern times, some monsters in medieval bestiaries provided explanations for death and disease. The dipsa was a snake too small to be seen but so deadly that its victims died before registering the pain of its bite. The bite of another snake-like creature, the asfodius, caused blood to pour from every bodily orifice. Since illness was often attributed to demonic forces, these creatures were inevitably described as evil or motivated by sin.

Forces for good

Some monstrous creatures, although feared, had positive associations, often linked to Christian virtues and ideals. The powerful and ferocious griffin, combining the characteristics of a lion and an eagle, was thought to carry off humans to feed its young. It was also, however, praised for its courage and role as a protector – an instructional exemplar of the need for Christians to defend their beliefs. One of the most famous creatures, the unicorn, hints at the complicated allegorical meanings associated with the bestiary beasts. A wild and dangerous inhabitant of distant lands, though not quite a monster, it was also venerated as the ultimate symbol – an incarnation of Christ.

Overcoming evil
In this 18th-century image symbolizing the victory of good over evil, St Martha calmly leads off a tarasque – a fearsome hybrid beast.

CHAOS AND EVIL IN KABBALAH

MEANING "RECEPTION" OR "TRADITION" IN HEBREW, THE JEWISH MYSTICAL PRACTICE OF KABBALAH SEEKS TO EXPLORE THE NATURE OF GOD WHILE TEACHING THAT THE DIVINE ESSENCE IS UNKNOWABLE.

Several spirits or demons within Kabbalah are associated with chaos and evil, and the most prominent are three unconquerable primordial creatures: Leviathan, Behemoth, and Ziz. All three beings are mentioned within the Zohar – the book of Splendour – the main canonical text of Kabbalah that emerged in 13th-century Spain. Although described as physical creatures, they were also understood in a metaphorical sense, representing ideas rather than reality.

Leviathan is a vast sea serpent that the Hebrew Bible describes as dwelling in the deep and embodying chaos. In the Zohar and later Jewish mysticism, it is depicted as immense in size, with scales like shields of iron, a thrashing tail, and the power to exhale smoke and flame, symbolizing untamed cosmic forces. According to the Talmud, after Leviathan drinks from the sea, the depths remain disturbed for 70 years.

According to some mystical Jewish traditions, there were originally two Leviathans, one male and one female. They were such fearsome and terrible creatures, however, that God killed the female so that the pair could not reproduce. It was said that her flesh was then salted and preserved in preparation for a meal that would be served to the righteous at the end of days. Some saw the eating of this flesh as a metaphor for the enlightenment at the end of the world.

In a similar vein, the primordial serpent appears in Kabbalah as both a symbol of temptation and evil and as a metaphor for enlightenment. It represents the cosmic struggle between light and darkness, embodying the forces that shape the spiritual universe, or non-physical realm.

Birds of the air, beasts of the earth

The creature known as Behemoth – sometimes interpreted as meaning "great beast" – is said to dwell in Duidain, the invisible desert that lies to the east of the Garden of Eden, and to rule over the land. Of insurmountable size, Behemoth is deemed invincible; at the time of the summer

The Devil takes a ride
While not traditionally linked in Kabbalah, the Devil and Behemoth are occasionally depicted together in some later sources, with Satan using the great beast as a mode of transport.

> "Every one among us has a thousand [demons] on his left hand and ten thousand on his right hand."
>
> RABBI HUNA, TALMUD, BERAKHOT 6A

solstice, he is particularly powerful, subduing all other animals for the year ahead with the loudest of roars. According to Jewish rabbinic legend, Behemoth and Leviathan will battle each other at the end of time, and their flesh will also be served to the righteous.

The final creature of the primordial triumvirate is the colossal, bird-like being known as Ziz. Revered as the ruler of the skies and all the birds that soar across them, Ziz is said to have wings so vast that when fully spread, they completely block out the Sun. A noble and majestic creature, Ziz is often equated with or closely linked to the legendary Bar Yochnei, a bird whose enormous eggs would bring catastrophe if ever they fell from the nest. According to tradition, when one such egg shattered, its contents drowned 60 cities and toppled 300 mighty cedar trees in its path.

Cosmic balance
The sea serpent Leviathan embodies the ancient cosmic forces that balance creation, destruction, and the unknown.

DANTE'S JOURNEY THROUGH HELL

RECOUNTING IN GRUESOME DETAIL A TOUR THROUGH NINE CIRCLES OF HELL, DANTE'S *DIVINE COMEDY* IMAGINES THE HORROR OF PUNISHMENTS METED OUT TO THE DAMNED.

Hell's mouth
This 15th-century illustration, by early Netherlandish painter Simon Marmion, shows the influence of Dante's powerful imagery on notions of Hell and the fiery torments within.

Italian poet Dante Alighieri's trilogy *The Divine Comedy* (called *La Commedia* at the time of writing) provided one of the most definitive depictions of Hell in medieval literature. Written between 1308 and his death in 1321, the epic sees Dante, as a character in his own work, travelling through Hell, Purgatory, and Heaven, where he encounters people from contemporary life and historical figures. The story is both a portrayal of the Christian cosmos, defined by sin on Earth and its consequences in the afterlife, and a political allegory commenting on the corruption and factionalism of contemporary Florence. Dante imagined Christian Hell as nine concentric circles, each representing a type of sin in order of increasing gravity. The first circle, and least horrible, is limbo, the realm of the virtuous but unbaptized. The second is for the lustful; the third for gluttons; the fourth for those who greedily pursued wealth; the fifth for the wrathful; the sixth for heretics; the seventh for the violent; the eighth for those who committed fraud; and the ninth for the treacherous. At the centre of the ninth circle lies Satan. Dante begins his journey through these circles of punishment in the trilogy's first

> "These did their faces irrigate with blood,
> Which, with their tears commingled, at their feet
> By the disgusting worms was gathered up."
>
> INFERNO, CANTO III

book, *Inferno*. Entering through the Gates of Hell, he reads the chilling inscription: "Abandon all hope, ye who enter here".

Hellish horrors

Admitted into Hell, Dante describes in graphic detail the horrific punishments meted out to sinners. In Canto XIII, for example, he traverses the Wood of the Suicides, where those who died by their own hand are transformed into twisted, thorny trees. The tree-people are torn apart by harpies, mythical bird-women from ancient Greek myth. Only when their branches are snapped can these trapped souls speak to tell their stories.

Demonic guard
Plutus, a monstrous demon based on the Roman god of wealth, guards the fourth circle of Hell, where the greedy are punished.

Swamp of sinners
This 19th-century illustration of the fifth circle of Hell shows Filippo Argenti, a Florentine politician known for his temper, immersed in the waters of the river Styx as punishment.

Caught in another circle, the lustful are swept into an "infernal hurricane", their bodies "molested" by strong winds as penance for their carnal sins on Earth; elsewhere the violent are submerged in a boiling river of fire and blood.

The greatest horrors lie at the centre of Hell, where Dante finds Satan, grotesque and three-faced, imprisoned in a frozen lake. This ninth circle punishes traitors, with those who have committed the worst betrayals buried deepest in the ice. The realm's coldness reflects a terrible penalty – the ultimate absence of God's love and warmth.

INTO THE INFERNO

Soon after Dante Alighieri completed his seminal work *The Divine Comedy* in 1321, artists began bringing his terrifying visions of Hell – the fiery *Inferno* – to life. Many illustrated copies of Dante's work were already circulating in manuscript form by the early 15th century, and the first printed versions were produced in 1472. Through these editions, images of Dante's nine desolate realms filled with grotesque demons and tortured sinners reached a new and wider audience. They also had a lasting impact on Western concepts of the afterlife.

Around 1485–95, Italian Renaissance painter Sandro Botticelli produced some of the most famous early illustrations of Dante's text. Among these, his "Map of Hell", which showed the structure of the *Inferno* as a spiralling three-dimensional funnel, provided an iconic interpretation that influenced later portrayals. His rendering of the horrific punishments inflicted on the damned also had lasting impact. With its meticulous detail and contemporary references, viewers were left in no doubt about the range and relevance of the terrible physical torments that might await them.

When members of the Romantic movement revived Dante's work in the 19th century, they laid greater emphasis on Hell's psychological and spiritual agonies. The illustrations by British poet and artist William Blake and French artist Gustave Doré were particularly celebrated. Doré used dramatic realism to make the horrors of Hell feel deeply personal, while Blake analysed the psychology of the damned as they wrestled with the consequences of sin. Both visions would greatly influence how future readers engaged with Dante's text.

Disgust and damnation
In this image of the eighth circle of Hell, William Blake shows Dante and his companion Virgil covering their noses to avoid an overpowering stench – the smell of moral corruption.

THE DANCE OF DEATH (DANSE MACABRE)

DEPICTIONS OF SKELETONS DANCING WITH PEOPLE FROM ALL WALKS OF LIFE WERE A SPUR TO REPENTANCE AND A REMINDER THAT DEATH COMES FOR ALL.

Evoking the horror and inevitability of death, the image of skeletons leading a dancing procession of the living became a popular theme in art and literature between the 14th and 16th centuries. It is unknown whether this *Danse Macabre* or "Dance of Death" was inspired by a real dance, but the motif's popularity coincided with a period of widespread death as famine, plague, and the Hundred Years' War ravaged much of Europe.

Before the emergence of the outbreak of plague known as the Black Death in 1347, death was usually illustrated as a monstrous, otherworldly creature – an embodiment of evil and sin. After the plague indiscriminately claimed the lives of millions across all social classes, including Church officials, skeletons became a more common representation. They served as a reminder that death was democratic, but also made death personal, reminding people that they should prepare their soul for the afterlife through repentance.

Scenes of death

A small number of 14th-century texts, including Jean le Fèvre's 1376 poem *Le Respit de la Mort* ("Respite from Death"), mention a "dance of death". The earliest visual representation may have been a large mural, later destroyed, on the south wall of the Holy Innocents Cemetery in Paris around 1424–25. This image showed a long procession of men, ranked according to social status, from peasant to pope, accompanied by dancing skeletons.

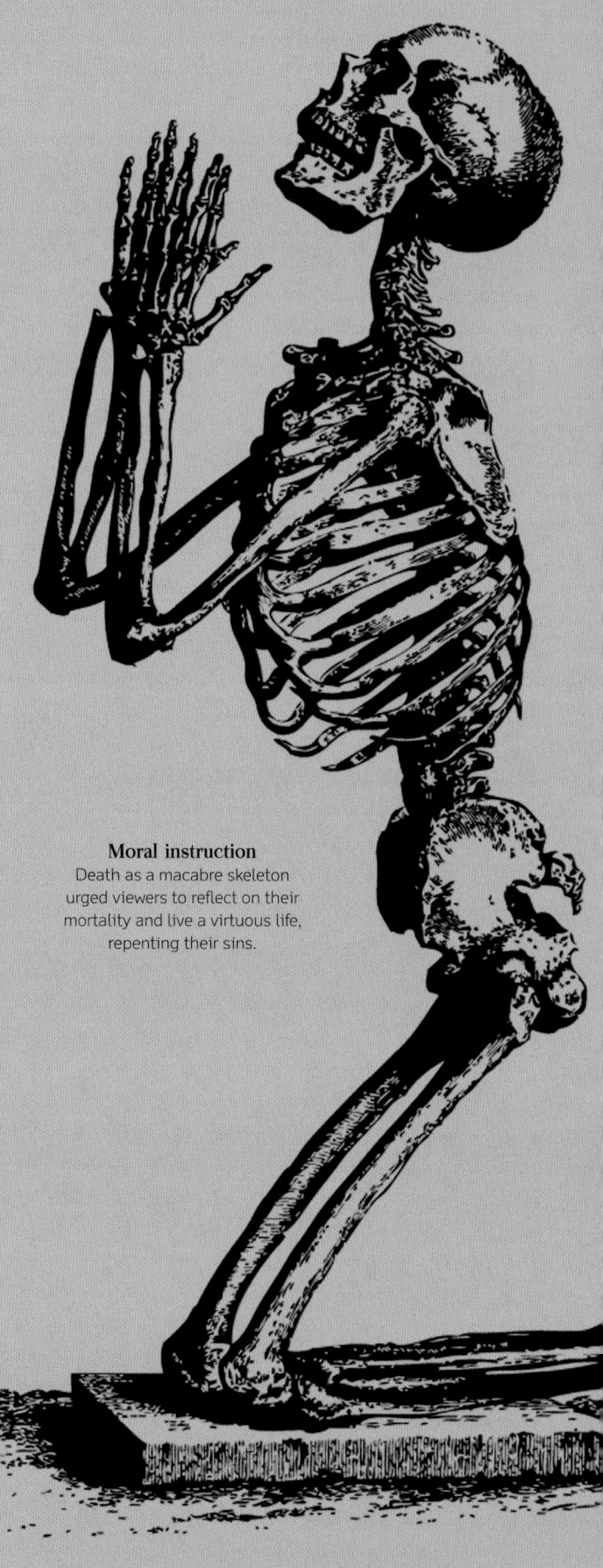

Moral instruction
Death as a macabre skeleton urged viewers to reflect on their mortality and live a virtuous life, repenting their sins.

Situated in a busy quarter of the city near to markets, this painting would have been seen by many. A print version of the images, along with accompanying verses, was published by French printer Guyot Marchant in 1485.

Holbein's dance

The theme of the *Danse Macabre* caught the public imagination and spread through Europe in the 15th and 16th centuries. One of the most famous iterations was a series of woodcuts titled *Dance of Death*, designed by German artist Hans Holbein the Younger around 1525. Each scene shows a victim from a different level of society surprised by death in the form of a skeleton. More than a simple reminder that death comes to all, the images provided a satirical social commentary. Death metes out punishments appropriate to each person's position and folly, with abusers of power at the top of the social scale coming off worst. Published in book form in 1538, the series became a definitive version of the *Danse Macabre* that would inspire artists and writers in the following centuries.

> "You who live: certainly, sooner or later, you will do this dance."
>
> GUYOT MARCHANT, *THE DANSE MACABRE*, 1485

Death and beyond
This 18th-century German painting shows the enduring popularity of the *Danse Macabre* motif beyond the medieval period. In a new twist, its central scene places individual death and afterlife in the wider context of Christian salvation.

FEAR OF THE PLAGUE

Causing horrific symptoms and an agonizing death, the plague inspired fear, horror, and a new form of realism as artists and writers captured its effects. Texts such as Giovanni Boccacio's *Decameron*, written in the late 14th century as the Black Death ravaged Europe, show an anxious society trying to deal with the deadly plague's terrible reality.

The beak of this 16th-century plague doctor's mask would have held herbs to filter "bad air".

AZTEC AND INCA DEATH GODS

BEFORE THE ARRIVAL OF THE CONQUISTADORS, THE GREAT INDIGENOUS EMPIRES OF SOUTH AND CENTRAL AMERICA HAD DISTINCT IDEAS ABOUT MORTALITY AND THE AFTERLIFE.

God of the Underworld
The skeletal Mictlāntēcutli, terrifying Aztec god of the Underworld, awaited those who were bound for Mictlān at the end of their lives.

For the Aztecs, whose empire in central Mexico flourished from 1325 until the Spanish conquest in 1521, death was a constant presence. According to their creation myth, the world began through the self-sacrifice of the gods, who gave their own blood to create humanity. The people felt compelled to honour this divine gift with their own offerings, either through bloodletting or the presentation of a human heart in ritual sacrifice. Those who gave their life in this way, whether voluntarily or not, were deified and held in the highest esteem. They would sometimes be referred to as the *teteo imixiptlahuan*, the "image of the gods".

Death was not the end for the Aztecs. The souls of the dead – referred to as *teyolía* – were believed to arrive in a place called Mictlān, where they were sorted into different groups, based on how each

Mummy Juanita
This Inca mummy is the remains of a young woman who was ritually sacrificed. Her exceptional preservation reflects the reverence for her sacred offering.

person had lived or died. Those who died in battle, through sacrifice, or during childbirth would go to Tonatiuhichan, the "heaven of the Sun"; casualties of accidents such as drowning or lightning strikes went to Tlālōcān, or "the place of the god of rain"; and children who died in early infancy went to Chichihuacuauhco, a special paradise for the very young. All other deceased had to spend four years navigating the nine treacherous levels of Mictlān, facing perilous tasks and supernatural creatures, including the daunting spirit dog Xolotl and fearsome demons with a craving for human hearts. In the ninth and deepest level, they would encounter Mictlāntēcutli, the ruler of death, along with his wife Mictēcacihuātl. After this arduous journey, the souls found their final resting place in the silent darkness of Mictlān.

As the ruler of Mictlān, Mictlāntēcutli was a fearsome and unsettling figure, with an appetite for human flesh. He is usually depicted as a decaying body, half flesh and half skeleton, often with a necklace of eyeballs and an owl-feather headdress. His clawed hands sometimes hold implements for removing the hearts of wandering or lost spirits.

Inca beliefs

The Aztecs shared some beliefs with the Maya, who previously dominated in Mesoamerica, and also with the major empire in precolonial South America, the Incas, who lived in what is now Peru between 1438 and 1533. Like the Aztecs, the Incas practised human sacrifice and worshipped Sun deities, but they had their own god of death, Supay. The Incas believed in life after death and venerated their ancestors. The dead were mummified and kept in sacred tombs called *huacas*.

In addition to death gods, these Andean peoples worshipped and feared a powerful cosmos of nature deities, reflecting their lives in the mountains, and used hallucinogenic plants to communicate with them. The beliefs of the Incas survive today in Quechua-speaking communities living in the Andes.

Purification fire
An Aztec priest oversees a ritual human sacrifice as the victim's heart is removed. The fire being held aloft symbolizes purification.

THE MALLEUS MALEFICARUM AND FEAR OF WITCHCRAFT

HEINRICH KRAMER'S NOTORIOUS DEMONOLOGY ENUMERATED THE MANY WAYS A WITCH COULD DESTROY THE LIVES OF THE GODLY.

In 1486, the most infamous witch-hunting manual – or "demonology" – was published in Speyer, Germany. Written by Catholic clergyman Heinrich Kramer, the *Malleus Maleficarum* ("Hammer of Witches") was a treatise on witches and how they should be identified and punished. Disseminated throughout Europe, it spread fear of witchcraft and caused a significant increase in the number of witch hunts. The recent invention of the printing press, which allowed texts to be mass-produced and widely distributed, meant that such treatises by supposed witchcraft experts quickly became gospel.

Deep-rooted fears

Belief in the existence of witchcraft was entrenched in scripture, with many Bible teachings attesting to witches' wickedness. Leviticus 19:31 declaims: "Regard not them that have familiar spirits, neither seek after wizards, to be defiled by them", while Exodus 22:18 states: "Thou shalt not suffer a witch to live". The Biblical story of the Witch of Endor (Samuel 28:3–25) cautions against dealings with witches. In the tale, King Saul breaks Old Testament prohibitions against necromancy (raising the dead) by asking the witch to communicate with the dead prophet Samuel. Rather than guidance, Samuel's spirit delivers a message of doom, foretelling Saul's defeat in battle and death.

Until the 13th century, however, the Church's official stance on witchcraft was that it was an illusion. The canon *Episcopi* – a text regarded as canonical law, compiled by abbot Regino of Prüm around 900 CE – called on churches to eject parishioners who believed in witchcraft. It was

Forbidden arts
Christian condemnation of witchcraft is rooted in the Old Testament. Here, King Saul breaks the law to consult the Witch of Endor.

> "The Witches ar servantes onelie, and slaues to the Devil... Necromanciers are his maisters..."
> KING JAMES VI, *DAEMONOLOGIE*, 1597

HÄXAN: WITCHCRAFT THROUGH THE AGES

Made by Danish director Benjamin Christensen in 1922, the silent horror film *Häxan* (released in English as *The Witches*) drew on the *Malleus Maleficarum* and other texts to chronicle the persecution of supposed witches from the medieval period onwards. Although it purported to be a documentary, the film included highly disturbing fictionalized scenes and shocking vivid reenactments, straddling a line between reality and horror. *Häxan* was heavily censored in multiple countries and initially banned in the US; it was finally released there in 1968 as *Witchcraft Through the Ages*.

Twice damned
A woodcut from a 1497 edition of the *Malleus* shows the torment awaiting a witch in Hell as punishment for consorting with the Devil.

heretical to think that there was any higher power in the world other than God. Usually, those accused of witchcraft were believed to be in league with Satan, but the *Episcopi* also mentions women performing rites to the pagan goddess Diana.

Trials after the publication of the *Malleus Maleficarum* similarly focused on satanic witchcraft, though there were a few exceptions. In the town of Vardø, Norway, in the 17th century, a group of Sami men were tried for practising Indigenous magical traditions.

A hammer against witches

Kramer was living in Innsbruck, Austria, when he encountered Helena Scheuberin, a woman known for associating with heretics and freethinkers. When Scheuberin denounced Kramer's teachings on witchcraft and encouraged others to avoid his sermons, he accused her of being a witch.

Kramer wrote to Pope Innocent VIII, who put out *Summis Desiderantes Affectibus* ("Desiring With Supreme Ardour", 1484), a papal bull on witchcraft that defined it as a crime against nature. It lamented that men and women alike had given themselves to devils, incubi, and succubi, and used their power for evil deeds. The edict gave many examples of what a witch might have the power to do, such as slay unborn children, kill calves, ruin harvests, cause illness and misfortune for people and animals, and even stop men from performing sexually or women from conceiving children.

The Pope empowered Kramer, along with Jacob Sprenger, a Dominican theologian, to act as inquisitors, bringing Scheuberin and others to trial in Innsbruck in 1485. Kramer led the trial, but his preoccupation with Scheuberin's sexual behaviour, which he had documented obsessively, alarmed the jury, and his arguments failed to convey a serious threat. Not only was Scheuberin acquitted, but Kramer was expelled from Innsbruck.

Unnatural act
Adam Elsheimer's painting (1598) depicts a witch riding on a goat. The night rides of witches – on animals and brooms – were attested by Kramer.

Humiliated, Kramer began to write the *Malleus Maleficarum* – a deeply misogynistic document that created a new legal framework for persecuting witches. He described witches as depraved women who had sexual relations with demons, rode broomsticks in the night (called "transvection"), and made deals with the Devil to do harm. Many of his ideas were not new – writing in 1154, English philosopher John of Salisbury, for example, discussed the idea of witches' night rides – but Kramer's manual formalized them as key tenets of witchcraft. As well as drawing on records of prior witch and heresy trials, Kramer was likely inspired by an earlier text: the fifth book of German theologian Johannes Nider's *Formicarius* ("The Ant Colony", 1475), a similarly misogynistic work that included examples of witchcraft described at the Council of Florence (1431–45).

Fanning the flames

The *Malleus* became a bestseller upon its release, spreading widely across Europe between the 15th and 17th centuries and ranking behind only the Bible in popularity. Alarmed by the wave of misogynistic fervour it helped ignite, the Church denounced the text in 1490. Nevertheless, secular courts across Europe embraced many of Kramer's recommendations for identifying, capturing, and punishing alleged witches.

In the 16th century, a series of anti-witchcraft laws enacted across Europe not only reflected the growing fear of witchcraft but also amplified it. In Germany, the Witchcraft Laws of the Holy Roman Empire, legislated in 1532 by Emperor Charles V, marked witchcraft as a capital crime. Only a decade later, England's Witchcraft Act of 1542 made practising any magic a crime, and though revised in 1563 to focus on *maleficium* (actual harm caused by witchcraft), it reinforced the perception of witchcraft as an existential danger.

Scotland's Witchcraft Act of 1563 not only criminalized witchcraft, leading to widespread persecution of suspects, but also laid the groundwork for mass executions. France followed suit with the Edict of 1583, which ordered the execution of witches by burning. These laws did more than reflect existing anxieties – they

> "And so in this twilight and evening of the world, when sin is flourishing on every side and in every place, when charity is growing cold, the evil of witches and their iniquities superabound."
>
> MALLEUS MALEFICARUM PART I, QUESTION II

intensified and institutionalized them, creating a legal framework that allowed society to act on its deepest fears, making individuals (often women) scapegoats. Sensationalized pamphlets describing witch trials added to the fear, which in some places grew into mass hysteria.

Witch-hunting handbooks

Evidence of the *Malleus*'s influence can be seen in other witch-hunting manuals, such as the *Daemonologie*, published in 1597 by King James VI of Scotland (who later became James I of England). Framed as a scholarly dialogue, this presented witchcraft as a real and present threat. Coming from a monarch, the text also carried significant authority and reinforced the belief that witches were agents of the Devil. It revealed how profoundly fear had permeated society, turning suspicion into state-sanctioned accusation.

The *Compendium Maleficarum* (*Book of Witchcraft*), published in Milan in 1608, also takes the form of rhetorical questions and answers about what witches can do. It cites many supposed cases of witchcraft uncovered by inquisitors all over Europe, including practices such as attending witches' sabbaths, making pacts with Satan, and sexual encounters with various types of demons. The *Compendium* contains multiple references to the *Malleus* as evidence for the beliefs it espouses.

A dark legacy

The influence of the *Malleus Maleficarum* only grew over time; although publication was halted from 1521 to 1573 in an unsuccessful effort to curb its appeal, the book was later reissued and was cited in witch-hunting trials for years. Individuals accused of witchcraft might fall under suspicion for any number of reasons. Historians now agree that there is no single factor driving the phenomenon of witch trials, with beliefs and methods varying based on time and regional characteristics. However, one component that all witch persecutions had in common was an element of fear – of both witches and those tasked with hunting them.

Unholy meeting
Witches offer Satan (in the form of a goat) children to devour at a sabbath in this 1798 painting by Spanish artist Francisco de Goya. The *Malleus* describes witches killing unborn and living children.

1500-1700

EARLY MODERN ENCOUNTERS

LATIN AMERICAN GHOSTS

Body in the water
La Llorona is depicted here in an open-air theatrical performance. In this telling, she takes the form of a skeleton, as evidenced by her fleshless fingers emerging from the sleeves of her white robe.

STORIES OF SPECTRAL WOMEN HAVE LONG CIRCULATED IN PARTS OF LATIN AMERICA, WITH MANY LEGENDS REFLECTING THE REGION'S COLONIAL TRAUMA.

A key theme links the phantasmic tales of Latin America – women lamenting the loss of their children, whether by their own hands or as the result of a terrible accident. The best known and most influential of these supernatural figures is La Llorona, or "The Weeping Woman", traditionally presented in folklore as an apparition.

While accounts vary, La Llorona's suffering is often rooted in the devastation caused by the Spanish conquistadors as they invaded the Aztec Empire and spread throughout Central and South America. The earliest documented references to La Llorona are found in testimonies gathered in the 16th century by Franciscan missionary Bernardino de Sahagún in his history of New Spain, now known as *The Florentine Codex*. Within the codex, the Aztecs recount the omens that foreshadowed the imminent suffering and death that Europeans would bring. In the sixth omen, a woman by a lake cries, "O, my children, we are about to be lost", lamenting her inability to protect them. This haunting voice was interpreted as that of Cihuacoatl, the Mexica mother goddess, mourning the death of her people.

Other stories link La Llorona to Indigenous women who became involved with the Spanish invaders. Such is the case of La Malinche, a woman sold into sexual slavery, who translated for Hernán Cortés and bore him a son. Willingly or otherwise, she aided the genocide of her own people. In an even more sinister version of the La Llorona tale, a young woman kills her children to punish the Spanish captain who left her for a wealthy new companion. In Colombian renditions of the story, it is the shame of being a single mother that compels the woman to drown her child. Her spirit supposedly roams riverbanks, wailing to express her regret.

Seeking revenge

While La Llorona often represents grief and guilt, other Latin American ghosts are more rooted in vengeance. In Honduran culture, La Cegua, or La Siguanaba, is a beautiful woman with long hair dressed completely in white, often seen bathing at night. She is sometimes associated with the spirits of washerwomen and called La Sucia ("The Dirty Woman"), in reference to the fact that she is always washing her clothes. While some legends characterize her as a child-snatcher, she is usually said to entice philanderers and adulterers, only to reveal her true face – that of a horse's skull – before drowning them. Similarly, in Colombian legend, La Muelona stalks unfaithful and sinful men, seducing her victims before devouring them.

A modern take on ghosts seeking vengeance has emerged in Argentinian fiction. Several stories in Mariana Enríquez's *Things We Lost in the Fire* (2016) reimagine the country's *desaparecidos* ("disappeared") as spectral presences, haunting a society whose silence and complicity enabled political oppression. Their spirits demand truth and justice. Through them, Enríquez preserves collective memory and ensures the disappeared – and their traumas – are never forgotten.

Inhuman visage
In her victim's last moments, La Cegua reveals her face – in some tales, this is a fully fleshed horse's head; in others, a skull with red eyes.

RENAISSANCE SCEPTICISM

UNTIL THE END OF THE 18TH CENTURY, MOST PEOPLE BELIEVED IN THE EXISTENCE OF DEMONS, SPIRITS, AND MAGIC. HOWEVER, THERE WERE ALWAYS RADICAL VOICES WHO REJECTED SUCH IDEAS.

It would be easy to suggest that those who did not believe in an all-present spirit world were "forerunners of modernity", but this would not be correct. Their scepticism was firmly rooted in their own time and their specific worldview.

One of the most influential opponents of the witch trials that were being held all over Europe was Dutch physician Johann Weyer. In his 1563 work *De Praestigiis Daemonum* ("On the Delusions Created by Demons"), Weyer rejected witch trials not because he did not believe in the Devil, but because he believed the Devil could manipulate human beings with ease. The witches, Weyer maintained, were merely feeble-minded old women. They were essentially harmless conduits confused and deceived by the Devil.

Miserable dispatches
In this 14th-century French illustration, women found guilty of witchcraft are burned at the stake and beaten with clubs.

Religious viewpoints

Another early critic of the witch trials was English politician Reginald Scot. His work *The Discoverie of Witchcraft* (1584) suggested that the concept of demonic witchcraft was ludicrous. He elaborated on this by saying that witch trials were wrong not because they were irrational or inhumane, but simply because there was insufficient proof of the existence of witches in the Bible. A radical Protestant, he also proposed that witches were merely Catholic inventions.

Discredited magics
The practice of necromancy, or ritual magic involving the dead – depicted here in a 1481 manuscript of natural history – also fell foul of sceptics such as Johann Weyer.

German Jesuit priest Friedrich Spee was the father confessor of a number of witchcraft suspects. His personal experiences with them, and with their judges and executioners, led him to believe that witch trials were generally miscarriages of justice, dependent on unreliable means to extract confessions. Spee was one of the first prominent figures to reject unconditionally the use of torture. Even though Spee was obliged to say that he believed in witches, he often hinted at a secret hidden in his 1631 book *Cautio Criminalis* ("Caution in Criminal Trials") that readers would have to discover for themselves: that not only most but all victims of the witch trials were innocent.

No material power

The Enlightenment, a radical reform movement that emerged at the end of the 17th century, challenged all traditional wisdom. A major attack on the belief in demons came with Protestant theologian Balthasar Bekker's *De Betoverde Weereld* (*The World Bewitch'd*), published between 1691 and 1693. Bekker claimed that pure spirits such as the Devil cannot influence the material world and that, therefore, witchcraft cannot exist. The belief in magic was, for Bekker, a primitive impulse that needed to be overcome.

In a similar vein, German lawyer Christian Thomasius wrote in *De Crimine Magiae* ("On the Crime of Magic"), published in 1701, that the Devil was just an evil voice one might hear in one's head and could not interfere with the material world. Thomasius maintained that the witchcraft doctrine was inherently Catholic and that all Protestant princes had to end the witch hunts immediately.

> "They… suffer awful torture until they would gladly exchange this… existence for death."
>
> JOHANN WEYER, *DE PRAESTIGIIS DAEMONUM*

An expert in his field
Johann Weyer – illustrated here in 1576, aged 60 – was a respected doctor who published several works on witchcraft and demons.

BOSCH'S HELLISH VISIONS

Filled with nightmarish scenes, fantastical creatures, and monstrous acts, the surviving works of early Netherlandish painter Hieronymus Bosch present a uniquely macabre vision of the world. Bosch was active at a time when popular beliefs and anxieties about the consequences of sin and temptation, as well as the nature of Hell, were well-established themes in both art and literature. Bosch embraced these topics but added a new element of satire mixed with the surreal to highlight moral failings within society and warn against earthly temptations.

Two of Bosch's most famous works, *The Last Judgement* (c.1482) and *The Garden of Earthly Delights* (c.1500), exemplify his use of grotesque imagery – a combination of horror and comedy – to create a moralizing narrative out of a hellish landscape. Arranged as triptychs, both paintings show Adam and Eve in the Garden of Eden on their left-hand panel; the earthly realm, with its opportunities for sin and judgement, in the centre; and the torments of Hell on the right. The terrible consequences of choosing vice over virtue are made clear: the damned are impaled, devoured, or tormented by a range of strange hybrid creatures and monstrous demons.

Bosch's disturbing fantasies forged a striking visual language that fed into later ideas of the afterlife, nightmares, and the genre of horror. Expanding on fears rooted in Christian teachings, they suggest that the unknown may be beyond even our wildest imagination.

Brutal punishment
Monsters in armour, symbolizing the battle against sin, torture the damned in this detail from Hieronymus Bosch's *Last Judgement*.

Swiss lycanthropy
In an attack in Geneva in 1580, a man is said to have killed 16 children while in the guise of a wolf, as depicted in this illustration.

EUROPEAN WEREWOLF TRIALS

IN THE 16TH AND 17TH CENTURIES, THERE WAS A SPATE OF WEREWOLF TRIALS. MANY OF THE ACCUSED WERE PROBABLY SERIAL KILLERS WHOSE CRIMES WERE VIEWED THROUGH A SUPERNATURAL LENS.

In December 1521, a dark tale unfolded in Poligny, a town in Franche-Comté, France. In a court case presided over by Jean Bodin, the prior of a Dominican convent, two shepherds named Pierre Burgot and Michel Verdun confessed – under torture – to killing and eating a number of people, including several children. They also claimed to have done this while in the form of wolves. The pair testified that they had made a deal with some mysterious men dressed in black: in exchange for food and watching the strangers' flock, they were given a magical ointment that would turn them into wolves. Burgot and Verdun were convicted of their crimes and burned at the stake. This was among the first of a handful of trials in the region aiming to punish supposed werewolves, or lycanthropes.

There were other French trials. A woman dubbed the "Werewolf of Auvergne" was identified by the wedding ring on her severed hand, which was reputedly cut off while she was a wolf and had reverted to human form. Another case concerned the "Werewolf of Châlons", a tailor who lured his child victims into his shop to sexually assault and murder them. He was also accused of chasing children in the forest while in the form of a wolf.

Beyond France

Werewolf trials were held in other countries, too. In Bedburg, Germany, a farmer called Peter Stubbe supposedly received a belt from the Devil that enabled him to shape-shift into a wolf. Official records state that, over 25 years, he murdered and ate at least two pregnant women, 13 children, and a number of cows. In 1589, he was executed for his crimes by having his skin torn off and his arms and legs broken, before being beheaded and burned.

In the Netherlands, a man named Folkert Dirks confessed that he and his family were able to change into wolves and cats when commanded to do so by Satan, again having been given a magical belt. Dirks's own teenage sons made the initial accusation, pointing not just at their father but also at their 17-year-old sister and their younger brothers, aged just 11 and 8.

Early Modern Encounters

Similar legal proceedings also took place in Eastern Europe, particularly Latvia and Estonia. In 1691, Thiess of Kaltenbrun, an elderly peasant who lived in Livonia (now Latvia), told a district court that he was a werewolf. However, far from being in league with the Devil, he insisted that he was one of the "hounds of God". During his trial in 1692, Thiess testified that he and other werewolves fought witches and the Devil in a bid to protect human crops and livestock. The man was flogged for heresy.

> "[The Devil] gave until him a girdle which being put about him, he was straight transformed into the likeness of a greedy devouring Wolf…"
>
> PAMPHLET ON THE TRIAL OF PETER STUBBE, REPRODUCED IN
> *THE WEREWOLF IN LORE AND LEGEND*, 1933

Werewolf attack
This woodcut from c. 1510 by Lucas Cranach the Elder shows a man on all fours with a hairy lower back; he has a baby in his mouth and is surrounded by previous victims.

THE GANDILLON WEREWOLVES

In 1598, in the Jura region of France, a peasant woman named Perrenette Gandillon was killed by an angry mob for supposedly attacking two children while she was in wolf form. When her brother and his children were also accused, he claimed they had been given a salve by the Devil that allowed them to turn into wolves. The trial of the Gandillon family was documented by judge and demonologist Henri Boguet, who wrote about it in his 1602 treatise *Discours Exécrable des Sorciers* (*An Examen of Witches*). The Gandillon case was taken as proof of the true existence and power of demonic lycanthropy.

THE GOLEM OF PRAGUE

THE TALE OF THIS HUMAN-MADE FIGURE THAT SERVES ITS MAKERS WILL REVERBERATE THROUGH EUROPEAN CULTURE.

Ambiguous creature
In Paul Wegener's *The Golem: How He Came into the World*, the monster saves the Jewish community, but then runs amok under the influence of an evil demon, Astaroth.

In 1883, the people of Prague took great interest in the renovation of the city's Old-New Synagogue. One of the earliest and most striking Gothic buildings in the city, it was rumoured to contain a secret in its attic. The dark, dusty enclave was believed to house the remains of the original Golem of Prague – a supernatural entity capable of wreaking havoc. Legend had it that the last man to ascend the ladder to the attic, a previous chief rabbi, had returned ashen-faced and trembling.

An ancient horror

The word "golem" was first used in the Bible, where it refers to anything that is incomplete or unformed. In the medieval era, stories emerged that put flesh on such a thing – creatures fashioned from inanimate material, often clay, and brought to life by arcane processes. By the 18th century, these supernatural beings, which could grow in size and serve as servants or protectors, were known as golems. They were animated by placing letters forming a "shem" (one of the names of God) on their foreheads or in their mouths, and deactivated by removing the shem. Importantly, they were neither good nor bad in themselves, being simply extensions of their animator's will.

Early tales about golems include that of the 16th-century Golem of Chełm, created by Rabbi Elijah Ba'al Shem, which grew uncontrollably, forcing the rabbi to destroy it. Most famous of all was the Golem of Prague, fashioned by Rabbi Judah Loew ben Bezalel, either to be a domestic servant or to protect the Jews of Prague from persecution. The rabbi dutifully removed the shem every sabbath, but one day he forgot, and the furious golem embarked on a spree of destruction. When the terrified rabbi managed to snatch the shem from the golem, it collapsed into a pile of dust, which the rabbi then stored in the attic of the Old-New Synagogue. He warned people to stay away from the remains, but added that the golem could be awakened when needed.

Modern fears

Mary Shelley's *Frankenstein* (1818) bears a striking resemblance to the tale of Prague's golem. Assembled out of inanimate objects (in this case, human body parts), animated by a mysterious process (the "spark of being"), and causing chaos, Shelley's creature shares many characteristics with the golem. Scholars have questioned the golem story's

> "That terrible life-giving word... I shall now call the golem to life."
>
> RABBI LOEW IN WEGENER'S *THE GOLEM: HOW HE CAME INTO THE WORLD*

influence in both Shelley's work and that of Johann Wolfgang von Goethe. Goethe's "The Sorcerer's Apprentice" (1797), a poem about the dangers of unleashing magical powers, was written after he made a series of visits to Prague.

Nothing out of the ordinary was found in the attic of the Old-New Synagogue. However, the myth retained its power, inspiring Gustav Meyrink's novel *The Golem* (1915), set in the ghetto of Prague, in which the titular monster may or may not be real. Then came Paul Wegener's silent film *The Golem: How He Came into the World* (1920), an early experiment in German Expressionism. Soon afterwards, clay was replaced by steel in Fritz Lang's acclaimed science fiction epic *Metropolis* (1927), which inaugurated cinema's obsession with robots and other machines threatening humanity. This eventually lead to the murderous, Jupiter-bound HAL 9000 computer in Stanley Kubrick's *2001: A Space Odyssey* (1968). Today, our fears about genetic engineering and artificial intelligence – effectively about human-made entities replacing us – show that reality has finally caught up with fiction.

Monster on the streets
An illustration for Gustav Meyrink's novel *The Golem* by artist Hugo Steiner-Prag shows the golem stalking the streets of Prague.

DEMONIC HIERARCHIES

THE IDEA THAT EVIL SPIRITS FORM COHORTS THAT CAN BE CLASSIFIED AND RANKED HAS A LONG HISTORY, ECHOING THE CONCEPT OF AN ANGELIC HIERARCHY.

Fire and brimstone
Haborym, a fire demon, appears in French occultist Jacques Collin de Plancy's *Dictionnaire Infernal* ("Infernal Dictionary") of 1863, a demonology organized by hierarchy.

The Seven Deadly Sins
In this 1510 woodcut print, by German artist Hans Burgkmair, each demonic figure personifies the sin it represents.

The Gospel writings of Matthew and Luke hint at organized groupings of angels and demons but the Bible does not explicitly describe a hierarchy; this notion would not take root until many centuries later. In the 11th century, Byzantine monk Michael Psellos integrated traditional beliefs about nature spirits and ghosts with demonology by identifying six types of demon. The Igneous, he maintained, inhabit the higher air; the Aerial, the lower air; the Earthly, nature. Lower down, he placed the Aqueous, which hide in water and drown whoever comes near them, then the Subterranean, which lie underground, and the Lucifugi, which lurk in darkness and seem barely sentient.

German theologian and writer Heinrich Cornelius Agrippa presented demons as ministers of God's punishment in his *De Occulta Philosophia* (*Three Books of Occult Philosophy*; 1533). He also described nine units of demons and their leaders. These included the false gods (under Beelzebub), the vessels of crime (led by Belial), the magicians who perform false miracles (under Satan), and the seducers (directed by Mammon).

The rise of demonology

Between the 14th and early 17th centuries, demonology began to ascribe certain tasks or spheres of influence to demons, in a similar manner to the belief that specific Catholic saints provided protection for particular groups of people or helped in certain crises. In 1589, German demonologist Bishop Peter Binsfeld connected the seven most powerful demons with the seven deadly sins: Lucifer stood for pride, Mammon for avarice, Asmodeus for lust, Satan for wrath, Beelzebub for gluttony, Leviathan for envy and Belphegor for sloth. According to Binsfeld, each of these demons had innumerable lesser demons to aid him. He also maintained that there were many others outside these units who haunted places and possessed humans or enticed them to blaspheme.

Johann Weyer, a Dutch opponent of the witch hunts, published the *Pseudomonarchia Daemonum* ("False Monarchy of Demons") in 1577, a long list of demons and their special powers. They were also ranked within a demonic hierarchy – from counts and dukes, to kings and presidents.

> "Their first king… is called Baëll who when he is conjured up, appeareth with three heads…"
>
> JOHANN WEYER, *PSEUDOMONARCHIA DAEMONUM*, 1577

THE FAUSTIAN BARGAIN

A RECURRING TROPE IN HORROR FICTION IS THAT OF A BARGAIN STRUCK WITH THE DEVIL — USUALLY BY A CHARACTER WHO THEN HAS HELL TO PAY.

Silent screams
A vivid example of German Expressionism, the silent film *Faust* (1926) depicted the conflict between good and evil using striking visuals.

Johann Georg Faust was a real practitioner of magic who lived in the 16th century, but his name is now more closely associated with legend. He was famously immortalized in Christopher Marlowe's tragedy *Dr Faustus* (finished in 1592–93 and published in 1604) and Goethe's two-part *Faust* (1790). The first known *Faustbuch* (a book of stories about Faust) was published in 1587, based on German folktales about a magician who makes a deal with a demon in exchange for power. Translated into various languages, and widely circulated, the book became an influential bestseller.

The notoriety of the Faust story was not limited to fiction. From the late 16th century to the 19th century, several *Höllenzwang* grimoires — a type of occult spellbook used to conjure and command spirits — were published in Germany and attributed to Faust. These texts purported to teach practitioners how to hunt for treasure with the aid of demons.

Faust in drama

Early modern audiences were thrilled by tales of the Faustian bargain and the demon Mephistopheles. According to traditional versions of the story, Faust, a scholar, becomes deeply frustrated with the limits of human knowledge and turns to magic. He summons Mephistopheles, a demon who offers him unlimited knowledge, pleasure, and power in exchange for his soul. Faust agrees to this deal, signing a contract in blood. With Mephistopheles as his guide, he experiences worldly delights and forbidden knowledge, but grows increasingly remorseful. In Goethe's

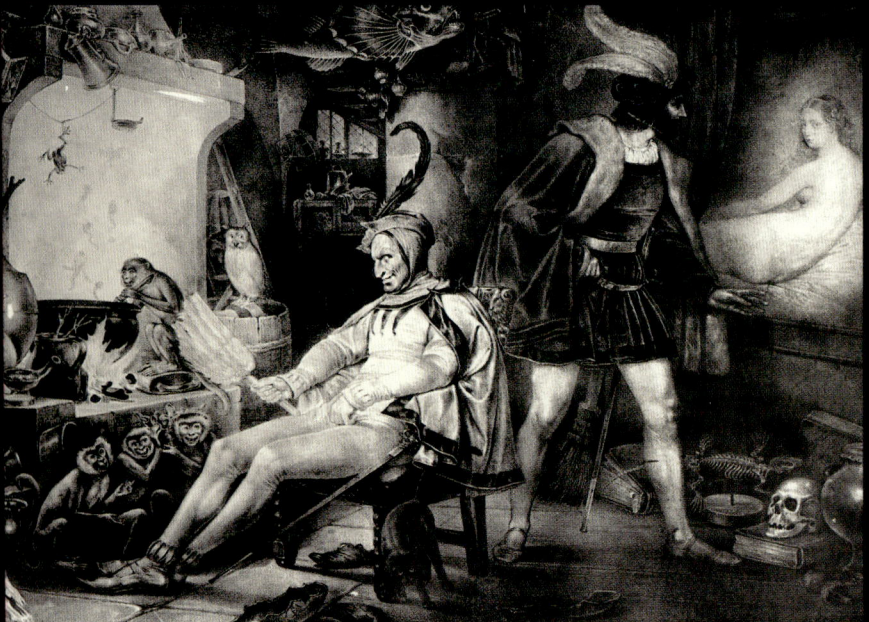

Promising the world
A lithograph from Goethe's *Faust* shows a fireside scene of Faust with Mephistopheles, who is conjuring an image of beauty in the magician's mirror.

version, Faust seeks redemption and is ultimately saved by divine grace, but in Marlowe's play, Faust is eternally damned – a darker ending that came to define later Faustian tales.

Modern depictions

The Faustian bargain became a common motif in Gothic and later horror fiction. In Oscar Wilde's *The Picture of Dorian Gray* (1890), the protagonist trades his soul for eternal youth and beauty. Stephen Vincent Benét's "The Devil and Daniel Webster" (1936) focuses on the contractual element: a farmer sells his soul to "Mr Scratch", then hires a lawyer to break the deal. Other 20th-century horror writers gave their own twists to the trope. Clive Barker's *The Hellbound Heart* (1986) follows a man whose pursuit of pleasure leads him to make a deal with demons, damning himself to an eternity of pain. In Stephen King's *Needful Things* (1991), townspeople make sinister deals with mysterious shop owner Leland Gaunt, who promises to sell them the thing they need most at the cost of a heinous deed.

Horror films often feature a protagonist who trades their soul for power, knowledge, or pleasure. Examples include the neo-noir *Angel Heart* (1987), in which a private detective trades his soul to escape his violent past, and horror comedy *Ready or Not* (2019), in which a bride is literally hunted by in-laws who have made a pact with the Devil to protect their wealth.

In hell
This sketch shows Ernest Klausz's set design for a 1933 production of Hector Berlioz's 19th-century opera *The Damnation of Faust*.

THE TERRORS OF THE NIGHT

SIXTEENTH-CENTURY TEXTS EXPLORING THE FEARS AND PHANTOMS THAT PLAGUE PEOPLE AT NIGHT TRIGGERED A FASCINATION WITH NIGHTMARES THAT WOULD FIND EXPRESSION IN THE HORROR GENRE.

For the people of Elizabethan England, belief in supernatural entities coexisted with Christian doctrines. Tales of demons, spirits, and other creatures inspired both fear and intrigue, and rumours circulated of witches serving the Devil in order to harm their neighbours. Malicious forces were particularly feared at night – a time when the soul was thought to be less guarded and open to spiritual attack and when demons, witches, and fairies were believed to roam under cover of the darkness.

In this ferment of myth and religion, and in lieu of scientific explanations, sleep disorders such as night terrors, which caused sufferers to scream, cry, and thrash around, were interpreted as demonic visitations. Nightmares were though to involve a demon – the *maere* – arriving at *niht* to sit on the chest of the sleeper, causing paralysis, a sense of suffocation, and vivid hallucinations of the sinister visitor. Popular writers such as Shakespeare and Thomas Kyd contributed to belief in such apparitions, often including avenging spirits and malevolent ghosts in their revenge dramas – a genre that became increasingly popular in the late 16th and early 17th centuries.

Superstition and scepticism

In 1594, playwright and poet Thomas Nashe published *The Terrors of the Night*, a pamphlet in which he challenged the prevailing superstitions and religious hypocrisy of Elizabethan England. Framed as a meditation on nightmares and nocturnal fears, it examined how darkness unleashes irrational anxieties, disturbed dreams, and visions. Nashe attributed such experiences to human imagination, arguing that at night the mind is vulnerable to suggestion and fears, especially of death, sin, and the Devil. Nashe maintained that

Tortured dreams
In this scene from Shakespeare's *Richard III*, drawn by English artist William Blake (1757–1827), Richard is visited in his sleep by the ghosts of the people he has murdered.

Sleep demon
Henry Fuseli's painting *The Nightmare*, in which an incubus sits on a woman's chest, shocked audiences at its debut in 1782.

most of the ghosts and spirits encountered at night are fabrications – the result of sins committed in daytime, or insinuations placed in the mind by evildoers. He also suggested that physiological factors, such as imbalances in the substances that make up the human body or the process of digestion, might play a role in causing nightmares.

Nightmarish fears

Nashe's work expressed scepticism about many supernatural entities, such as ghosts and fairies, but it also painted a vivid picture of the Devil exercising his powers at night – paradoxically stimulating the reader's imagination rather than dispelling fears. God is described as the "father of the light", implying the spiritual safety of daytime, while the Devil is the "prince of darkness".

Fears of nighttime persisted after Nashe, but his work laid the foundations for a more rational interpretation of night terrors and nightmares based on scientific and psychological understanding. By the 18th century, Enlightenment thinkers were attributing sleep disturbances to mental and physical factors rather than demonic activity, and beginning to classify them as medical rather than moral conditions.

> "The night is the devil's black book, wherein he recordeth all our transgressions."
>
> THOMAS NASHE, *THE TERRORS OF THE NIGHT*

NIGHTMARES AS A HORROR TROPE

Nightmares are a recurring theme in the horror genre, often blurring the line between dreamscapes and reality to heighten fear and suspense. In *A Nightmare on Elm Street* (1984), the spirit of murderer Freddy Krueger attacks victims in their sleep, making the subconscious a battleground. Nightmares can also reflect psychological torment, as in *Before I Wake* (2016), about a grieving boy whose nightmares become reality.

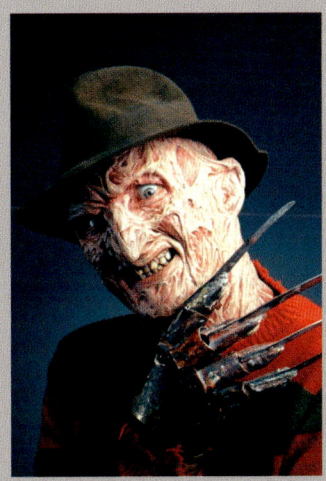

SUPERNATURAL FEARS IN COLONIAL AMERICA

Ritual ceremony
This English depiction shows an Indigenous ceremony on Roanoke Island, Virginia, in 1590. Roanoke is famous for the mystery of the "lost" English colony that disappeared from the area.

EUROPEAN COLONISTS ARRIVING IN NORTH AMERICA BROUGHT WITH THEM BELIEFS ABOUT WITCHCRAFT AND THE SUPERNATURAL, AND DEEP-SEATED FEARS THAT WERE INTENSIFIED BY THEIR NEW HOMELAND.

The Europeans who colonized the East Coast of North America in the early 17th century travelled there for a new life, in many cases seeking freedom from religious persecution. They hoped to build a new society, but they also brought aspects of their own cultures, including superstitions, with them.

Indigenous encounters
European beliefs in the supernatural mingled with new fears in colonial North America, some of which related to the American landscape and its Indigenous inhabitants. Colonial folktales often incorporated Indigenous elements such as spirit guardians and shape-shifters into their narratives, but in ways that distorted or misinterpreted their true meaning and significance.

Colonists were entering unfamiliar territories, and Indigenous cosmologies were tied closely to the land in systems settlers could not understand. Rituals connected to nature, animal spirits, and the dead were foreign and unsettling to Europeans steeped in Christian orthodoxy. Ignorance and misunderstanding gave rise to mythologies that the land itself was spiritually dangerous or cursed. Charles Island, in Milford, Connecticut, for example, came to be known as the "Thrice Cursed Island" after three legends linked it to ill fortune. The first curse was allegedly placed by members of the Indigenous Paugussett Nation after the island was taken by European settlers. The second was said to have been laid by Scottish pirate Captain Kidd in 1699 to protect his buried treasure, while the third curse was reputedly inflicted by sailors hoping to hide looted Aztec gold on the island. The New England coast was also believed to be haunted by ghost ships. Reported sightings of these phantom galleons led to theories that they protected sites of buried treasure, guarded by the spirits of sacrificed sailors.

Wonders and apparitions
In 17th-century England, religious anxiety and political turmoil stoked fears, superstitions, and a fascination with the supernatural. Pamphlets containing stories of ghostly apparitions and strange events circulated, including one in 1642 that described a meeting between the ghosts of King James I of England and the Duke of

Cursed treasure
This 19th-century engraving shows the enduring myth of Captain William Kidd and his pirate accomplices burying their treasure on Charles Island, Connecticut in 1699.

Witchcraft at work
A girl writhes on the floor of the courtroom in this image capturing the climate of hysteria that overtook the Salem community in 1692.

Buckingham to discuss a treasonous plot. Another, from around 1690, alleged that the Devil had appeared on Earth to identify a murderer.

Similar reports began circulating in the British colonies of North America. During the 1630s and 1640s, John Winthrop, Puritan leader and governor of the Massachusetts Bay Colony, noted several mysterious occurrences in his diaries, including apparitions and unexplained lights. In 1689, Puritan clergyman Cotton Mather documented the demonic possession of four children in Boston, which resulted in the trial and execution of a neighbour for witchcraft.

Under attack

Following the witch trials that spread through Europe in the late 16th and early 17th centuries, fears of witchcraft prompted a wave of hunts for malefactors in the American colonies during the 17th and 18th centuries. European colonists brought knowledge of witches and their abilities and introduced ideas sourced from European witch-hunting manuals, such as Heinrich Kramer's *Malleus Maleficarum* (1486), which provided a framework for persecution. Just as King James VI's *Daemonologie* (1597) had depicted Britain as a land under supernatural threat, clergyman Cotton Mather's *Wonders of the Invisible World* (1693) framed New England as a chosen land under attack from Satan, providing numerous examples of witchcraft and possession. He suggested that the Devil was targeting the colonies specifically because of their religious purity and commitment to building a godly society.

Belief on trial

One of the first witch hunts in North America took place at Hartford, Connecticut, between 1647 and 1663, with Alse Young becoming the first person to be executed for witchcraft in the colonies in 1647 as a result. Other trials took place in Albany, New York (1665); Exeter, New Hampshire (1656–58); and Virginia, where in 1706 Grace Sherwood, the "Witch of Pungo", was thrown into a river to see if she floated – a sure sign of witchcraft.

The most infamous witch trials in North America began in Salem, Massachusetts, in 1692, sparked by the strange behaviour of four young girls who displayed symptoms that included screaming, contortions, and entering trances. Under pressure from officials, the girls testified that three local women had bewitched them. One of these, an enslaved woman named Tituba, confessed under duress that she had made a "witch cake" – a remedy from English folk magic traditions – and that she was in league with the Devil.

> "Several testifi'd, That the Shape of the Prisoner did oftentimes very grievously Pinch them, Choak them, Bite them, and Afflict them."
>
> TRIAL OF BRIDGET BISHOP, THE FIRST WOMAN HUNG AT SALEM, 2 JUNE 1692

A witch panic quickly escalated as the community turned on itself. Many in Salem testified to being haunted in dreams or visions by those accused of witchcraft. This "spectral evidence" was founded on the belief that the Devil co-opted human agents (witches) and used their spirit forms to torment people. The trials' reliance on spectral evidence, which could not be substantiated, became their undoing. People became increasingly sceptical as the number of accusations based on flimsy evidence mounted and even respected community members were charged. Faced with prosecuting his own wife, the Governor of Massachusetts, William Phips, shut down the trials in October 1692. Overall, more than 200 people were accused of witchcraft in Salem, and 19 were executed by hanging, most of them women.

Spectres of Salem

The witch trials in North America have inspired literature, film, and popular culture, particularly in the horror and supernatural genres. One of the most famous portrayals of the trials is American playwright Arthur Miller's drama *The Crucible*. The play has been staged repeatedly since its premiere in 1953, often with lighting, stage, and sound designs to heighten horror elements such as fear, dread, and a sense of the occult.

Several horror films have also drawn on the Salem witch trials, including Rob Zombie's *The Lords of Salem* (2012), centring on a modern woman cursed by the 17th-century witches of Salem. The Puritan worldview reflected in the trials – restrictive and obsessed with sin – has also become a horror trope. Robert Eggers's *The VVitch* (2015), for example, features a Puritan family that falls apart when threatened by an evil force in woods next to their home. The film ends when the young daughter is seduced by the Devil into signing her name in his book and joining a witches' sabbath.

Salem is not the only witch trial that has been represented in horror, but it is the most recognizable. Some interpretations, such as R.L. Stine's *Fear Street* novels and their film adaptations, describe witch trials that are only loosely based on the events in colonial America. What unites many of these depictions is their portrayal of historical events in the context of a perceived supernatural threat. Within the horror genre, the accused are portrayed as actually practising dark magic, associating with spirits and demons, or placing curses on people. Only rarely is the true source of fear in these books, films, and television series the terror of false accusation or forced confessions, or the damaging psychological effects of the imprisonment and torture the victims faced.

False accusations
Winona Ryder portrays the young accuser Abigail Williams in this still from the 1996 film adaptation of Arthur Miller's *The Crucible*.

Death's warning
In an illustration by British artist Henry Weston Keen (1899–1935), the ghost of Brachiano appears to Flamineo, a character who murders his own brother, among others, in *The White Devil*.

REVENGE TRAGEDIES

THE THEATRE-GOERS OF LATE 16TH- AND EARLY 17TH-CENTURY ENGLAND RELISHED STORIES ABOUT MURDER AND VENGEANCE, LEADING TO THE GENRE OF PLAYS NOW KNOWN AS REVENGE TRAGEDIES.

Also known as "tragedies of blood", revenge tragedies revolve around a protagonist's quest for vengeance, and often feature the ghost of a murdered loved one and scenes of illicit affairs, madness, and murder. The genre rose to popularity in England in the last decades of the Elizabethan era (1558–1603), and continued to flourish in the Jacobean period – the reign of James I (1603–25). Two of the most popular examples from this time are John Webster's *The Duchess of Malfi* (1614) and *The White Devil* (c. 1612). In *The Duchess of Malfi*, a young widow secretly marries her steward, Antonio. Her two brothers, a jealous duke and a corrupt cardinal, believe she has dishonoured their family and plot to punish her. They have her imprisoned and eventually killed, after subjecting her to psychological torture.

The White Devil also focuses on corruption among the nobility and the fatal consequences of revenge. The play centres on the character of Vittoria Corombona, a beautiful woman caught in a web of murder, deceit, and infidelity. Her affair with the villainous Duke of Brachiano leads to the murder of her husband, and she is eventually implicated in a series of violent deaths. The play explores the dark psychology of its characters, revealing how vengeance and unchecked desire lead to a spiral of horrific events. Like *The Duchess of Malfi*, *The White Devil* uses a complex interplay of power, betrayal, and moral corruption to create an atmosphere of fear and dread. Webster's plays were staged in the Blackfriars Theatre, a shadowy and intimate indoor venue where audiences were close to the fake blood and gore.

Blood and drama

Shakespeare made his own contributions to the tragedy genre, with his plays *Titus Andronicus* (1588–93) and *Hamlet* (1599–1601) both exploring the themes of vengeance, justice, and moral corruption. In *Hamlet*, a prince seeks revenge for his father's murder, leading to a tragic cycle of betrayal and death. In *Titus Andronicus*, a Roman general cuts off his own hand and prepares a cannibalistic feast with the bodies of his enemies.

Revenge tragedies captured the imagination. Other examples of the genre include Thomas Middleton and William Rowley's *The Changeling* (1622), Christopher Marlowe's *The Jew of Malta* (c. 1589), and *The Revenger's Tragedy* (c. 1606; also attributed to Middleton). While the category of "horror" did not exist in the Elizabethan and Jacobean eras, the bloody and psychological elements of these stories can be traced in later tales, from the Gothic literature of the 18th and 19th centuries to modern horror fiction.

> "When the bad bleeds, then is the tragedy good."
>
> VINDICI IN THOMAS MIDDLETON'S
> *THE REVENGER'S TRAGEDY*

Revenge Tragedies

THE SPANISH TRAGEDY

Thomas Kyd's *The Spanish Tragedy* (c. 1587), written in the late Elizabethan era, was an important precursor to Jacobean revenge dramas. It features the ghost of Spanish nobleman Don Andrea, who has been killed in battle by a man named Balthazar, and a web of relationships at the Spanish court. Revenge is both a theme and the name of a character in the play, as the figure of Hieronimo seeks revenge for the murder of his son, with bloody consequences. Kyd's play set the stage for several other tragedies in the following decades, and is believed to have served as the model for Shakespeare's *Hamlet*.

Power, corruption, and murder
Graphic artist and lithographer Henry Weston Keen produced this macabre illustration of a skull crowned with snakes and flowers for the 1930 edition of John Webster's greatest plays.

THE WEIRD SISTERS

During the early 17th century, belief in witches was widespread in England, particularly under King James I, who was deeply concerned with the dangers of witchcraft. James himself had a personal interest in the subject, writing *Daemonologie* in 1597. This work – along with Scotland's North Berwick witch trials of 1590–91, which the king directly investigated – contributed to the climate of fear and fascination surrounding witchcraft at the time.

The inclusion of the three witches in Shakespeare's *Macbeth* (first performed around 1606) reflects that obsession. In the play, the witches – or "weird sisters" – foretell Macbeth's ascension to the throne, setting off a chain of violent events. They throw gruesome ingredients into a cauldron to bring forth chilling apparitions, including a floating soldier's head, a bloody child, and a line of ghostly kings. The cryptic nature of their predictions mirrors the confusion and fear surrounding witchcraft, because such women were believed to wield knowledge that was both dangerous and forbidden.

The witches' physical descriptions – "so wither'd and so wild in their attire", with "skinny lips" and "chappy" fingers – call for actors to play them as feral and otherworldly, not human, reinforcing assumptions about the women accused of being witches. In reality, these women varied in age, marital status, and appearance, but the enduring image of the "witch" is an ugly and elderly hag, marginalized by society. *Macbeth*'s witches heavily influenced later depictions in literature and horror.

Three witches, one force
In Joel Coen's 2021 film *The Tragedy of Macbeth*, all three witches were played by the same actress – Kathryn Hunter – reflecting their presence as a singular force.

THE LOUDUN POSSESSIONS

FRENCH NUNS CLAIMING DEMONIC POSSESSION SPARKED ONE OF THE MOST SIGNIFICANT WITCHCRAFT TRIALS OF THE 17TH CENTURY.

Passionately possessed
Vanessa Redgrave plays Prioress Jeanne des Anges in the controversial film *The Devils* (1971), directed by Ken Russell.

On the night of 22 September 1632, three nuns, Prioress Jeanne des Anges, Sister de Colombiers, and Sister Marthe de Saint-Monique, were visited by an apparition of a "man of the cloth" asking them for help. This event would be taken as the first sign that a demon was at work in the Ursaline convent of Loudun, France. The nuns claimed to hear voices, their bodies convulsed, and Jeanne des Anges was plagued by nightmares of a priest commanding her to perform sexual acts. The Loudun nuns believed they were possessed by the Devil.

Pointing fingers
After an exorcist who was called in failed to eject the demons in a series of public spectacles, suspicions turned to Urban Grandier, parish priest of the Church of Saint-Pierre-du-Marche in Loudun. Grandier had previously clashed with local authorities and the powerful Cardinal Richelieu, chief minister to King Louis XIII.

Notably, Grandier had refused to become the spiritual director of the Ursuline convent, which may have contributed to resentment against him. He was also rumoured to have conducted several illicit affairs with women in town, further tarnishing his reputation.

The nuns accused Grandier of using witchcraft to summon demons to torment them. They produced a document at his trial in 1634 allegedly containing the signatures of Satan, Leviathan, Astaroth, and other demons. In the face of this evidence, Grandier was found guilty and burned at the stake. Jeanne des Anges, supposedly possessed by seven different demons, continued to be tormented until a new exorcist managed to free her. She later wrote an autobiography in which she described her intense sexual fascination with Grandier.

Possession was regarded as the most extreme form of demonic attack, as determined by Christian theologians such as Thomas Aquinas and Albertus Magnus in the late medieval period. Demons were also believed capable of inducing "obsession" – able to "besiege" a person's senses through dreams or apparitions, possibly involving physical attacks. If an individual failed to resist demonic obsession, complete possession might follow. By December 1634, nine of the Loudun nuns were deemed to have been possessed, while eight more were declared subject to demonic obsession.

Lurid legacy
Enduring fascination with the story of the Loudun nuns has inspired several horror films. The Polish film *Mother Joan of the Angels* (1961) drew on the tale, but focused on a priest's attempt to exorcise the demons, culminating in the axe murder of some local men. Another retelling, Ken Russell's *The Devils* (1971), was a more faithful reproduction of the historical events, but featured such graphic depictions of gore and sexual violence that it was banned in several countries and heavily edited in others.

Public punishment
Urbain Grandier is burned at the stake in 1634 after being tried for witchcraft. His request to be hanged beforehand was ignored.

> "[The nuns'] tongues issued suddenly from their mouths, horribly swollen, black, hard, and covered with pimples."
>
> CONTEMPORARY ACCOUNT OF THE LOUDUN POSSESSIONS

THE GREAT WITCH HYSTERIA

THE WITCH TRIALS OF WÜRZBURG WERE AMONG THE LARGEST AND DEADLIEST IN EUROPE, SHOWING HOW BELIEF IN MAGIC COULD IGNITE WIDESPREAD PANIC.

During a period of intense witch hysteria between 1626 and 1631, a series of trials were held in the prince-bishopric of Würzburg, Germany, which was part of the Holy Roman Empire at that time. The belief that demonic magic and Satanic pacts were being carried out by the region's citizens led to a programme of mass persecution.

At the heart of the frenzy was a deeply ingrained belief that witches were responsible for all forms of misfortune – from crop failure and infant deaths, to variable weather. In the early 17th century, Würzburg was burdened by war, famine, and disease, particularly during the Thirty Years' War, which ravaged the Holy Roman Empire from 1618 to 1635. The heightened social tension and hardships of war created fertile ground for

> "Ah, the woe and the misery of it – there are still four hundred [witches] in the city… of every rank and sex, nay, even clerics."
>
> THE CHANCELLOR OF THE PRINCE-BISHOPRIC OF WÜRZBURG, 1629

A fiery end
A group of men prepare to burn a Swiss woman found guilty of practising witchcraft. She is tied to the stake in readiness, while spectators gather around.

European persecution
This illustration of 1594 depicts the witch trials and some of the various punishments meted out in the German city of Trier.

scapegoating, and people began to blame perceived witches for their suffering. Würzburg was not the only German town to fall under the spell of hysteria.

Fear leads to panic

The initial accusation that triggered the trials is lost to history, but the panic in Würzburg became a vicious cycle. Empowered by Prince Bishop Philipp Adolf von Ehrenberg, commissions were established to prosecute alleged witches. Accusations were often given under torture, which encouraged accused individuals to name others to end their own suffering. This led to a chain reaction of suspicion and denunciations.

There was little logic in who was targeted. Fear overrode rationality, and a third of the population was said to be attending witches' sabbaths to worship the Devil, in a demonic parody of a mass. Estimates suggest that, across the prince-bishopric in this period, up to 900 people were executed or died in custody, 19 of whom were Catholic priests, and several were children accused of having sex with the Devil. Only the taking of Würzburg by Sweden in 1631 brought the mania to an end.

Europe's witch craze

While exact figures are impossible to ascertain, historians believe that around 110,000 people were tried for witchcraft in Europe between 1450 and 1750, leading to 60,000 executions. The fear of witchcraft spread through Europe in these centuries, fuelled by salacious stories in demonologies and the belief that the Devil was the root of all adversity. The hysteria would only reach a conclusion during the Age of Enlightenment, which prioritized reason and science over superstition and religion.

Today, the phrase "witch hunt" is synonymous with unmerited persecution. While it is possible that some victims of Europe's trials were attempting to practice witchcraft, it seems clear that most faced the horrifying prospect of a trial where the truth did not matter.

Hanged until dead
Torture and death often awaited those accused of witchcraft. While public hangings were common in England, burning at the stake was more usual across mainland Europe.

Vodou vigil
Participants in this Vodou ceremony have made symbols from maize flour on the floor to invoke the *loa*. Offerings of alcohol and candles accompany the ritual.

VODOU AND ZOMBIES

VODOU, A RELIGION WITH ROOTS IN WEST AFRICA AND HAITI, BECAME FICTIONALIZED AS HARMFUL MAGIC, OR "VOODOO".

French settlers on the Caribbean island of St-Domingue (now Haiti) referred to the religious practices of enslaved West African people there as *vaudoux* – probably mishearing the word *vodun*, which means "spirit" in the Fon language. Over centuries, Vodou (as it is now called in Haiti) has become an elaborate, ritualized belief system in which ceremonies culminate in ecstatic dancers possessed by a panoply of spirits (*loa*, or *lwa*). Haitian vodou also includes belief in the *zombi* (or *zonbi*), a bodiless soul (*zombi astral*) or soulless body (*zombi cadavre*). The latter is a reanimated corpse, forced to do the bidding of a Vodou sorcerer, or *bokor*, and reflects the Haitians' fear of eternal enslavement. The modern concept of the zombie comes from these Haitian beliefs.

Haiti was demonized by colonial powers as a place of savagery, cannibalism, and black magic. They claimed that Vodou rituals involved human sacrifice and debauchery, and that priests were masters of poisons who practised targeted magic by using dolls. When Haiti was occupied by US forces between 1915 and 1934, there was an attempt by the army and missionaries to stamp out "secret cults" centred on Vodou temples.

Sensationalized views of Vodou, or "voodoo", fed back to the US via written accounts. In his 1929 travelogue *The Magic Island*, American journalist William Seabrook claimed to have met workers who had been put under the power of Vodou priests. American author Zora Neale Hurston made a similar claim in her book on Haiti, *Tell My Horse* (1938).

Separating fact from fiction

The perception of Voudou shaped by fantasy projection has been present in Gothic fiction since the 1880s. Examples include "The Beckoning Hand", an 1887 short story by Grant Allen, and *The Parasite* (1894) by Arthur Conan Doyle. Henry Whitehead, who was archdeacon of the Virgin Islands in the 1920s, also wrote many horror stories about so-called voodoo practices.

Early horror films, made during and directly after the occupation of Haiti, wove together American beliefs about voodoo and Haitian *zombi* lore. Early 20th-century examples include *Chloe, Love is Calling You* (1934), *Ouanga* (1936), *King of the Zombies* (1941), and *I Walked with a Zombie* (1943). Voodoo portrayals in later films, however, moved increasingly further away from the reality of Vodou practices. Blaxploitation films such as *Scream Blacula Scream* (1973) and *Sugar Hill* (1974) reflected a new Hollywood standard: portraying voodoo not as a religious system but as evil, ritual magic that granted control over other bodies – dead or alive.

Enslaved bodies
Alexander King created a series of evocative illustrations for William Seabrook's *The Magic Island*, here depicting soulless workers (note the empty eyeballs) walking towards the plantation.

WHITE ZOMBIE

The 1932 film *White Zombie*, the first feature-length entry in the zombie genre, was based primarily on William Seabrook's *The Magic Island*. Seabrook wrote of "dead men working in the cane fields" – people believed to be dead, who were buried but then reanimated by sorcery to perform forced labour. His use of the term "zombie" marked its first appearance in English and introduced these undead Vodou figures to Western audiences.

"The zombie… is a dead body which is made to walk and act and move as if it were alive."

WILLIAM SEABROOK, *THE MAGIC ISLAND*

1700-1900

THE GOTHIC ERA

VAMPIRE PANICS

AT TURNS BEAUTIFUL AND FRIGHTENING, VAMPIRES ARE POPULAR FIGURES IN HORROR WRITING AND FILM, BUT SOME PEOPLE IN THE 18TH CENTURY, SAW THEM AS A REAL-LIFE THREAT.

Teenage vampire
When Mercy Brown died of tuberculosis, years after her mother and sister, local townsfolk believed she had been a vampire responsible for their deaths and exhumed her body.

The modern understanding of a vampire is a fictional predator that is "undead" — technically dead but reanimated by supernatural means. These beings are equipped with fangs to puncture the skin of their human victims and feed on their blood: the carotid arteries in the neck are the most common site of attack. However, almost a century before the first vampire appeared in a work of fiction — in 1819's "The Vampyre" by John William Polidori — belief in the existence of such creatures sparked a series of vampire panics in Europe.

Rather than being caused by some of the ruthless historic killers who influenced vampire lore — Vlad the Impaler, most famously, or Hungarian "Blood Countess" Elizabeth Báthory of Ecsed — these upsets centred on ordinary, recently deceased people, who were accused of returning to kill the living.

Fear spreads

The so-called Great Vampire Epidemic swept through parts of Eastern Europe in the early to mid-18th century, triggered in 1725 when a Serbian peasant called Petar Blagojević was accused of being a vampire within days of his burial because of a spate of unexplained deaths. When his body was exhumed, signs of hair and nail growth, the lack of decomposition, as well as fresh blood on his mouth were taken as signs of vampirism. To kill him once and for all, a group led by government official Ernst Frombald put a stake through the corpse's heart.

Frombald's report to the authorities in Austria, the imperial power that ruled over Serbia, claimed that blood subsequently came from Blagojević's ears and mouth. This sensational document was

Prevention is better than cure
Unearthed by archaeologists working in southeast Bulgaria in 2014, this skeleton dates from the Middle Ages. Its heart has been staked with an iron rod in a practice said to prevent the dead from becoming vampires.

Straight to the heart of the matter
Plunging a stake into the heart of a vampire is the best-known way to kill it. Modern fiction often depicts the stake as a pointed wooden post, but in this engraving a red-hot iron rod is deployed.

widely published, creating a panic that was only subdued in 1768, following a report from Empress Maria Theresa's personal physician, who had investigated (and disproved) the claims at her request. Several treatises on vampirism were written at the height of the panic. In France, Augustin Calmet, a Catholic monk, compiled a work dedicated to cases of vampirism in Hungary, Bohemia, Moravia, and Silesia.

Hysteria regarding vampires tended to peak when new diseases emerged, but folklore also played a part. In fact, the 18th century was not the first time that supposed vampires had been identified in Eastern Europe – in the 14th century, Serbian laws banned "vampire burials", which involved staking the corpse through the heart or other methods designed to prevent a vampire from returning from the dead. Vampire-like figures also feature in Slavic tales of creatures such as the *upiór*, a possessed corpse condemned to drink blood, and the demon *strzyga*, which returns from death to feast on the living.

Into the Americas

Vampire panics gripped towns in the US in the late 18th and 19th centuries. Among the most famous examples is the terror caused by Mercy Brown, a Rhode Island woman who died of tuberculosis in 1892. At the time, tuberculosis was associated with vampire attacks, because both presented similar symptoms of physical wasting. When Mercy's brother Edwin also fell ill with the disease, her body was exhumed and her heart was found still to be bloody, sparking fears that she was indeed a vampire.

In a bid to save Edwin's life, the townsfolk burned Mercy's organs and made him consume them – a ritual rumoured to strike a vampire dead and stop them from claiming another victim. Unsurprisingly, this did not cure the boy, and he died less than two months later.

> "[Vampires] return either by night or by day, disturb the living, suck their blood, kill them, appear in their clothes… and do a thousand other things; then return to their graves…"
>
> FRENCH MONK AUGUSTIN CALMET, *THE PHANTOM WORLD*, 1746

CATHEDRALS OF FEAR

THE DARK, MELANCHOLY FEEL OF MEDIEVAL "GOTHIC" ARCHITECTURE MADE SUCH BUILDINGS THE PERFECT SETTINGS FOR HORROR FICTION.

Dizzying heights
The vaulted ceilings of large Gothic cathedrals seem to rise toward the heavens, as seen here at Cathedral of Saint Cecilia of Albi (built in the Southern French Gothic style).

The key features of Gothic architecture include a pointed arch and decorative excess in ribbed ceilings, spires, and flying buttresses. The Gothic style – named by Renaissance writers, who found it to be ugly and associated it with the barbarian Goths' destruction of Rome and its culture – lasted from 1180s until 1520, when it was followed by renewed interest in Greek and Roman styles.

The Gothic Revival dawned in Britain in the early 19th century. The Gothic was now claimed (inaccurately) to be an architectural style rooted in the deep history of England, a mark of its institutions of Church and democratic state. The Houses of Parliament in London were rebuilt in full Gothic Revival style, from 1840 to 1860. Influential art critic John Ruskin wrote an essay

> "... it was not easy for one under so much anxiety to find the door that opened into the cavern."
>
> HORACE WALPOLE, *THE CASTLE OF OTRANTO*, 1764

Eerie sentinels
The spires on the rooftops of Milan's Duomo (cathedral) pierce the sky like silent stone sentinels, in keeping with the eerie menace of Gothic horror writing.

"On the Nature of the Gothic" in his *Stones of Venice* (1851–53), which further fostered an embracing of the Gothic style in the Victorian era.

Suggesting fear

Even before the reappraisal of the Gothic style, fiction writers associated its architecture with northern European Protestants' commonly held fear of the Catholic south. For them, Catholicism represented superstition, the tyranny of priests, and the tortures of the Spanish Inquisition.

Many early Gothic novels were set in Spain or Italy and featured ruined castles, monasteries, or churches teeming with murderous monks, deviant nuns, and damsels in distress. Ann Radcliffe's *The Mysteries of Udolpho* (1794), which helped define the Gothic "terror novel", is set in a crumbling labyrinthine castle with dungeons, hidden passages, twisting corridors, and apparent ghosts. The book was key in shaping haunted-house conventions.

Other important texts set in Gothic buildings include Victor Hugo's *The Hunchback of Notre Dame* (1831), which takes the famous Paris cathedral as its setting and even makes the hunchback Quasimodo a gargoyle-like presence.

In *The Monk* (1796), by Matthew Lewis, Gothic architecture embodies oppression and secrecy: dark cloisters, shadowy chapels, and imprisoning convents mirror corruption, repression, and forbidden desire, intensifying the terror and transgression of the story. At the end of the 19th century, Bram Stoker's *Dracula* (1897) opens with a journey to a Transylvanian castle that looms over the landscape, evoking the terrorizing, supernatural power that the vampire count holds over the superstitious peasants below.

Ruined edifices signal a comforting victory over the past – but also a deep fear that the superseded dark age might return. This theme continues in many more recent classic works of horror, including Shirley Jackson's *The Haunting of Hill House* (1959), Stephen King's *The Shining* (1977), and Mark Danielewski's *The House of Leaves* (2000).

Iconic figures
Demonic gargoyles, like this one on Notre Dame cathedral, are iconic features of Gothic architecture.

HORROR IN ROMANTIC ART

The European Romantic movement of the late 18th and early 19th centuries saw artists and writers drawn to heightened emotions and darker themes, a fascination that led to the birth of the Gothic novel. Romantic paintings also incorporated ideas from the Gothic aesthetic and introduced elements that would later become central to horror: madness, death, decay, isolation, and the supernatural, as well as the sublime terror inherent in the natural world. These atmospheric artworks often used gloomier palettes than the light-infused scenes of the Enlightenment.

Some of the major Romantic paintings that explore dark themes include Swiss artist Henry Fuseli's *The Nightmare* (1781), which depicts a grotesque demon sitting on a sleeping woman's chest (possibly alluding to a disturbed mental state); the occult and mythological scenes of Spaniard Francisco Goya; and the works of Germany's Caspar David Friedrich, often featuring the crumbling ruins of man's creations in a beautiful, wild landscape, as in *The Abbey in the Oakwood*. British artist John Martin portrayed the chaos and destruction of the apocalypse, as did some of the works of William Blake, such as *The Great Red Dragon and the Woman Clothed with the Sun* (c. 1805–10).

Several Gothic paintings emerged from the Dresden Romantic circle, a group of artists living in the German city in the early 19th century. Key members were Friedrich, his pupil Ernst Ferdinand Oehme, and Norwegian artist Johan Christian Dahl. Their moody landscapes and Gothic structures created an aesthetic that is still visible in the horror genre today.

An eerie scene
In his 1828 painting *Prozession im Nebel* (*Procession in the Fog*), Ernst Ferdinand Oehme conjures up an eerie and melancholy atmosphere.

THE BIRTH OF BRITISH GOTHIC LITERATURE

EMERGING IN THE MID-18TH CENTURY, BRITISH GOTHIC LITERATURE FUSED TERROR, ROMANCE, AND THE SUPERNATURAL. IT FORGED A DISTINCT LITERARY GENRE THAT IS STILL INFLUENTIAL TODAY.

While the birth of Gothic literature has been attributed to the classic works of British writers, the genre is rooted to some degree in French history and literary traditions. Gothic literature emerged in the aftermath of the Seven Years' War (1756–63), a conflict across Europe and beyond. Three decades later, the French Revolution stimulated a second wave of Gothic fiction – an offshoot of the Romantic movement (c. 1790–1850) – inspired by the terrors of that upheaval and the uncertainty plaguing France and the rest of Europe.

Awe and terror

In Britain, *The Castle of Otranto*, by politician and writer Horace Walpole, is considered the first Gothic novel. Published in 1764, and subtitled "A Gothic Story" for a second edition the following year, it was born out of increasing tensions between the British and French, and Walpole's own frustration at having to return to Britain from France after the war between the two nations. *The Castle of Otranto* was written in direct opposition to French neoclassical traditions – favouring the supernatural over the rational – yet the novel has a distinctly European tone, setting a precedent for many Gothic novels that followed.

Presented as a medieval manuscript found and translated by Walpole, the novel is set in a derelict castle in 12th-century Italy. It centres on Manfred, the head of the Otranto royal family, who has been

Misattributing the macabre
The anonymous 1801 anthology *Tales of Terror* was long thought to have been written by Matthew Lewis, author of *The Monk*. However, in the early 1920s, scholars successfully disproved the idea.

The Birth of British Gothic Literature

A ghostly encounter
Isabella's father Frederic meets a skeleton in this scene from Walpole's *The Castle of Otranto* drawn by artist Bertie Greatheed.

Gothic trope
Dramatic natural scenery is a hallmark of Gothic literature. In the ravine scene of *The Mysteries of Udolpho*, it represents Lady Blanche's courage as she overcomes her fear.

plagued by visions and prophecies that predict his family's ruin. When his heir dies unexpectedly, Manfred pursues his son's wife-to-be, Isabella. As the young woman tries to avoid the prince's advances, Manfred finds himself increasingly tormented by the spectral reminders of his past crimes and the shadow of a prophecy that refuses to release him.

Like Romantic literature, early Gothic works evoke the sublime — a sense of overwhelming awe and terror. The effect in Walpole's novel is enhanced by the grand architectural setting, inspiring later authors to locate their tales within similarly formidable structures. These include religious spaces, such as cathedrals, which were often shrouded in mystery for ordinary people.

Psychological dimension

As in Walpole's story, early Gothic novels often revolve around a female character threatened by supernatural entities or the people around her.

A villainous prototype
In "The Vampyre", a short story written in 1819, John William Polidori presented a charismatic bloodsucking fiend 78 years before Bram Stoker's *Dracula* was published.

While these protagonists tend to suffer from some form of emotional turmoil, the psychological element of Gothic fiction became a key factor of the genre in the early 19th century. Ann Radcliffe's *The Mysteries of Udolpho*, published in 1794, was the first psychological thriller. It centres on a young orphan called Emily sequestered in a remote castle haunted by what she believes are phantoms; these are later revealed to be manifestations of her own memories of people and events. This psychological twist exemplifies the "explained supernatural" form of Gothic for which Radcliffe is known. Three years later, she followed up with *The Italian*, another Gothic work. The distinctly female-centric focus in Radcliffe's writings would be preserved in Gothic literature in the centuries to come.

Sensationalist writings

In the same decade that Radcliffe established herself as a Gothic author, the unrest caused by the French Revolution (1789–99) attracted more writers to the genre. Gothic fiction became a fitting outlet through which to explore the turbulent political and social climate. Published in 1796, Matthew Lewis's *The Monk* shocked readers with its depiction of corruption within the Church. In the novel, Ambrosio, a celebrated Spanish monk, is gradually corrupted after a novice named Rosario — later revealed to be a woman, Matilda — enters the monastery in disguise and eventually seduces him. Their clandestine affair is interrupted by the arrival of another young woman — Antonia — with whom Ambrosio becomes obsessed. Resorting to witchcraft and conspiring with the Devil to win her affection, Ambrosio commits rape and murder. Eventually sentenced to death by the Inquisition, he is condemned to eternal damnation alongside Lucifer.

Sisterly sacrifice
In *Goblin Market* (1862), Christina Rossetti fuses Gothic horror with sisterly love when Lizzie has to sacrifice herself to save Laura from seductive "goblin men".

The graphic violence of *The Monk* made it one of the most popular Gothic novels of the period, in turn leading to a surge in Gothic literature published between 1796 and 1806. However, the sensationalist tone and moral ambiguity of Lewis's work, paired with an explosion of interest in the genre, prompted criticism and derision by authors and readers alike.

Threat to morality

The growing female readership for Gothic novels contributed to the genre being dismissed for being merely popular, overly dramatic, and trivial. At the same time, the sensationalist and immoral elements led to concern about the influence such books might have on their readers.

In 1798, Jane Austen finished writing *Northanger Abbey*, a novel that satirizes the Gothic genre and its impressionable enthusiasts. Within the story, the young Catherine's deep infatuation with Gothic literature (particularly *The Mysteries of Udolpho*) leaves her convinced that she is the protagonist of her own Gothic adventure, her imagination breaking from reality and running wild. In 1818, the same year that Austen's *Northanger Abbey* was belatedly published, Mary Shelley produced *Frankenstein*, reviving interest in the form, and anticipating another resurgence of British Gothic fiction during the Victorian era.

> "A terror of this nature, as it occupies and expands the mind… is purely sublime."
>
> ANN RADCLIFFE, *THE MYSTERIES OF UDOLPHO*

AMERICAN GOTHIC

RISING FROM THE VIOLENT BIRTH OF THE US, THIS LITERARY GENRE OFTEN EXAMINES THE NATION'S TROUBLED PAST THROUGH THE EYES OF THOSE WHO HAVE BEEN CAST AS OUTSIDERS OR MONSTERS.

A symbol of strength
In *The Scarlet Letter*, Hester Prynne wears a red "A" as punishment for adultery but shifts its meaning through dignity and defiance.

Tapping into fears
This imagining of "the nightmare, with her whole ninefold" from "The Legend of Sleepy Hollow" evokes the tale's folkoric terrors.

European settlement of North America is rooted in horror. In the winter of 1609–10, the New World's first white settlers, in the eastern colony of Jamestown, faced a harsh winter and the prospect of starvation. Archaeological evidence shows that the small number of survivors resorted to cannibalism to save themselves. Other settlements disappeared entirely or fought with the Indigenous tribes. The settlers saw it as a Biblical imperative to cultivate this land and, if necessary, to eliminate what they perceived as the "godless heathens" living on it.

Later in the 17th century, the superstition and religious zealotry of settlers led to accusations of witchcraft or Devil worship. During the Salem witch trials of 1692–93, 19 people were found guilty of witchcraft and hanged; many others were imprisoned in an atmosphere of escalating fear.

Haunted by the past

It could be argued that all American fiction is Gothic, given that it has been underpinned by such traumatic events. One of the country's first professional authors, Charles Brockden Brown, wrote a cluster of works that were Gothic in tone. His novel *Wieland* (1798) brims with paranoia and persecution as a man murders his wife and children under the influence of mysterious voices. *Edgar Huntly* (1799) is about sleepwalking, irrationality, and murder on the Pennsylvania frontier; it contains some compelling early depictions of violent conflict between local Indigenous people and white settlers.

The early 19th century produced a number of notable Gothic writers. Washington Irving's 1820 story "The Legend of Sleepy Hollow" illustrates how German "terror novels" and dark fairy tales were transposed to the American landscape. Nathaniel Hawthorne – a descendent of one of the hanging judges of the Salem trials – offered echoes of the witch-hunt era in his 1850 book *The Scarlet Letter*, while *The House of the Seven Gables* (1851) is a haunted-house story of an old building saturated by dark deeds going back two centuries. Both Irving and Hawthorne travelled in

Gothic commentary
In this Civil War cartoon, Confederate president Jeff Davis harvests skulls – a dire commentary on the human cost of the war.

> "There was a contagion in the very air... infecting all the land."
>
> WASHINGTON IRVING, "THE LEGEND OF SLEEPY HOLLOW"

Europe, bringing back Gothic themes and styles. This is also true of the most important writer of Gothic fiction during this period, Edgar Allan Poe.

The dark romanticism of German literature sat uneasily in the US, and Poe's stories were disdained in his lifetime for their psychological and physiological extremes. He explored macabre subject matter, including premature burial, and extreme psychological states of horror, guilt, or perversity. In his early short story "Berenice" (1835), the narrator obsesses over his cousin's teeth; after she has a seizure and seemingly dies, he extracts all 32 of them from her mouth as she lies – still living – in her grave.

New inspiration

Poe's work inspired Irish-American writer Fitz-James O'Brien, who wrote several psychological horror works, including "What Was It? A Mystery" (1859). His career ended when he died fighting for the North in the American Civil War. Another key writer in US Gothic horror was war journalist Ambrose Bierce, famous for "An Occurrence at Owl Creek Bridge" (1890). In this Civil War story, a Confederate sympathizer escapes a hanging, but the ending reveals that this escape is a hallucination, all experienced in the moment between stepping from the bridge and the noose breaking his neck.

Distorted reality
"An Occurrence at Owl Creek Bridge", an American Gothic tale of war, death, and distorted reality, inspired an Oscar-winning French short film of 1961.

In the mid-19th century, there was a boom in women writing in a professional capacity. Louisa May Alcott, best known for *Little Women* (1869), made a career crafting horror tales for illustrated magazines; examples of this work include *Behind a Mask, or A Woman's Power* (1866) and *Pauline's Passion and Punishment* (1862). Gothic devices were sometimes adapted for the female experience. One of the most effective accounts of a woman confined and driven mad by her husband and doctor is Charlotte Perkins Gilman's *The Yellow Wallpaper* (1892), based on the treatment she received for post-natal depression.

Racism and fear

Gothic works tend to turn fear and hatred into monsters. Writer H.P. Lovecraft depicted people of colour as inhuman threats. In his 1925 short story "The Horror at Red Hook", he describes the Satan worshippers hidden in Brooklyn's tenements as a terrifying mix of races, reinforcing xenophobic anxieties. For their part, early Black writers in the 19th century – such as Harriet Jacobs, Frederick Douglass, Hannah Crafts, and Harriet Wilson – used Gothic tropes to make it clear that the system of slavery and white enslavers were the monsters.

Race is also at the heart of the Southern Gothic tradition, a subgenre shaped by writers such as William Faulkner, Carson McCullers, Flannery O'Connor, and Toni Morrison; their works highlight the horrors and violence of the South's past. Morrison's *Beloved* (1987) is a modern classic that reconfigures the genre's traditional boundaries by rooting Gothic terror in the legacy of slavery and racism. Charles W. Chestnutt's 1899

Family feud
Vincent Price stars in an eerie film adaptation of *The House of the Seven Gables*, in which a family is cursed by ancestral greed and guilt.

> "His imagination... was fraught with an incurable persuasion that his death was at hand."
>
> CHARLES BROCKDEN BROWN, *WIELAND*

anthology *The Conjure Woman* features many of Southern Gothic's hallmarks in an exploration of folkloric beliefs among the Black population.

American Gothic has diversified and entered mainstream fiction through Black American writers such as Zora Neale Hurston, Octavia Butler, Victor LaValle, and Tananarive Due. Like Morrison, Stephen Graham Jones, a Blackfeet Native American writer, reimagines the genre through an Indigenous lens with works such as *The Only Good Indians* (2020).

In 1964, US historian Richard Hofstadter suggested that a "paranoid style" has shaped the American republic, casting diverse groups as existential threats. With such rich sources, Gothic horror is well adapted to the American experience.

A GUIDING LIGHT

Central to the Southern Gothic subgenre, William Faulkner's work explores the legacies of slavery and the lingering stain of the Civil War – forces that haunt the present and drive characters to extremes. His 1932 novel *Light in August* inspired others to follow similarly twisted paths. In film, *Deliverance* (1972) typifies Southern Gothic through isolation, guilt, and grotesque violence.

Faulkner's *Light in August* became a template for later writers of the Southern Gothic.

EDGAR ALLAN POE

THE DARK TALES OF EDGAR
ALLAN POE ARE MASTERPIECES
OF PSYCHOLOGICAL HORROR
AND THE MACABRE.

He shrieked once – once only
The frontispiece of the 1923 coloured edition of Poe's *Tales of Mystery and Imagination* featured Harry Clarke's classic illustration of "The Tell-Tale Heart".

Unlikely culprit
Daniel Vierge's 1870 illustration of "The Murders in the Rue Morgue" depicts an orangutan – the mysterious murderer in Poe's tale – attacking a woman with a straight razor.

Boston's Edgar Allan Poe is considered the first great American short-story writer. He believed that fiction should be short enough to be read in one sitting, and that writers should follow the principle of the "unity of effect" – the concept that every word of a story, including its first, should be focused on its ending. Applying this approach, Poe took horror and science fiction into frightening new territory, and with *The Murders in the Rue Morgue* and *The Mystery of Marie Rogêt* single-handedly invented the detective story.

Broken minds

Like lightning illuminating a hellish landscape, "The Tell-Tale Heart" is over in just 2,000 words or so. An unnamed narrator, who tries to convince us that he is sane, describes murdering an old man, not in revenge or out of greed, but to shut off the man's eye – a "vulture eye" – which the narrator fears. The narrator hides the man's body under the floorboards, then panics later while entertaining some policemen, sure that he can hear a heartbeat (possibly his own), which he believes to be his victim's. Convinced that the policemen can hear it too, and that they know exactly what he has done, the narrator tears up the floorboards and confesses his crime – as if a sleepless eye, his own conscience perhaps, has always been watching him.

In "The Masque of the Red Death", Prince Prospero and 1,000 nobles hide in Prospero's castle, welding the doors and windows shut, to wait out a ravaging plague. For months, they live in luxury, until a stranger appears at a masquerade ball wearing a bloodied robe and a death mask. Enraged, Prospero removes the mask to find nothing beneath, and one by one the people around him die. In "The Fall of the House of Usher", a crumbling house and its surrounding landscape are the malign forces that instigate and mirror the demise of twins Roderick and Madeline, the last members of the Usher family.

Poe perfected his Gothic tales by adding acute psychological twists. Some stories, such as "The Black Cat", use a first-person narrative to expose the mechanics of the psychopathic mind and create a growing sense of dread. In this story, a man is overwhelmed by hatred for his cat, but kills his wife by mistake while pursuing it. When he unknowingly immures the living cat with his wife, its cries alert the police to the killing.

> "I became insane, with long intervals of horrible sanity."
>
> EDGAR ALLAN POE, LETTER TO GEORGE WASHINGTON EVELETH, 1846

FRANKENSTEIN AND SCIENCE FICTION

MARY SHELLEY'S NOVEL ABOUT A SCIENTIST WHO CREATES LIFE IS ONE OF THE MOST INFLUENTIAL STORIES EVER WRITTEN. IT SPARKED A GENRE OF STORIES ABOUT THE HORRORS OF EXPERIMENTATION.

On a stormy night in June 1816, a group of literary friends gathered at the Villa Diodati, on the shores of Lake Geneva. The group were guests of Lord Byron, who was renting the property for the summer. Due to the poor weather, the friends decided to hold a competition – to conjure a ghost story that would terrify those in attendance. That night, the ideas for two defining works of the horror literary genre were conceived: the first vampire novel, John Polidori's *The Vampyre*, and Mary Shelley's *Frankenstein*.

Published in 1818, *Frankenstein; or, The Modern Prometheus* follows an inventor named Victor Frankenstein who is obsessed with testing the boundaries between life and death. When he successfully creates a living being – called the Creature – out of body parts from stolen cadavers, he is quickly horrified by what he has done. His abandonment of his creation has devastating consequences, leading to a chain of events that result in pain, revenge, and ultimately death.

Humanity and creation

In popular culture, the name "Frankenstein" is frequently misattributed to the inventor's creation. What this error underscores is the monstrous behaviour of Victor throughout the novel. His lack of ethical consideration along with his rejection of and intentional cruelty towards his creation all show the darker side of humanity. Although a number of people are killed by the Creature, the novel puts the onus on his maker.

CYRANO DE BERGERAC'S THE OTHER WORLD

Although Shelley is credited as the progenitor of science fiction horror, the genre's origins can be traced back to the mid-17th century. French writer Cyrano de Bergerac wrote three novels collectively published in 1657 as *L'Autre Monde* (*The Other World*). Defying the genres of the time, de Bergerac's novels depict a man's attempts to travel to the Moon and later the Sun to prove there are other civilizations beyond our own. These novels are often characterized as satirical, as they sought to criticize the understanding of the Universe put forward by the Church and scientific followers of Aristotle. Nevertheless, the cosmic themes, including the visions of other worlds and life forms, show the great influence that scientific debate had on the imagination.

This 19th-century chromolithograph illustrates de Bergerac's *The Other World* and its imagined alien civilizations.

The Gothic Era

> "All men hate the wretched; how, then, must I be hated, who am miserable beyond all living things!"

THE CREATURE TO HIS CREATOR, *FRANKENSTEIN; OR, THE MODERN PROMETHEUS*

The power of nature
Victor Frankenstein meets the Creature near Mont Blanc in the Alps – a setting that highlights the futility of his attempts to control nature.

Written during a time of great change, brought about by industrialization, scientific discovery, and rationalism, *Frankenstein* not only questions humanity's capabilities, but also highlights the moral and ethical concerns around our pursuit of knowledge. Despite Victor's success in bringing the Creature to life, his ugliness represents Victor's failures and reminds the inventor that he is not God. The Creature's murderous acts stress the danger that both Victor and his creation present to humanity. At the same time, however, sections of the novel are written from the point of view of the Creature, demonstrating his intellect and humanity as well as his feelings of pain and rejection. His request that Victor create him a female companion reveals his isolation and desire for affection, evoking pity.

Frankenstein's monsters

Since its initial publication, Shelley's tale has been adapted for the stage and screen multiple times. Five years after the novel's release, a stage adaptation was produced at the English Opera House. The first film version arrived in the silent era, with director J. Searle Dawley's short movie depicting the creation of the Creature in 1910. While Shelley called him "the Creature", he has become better known as "Frankenstein's monster", with some adaptations playing down the Creature's intellect and emotions.

The most iconic depiction of the monster comes from James Whale's *Frankenstein* (1931), a Universal Pictures film, which famously gave Boris Karloff's Creature bolts in his neck to conduct electricity during reanimation. Several more Universal projects starring the Creature followed. Other films have ranged from parodic, such as *Young Frankenstein* (1974), to melodramatic, like Kenneth Branagh's *Mary Shelley's Frankenstein* (1994). In 2025, Mexican director Guillermo del Toro released his own adaptation with Oscar Isaac and Jacob Elordi (an actor known for playing romantic leads) as the creator-Creature duo.

Gothic legacy

Frankenstein's influence on the Gothic genre was enormous. The horrors of transgressive science, fear of the unknown or forbidden knowledge, and feelings of isolation or alienation were themes picked up by other Gothic stories, including

Alien technology
Henrique Alvim Corrêa's 1906 illustrations for *The War of the Worlds* showed Martians as terrifying mechanical creatures.

Iconic appearance
Makeup artist Jack Pierce's design for Boris Karloff's Creature set a visual identity for the monster that still influences portrayals today.

> "Oh, in the name of God! Now I know what it feels like to be God!"
>
> HENRY FRANKENSTEIN IN UNIVERSAL PICTURES' *FRANKENSTEIN*, 1931

Robert Louis Stevenson's novella *The Strange Case of Dr Jekyll and Mr Hyde* (1886). Curious about humanity's "darker side", Jekyll, a scientist, experiments on himself, unexpectedly releasing a violent alter-ego, Hyde.

The protagonist of H.G. Wells's *The Invisible Man* (1897) also experiments on himself, embarking on a reign of terror when he realizes that he can make himself invisible. In *The Island of Doctor Moreau* (1896), Wells explores the moral corruption that scientific experimentation can breed. He turns to aliens to inspire fear and highlight human hubris and vulnerability in his Gothic science fiction classic *The War of the Worlds* (1895-97). In this book, the cosmic creatures wreak havoc on Earth and inspire fear and disgust with their thirst for blood.

A horror legacy

Beyond Gothic science fiction, dark themes drawn from *Frankenstein* have fed into several subgenres of modern horror, including the "new weird" fiction series by authors such as China Miéville and Jeff VanderMeer. Works of psychological horror, such as Darren Aronofsky's film *Black Swan* (2010), have reflected *Frankenstein*'s study of identity, alienation, guilt, and ambition, while the unease provoked by the assembly of the Creature from dismembered corpses has underpinned works of body horror including David Cronenberg's films *The Brood* (1979) and *The Fly* (1986).

Frankenstein itself has also been reimagined multiple times, including in Scottish writer Alasdair Gray's *Poor Things* (1992), in which a scientist brings a pregnant woman who dies by suicide back to life by replacing her brain with her unborn child's. The novel, set in late Victorian Glasgow, has been characterized by some as a feminist retelling of *Frankenstein*, focusing on female empowerment, bodily autonomy, and sexual liberation through the story of its protagonist's self-discovery.

Adult rebirth
Emma Stone stars as the protagonist Bella Baxter in the 2023 film of *Poor Things*. The movie traces her rapid development from an infant-like state to an independent woman.

PENNY DREADFULS AND THE NEW NEWGATE CALENDAR

THE FIRST MASS-MARKET HORROR, PENNY DREADFULS BROUGHT TALES OF VIOLENCE AND TRUE CRIME TO A NEW AUDIENCE, CHANGING THE LITERARY LANDSCAPE OF BRITAIN.

Arctic terrors
The Frozen Crew of the Ice-bound Ship was published in 11 weekly instalments in 1868. It was among the first to feature a colour cover, made possible by the invention of a new printing technique, chromolithography, in the 1860s.

Rapid developments in printing technology at the turn of the 19th century allowed books and other printed material to be produced and sold cheaply. This publishing boom, along with rising literacy rates, spawned a new genre of horror fiction aimed at the masses. First appearing in the 1830s, pamphlets called "penny bloods" – so named for their cheap price and grisly subject matter – offered working-class readers in Britain short-form doses of violence and terror. By the 1860s, these immensely popular publications had become known as "penny dreadfuls".

Serial horror

Presented in serialized form, penny dreadfuls were usually released weekly in eight- or sixteen-page instalments, often with a lurid black-and-white illustration on the front page to draw in readers. The first one appeared in 1836; it was titled *Lives of the Most Notorious Highwaymen, Footpads, &c.* and had 60 parts. Less than a decade later, George W.M. Reynolds's *The Mysteries of London* became the most popular penny dreadful ever produced. First published in 1844, it would be published in 624 instalments, released over the course of 12 years.

While early penny dreadfuls were retellings of 18th-century Gothic fiction, later publications offered original stories. One of these was James Malcolm Rymer's tale of Sweeney Todd, about a

High drama and adventure
As well as tales of true crime, penny dreadfuls told sensationalist adventure stories full of action, exotic locations, and colourful characters. Pirates, highwaymen, and wayward aristocrats were particularly popular subjects.

> "'They shall die,' said Sweeney Todd, 'dead men tell no tales, nor women nor boys either, and they shall all die!'"
>
> JAMES MALCOLM RYMER, *THE STRING OF PEARLS*

demon barber who murders his customers and eats their remains in pies. It first appeared under the title *The String of Pearls* in 1846 and quickly gained a large following. Despite this being a fictional tale, a growing fascination with true crime appears to have fuelled the popularity of this story. Soon, other penny dreadfuls began detailing real-life events to thrill readers.

One series that blurred fact with fiction was *The New Newgate Calendar* (1863–66). Inspired by an 18th-century collection of the same name, it documented the heinous acts of criminals throughout history, while warning readers of the consequences of succumbing to a life of crime. A runaway success, this type of penny dreadful caused moral panic in the last decades of the 19th century. Accused of glamorizing violence and encouraging copycat crimes, they reinforced the notion of a criminal and immoral underclass ready to attack respectable society.

By this time, it is estimated that as many as 30,000 penny dreadfuls were being sold every week, many to young working-class boys – now literate thanks to the establishment of public schools in Britain. These impressionable minds, it was argued, were being corrupted by a diet of literary horror. The fears appeared to be justified by numerous newspaper reports of children committing gruesome crimes, including attacking and killing their mothers, as well as an increase in suicide rates among adolescents. In 1886, the *Pall Mall Gazette* described penny dreadfuls as "the poison which is threatening to destroy the manhood of the democracy".

SAWNEY BEAN

Penny dreadfuls such as the *New Newgate Calendar* revived and popularized a number of chilling ancient tales, including the notorious legend of Sawney Bean. Allegedly born in 16th-century Scotland, Bean was said to have lived with his wife and many offspring in a cave near the Ayrshire coast. Here they attacked, robbed, and murdered passing travellers, eating those they ambushed and throwing their remains into the sea.

An enduring tale
Actor Johnny Depp plays the eponymous barber in Tim Burton's 2007 film *Sweeney Todd: The Demon Barber of Fleet Street*, one of the many modern retellings of the story.

VICTORIAN GOTHIC

AS CITIES EXPANDED AND SCIENCE CHALLENGED TRADITIONAL BELIEFS, VICTORIAN GOTHIC TALES REFLECTED THE FEARS AND ANXIETIES CAUSED BY THESE SOCIETAL SHIFTS.

> "I came here, robbed of my character, and determined to claim it back."
>
> ANNE CATHERICK TO WALTER IN WILKIE COLLINS'
> *THE WOMAN IN WHITE*

When the Gothic genre first emerged in the late 18th century, its stories followed set patterns of content, structure, and style. Ominous edifices and phantom sightings were key ingredients, and a young woman in distress was often at the heart of the narrative. During the Victorian era (1837–1901), however, the genre found a renewed readership and took on a darker, more psychological tone, most clearly demonstrated in changes to settings and characterization.

Domestic horrors

While early Gothic tales were often set in the cold confines of a formidable monastery, mansion, or castle, Victorian Gothic broke away from these spatial constraints. Eschewing distant, exotic settings, Victorian tales revolved around the dark secrets and scandals of domestic life and took place in ordinary suburban homes. Wilkie Collins's *The Woman in White* (1859–60), for example, centres on a regular working man — an art teacher — who falls in love with a woman already betrothed by her late father to a villain, Sir Percival Glyde. A tale of entrapment, identity theft, murder, and madness unfolds, made more disturbing by the pretence of respectable normality.

Like the popular penny dreadful serializations that emerged during the 1830s, many Victorian Gothic novels were set in cities. Works such as Charles Dickens's *Bleak House* (1853) and Robert Louis Stevenson's *The Strange Case of Dr Jekyll and Mr Hyde* (1886) captured the horrors of urban living, with city architecture and atmosphere often acting as a metaphor for the disturbed mind.

Madwomen in the attic

As in the first wave of Gothic literature, women featured strongly in Victorian Gothic. Many stories have female protagonists who are accused of, or

MAGIC LANTERN SHOWS

First invented in the 17th century, the magic lantern show became a popular form of entertainment for Victorians, both in their homes and in taverns and halls. People gathered to listen to horror stories brought to life by images depicted on glass slides and projected onto walls, screens, or simply white sheets. At the end of the 18th century, French magician Étienne-Gaspard Robert's *Phantasmagorie* used the technique, and other optical effects, to produce convincing apparitions. This led to a new type of horror theatre called phantasmagoria: large-scale productions in which magic lanterns created the illusion of phantoms performing onstage alongside actors.

The audience of a 19th-century phantasmagoria show gasp in horror as the magic lantern is used to project the image of a demon onto the stage.

Cloaked in innocence
This 1870s poster for *The Woman in White*'s stage adaptation depicts Anne Catherick – the woman in white – who is persecuted by the villain, Sir Percival Glyde, because she knows he is illegitimate.

Changing faces
Dr Jekyll transforms into the immoral Edward Hyde in Edmund J. Sullivan's illustration from the 1928 edition of *The Strange Case of Dr Jekyll & Mr Hyde*. Jekyll created an elixir that enabled him to slip between the two characters.

experience, episodes of "madness", making them unreliable narrators. These psychological breakdowns can be a consequence of societal transgression, acts of resistance, or supernatural encounters. *The Woman in White* and J. Sheridan Le Fanu's *The Rose and the Key* (1871) depict women committed to asylums on account of their suspected madness, when really they are being trapped by men who wish to control them.

American writer Charlotte Perkins Gilman explored the toll of patriarchy on a woman's psyche in *The Yellow Wallpaper* (1892), in which a woman convalescing after giving birth becomes transfixed by what she believes to be a woman trapped behind her room's wallpaper. The preponderance of female characters who are similarly isolated or hidden away, due to (perceived) madness caused by societal pressures, led to the Gothic trope of the "madwoman in the attic", identified by literary critics Sandra M. Gilbert and Susan Gubar in 1979. The most famous example is Bertha Mason, Mr Rochester's Creole first wife, in Charlotte Brontë's *Jane Eyre* (1847).

These "mad" women represent a shift from the external supernatural forces that dominate early Gothic works, such as ghosts and monsters, to internal horrors – projections of psychological states such as anxiety, trauma, repressed desire, and moral turmoil. Henry James blended these threats in *The Turn of the Screw* (1898), creating a tale that taps into a range of contemporary fears. Framed as a true story told amongst friends wishing to scare one another with ghostly tales, the novel follows a young governess who becomes convinced that she is being haunted by the spirits of two former employees. Her fear that the ghosts will corrupt the children in her care highlights Victorian anxieties around the susceptibility of children to moral and spiritual decay, and the power of demonic forces. The novel's ambiguous conclusion leaves readers unsure whether the protagonist is a victim of a real haunting or simply her own imagination.

Decadent Gothic

By the late 19th century, fears that society was becoming morally degenerate were manifesting in new Gothic monsters, such as the vampire. Depicted in Le Fanu's *Carmilla* (1872) and Bram Stoker's *Dracula* (1897), the vampire epitomized fears that monstrosity was hiding in plain sight – in the guise of characters who appeared to be ordinary people. Unable to curb their deadly appetites, vampires symbolized excess and a flagrant disregard for social, sexual, and moral boundaries. Tales exploring these darker recesses of the human soul are now categorized as "decadent gothic".

The Strange Case of Dr Jekyll and Mr Hyde and Oscar Wilde's *The Picture of Dorian Gray* (1890) exemplify this type of story. Both employ the trope

> "It becomes bars!… the woman behind is as plain as can be."
>
> CHARLOTTE PERKINS GILMAN, *THE YELLOW WALLPAPER*

of the double self, or doppelgänger, who becomes integral to each character's struggle with good and evil and their own mortality. *The Picture of Dorian Gray* sees Gray's desire to stay young and beautiful granted by a magical (or cursed) portrait, which comes with a heavy price. His hedonistic lifestyle and immorality leave no trace upon his physical appearance, while the painted Dorian withers, revealing his true base nature.

Sign of the times

By the end of the 19th century, Gothic horror had developed into a rich and varied genre with serious underlying themes. It no longer relied solely on the supernatural to entertain audiences, but exploited contemporary anxieties related to social, cultural, and religious change. Rapid advances in science were also a cause for concern, reflected in works that built on the combination of Gothic horror and science fiction pioneered by Mary Shelley's *Frankenstein*. Published in 1894, towards the end of the Victorian era, Welsh author Arthur Machen's *The Great God Pan* reflects these diverse fears. It tells the story of a girl whose brain is tampered with in order to amplify her perception of the supernatural world, setting her on a path of misery, persecution, and pain.

His true self
American artist Ivan Albright painted the rotting visage of Dorian (right) used in the 1945 film adaptation of *The Picture of Dorian Gray*. Directed by Albert Lewin, the film starred Hurd Hatfield (above) as the narcissistic anti-hero.

GOTHIC OPERA

EMERGING IN GERMANY IN THE MID-19TH CENTURY, GOTHIC OPERA THRILLED EUROPEAN AUDIENCES WITH ITS SPINE-TINGLING STORIES, DRAMATIC SCORES, AND ATMOSPHERIC SETS.

Characterized by intense emotion, Gothic operas often involved the mysterious figures, tragic fates, and paranormal elements of the Gothic literary tradition, but they also incorporated ideas from older European folk beliefs. One early standout work — inspired by an 1821 play based on John Polidori's short story "The Vampyre" (1819) — was Heinrich Marschner's *Der Vampyr*, which premiered in 1828. Marschner's dramatic score represents the protagonist's inner torment and the looming presence of evil. Popular in its time, the piece contributed to the Gothic craze in opera and is frequently staged in German-speaking countries to this day.

One of the most significant Gothic operas of this early period was Richard Wagner's *Der Fliegende Holländer* (*The Flying Dutchman*), which premiered in 1843. The story is based on the legend of a cursed Dutch captain condemned by Satan to sail the seas forever, in a ship crewed by the corpses of dead sailors, and unable to die unless he is redeemed by true love. The opera raised questions about destiny and the boundaries of human suffering. Other important German contributions to the Gothic opera genre include Carl Maria von Weber's *Der Freischütz* (*The Marksman*; 1821), a Faustian-bargain tale that is famous for its supernatural night scene in the eerie Wolf's Glen, and Louis Spohr's *Der Berggeist* (1824) about a mysterious mountain spirit.

Further afield

Gothic tales also flourished in operas beyond Germany's borders. Jacques Offenbach's French opera *Les Contes d'Hoffmann* (*The Tales of Hoffmann*), which premiered in 1881, diverged from the dark seriousness of Wagner and Marschner by introducing a more fantastical and ironic approach to the Gothic genre. Based on the

Devilish opera-ballet
Jacques Mars cuts a fearsome figure as Mephistopheles, "the Devil disguised as a gentleman", in rehearsal for the 1964 Paris production of Hector Berlioz's *The Damnation of Faust*.

Evoking isolation
The staging of Wagner's *The Flying Dutchman* often features dramatic lighting and stark sets that help evoke isolation and heighten the tragic inevitability of the tale.

short stories of German Gothic author E.T.A. Hoffmann, it is a journey through the failed loves and strange adventures of the protagonist. *The Tales of Hoffmann* centres on four supernatural women, each embodying a different aspect of the protagonist's relationships – from a mechanical doll, to a demonic temptress. It includes Hoffman's popular 1816 tale "Der Sandmann" ("The Sandman"), about a figure from German mythology who stole children's eyes if they would not go to sleep.

Inspired and inspiring

Other popular works took inspiration from Romantic literature. Russian composer Anton Rubinstein based *The Demon* (1871) on the poem of that name by Mikhail Lermontov. It centres on a fallen angel cursed to wander Earth spreading corruption and destruction. With its melodic complexity and psychological depth, *The Demon* made a notable contribution to the Gothic opera tradition, though its popularity later declined with the rise of more innovative 20th-century works.

> "Her blood gives me new courage; Her death tremor gives new life!"
>
> LORD RUTHVEN, IN HEINRICH MARSCHNER'S *DER VAMPYR*, 1828

By evoking the psychological and emotional undercurrents of the plot, composers made important contributions to the development of Romantic orchestral techniques. Furthermore, these operas were typically staged in grand European theatres with elaborate sets and lighting effects that heightened the stories' eerie atmosphere. With their supernatural themes, emphasis on fate, and exploration of the darker side of human nature, Gothic operas resonated deeply with 19th-century audiences. They expressed broader societal anxieties through sensational visual spectacle, thereby creating an explosion of interest in the supernatural.

Unique staging
In 2018, Barcelona's Liceu theatre put on a visually striking production of *The Demon*, staged in a wooden tunnel and inflatable sphere.

GHOSTS AND BLOODY PICTURES

DURING JAPAN'S EDO PERIOD, SOCIETY BECAME INCREASINGLY URBANIZED, CREATING SOCIAL ANXIETIES THAT WERE PERFECT SUBJECTS FOR JAPANESE HORROR ART AND *KAIDAN* — "GHOST STORIES".

The rise of literacy during Japan's Edo period (1603–1868) led to a flourishing of popular culture and a boom in horror literature, plays, and art. This new interest in gory subject matter even influenced *ukiyo-e*, the traditional form of woodblock art dedicated to creating "pictures of the floating world". In the 1860s, masters of this practice, such as Tsukioka Yoshitoshi and Utagawa Yoshiiku, began to paint works that depicted extreme violence, including bloody murder, establishing a growing genre known as *chimidoro-e* ("bloody pictures") and *muzan-e* ("cruel pictures"). In *yūrei-zu* ("ghost art"), female *yūrei* ("ghosts") were often depicted with long, black hair and dressed in a white kimono – the funeral attire of the dead.

Spirited tales

Telling *kaidan* ("ghost stories") was a popular pastime in the Edo period. A Buddhist-inspired party game was *Hyakumonogatari Kaidankai* ("A Gathering of One Hundred Supernatural Tales"), in which people gathered in a room to tell ghost stories in turn, each person leaving to blow out a lantern in an adjoining room after they had told their tale. The storyteller would then look in a mirror, where a *yūrei* was meant to appear, drawn by the tales and the encroaching darkness. These *yūrei* had many forms, each with its own name and character. There were *onryō*, vengeful phantoms who returned to seek justice;

Extreme art
In this 19th-century "bloody picture" by woodblock print master Tsukioka Yoshitoshi, a man drinks blood from the severed head of his enemy.

GHOST THEATRE

Japanese *kabuki* theatre blends drama and dance. In the Edo period, it featured numerous ghost stories, with actors playing apparitions wearing frightening *kumadori* (stage makeup). A *suppon* (lift) enabled them to appear and disappear like ghosts.

At night, the spirit of a dead monk visits the woman he loves.

In this early 20th-century painting by Takayama Umpo, a female ghost ties up a mosquito net – a symbol of the fragile border between the living and spirit worlds.

kosodate-yūrei, the spirits of mothers who had died during childbirth; *funa-yūrei*, the ghosts of those who had died at sea; and *zashiki-warashi*, the mischievous ghosts of children.

Three great ghosts

The most famous ghost stories of the time were compiled as the *Nihon san dai kaidan* (*Japan's Three Great Ghost Stories*). *Yotsuya Kaidan* (*The Ghost Story of Yotsuya*), written for the stage by Tsuruya Nanboku IV in 1825, was particularly popular. In the story, a bad husband, Iemon, plots to kill his wife, Oiwa, and marry someone else. He poisons Oiwa with a disfiguring face cream, causing her to kill herself with her husband's sword. Iemon is then haunted by her disfigured form, and even kills his new wife when Oiwa appears in front of her. Like Shakespeare's play *Macbeth* in the Western world, the very story of Oiwa was thought to be cursed, and was associated with numerous accidents, such as stage lights falling and actors being injured. It was also based on a true story, so actors visited Oiwa's grave to pay homage and protect themselves from her wrath.

The *Nihon san dai kaidan* also included the ghost stories of Okiku and Otsuyu. Okiku was a servant who continued to count the plates in her master's mansion after he had killed her for spurning his advances, while lantern-bearing Otsuyu seduced a man after her death.

> 'From the bottom of the well came a woman's voice: 'One… Two…' counting the plates.'
>
> BABA BUNKO'S VERSION OF OKIKU'S TALE, 1741

GHOST ART

Japanese *ukiyo-e* ("woodblock art") from the mid- to late 19th century reflected the nation's fascination with terrifying supernatural tales. Subgenres emerged to represent different subjects – from the crime and retribution imagery of *chimidoro-e* ("bloody pictures"), to prints depicting *yōkai* (demons and creatures).

Images that illustrated ghost stories were called *yūrei-zu*, with the word *yūrei* applying to all manner of ghosts. Masters of this genre included Hokusai, whose five prints for a *Hyakumonogatari* (*One Hundred Ghost Stories*) anthology depicted some of the most popular contemporary tales; Kunisada Utagawa and Kuniyoshi Utagawa, both prolific artists and students of the Utagawa school; and Yoshitoshi Tsukioka, whose own version of the *One Hundred Ghost Stories* was published in 1865.

Kuniyoshi, who was particularly known for his vivid and dynamic prints of supernatural tales, took his inspiration from history and legend, as in the triptychs *Ghosts of the Taira at Daimotsu Bay* and *Takiyasha the Witch and the Skeleton Spectre*. Many of Kuniyoshi's prints feature scenes from kabuki theatre, giving an insight into how scary stories were portrayed on the Edo stage. They also cover themes expressed in contemporary popular literature, kabuki performances, and oral storytelling. The nightmarish imagery and the exaggerated features of the characters reflected deep cultural anxieties about death, karma, and the afterlife, making them ideal as cautionary tales for Edo-period audiences.

The Ghosts of Tōgo and His Wife
This print by Kuniyoshi shows the vengeful spirits of Asakura Tōgo and his wife returning from the dead to haunt the corrupt official who ordered their unjust execution.

CELEBRATING HALLOWEEN

WHEN IRISH AND SCOTTISH IMMIGRANTS TOOK THEIR ANCIENT FOLK TRADITIONS TO THE US IN THE LATE 19TH CENTURY, THEY LAID THE FOUNDATIONS FOR A SPOOKY AND SPINE-TINGLING FESTIVAL OF THE OCCULT.

Repelling spirits
This plaster cast of a turnip carved to look like a ghost, from Donegal, Ireland, shows the type of "jack-o'-lanterns" that preceded lighted pumpkins in the US.

From pumpkin lanterns to terrifying costumes, many of the modern traditions we associate with Halloween gained popularity in the 19th century. Their origins, however, are much older, probably linked to the ancient Celtic festival of Samhain. On this night, which celebrated the end of harvest and marked the start of winter, the barrier between the realm of the living and the dead was believed to thin, allowing spirits to roam freely. Bonfires were lit and costumes adopted to ward off harmful ghouls.

With the supernatural world so accessible, this was also considered an opportune time to gain insights into the future through divination practices such as scrying (gazing into a reflective surface).

Celtic imports

Between 1845 and 1855, a mass wave of Irish and Scottish immigrants escaping famine arrived in the US, bringing Celtic traditions with them. Among these were Halloween customs rooted in Samhain,

Community fun
Parades became a popular part of Halloween festivities, as depicted in James Elder Christie's *Halloween Frolics*, painted in the 1890s.

The Gothic Era

Trick or treat
Photographed around 1925, three costumed children prepare for "trick or treating", a sign of Halloween's transition from an adult festivity to one almost exclusively celebrated by children.

as well as newer practices that had emerged after the pagan festival was absorbed into Catholic celebrations for All Hallows' Eve, All Saints' Day, and All Souls' Day during the medieval period. The act of carving pumpkin lanterns, or "jack-o'-lanterns", is one example of how these traditions evolved and gained popularity in the context of the US. These lights reflected the ancient belief that fire repels spirits, but were also linked to the Irish legend of Stingy Jack. In this tale, Jack is banished from Heaven and Hell and left to wander Earth with a burning coal in a carved out turnip. Once in the US, widely available pumpkins offered Irish immigrants a perfect alternative.

Games and trickery

By the end of the 19th century, Halloween parties featuring games, mostly aimed at matchmaking, were popular. These replicated ancient divination rituals, including bobbing for apples, in which the first person to catch a floating apple was believed to be the next to wed; sometimes each fruit was given the name of a potential partner. Mirrors were another common component of such games: gazing into a mirror on the night of Halloween was said to reveal the image of a future spouse.

Fate and fears for future happiness are also tied into the origins of "trick-or-treating". While the term was not coined until the 1920s, the custom has links to older practices, such as leaving food out to appease spirits on Samhain, and the medieval tradition of "souling", in which people went door-to-door asking for "soul cakes" in exchange for prayers for the dead. In another tradition, "guising", visitors donned costumes and put on a show in return for treats. The sinister inference, carried through to the modern "trick", is that misfortune follows if the visitors are not satisfied.

> "From gate posts glared the grinning Jack-o'-lantern, with its flickering tallow candle within."
>
> NEWS FEATURE IN *THE SAINT PAUL GLOBE* NEWSPAPER, 31 OCTOBER 1897

Hostile environment
In Russell Drysdale's 1945 painting *The Drover's Wife*, a lone figure stands against a barren landscape that evokes isolation, dread, and the hostility of the outback.

AUSTRALIAN HORROR

THE COLONISTS WHO ARRIVED IN AUSTRALIA STRUGGLED TO ADJUST TO THEIR NEW SURROUNDINGS. THEIR ANXIETIES WERE REFLECTED IN THEIR STORIES, WHICH OFTEN PORTRAYED THE LAND ITSELF AS HOSTILE.

Written in 1856, settler Frederick Sinnett's essay "The Fiction Fields of Australia" rued that, in the absence of Europe's grand ruins, Australian Gothic fiction would be impossible to write. Australia nonetheless developed its own traditions: its tales drew their horrors from the vastness of the outback, physical and psychological isolation, and themes of guilt and retribution. Marcus Clarke's *For the Term of His Natural Life* (1874), for example, portrays the brutal convict system through Gothic imagery of moral decay and entrapment. Gothic elements also feature in stories by writers such as Henry Lawson and Barbara Baynton. Baynton's *Bush Studies*, written in the 1890s, presents the bush as indifferent and threatening, especially to women.

A spiritual and dangerous land

Indigenous Australians have long understood their lands as places of spiritual power and potential danger. The Dreaming — their sacred creation narrative — features numerous cautionary tales populated by supernatural beings and shape-shifting monsters. For the Martu people of Western Australia, these include *ngayurnangalku*, flesh-eating spirits that dwell beneath the desert, surfacing to feed on the living; while the Bunyip, most widely associated with southeastern Australia, is a semi-aquatic creature of swamps and billabongs, sometimes said to drown or "hug" its victims to death in folkloric accounts. Such stories acted as cultural anchors that enforced taboos, demarcated sacred spaces, and offered a means by which to explain sudden loss.

While early Gothic writers in Australia rarely engaged authentically with First Nations beliefs, their understanding of the land itself was shaped by Indigenous presence, resistance, and spirituality. The idea of the land as unknowable, ancient, and spiritually charged is central to Australian Gothic, reflecting Indigenous conceptions of country as a living entity. However, settler writers often recast this in Gothic terms, depicting the landscape as

> ### THE "GHOST HOAXERS" OF AUSTRALIA
>
> In the late 1800s, a number of Australians (usually young men) began donning white sheets or wearing nightmarish costumes around their communities with the intention of terrorizing other locals. This bizarre form of public horror straddled both performance art and social provocation, although some "ghost hoaxers" also committed violent crimes. While these acts were initially met with fear or amusement, they eventually led to vigilante reprisals. As policing in Australia improved, the phenomenon declined, and it had died out completely by the 1920s.

The Gothic Era

> "The Australian mountain forests are funereal, secret, stern… They seem to stifle in their black gorges a story of sullen despair."
>
> MARCUS CLARKE, *THE ANTHOLOGY OF COLONIAL AUSTRALIAN GOTHIC FICTION*, 2007

hostile, mysterious, or cursed. Gothic fiction would influence Australian horror, which often explores alienation and post-colonial guilt. Patrick White's novel *Voss* (1957) portrays the bush as a Gothic void in which the protagonist descends into madness — a comment on the futility of colonialism. Randolph Stow's *To the Islands* (1958) sees a Christian missionary disappear into the Australian wilderness after a violent confrontation with an Indigenous man.

The hostility of the landscape is a key factor in a number of Australian horror films. In Peter Weir's *Picnic at Hanging Rock* (1975), a looming rock formation is the backdrop for vanishing schoolgirls, while Colin Eggleston's *Long Weekend* (1978) sees the bush turn against a bickering couple. Russell Mulcahy's cult success *Razorback* (1984) imagines the outback as home to a monstrous boar, which takes revenge on the human characters.

Picnic at Hanging Rock
While on a school trip, three girls and a teacher vanish mysteriously. This event fuels a tale of psychological horror, obsession, and a lingering sense of dread.

Into the unknown
This 1856 painting of Cunningham's Gap, Queensland, reflects the notion of the settler as a brave explorer, facing the terrors of unknown lands.

VAMPIRE FICTION

WHILE THE WORD "VAMPIRE" BRINGS TO MIND A CERTAIN TRANSYLVANIAN COUNT, MODERN VAMPIRE FICTION WAS BORN ALMOST 80 YEARS BEFORE BRAM STOKER'S IMMORTAL FIGURE ARRIVED ON THE SCENE.

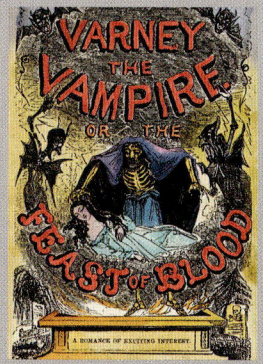

Popular periodical
The penny dreadful *Varney the Vampire* ran for two years from 1845, detailing the heinous acts of the titular bloodsucker.

And so it begins
Jonathan Harker's coach approaches the sinister setting of Count Dracula's castle in Bram Stoker's genre-defining novel.

In his short story "The Vampyre", published in 1819, John William Polidori introduced a sinister aristocratic figure whose immortal status is revealed in the final line of the book. This first piece of vampire fiction was part of the same competition among friends that resulted in Mary Shelley's *Frankenstein*.

Further tales of bloodsucking figures followed. In 1872, Irish author J. Sheridan Le Fanu's *Carmilla* offered readers a fresh perspective on vampire lore by depicting two female protagonists. However, in 1897, fellow Irishman Bram Stoker published *Dracula*, a book that defined the vampire genre and established the classic ingredients of vampire mythology that are still familiar today. A significant feature was Stoker's incorporation of folklore superstitions about vampires and their supposed vulnerabilities, such as aversion to sunlight, garlic, and religious symbols, as well as their inability to see their own reflection or to enter a new space unless invited in.

Structure and form
Since its inception, vampire fiction has often experimented with narrative structures. *Carmilla*, for example, is presented as a medical case study of protagonist Laura's experiences, while *Dracula's* epistolary style uses letters, diary entries, and news reports. In Anne Rice's *Interview with the Vampire* (1976), vampire protagonist Louis reveals the story of his 200-year mortal and immortal life to a reporter.

In addition to playing with form, the genre has occasionally merged with science fiction, as in Richard Matheson's *I Am Legend* (1954) and Octavia E. Butler's *Fledgling* (2005). The possibility of vampires overtaking towns is explored in Stephen King's *'Salem's Lot* (1975). Authors of speculative fiction have also delved into the vampire world: Jewelle Gomez's *The Gilda Stories* (1991) follows a formerly enslaved woman-turned-vampire across two centuries, challenging many common tropes.

Forbidden love
While contemporary vampire fiction continues to explore fear, it has also developed a more sensual and romantic tone. The forbidden love between an immortal vampire and mortal human continues to fixate readers. The publication of Stephenie Meyer's *Twilight* in 2005 (the first in a saga with wildly successful film adaptations) led to the revival of earlier series such as L.J. Smith's *The Vampire Diaries* (1991–2014) and Charlaine Harris's *The Southern Vampire Mysteries* (2001–13), which were also adapted as long-running TV shows, the latter as *True Blood*.

A new twist
Carmilla (1872) was a groundbreaking work about a female vampire who only preys on women – and falls for the female protagonist. Modern versions frame it as a lesbian love story.

LATIN AMERICAN GOTHIC

WITH ITS BLEND OF FOLKLORE, HISTORY, AND THE SUPERNATURAL, LATIN AMERICAN GOTHIC CONFRONTS COLONIALISM AND VIOLENCE IN DARK, ATMOSPHERIC STORYTELLING.

Horrors of youth
In *Jawbone* (2018), Mónica Ojeda uses teenage cruelty, isolation, and the occult to explore themes of power and trauma in an elite school.

Latin American horror fiction is currently flourishing, but it has taken a long time for authors to fully embrace the notion of Latin American Gothic. British Gothic fiction was famously set in grand castles and churches, which did not translate within the Latin American context. Neither did the genre's archetypal characters, who existed within the rigid and hierarchical social frameworks of European class systems.

The genre's European origins led to some Latin American authors outrightly rejecting the Gothic, instead looking to create new traditions with distinctly Latin American paranormal elements, inspired by folklore. Many authors opted for magical realism – a popular literary style in which magical or fantasy elements are treated as if they are normal within an otherwise realistic setting – to bridge the real and the supernatural. Latin American Gothic includes supernatural elements but, unlike magical realism, focuses on dark themes and creating fear and suspense. In its supernatural elements, the genre takes its cues from the most sinister of regional folktales, but it also portrays the horrors of real life: colonialism, poverty, and political oppression.

Some early traces of the genre can be found in short stories from the 1850s and 60s. Cuban author Gertrudis Gómez de Avellaneda wrote "La Ondina del Lago Azúl" ("The Nymph of the Blue Lake") in the 1850s based on Pyrenean folklore

THE HORRORS OF DICTATORSHIPS

The Gothic tradition has helped Latin American writers to process the horrors endured under dictatorships. In 2019, Argentinian writer Mariana Enriquez published her fourth novel, *Nuestra Parte de Noche* (*Our Share of Night*). While the tale spans some 40 years, much of it is set during and immediately after the Pinochet dictatorship of 1976–83, which terrorized and took away opponents of the regime. In the novel, Enriquez ties the history of the *desaparecidos* ("the disappeared") to a secret order that worships a supernatural phenomenon called "the Darkness".

Family members of "the disappeared" take to the Plaza de Mayo in Buenos Aires every Thursday – a protest that began in 1977 and is ongoing even today.

Ghost town
Juan Rulfo's *Pedro Páramo* is one of the most important works of Mexican literature. It was adapted for film by Carlos Velo in 1967.

about a deceitful water spirit; while *Sueños y Realidades* ("Dreams and Realities"), an 1865 collection by Argentinian author Juana Manuela Gorriti, included Gothic tales such as "El Guante Negro" ("The Black Glove").

The first Latin American work to be overtly characterized as Gothic was Chilean writer María Luisa Bombal's 1938 novel *La Amortajada* (*The Shrouded Woman*), in which a recently deceased woman reflects on her own life and death from inside her coffin. Bombal's work inspired many others, such as Mexican writer Juan Rulfo's *Pedro Páramo* (1955), about a literal ghost town.

Women lead the charge

The 21st century has seen a considerable number of Latin American writers, particularly women, thrive in the horror genre, gaining both national and international recognition. Their novels explore gender violence, women's rights, (Catholic) religion, and abuse. Today, Latin American writers have carved out Gothic subgenres unique to their cultural heritage: Ecuador's Mónica Ojeda, for example, characterizes her 2020 collection *Las Voladoras* ("The Flying Women") as "Andean Gothic". Some Argentinian Gothic writers, such as Mariana Enriquez and Samanta Schweblin – particularly known for her novel *Fever Dream* (2017) – are also considered part of the "new Argentine narrative" movement, reflecting on life after the 2001 economic crisis.

> "Mysterious clappings as of frightened wings rustled as we passed through the foliage. From the depths of the ravine came a gentle murmur."
>
> MARIA LUISA BOMBAL, *LA AMORTAJADA* (*THE SHROUDED WOMAN*)

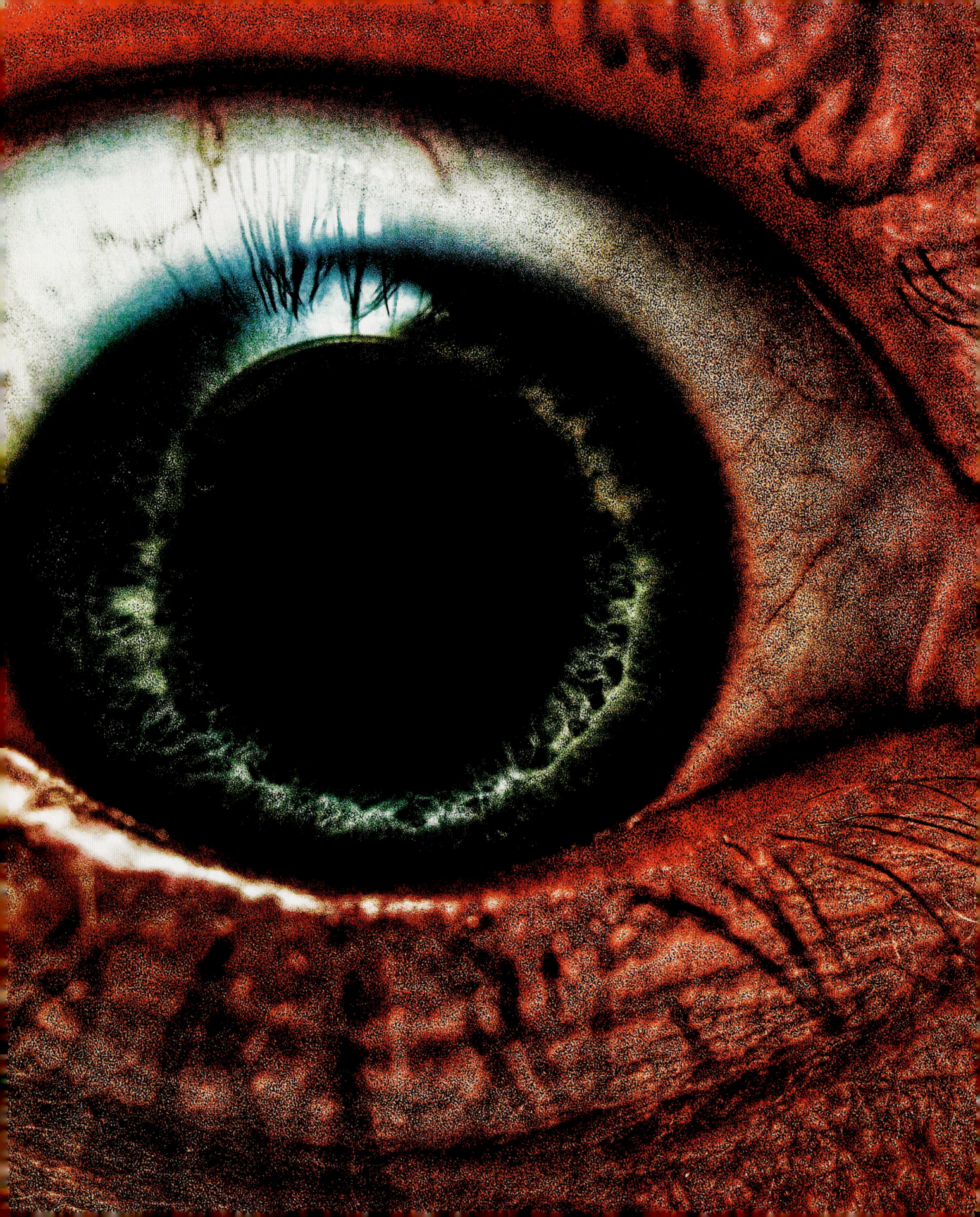

THE SCIENCE OF FEAR

IN THE EARLY 19TH CENTURY, THE SCIENTIFIC REVOLUTION HERALDED NEW INSIGHTS INTO THE BIOLOGY AND PSYCHOLOGY OF FEAR.

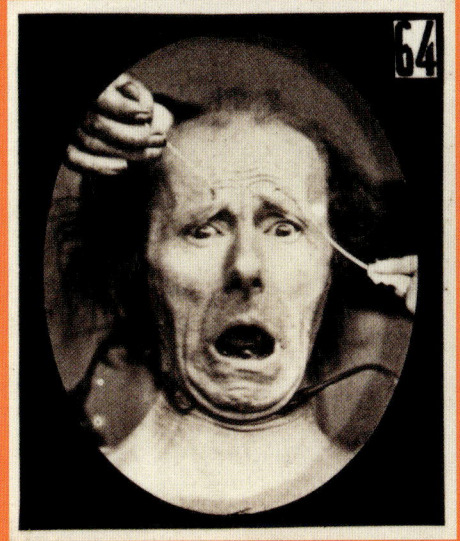

Muscle manipulation
Neurologist G.B. Duchenne's 1862 photograph shows how electrical currents could provoke a fearful facial expression in his subject.

In the eyes
Fear causes physical responses in human eyes, including dilated pupils and raised eyelids.

Canine subject
Ivan Pavlov is pictured here with one of the dogs that took part in his scientific experiments.

In the wake of Charles Darwin's theory of evolution, which placed humans within the animal kingdom, scientists started to consider how evolution had shaped the human mind. In 1872, Darwin's *Expression of the Emotions in Man and Animals* showed how human emotions, such as fear, are universal and can be traced to our animal ancestors. He made the distinction between fear, an appropriate response to a sudden stimulus, and terror, a more extreme response.

Around the same time, American psychologist G. Stanley Hall proposed that children's development mirrors the stages of human evolution. This implied that young children could be viewed as "primitive" or "savage" people who experienced the world, including fears, as our ancient ancestors did. Hall's theory maintained that fear was just the anticipation of pain – with some fears being natural and inherited genetically, and others learned through painful events.

Learned response

Scientific research at the turn of the century seemed to corroborate Hall's theory of fear. Ivan Pavlov, a Russian scientist studying canine digestion, found that ringing a bell when he presented dogs with food led them to link the sound with eating. Once the association between the stimulus and food had been created, Pavlov could stimulate the physiological response (salivating) with just the bell alone. He also found that he could produce a fear response in the dogs. When he started a metronome ticking and then squirted a diluted acid onto their tongues, causing pain and unpleasant sensations, the dogs would shake their heads and back away. Soon just the ticking of the metronome caused the dogs to display fear.

In the early 20th century, new research suggested that humans were more psychologically complex than animals. Sigmund Freud, the father of psychoanalysis, believed that many fears and phobias were caused by sublimated anxieties that could be traced to subconscious desires. In his 1909 study of a five-year-old boy referred to as "Little Hans", Freud thought that a phobia of horses was actually caused by the boy's Oedipus

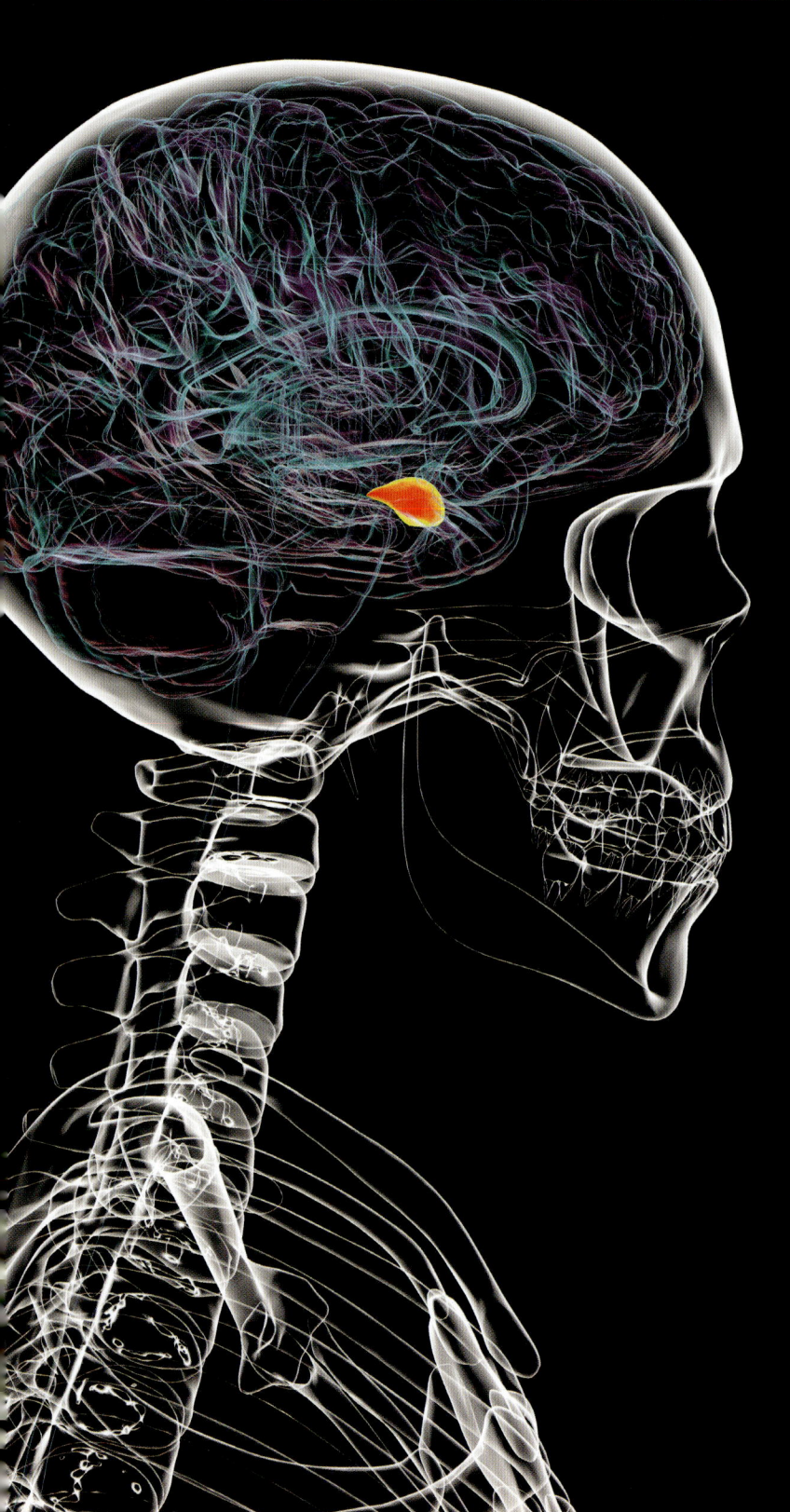

Panic button
This shows the placement of the amygdala within the human brain. The amygdala is responsible for fear and is overactive in fear-related disorders such as PTSD and anxiety.

complex. According to this interpretation, Hans's subconscious hatred of his father was manifesting as a fear of large and powerful animals. Freud's theories were highly influential – though many psychiatrists today disagree with his conclusions.

Modern research

The science of fear became a vital area of research during World War I (1914–18). To keep soldiers fighting in the horrific conditions of trench warfare, it was necessary to understand and control fear. Constant bombardment and the ever-present threat of death led hundreds of thousands of soldiers to develop shell shock. This manifested in several ways: from loss of speech, to panic attacks, to tremors. Survivors of the war often found everyday sounds, such as bells, triggered feelings of horror and intense fright. More recent research has identified these soldiers' ailment as post-traumatic stress disorder (PTSD), the consequence of having witnessed traumatic events.

After the war, doctors wishing to know more about how fears develop conducted a number of experiments, some of them of a dubious ethical nature. One such test, conducted in 1920 by American psychologists John B. Watson and Rosalie Rayner, attempted to stimulate a phobia in an infant using Pavlov's techniques. When the nine-month-old child, referred to as "Little Albert" (an alias),

THE HORROR "HIGH"

Fear junkies crave the psychological and physiological states caused by fear. Once an immediate threat passes, the stress produced by fear dissipates, bringing relief, and chemicals that cause pleasure flood the body. Our minds also get a mental boost from mastering fear and a sense of exhilaration from surviving. Research into "recreational fear" suggests that experiences such as watching horror films can also help to prime our bodies to process real-life fear stimuli.

The thrill of fear
Children scream on board a funfair "ghost train" in this 1950s photograph. Such attractions are popular because of the rush of adrenaline they produce.

> "Chasing fright for fun helps us confront real-life fears."
>
> MATHIAS CLASEN, DIRECTOR OF THE RECREATIONAL FEAR LAB AT AARHUS UNIVERSITY, 2023

amygdala, a neural network in the brain, which sends a rush of chemicals to nerve cells to prepare the body to react. The amygdala also sends signals to the hypothalamus, which releases the stress hormones adrenaline and cortisol.

Such knowledge can help to explain the emergence and development of the horror genre in art, film, and literature, as well as the appeal of recreational fear. Evolutionary scientists have shown that humans are primed for fear, but gaining a fuller understanding of how the brain and body process fear at a chemical and neurological level may clarify questions such as why horror is so compelling, whether it causes or allays anxiety, and what type of horror evokes the most fear or dread. The answers may allow future creators of horror to engage and manipulate their audiences on a deeper level, tapping into inbuilt physiological responses and their related psychological effects to heighten the experience of fear.

was given a rat to play with, he showed no fear. The next time he was given the rat, the researchers made a loud noise, which made him cry and retreat from the animal. After repeatedly exposing him to the rat and noise, the scientists could elicit the same fear response to the rat alone. They also found Albert was now afraid of other small furry things.

When American psychologist Mary Cover Jones heard about this experiment, she began researching how a child might be freed from a phobia. She started exposing a child patient with a fear of rabbits to rabbits at shorter and shorter distances and pairing their appearances with sweets. Soon the child identified rabbits with pleasant experiences and eventually could calmly play with them. Fears could be learned, but also unlearned through desensitizing a person to the stimuli that would normally provoke fear. Fear was not a moral failing but a condition of the body that could be treated.

From science to horror
Today, scientists can study how fear works through imaging responses within the brain and the biochemical changes behind these responses. They know that the body's reaction to fear begins in the

Unfair consequences
The Little Albert experiment is considered one of the most unethical experiments ever. Inducing a fear of all furry animals, it may have affected the participant for the rest of his life.

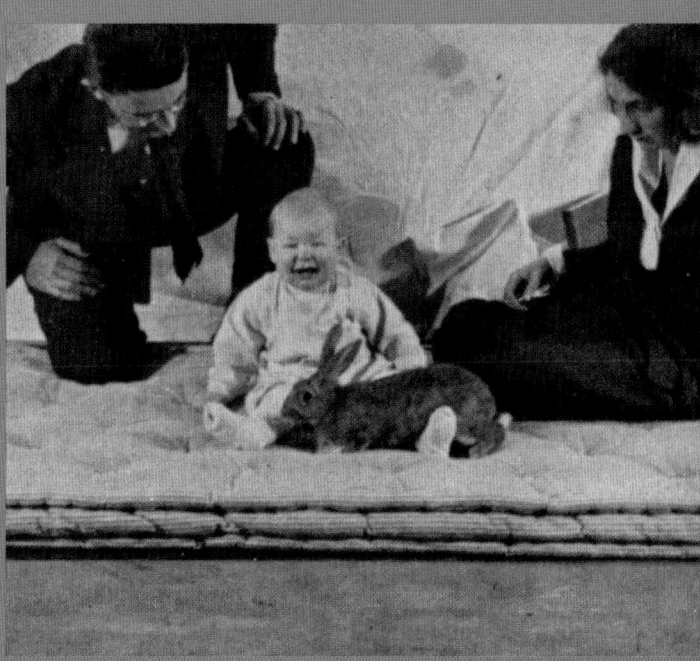

THE ALLURE OF HORROR

It might seem counterintuitive that people enjoy being scared, but deriving pleasure from how the body responds to fear – initially a negative emotion – is an example of what psychologists call a hedonistic reversal. In the 21st century, scholars have investigated this process by looking at what draws people to horror – or, as in the title of the 2017 study by Mathias Clasen, *Why Horror Seduces*. Clasen and his colleagues at the Recreational Fear Lab, based at Aarhus University, Denmark, have studied how and why people seek out things designed to frighten them and enjoy being scared.

Even among thrill-seekers, there are different approaches to relishing fear. In one study, Clasen took 280 people to a haunted-house attraction and divided them into two groups: "adrenaline junkies", who preferred to maximize their fear during the experience, and "white knucklers", who strove to minimize fear as a coping strategy. The two groups reported equal enjoyment of the haunted-house experience, but for different reasons – adrenaline junkies prized the excitement, while white knucklers were relieved to have faced their fears.

The huge appeal of haunted-house attractions among horror fans has led to bigger budgets and more complex storylines, often inspired by recent horror films. Their immersive nature is a key factor in their popularity – they are horror stories playing out in real time, with realistic sights and sounds, and unpredictable jump scares.

Chasing down fear
Clasen studied participants at Dystopia, a haunted-house attraction in a former fish factory in Vejle, Denmark. This photograph shows a Dystopia scare actor dressed as Mr Piggy, the main villain of the 2017 experience *Dystopia Horror Run – Zombie Massacre*.

THÉÂTRE DU
GRAND GUIGNOL

20 bis Rue Chaptal C. CHOISY & J. JOUVIN Directeurs

L'HOMME QUI A TUÉ LA MORT

DRAME EN 2 ACTES DE M. RENÉ BERTON — MISE EN SCÈNE DE C. CHOISY

Melle MAXA – MM. GOUGET, ORVAL, LERICHE, DE NÉVRY, ETC

THE GRAND GUIGNOL THEATRE

A SMALL THEATRE FAMED FOR ITS PRODUCTION OF HORROR, GORE, AND DEPRAVITY ONCE STOOD AT THE END OF A COBBLED ALLEYWAY IN PARIS.

Further afield
To take its productions beyond the Paris city limits, the Grand Guignol also had a touring company, advertised in this poster for *Les 3 Masques*, a tale of bloody revenge.

The Théâtre du Grand Guignol operated from 1897 to 1962. It took up residence in a deconsecrated chapel and retained the original architecture and Gothic embellishments — a choice that heightened the eerie atmosphere before the curtain even rose. Although the theatre began by putting on realist dramas about the everyday lives of ordinary people, it quickly found that its audiences craved more bloodthirsty fare.

A short play in the theatre's opening season, *Mademoiselle Fifi* — in which a Parisian sex worker murders a Prussian officer — became a must-see sensation, albeit "not for the faint-hearted". Following this success, the Grand Guignol began to specialize in gore, sometimes interspersed with comedies for a little light relief.

Authenticity at every turn

The playwrights at the Grand Guignol drew inspiration from true crime stories and avoided the supernatural: horrors were always real or, at least, disturbingly plausible. A night at the theatre plunged its audience into the depths of human depravity through tightly paced short dramas that built to shocking climaxes. Viewers might witness the effects of sulphuric acid hurled into someone's face, a sex worker skinned alive while her client watches in ecstasy, or a group of lunatics gouging out a sane woman's eyes. The repertoire was imaginative, visceral, and unrelenting.

Special effects reached an unprecedented level of authenticity. The company made its own stage blood using secret recipes and employed prosthetic limbs, heads, and eyeballs to horrific effect. Some audience members vomited or fainted and were revived by the resident doctor. Others roared with laughter or found intimate pleasures in the private booths at the back of the auditorium.

An array of talent

Great talent was drawn to the Grand Guignol. André de Lorde, the "Prince of Terror", was its most prolific playwright, often consulting surgeons and psychologists to ensure medical and psychological accuracy. The theatre's greatest performer, Paula Maxa — the original scream queen — was dubbed "the most assassinated woman in the world" and was famously slaughtered in countless creative ways, except when she was doing the killing herself.

Although the term "Grand Guignol" is now shorthand for over-the-top horror, generations of writers, actors, and technicians contributed meticulous craftsmanship to this thrilling, salacious theatre. The original Grand Guignol is long gone, but its phantom still haunts horror culture across all media. Its legacy looms especially large over horror theatre, immersive experiences, Halloween events, and every time someone offers, in hushed tones, to recount a blood-drenched true story.

Perfect match
Adrien Barrère's poster for *L'Homme Qui a Tué la Mort* ("The Man Who Killed Death") encapsulates the theatre's gory aesthetic.

1900-1969

THE DAWN OF MODERN HORROR

M.R. JAMES

WIDELY REGARDED AS THE FINEST WRITER OF GHOST STORIES IN THE ENGLISH LANGUAGE, M.R. JAMES WAS A CAMBRIDGE ACADEMIC WHO UPDATED THE FOLKTALE FOR MODERN READERS.

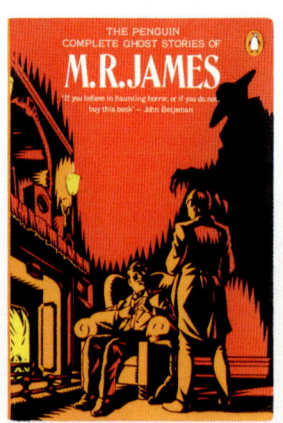

Compendium of horror
Published in four separate volumes during his lifetime, James's tales were later issued as a single collection, such as this 1987 release by Penguin.

The stories of M.R. James (1862–1934) typically feature a scholar discovering an ancient artifact and then naively awakening an evil spirit. Their setting is usually an English village or university town, with trips to country houses, libraries, and cathedrals – far removed from the crumbling castles and exotic locations of much traditional Gothic fiction. An admirer of Edgar Allan Poe, James was more interested in psychology than in vampires, and focused on ordinary people becoming mired in the occult. About half of his stories involve pagan rituals, a fact that has earned him the title "the father of folk horror". "Casting the Runes" is one of these pagan-themed tales.

In this story, a writer tries to kill a man who has derided an article he has written on alchemy. He slips the man some runes in the belief that their bearer will die within three months. The day before the curse expires, the man returns the runes to the writer, who is then killed in a freak accident.

Ordinary fears

Supernatural beings in James's stories inspire terror through fear of the unknown or the unseen. In "A Warning to the Curious", an antiquarian unearths a Saxon crown that is said to keep enemies away from England but also to have a guardian. When the man goes missing, friends find his body

The Suffolk coast
M.R. James was a native of Suffolk, England, which inspired many of his tales. "'Oh, Whistle, and I'll Come to You, My Lad'" is likely to have been set near the Deben Estuary – an area that can be misty at dusk and marshy at low tide.

on a beach – beside footprints that show "more bones than flesh". In "'Oh, Whistle, and I'll Come to You, My Lad'", a professor visits a seaside town, where, in spite of ridiculing the supernatural, he is disturbed by the twin room he is given – especially its second bed. He finds a whistle while exploring some ruins, after which something follows him back to his lodgings. On discovering the words "Who is this who is coming?" on the whistle, he blows it and is besieged by visions of a pale figure darting about a beach. He also hears scratching at the floor. In the end, whatever it is rears from the second bed, with a "face of crumpled linen". The professor survives, but only just. We learn that he is frightened by ordinary things, such as coats hanging on doors, for the rest of his life. In this manner, James gave horror tales a much-needed blood transfusion, injecting them with a realism that makes the reader feel *This could happen to me…*

Modern adaptations

Although partially eclipsed by the works of Shirley Jackson and Stephen King, James's tales remain influential today, having been immortalized by numerous adaptations. These include Jacques Tourneur's *Night of the Demon* (1957), based on "Casting the Runes" – widely regarded as one of the best classic horror films ever made – and *Whistle and I'll Come to You* (1968) directed by Jonathan Miller. Most memorable, perhaps, were the Christmas-timed television adaptations, some of which featured Christopher Lee re-enacting James reading his tales as he originally did – to a select group of students and friends.

Figure on the beach
British actor Michael Hordern plays the haunted professor in Jonathan Miller's spine-tingling *Whistle and I'll Come to You*.

> "Do I believe in ghosts?… I am prepared to consider evidence."
>
> M.R. JAMES, *THE COLLECTED GHOST STORIES OF M.R. JAMES*, 1931

COSMIC HORROR

THERE ARE PLENTY OF WEREWOLVES, VAMPIRES, AND OTHER MONSTERS IN HORROR, BUT THIS SUBGENRE OFFERS FEAR ON A FAR MORE PROFOUND AND TERROR-INDUCING SCALE.

A library of the weird
Launched in 1939, Arkham House published close to 200 books, many by Lovecraft or inspired by his canon. Other authors included Clark Ashton Smith and August Derleth.

Gaining in prominence and popularity over the past century or so, cosmic horror – a subgenre of weird fiction – transcends the traditional, swapping tangible monsters and phenomena for an existential dread rooted in our deepest fears of the unknown. It emphasizes the insignificance of humanity in the face of vast, incomprehensible forces – powers so alien that even glimpsing them can unravel the mind.

These forces are not merely evil; they are indifferent – utterly beyond human morality or understanding. Cosmic horror confronts the limits of knowledge, belief, and reason, where terror arises not from what is seen but from what cannot be seen, explained, or named.

Creating a genre

Prolific writer H.P. Lovecraft is both the originator and the best-known exponent of cosmic horror. His mythology of the Great Old Ones – malign, godlike entities such as Cthulhu – established a canon in which the pursuit of forbidden knowledge inexorably leads to madness. The protagonists in his tales often uncover sinister truths that defy scientific and religious frameworks. His stylistic use of words such as "indescribable" or "unnameable"

Cosmic pioneer
William Hope Hodgson was a pioneer of weird fiction. This illustration is from a 2024 collector's edition of his work, *The House on the Borderland & Others*.

A rich vein to tap
Color Out of Space is one of the most recent film adaptations of Lovecraft's work, which has inspired the industry since the 1960s.

indicates a breakdown of language and perception, highlighting humanity's fragile grasp on reality and exploiting a primal fear of the unfathomable.

The impact of the author's work led to the establishment of a loosely connected group known as the Lovecraft Circle, which began to take shape in the early 1920s. This included writers who shared ideas and themes, codifying an earlier horror genre that Lovecraft dubbed weird fiction. Weird-fiction works such as Robert W. Chambers's *The King in Yellow* (1895) and William Hope Hodgson's *The House on the Borderland* (1908) can be seen as precursors to Lovecraft's signature subgenre, anticipating the destabilizing metaphysical dread that would become central to cosmic horror.

Key figures in the Lovecraft Circle were August Derleth and Donald Wandrei, who cofounded Arkham House, a publishing company that did much to keep Lovecraft and other weird-fiction writers in print. These included Clark Ashton Smith (famed for his work in *Weird Tales* magazine), Robert E. Howard (best known now for Conan the Barbarian), horror writer and poet Frank Belknap Long, and Robert Bloch, who would later write the classic 1959 novel *Psycho*. This network helped build the link from weird fiction to cosmic horror.

From the ashes of war

It is no coincidence that cosmic horror took shape at a time of immense philosophical and cultural uncertainty. The birth of psychoanalysis unsettled society by revealing the irrational forces within the human mind, while the industrialized slaughter of World War I, coupled with rapid modernization, led to anxiety and disillusionment, as well as progress and innovation. Viewed in its historical context, Lovecraft's vision is powerful and symbolic: he depicts humans as irrelevant specks.

Today, even as Lovecraft's influence has waned, the essence of cosmic horror continues to permeate contemporary horror. It has fed into literature, television, radio, podcasts, music, comics, and games. Its philosophical scope and aesthetic of existential dread have eclipsed more traditional Gothic and horror tropes, proving both enduring and endlessly adaptable.

> "Abruptly, the Thing turned and gazed hideously in my direction… I was borne helplessly to meet it."
>
> WILLIAM HOPE HODGSON, *THE HOUSE ON THE BORDERLAND*

THE PHANTOM OF THE OPERA

The mystery of the masked Opera Ghost reputed to haunt the Palais Garnier, the main opera house in Paris, has captured people's imaginations for over a century. French readers first learned of the story in September 1909, when newspaper writer Gaston Leroux published the first instalment of *Le Fantôme de l'Opéra* in *Le Gaulois* newspaper. It was a sensational tale inspired by a mixture of historical events and hearsay.

Set in Paris in 1881, the story relates the strange events that are happening at the Palais Garnier. Dead stagehands, unexplained illnesses, collapsing chandeliers, and curses are just some of the horrors that are attributed to a ghost that haunts the theatre. At the centre of each misfortune is Swedish soprano Christine Daaé, who, it turns out, is tutored by the ghost itself – a figure she refers to as the Angel of Music. Her success is partly due to the ghost, who demands that she is given the lead roles.

The ghost's obsession with the opera singer takes a dangerous turn when Vicomte Raoul de Chagny declares his love for her. Consumed by jealousy, the ghost kidnaps her and reveals itself to be a man – a magician, illusionist, and opera aficionado named Erik. Facially disfigured from birth, and abandoned by his mother, he has spent his life living beneath the theatre, having built his lair in its foundations. Desperate for affection, he tries to woo Christine, but finally lets her go. He dies, and Christine and Raoul are married.

Stage fright
This still from the classic silent film *The Phantom of the Opera* (1925) shows actor Lon Chaney as Erik. Erik creates mayhem while trying to turn the woman he loves into a star.

DARK FANTASY AND HORROR

Mixing the ordinary and extraordinary
In *Weaveworld*, the cover art of which is shown above, Clive Barker blends horror and the everyday in a tale about a magical world threatened by a sorceress and a corrupt salesman.

SINCE ITS INCEPTION, DARK FANTASY, OR FANTASY HORROR, HAS PROVED DIFFICULT TO DEFINE. AS A RESULT, MANY WORKS HAVE BEEN BOTH ACCEPTED AND REJECTED AS BELONGING TO THIS PARTICULAR GENRE.

Works that have been characterized as dark fantasy combine elements of fantasy and horror. Although both genres can feature imaginary settings and supernatural creatures, the way in which they are handled varies significantly. While fantasy often offers escapism for the reader, presenting a hypothetical world far beyond the human realm, horror describes the terror found in scenes and situations that are more familiar. Combining these two approaches, works of dark fantasy conjure environments that feel familiar but feature otherworldly creatures or lore. Horrific elements may be introduced to create suspense, but the aim is not solely to terrify the audience.

The earliest examples of dark fantasy appeared after World War I, when science fiction writers were beginning to explore more horrifying themes. Francis Stevens, H.P. Lovecraft, and Clark Ashton Smith are all considered early proponents of the genre, creating imagined worlds that are not too dissimilar from our own, but plagued by terrifying creatures or events.

A later classic is Ray Bradbury's *Something Wicked This Way Comes*, published in 1962. In this second instalment in the author's Green Town Trilogy, teenagers Jim and Will find their lives – and the whole town – threatened when a travelling carnival led by Mr Dark arrives for Halloween. The novel would go on to influence Stephen King's *It*, among other works.

An evergreen genre

During the 1980s, there was a surge in works that experimented with this hybrid genre, including King's nine-part series *The Dark Tower* (which took 30 years to complete) and Clive Barker's *Weaveworld* (1987). Another long-running series with dark fantasy elements began the following decade, with the publication of *A Game of Thrones* (1996), the first in George R.R. Martin's *A Song of Ice and Fire* cycle of novels.

Despite the lack of consensus among fans and critics about the genre's essential attributes, novels that blend horror and fantasy tropes continue to be catalogued as dark fantasy. Examples from the 21st century include Silvia Moreno-Garcia's *Certain Dark Things* (2016) and Leigh Bardugo's *Ninth House* (2019), which was praised by King as "the best fantasy novel" he had read in years.

DARK FANTASY'S FORGOTTEN ORIGINS

When discussing the history of dark fantasy, many look to H.P. Lovecraft as an early master of the genre. However, dark fantasy's origins can be traced back to a largely forgotten woman who wrote under the pseudonym Francis Stevens. Born Gertrude Barrows in 1883, Stevens wrote both short and full-length dark fantasy stories that were sold as pulp fiction. Her 1918 novel *The Citadel of Fear*, mainly set within the lost Mesoamerican city of Tlapallan, was praised by Lovecraft himself. In 2004, a series of Stevens's short stories was published in a collection titled *The Nightmare and Other Tales of Dark Fantasy*.

Dark debut
US author Ray Bradbury's short-story collection *Dark Carnival*, published in 1947, established him in dark-fantasy circles.

SIGMUND FREUD AND THE UNCANNY

> "The frightening element can be… something repressed which recurs."
>
> SIGMUND FREUD, *THE UNCANNY*

IN HORROR, THE UNCANNY EVOKES DISCOMFORT BY REVEALING THE STRANGE WITHIN THE FAMILIAR. COMMON EXAMPLES INCLUDE EERIE DOUBLES, REPRESSED MEMORIES, AND DISTORTED REALITIES.

"Uncanny" is a word that is difficult to pin down precisely. Not quite scary, different from creepy, and more than strange, it captures an uneasy sense of both the familiar and the unfamiliar. A doll so lifelike that it seems as though it might suddenly move is a good example of an unnerving object that might be described as uncanny.

The idea of the uncanny in psychology was first explored by Ernst Jentsch in a 1906 essay. Sigmund Freud probed further in his book *The Uncanny*, published in 1919. He suggested that uncanny experiences are produced by the occasional reemergence of childhood fears or desires that have been abandoned in light of adult rationality. For example, while children might believe that a doll could come to life, a rational adult knows that dolls are inanimate objects. Despite this, the original childhood beliefs are not erased; they are merely repressed and remain in the subconscious. The sense of uncanniness, according to Freud, comes from the simultaneous experience of the *heimlich* ("homely") and *unheimlich* ("unhomely"). He said, "The uncanny is that class of the terrifying which leads back to something long known to us, once very familiar."

Strangeness and discomfort

Freud identified how powerful the uncanny could be in art and literature. He used the example of E.T.A. Hoffman's "The Sandman", but authors as diverse as Edgar Allan Poe, Franz Kafka, and Daphne du Maurier have also played on Freudian ideas of an interwoven familiarity and strangeness. Freud's theories in *The Uncanny*, together with his book *On Dreams* (1901), influenced the Surrealist artists of the early 20th century, who often transformed everyday objects into distortions of themselves – for example, Dalí's melting watches or Man Ray's domestic iron with added thumb tacks.

Stanley Kubrick's 1980 film *The Shining* mines Freudian notions of the uncanny particularly effectively. The empty rooms and corridors of the Overlook Hotel seem at once familiar and strange, just as Jack Torrance increasingly does. The hotel's previous guests seem present, but only in spectral form. Jack's young son Danny seems to see the true (unrepressed) nature of the hotel through his supernatural powers (the "shining" of the title), while his rational adult mother does not. The result is a rising feeling of dread and a powerful sense of the uncanny.

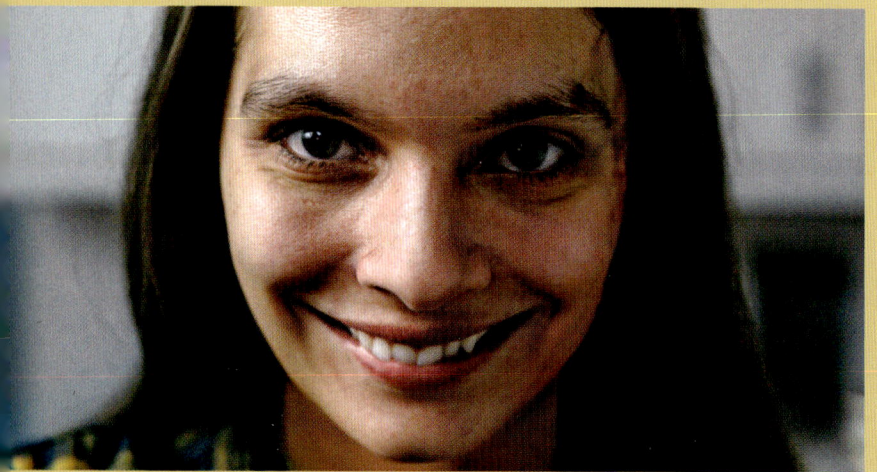

A creepy smile
The 2022 film *Smile* turns the most pleasant of facial expressions on its head. An eerie grin marks those under the control of an uncanny entity – moments before they die and pass the curse to the next victim.

The Dawn of Modern Horror

The young Nathaniel watches as Coppelius passes by.

THE SANDMAN

In E.T.A. Hoffmann's short story "The Sandman" (1817), young Nathaniel's mother tells him of the Sandman, a monstrous figure who pours sand in children's eyes if they do not sleep. When Nathaniel hears feet thudding up the stairs, it turns out to be a scary family friend, Coppelius, who Nathaniel fears is really the Sandman. Later, as an adult, he meets an optician named Coppola, who closely resembles Coppelius. The resemblance disturbs Nathaniel greatly: the encounter with a doppelgänger brings on a reawakening of Nathaniel's childhood fears.

Human-like doll
German Surrealist Hans Bellmer made several photographs called *The Doll* (*Die Puppe*) throughout the 1930s and beyond, each featuring a disturbing, manipulated version of the female form.

"I must know everything...
I must penetrate his secrets...
I must become Caligari!"

DR CALIGARI ON CALIGARI, *THE CABINET OF DR CALIGARI*

Night flight
Cesare the somnambulist, played by Conrad Veidt, abducts a sleeping woman in the middle of the night. He then flees through a village composed of stylized, distorted, Expressionist sets.

THE CABINET OF DR CALIGARI

PRODUCED IN GERMANY IN 1920, *THE CABINET OF DR CALIGARI* IS WIDELY CONSIDERED THE FIRST TRUE HORROR FILM. NARRATED BY A MADMAN WHO MAY BE HALLUCINATING THE ENTIRE STORY, IT TELLS THE TALE OF A VILLAGE TERRORIZED BY A HYPNOTIST NAMED CALIGARI.

Directed by German Expressionist film-maker Robert Wiene, *The Cabinet of Dr Caligari* is set in the small village of Holstenwall. Portrayed using a labyrinth of cramped theatrical sets and dramatic lighting, the location takes on a disturbing character. At the annual fair, Caligari, a mysterious doctor, presents a show in which a sleep-walker called Cesare can be summoned from a coffin to answer questions about the future. A man named Alan asks, "How long shall I live?" and Cesare whispers "Until dawn tomorrow". True to the prediction, Alan dies in the night – murdered by Cesare himself.

The horror of Alan's death is not just that of a monster stalking its prey, but of a victim being implicated in their own killing. Would Alan have died if he had not asked the question? Worse still, when he learns of his imminent death, Alan seems shocked, but then elated – as if a dream has come true. Who is to blame for the killing? The question echoes throughout the film as more crimes are committed and the police chase Caligari to an asylum – where, it turns out, he is the director.

Terrifying realities

Further questions – whose version of events reflect the "truth" and who is really in charge – fuel the horror in the remainder of the film. A found diary shows that Dr Caligari is obsessed with replicating the acts of an 18th-century murderous mystic, also called Caligari. When confronted, Caligari becomes violent and is confined in his own institution. A final twist, however, shows that none of these events can be taken at face value. They have been fabricated or hallucinated by the film's unreliable narrator, who is also an inmate of the asylum.

In his book *From Caligari to Hitler* (1947) Siegfried Kracauer, who fled Germany in 1933, argues that *Caligari* is about a nation sleep-walking into ruin at the hands of an insane dictator – a premonition of Nazi Germany. The film's popularity may well have been due to this self-critique. However, there is also the production's visual ingenuity, including its nightmarish sets designed by legendary Expressionist Hermann Warm. It was a style that greatly influenced other German directors, including F.W. Murnau and Austrian-born Fritz Lang.

M for murderer
Fritz Lang's *M* (1931) stars Peter Lorre as a serial killer who targets children. Its innovative use of light, shade, and reflection help make it an Expressionist masterpiece.

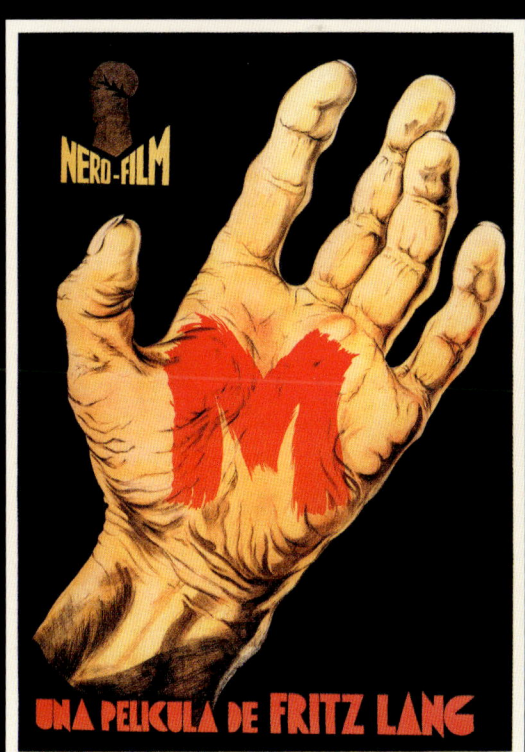

NOSFERATU AND DRACULA FILMS

NOSFERATU: A SYMPHONY OF HORROR WAS BOTH A RECOGNIZABLE DRACULA FILM AND A SILENT MASTERPIECE BORN OF THE HORRORS OF WAR.

Distorted reality
Nosferatu, like *The Cabinet of Dr Caligari* before it, used the angular, distorted aesthetic of German Expressionism to create a sense of unease for viewers.

In 1922's *Nosferatu*, Bram Stoker's plot remained intact, but Jonathan Harker became Thomas Hutter and Dracula became Orlok. In this guise, the vampire was described as a *nosferatu*, a term meaning "undead" or "living dead". Dracula's Transylvanian home was swapped for the mid-19th-century setting of Wisborg, Germany, but it was the Count himself who underwent the biggest change.

Director F.W. Murnau, producer (and occultist) Albin Grau, and star Max Schreck all fought in World War I and were influenced by its real-life

> "This monstrous event… swooped down on the Earth like a cosmic vampire to drink the blood of millions…"
>
> ALBIN GRAU ON WORLD WAR I TRENCH WARFARE

horrors. They set aside the seductive Dracula of Stoker's novel to portray Orlok as Death itself. Schreck's Count, whose grotesque appearance was Grau's own invention, is truly repellent. Some critics have speculated that it may have been inspired by the disfigurements of soldiers returning from war – a visual reminder of people's suffering. The film also references the flu pandemic of 1918–20 that killed up to 50 million people: as Orlok approaches Germany in a rat-infested coffin, news breaks of a spreading plague.

Adaptations and spin-offs

Upon *Nosferatu*'s release, the estate of Bram Stoker sued the film-makers for copyright infringement. Grau had wanted to make a vampire film based on *Dracula*, but Stoker's estate had refused to give him the rights. *Nosferatu*'s opening title cards acknowledged *Dracula*'s influence, but this was not enough. The ensuing lawsuit led to the closure of Grau's production company, and a judge ordered all copies of the film to be destroyed. Some survived, however, because copies had already been sent out for distribution.

In 1930, the Stoker estate granted film rights to Universal Pictures; this resulted in several films in which Dracula was either a main or supporting character, including *Dracula* (1931), *Dracula's Daughter* (1936), and *Son of Dracula* (1943). In 1958, Hammer Films released its own version of the story – the first vampire film in colour.

Just as the 1922 *Nosferatu* drew inspiration from World War I, modern *Dracula* adaptations have reflected their times to varying degrees. Francis Ford Coppola's 1992 film embraced flashy MTV-era visuals and marked a return to a more romantic portrayal of the eponymous vampire. In contrast, Robert Eggers's *Nosferatu* of 2024 featured a hideous Orlok whose corpse-like design was inspired by Ötzi the Iceman, Europe's oldest natural mummy, unearthed just three decades earlier.

The Count returns
After a somewhat fallow period in the 1980s, the Count returned to the big screen in Coppola's 1992 version, with Gary Oldman in the title role.

THE TWO COUNTS

Nine years after *Nosferatu*, Universal Pictures released *Dracula* (1931). This reinstated the Count of the novel, who stood alone for several decades, as played by Bela Lugosi in the 1930s, Christopher Lee in the 1950s, 60s and 70s, and Frank Langella in 1979. However, his death-like twin was resurrected by actor Klaus Kinski in *Nosferatu the Vampyre* (1979), Willem Dafoe in *Shadow of the Vampire* (2000), and Bill Skarsgård in Eggers's *Nosferatu*.

Almost 100 years after playing the character on film, Bela Lugosi remains the archetypal Dracula.

H.P. LOVECRAFT

FEW WRITERS' NAMES ARE USED AS ADJECTIVES, BUT SUCH WAS THE INFLUENCE OF AMERICAN WRITER H.P. LOVECRAFT THAT HIS BRAND OF COSMIC HORROR – INCLUDING UNIQUE MONSTERS AND SETTINGS – HAS BEEN TERMED LOVECRAFTIAN HORROR.

A Lovecraftian book, film, or design is concerned not solely with monsters but also with the monstrously alien. H.R. Giger's xenomorph in *Alien* (1979) is Lovecraftian, as is John Carpenter's *The Thing* (1982), the creatures in Stephen King's novella *The Mist* (1980), and Area X in Jeff VanderMeer's *Annihilation* (2014). With Lovecraft, there is a twist, though: however alien they are, his creatures are bound to humans historically and psychologically – and yet are indifferent to them.

A key concept in Lovecraftian horror is that of the Old Ones – cosmic creatures of unimaginable age that once ruled Earth. Now dormant, they can still be disturbed, and may be influencing the thoughts of human beings, who are descended from life forms that the Old Ones seeded on Earth.

Enter Cthulhu

One such cosmic creature is Cthulhu, which is introduced in "The Call of Cthulhu" (1928), a tale that begins with the sentence, "The most merciful thing in the world, I think, is the inability of the human mind to correlate all its contents." The narrator tells of inheriting his murdered grand-uncle's estate, which includes a box containing a bas-relief of a creature seen by its sculptor in a dream. The box also includes newspaper clippings about strange events in different parts of the world, all involving the same creature. As a manuscript clarifies, the uncle had helped to investigate a series of

Author's sketch
Lovecraft made many drawings of his monsters, including this 1934 pencil sketch of the Cthulhu with wings and a tentacled face.

The Dawn of Modern Horror

murders, one of which involved a chanted ritual that translated as "In his house at R'lyeh dead Cthulhu waits dreaming."

On making enquiries, the narrator learns that an earthquake had occurred on a Pacific island at around the time the sculptor made his carving. He also discovers that a ship's crew inadvertently released a "Thing" from its lair – the buried Cyclopean city of R'lyeh, which had risen briefly as a result of the quake. Cthulhu has been released, and the story ends with the narrator awaiting his own doom. As with so many of Lovecraft's characters, his curiosity destroys him.

The Lovecraft legacy

Although Lovecraft never intended his creatures to be ranked in a pantheon – one of their key characteristics being their unknowability – his friend and posthumous publisher August Derleth did exactly that, creating what he called the "Cthulhu mythos" to enable other authors to write consistently in Lovecraft's universe. Azathoth became the god that is the source of all creation and his three sons, Nyarlathotep, The Nameless Mist, and Darkness, spawned everything else. Yog-Sothoth, born of The Nameless Mist, became the god or embodiment of time. Key contributors to the mythos have been Robert E. Howard, Clark Ashton Smith, Brian Lumley, and Ramsey Campbell. In the tales, much of the information about the gods comes from the *Necronomicon*, a fictional forbidden tome written in Damascus in the early 8th century by the so-called mad poet Abdul Alhazred.

> " ... it was the general outline of the whole which made it most shockingly frightful."
>
> H.P. LOVECRAFT ON CTHULHU, "THE CALL OF CTHULHU"

The Great Old One
This digital illustration shows Cthulhu rising up from the watery depths to face a single man, whose weapons will not save him.

UNIVERSAL MONSTERS

THE 1930s WERE A BOOM TIME FOR HOLLYWOOD'S UNIVERSAL PICTURES, WHICH PUT OUT A SERIES OF ATMOSPHERIC HORROR FILMS BASED ON CLASSICS OF GOTHIC LITERATURE.

Horror icon
Lon Chaney Jr brought depth and tragedy to the title role in *The Wolf Man* (1941). His performance helped define Universal's classic legacy.

Breakout role
Bela Lugosi shot to fame playing Dracula on Broadway in 1927, but his casting in the film adaptation by Tod Browning took him to a whole new audience all around the world.

Two years into the Great Depression, Universal Pictures struck gold when it released *Dracula* (1931), a film that distracted audiences from the global crisis. The cinema industry was in the early days of the talkies era, so an all-sound *Dracula* was expected to be a success, given that its silent predecessors *Dr Jekyll and Mr Hyde* (1913), *The Hunchback of Notre Dame* (1923), and *The Phantom of the Opera* (1925) had done well. The film was so popular that Universal made a host of successors — *Frankenstein* (1931), *The Mummy* (1932), *The Invisible Man* (1933), and *Bride of Frankenstein* (1935) among them — that made household names of Bela Lugosi and Boris Karloff, who played Dracula and Frankenstein's monster respectively. Karloff's monster remains the defining image of Universal horror — a reanimated giant in a tattered suit, with a flat head and electrodes in his neck.

Villain and victim

Between them, the vampire and the monster were perfect symbols of the time: an evil sucking the life out of innocent people, and an outcast trying to make sense of the world. Likewise, the Mummy, who searches for a life he cannot live, and the Invisible Man, whose existence is felt but not seen, express the anxiety of a nation plunged into uncertainty.

A similar phenomenon occurred in Germany in the aftermath of World War I, when audiences flocked to see *The Cabinet of Dr Caligari* (1920) and *Nosferatu* (1922), films that reflected a society that had been thrown into turmoil.

Karloff's mummy

A year after *Frankenstein*, Boris Karloff starred in the follow-up hit *The Mummy*. It became the template for horror movies set in Egypt.

However, Universal's films remained Gothic at heart, offering horror for escapism rather than the nightmarish intensity of German Expressionism.

The Wolf Man came in 1941, making a star of Lon Chaney Jr, whose father played the title roles in Universal's *The Hunchback of Notre Dame* and *The Phantom of the Opera* in the 1920s. This was followed by a slew of "mash-ups", such as *Frankenstein Meets the Wolf Man* (1943) and *Abbott and Costello Meet Frankenstein* (1948) – light-hearted fare that offered respite from the memory of another world war.

Universal's next new monster arrived in *Creature from the Black Lagoon* (1954). A beautiful woman goes boating with two men who are both in love with her. In the ensuing confusion, the aquatic Gill-man attacks and drags her into the deep. For all its Freudian symbolism, the film is also an eco-horror, and its underwater shots inspired the opening scenes of *Jaws* (1975). Two sequels followed, *Revenge of the Creature* (1955) and *The Creature Walks Among Us* (1956), bringing an end to the classic era of Universal films.

> "I felt its breath on my face and then its lips…"
>
> MINA SEWARD IN *DRACULA*

"IT'S ALIVE! IT'S ALIVE!"

When Henry Frankenstein – known as Victor in Mary Shelley's novel – brought his creature to life in 1931, he shouted, "It's alive! It's alive!" in what became one of the most famous lines in film history. He added, "In the name of God, now I know what it feels like to be God!", but that phrase was cut when the film was re-released in 1938. The full line, now that it is no longer deemed scandalous, has since been reinstated.

LIVE HORROR RADIO

BEFORE THE ARRIVAL OF TELEVISION, ICONIC RADIO SHOWS ENGAGED LISTENERS' IMAGINATIONS WITH TERRIFYING TALES OF MURDER, MYSTERY, AND THE SUPERNATURAL.

For Halloween 1938, the Mercury Theatre on the Air – a radio drama series created and hosted by American director Orson Welles – presented a live adaptation of H.G. Wells's novel *The War of the Worlds*. The broadcast mimicked "breaking news", confusing – and even panicking – some listeners. Its impact became a major news story and demonstrated the extraordinary power of the nascent medium of radio to convey uncanny stories.

Although the Mercury Theatre dramas are justifiably famous for their innovatory approach, they were part of a much broader landscape of radio programming featuring suspense and horror. Following the popularity of early one-off thrillers and plays focusing on the supernatural, the early 1930s brought *The Witch's Tale* (1931–38), the first fully-fledged horror show on US radio.

War on the airwaves
Orson Welles broadcasts at CBS Radio, just days after the transmission of *The War of the Worlds* hit the headlines for generating fear and panic across the US.

Radio murder
Actors in a radio drama play dead after being "killed" by a mass murderer on an NBC *Lights Out* broadcast. A sound effects man provides dramatic tension in the background.

Introduced by "Old Nancy, the Salem Witch", the show drew millions of listeners with its tales of terror, ranging from Gothic adaptations to original scripts. The success of *The Witch's Tale* inspired similar shows with memorable hosts, including *The Hermit's Cave* (1935–44), *Inner Sanctum Mystery* (1941–52), *The Mysterious Traveler* (1943–52), and in Britain, *Appointment with Fear* (1943–55), presented by "The Man in Black".

Deeply disturbing

Other radio programmes pushed the boundaries of horror even further. In the US, *Lights Out* (1934–47) was renowned for its ingenious and unsettling scenarios: a malevolent force turns people inside out ("The Dark"); a woman is forced to share a bed with her undead mother-in-law ("Knock at the Door"); and a beating chicken heart grows until it consumes the world ("Chicken Heart"). Similarly inventive, *Quiet, Please!* (1947–49) delivered some of the most original and haunting plays in radio history, using long pauses to build suspense and mood rather than elaborate sound effects. Terrifying stories included an episode about sentient plants that begin to communicate ("Let the Lilies Consider"), the horrifying tale of an Egyptologist trapped in a tomb ("Whence

"It... is... later... than... you... think!"

OPENING TAGLINE FOR *LIGHTS OUT*

Came You?"), and "The Thing on the Fourble Board", a frightening story about a worker on an oil rig who discovers a sinister creature.

Horror radio often ventured into gruesome, daring, and darkly comic territory. Exploiting the live nature of the medium (shows were not pre-recorded), programmes were often scheduled late at night, adding to the spooky atmosphere and allowing for storylines unsuitable for younger listeners. Ironically, the absence of visuals made it possible to present shockingly graphic scenarios that cinema at the time could not, such as zombies dripping with decay or bodies violently and gruesomely dismembered.

Though many radio recordings have been lost, a significant number survive and remain surprisingly chilling. Their legacy also lives on in a new era of audio horror, in which podcasting has become the prime vehicle of storytelling. From the American zombie survival epic *We're Alive* (2009–14), and its various spinoff series, to the British drama *The Lovecraft Investigations* (2019–23), today's audio horrors demonstrate the continuing power and immersive appeal of the form. As horror author Stephen King has noted, radio's ability to engage the deepest recesses of our imagination allows it to conjure the "perfect monster" in ways that visual mediums cannot match.

Sinister sounds
Peter Lorre and a member of the sound effects crew record an episode of the *Inner Sanctum Mystery* series for NBC Radio in 1944.

DISABILITY IN HORROR

> "The horror genre [offers] potential for the representation of disabled people."
>
> CHARLIE LITTLE, FILM-INDUSTRY ACCESS CONSULTANT, 2020

THE WAY IN WHICH DISABLED PEOPLE ARE PORTRAYED IN HORROR STORIES HAS COME FULL CIRCLE — FROM BEING THE CHARACTERS YOU SHOULD FEAR, TO SAVIOURS WHO OFFER A FRESH PERSPECTIVE.

Historically, people with physical and learning disabilities have been othered by the horror genre in order to evoke fear and repulsion in the audience. From Mary Shelley's *Frankenstein* to Gaston Leroux's *The Phantom of the Opera*, such characters have been marginalized and demonized. These overwhelmingly negative depictions of disabled and disfigured bodies have only served to reinforce negative real-life stereotypes.

The film industry has long exploited the disabled community for the purpose of entertainment. Such was the case in 1932, when Tod Browning's *Freaks* was released. Featuring a cast of actors with varying disabilities, this horror film revolves around the everyday lives and relationships of performers working in what was then called a freak show. When two of the carnival's able-bodied stars try to steal the inheritance of one of the disabled performers, the other entertainers punish the couple by mutilating them both. The film divided critics: some felt that it humanized the disabled cast; others thought that it demonized them. It was banned in the US after an adverse reaction from audiences, and refused a rating by the British Board of Film Censors (BBFC), in effect banning it in the UK.

From outcasts to heroes

Even in the 21st century, disability is sometimes still used to instil horror by accentuating physical or mental divergence from the established "norm". The subgenre of body horror frequently focuses on

Ahead of its time
Despite facing bans on release in the 1930s, *Freaks* was reappraised and found an appreciative audience 30 years later. It remains a powerful piece of cinema.

Inclusive casting
In the first two *A Quiet Place* films, deaf actor Millicent Simmonds (right) plays the deaf daughter of Emily Blunt (left) and John Krasinski.

deformity or mutilation, while psychological horror centres on characters suffering from psychiatric disorders that are often the result of unresolved trauma. Ryan Murphy's anthology TV series *American Horror Story* (2011–), for example, includes seasons *Asylum* and *Freak Show*, finding horror in both of these settings.

Disability viewpoint

Some horror films have tried to move away from the "abled gaze" by telling stories from the perspective of disabled characters. A notable early example is the 1967 Audrey Hepburn vehicle *Wait Until Dark*, in which a blind woman is terrorized by a gang of crooks – a premise given an extreme update in *Don't Breathe* (2016), when invaders break into the home of a blind army veteran only to find him more than able to defend himself.

Other films that cast disabled people in a non-stereotypical way include Mike Flanagan's *Hush* (2016), a slasher film in which a deaf-mute woman is the target of a masked killer. The post-apocalyptic 2018 film *A Quiet Place* by John Krasinksi is set in a world overtaken by blind extraterrestrial creatures that are extremely sensitive to sound. The plot focuses on a family that primarily communicates in sign language on account of deaf daughter Regan. Ultimately, the family's ability to communicate – and so to survive their ordeal – is a direct result of Regan's disability.

DEAFULA

A Quiet Place was not the first film to pair horror and American Sign Language (ASL). In 1975, Deaf director, writer, and actor Peter Wolf brought members of the Deaf community together to create a vampire film for a Deaf audience. *Deafula* was the first feature-length film to be shot in ASL, with a voice-over added in post-production for those unable to understand sign language. The independent film went one step further by re-creating a world familiar to Deaf viewers, featuring visual prompts (such as flashing light doorbells) instead of sound cues. Since its initial release, *Deafula* has been recognized as a hallmark of inclusivity in film.

THE GOLDEN AGE OF HORROR COMICS

Moral crusade
Thirteen-year-old David Mace officiates as grade school children burn 2,000 comic books in Spencer, West Virginia, on 26 October 1948. The children had collected the comics for weeks.

FOR A DECADE OR SO IN THE 1940S AND 50S, THE PULP COMIC WAS THE GO-TO MEDIUM FOR HORROR IN THE US. ITS HEYDAY WAS BRIEF, BUT ITS INFLUENCE WAS WIDELY FELT.

In New York State, on 10 May 1954, *The Buffalo Evening News* began an exposé of a shocking new menace to American youth – horror comic books. "Horror For Young Readers!", the headline read, "All for the price of a dime!"

It was not alone. Across the country, newspapers ran appalled stories about the depravities that the nation's children were being exposed to. Sparked by the best-selling book *Seduction Of The Innocent* by psychiatrist Fredric Wertham, community and church groups burned piles of the offending publications, alarmed parents searched teenage bedrooms, and there were even hearings in Congress. It was a classic moral panic – similar to the one that broke out in the UK during the 1980s over Video Nasties, low-budget horror films released straight to home video.

From the Bible to the crypt

The panic concerned all comic books – Superman, for example, was accused of covert fascism – but horror titles aroused particular ire. The genre had its roots in so-called "shudder pulps", but came into its own in the 1940s with the first long-running horror comic *Adventures Into The Unknown*. Published in 1948 by The American Comics Group, its first issue featured stories about werewolves, ghosts, and the living dead.

The floodgates opened with EC Comics, which was founded in 1944 but originally published wholesome fare, such as *Picture Stories From The Bible*. By the late 1940s it had pivoted to horror, producing titles such as *Tales From The Crypt*, *The Vault Of Horror*, and *The Haunt Of Fear*. The new magazines boasted lurid covers, often featuring grinning ghouls or corpses emerging from graves.

In October 1954, the comic book industry acted to save itself from annihilation by state legislation. It established a self-censorship system known as the Comics Code, which stated: "All scenes of horror, excessive bloodshed, gory or gruesome crimes, depravity, lust, sadism, and masochism shall not be permitted". At a stroke, the golden age of horror comics was at an end – but the genre never really died. Films such as Amicus's *Tales*

SHUDDER PULPS

A key influence on the development of horror comics in the 1950s were so-called "shudder pulps". First published in the late 1800s, pulps were named after their low-grade paper, and originally featured crime and science fiction stories. However, the public was eager for darker fare, delivered by magazines such as *Dime Mystery Magazine* (1932–50) and *Terror Tales* (1934–41). These began to publish "weird menace" stories – tales characterized by graphic violence, sadistic villains, and mysterious events.

From The Crypt (1972) and George A. Romero's *Creepshow* (1982) captured the tone of those lurid publications, keeping their memory alive. At the same time, popular heavy metal bands such as Iron Maiden featured imagery influenced by EC Comics on their record covers.

Second wave

From the late 1980s, the comic in general became accepted as a legitimate art form and the horror comic achieved a new-found respectability. Titles such as *The Crow* (1989), *Sandman* (1989), *Hellblazer* (1988), and *Hellboy* (1993) became hugely successful, sparking film and television adaptations. In many ways, they inaugurated a second golden age.

Creepy nights
Comic book artist Edvard Moritz designed this cover for the first issue of *Adventures Into the Unknown* (1948–67). The publication ran to a total of 174 issues.

Undead frights
Each of the 27 issues of *Tales From the Crypt* (1950–55) contained stories told by The Crypt-Keeper and other guest hosts. In this, the 20th issue, he is joined by The Old Witch and The Vault-Keeper.

HORROR IN MODERN ART

FROM THE END OF THE 19TH CENTURY, HORROR CREPT INTO THE WORLD OF FINE ART, AS ARTISTS BEGAN TO INNOVATE AND EXPERIMENT IN THE FACE OF AN UNCERTAIN WORLD.

The startling paranoia of Edvard Munch's *The Scream* (1893) is emblematic of things to come with the rise of Modernism: breathtakingly experimental visions that often present discord and despair. By the mid-1940s, depictions of horror and the horrifying were dominating modern art, reflecting the exhaustion and destruction caused by World War II (1939–45).

Existential fears

At the forefront of the exploration of profound horror was Irish artist Francis Bacon, whose paintings present the human form as a site of suffering and psychic disintegration – distorted, corporeal, and violent. His *Three Studies for Figures*

Chilling portrait
Every five years since 1991, British artist Marc Quinn has made a self-portrait using his own blood. This version of *Self* dates from 2006.

 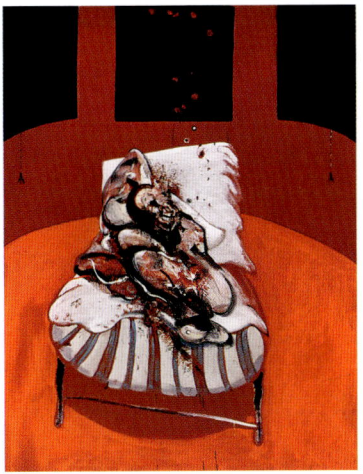 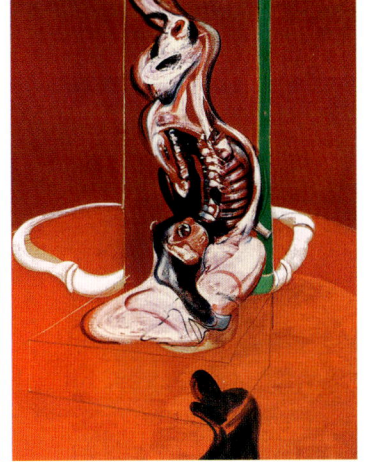

Sinew and meat
Francis Bacon's crucifixion triptych is a study in pain and suffering. The exposed flesh references animal carcasses in an abattoir.

at the Base of a Crucifixion (1944) presents three grotesquely dysmorphic creatures, while his *Study after Velázquez's Portrait of Pope Innocent X* (1953) reimagines the Holy Father as a contorted figure screaming in a realm of darkness and oppression. These are visions of existential horror, representing terrors of flesh, disintegrating identity, and an absence of God.

Bacon's influence on figurative painting was — and is — colossal, showcasing horror as a potent aesthetic and thematic force. Horror in modern art is rarely straightforward representation or narrative. At its best, it raises deep and unsettling questions through visions that are provocative, disturbing, and unforgettable.

Discomfort and dysfunction

Later artists have sought to shock in order to create a visceral confrontation with human mortality. Such work has often been highly controversial, both in subject and material. Photographer Joel-Peter Witkin has used dead and dismembered bodies to macabre effect in some of his images, while sculptor Rick Gibson experimented with freeze-dried body parts in the 1980s, producing *Human Earrings* (1987) made from human foetuses. Several artists have used human blood as a medium. These include Marc Quinn, who has cast self-portraits using his own frozen blood, and Teresa Margolles, who has incorporated artefacts and blood from crime scenes and morgues into her installations. These works challenge viewers to consider what it means to be human. They speak to horror's common themes of bodily mutation, psychological disintegration, and the terrifying inevitability of death.

The scale of these disturbing works can be monumental. Gregor Schneider's *Haus u r* (1985–present) elaborately reworks an entire house to create an unstable labyrinth of additional rooms, false walls and doors – a claustrophobic installation that turns domestic comfort into disorientating terror. The Chapman Brothers' *Hell* (1998–2000) and its follow-up installation feature tens of thousands of toy Nazi soldiers and skeletons in sweeping scenes of cruelty, alluding to the nightmarish visions of Bosch and Goya. Jordan Wolfson's *Colored Sculpture* (2016) features a huge puppet of a child with animatronic eyes that meet the gaze of spectators. Brutally contorted and tortured by chains attached to its head and limbs, it confronts viewers with an unsettling impression of abuse and complicity.

A thousand heads
This detail from *Hell* by the Chapman Brothers shows helmeted Nazi soldiers and their victims. At the centre is a grisly scene of crucifixion.

HORROR IN SURREALIST ART

Surrealism, an art movement that emerged in Europe after World War I, delved deep into the unconscious mind and pushed the boundaries of human thought. Inspired by the work of Sigmund Freud, Surrealist art did not depict reality, but imagination. In particular, it took inspiration from dreams and nightmares (a gateway to the subconscious mind) leading to unsettling images and juxtapositions. Between the 1920s and 1950s, Surrealist art reflected the trauma of war, societal upheaval, and its artists' fascination with the growing field of psychology. The movement has influenced horror films, such as Luis Buñuel's *Un Chien Andalou* (1929) and David Lynch's *Eraserhead* (1977), which take cues from its aesthetic to inspire unease and depict the uncanny.

The work of Salvador Dalí, whose name is synonymous with the Surrealist movement, featured monstrous figures and strange configurations to reflect his own anxieties. From the 1930s, he employed what he called the "Paranoiac-critical method", whereby he deliberately provoked a paranoid state to encourage his brain to make irrational connections, which he called the "spontaneous method of irrational knowledge".

The results were horrifying scenes. He frequently depicted death, decay, and the grotesque, using recurring motifs, such as skulls and distorted human forms. In *Daddy Longlegs Of The Evening – Hope!* (1940), a painting made shortly after he fled to the US in World War II, Dalí represents himself as one of these forms – a melting figure in an apocalyptic landscape that evokes wartime destruction.

Unsettling creation
A cherub looks away as a wrath-like human figure hangs over a branch, an instrument limp in its hands in Dalí's *Daddy Longlegs of the Evening – Hope!* Amidst the terror, a spider provides a shred of optimism – spiders are a token of good luck according to French folk belief.

COMEDIC HORROR

THEY MIGHT BE POLAR OPPOSITES, BUT COMEDY AND HORROR HAVE OFTEN GONE HAND IN HAND IN PARODY. A FEW FILMS MANAGE TO BE BOTH FUNNY AND GENUINELY FRIGHTENING.

American director Jordan Peele, director of the critically acclaimed *Get Out*, has compared comedy and horror to conjoined twins. Both rely on timing, from their pacing to their reveals, and the ability to anticipate how the audience is feeling. Despite these similarities, explicitly combining the two genres can be a challenging prospect – while there have been a handful of hits, some comedy horrors have failed to find commercial success.

Comic tributes

Abbott and Costello Meet Frankenstein (1948) established the comedy horror genre. Bud Abbott and Lou Costello were a celebrated comedy duo, but their careers were dwindling when they agreed to star in the horror mashup. The movie, in which the pair interact with famed monsters from the Universal franchise was a big hit. Sequels followed in which Abbott and Costello meet *The Killer,*

Unleashing mayhem
Gremlins (1984) features initially adorable creatures who quickly replicate and evolve into chaotic monsters.

A perfect candidate
Promotional material for the 1948 hit shows Lou Costello's character trapped in a vice, about to lose his brain to Frankenstein's monster.

Boris Karloff (1949); *The Invisible Man* (1951); *Dr. Jekyll and Mr. Hyde* (1953); and finally *The Mummy* in 1955.

Comic tributes to classic horror flourished in the 1960s and 70s. Roman Polanski directed the Hammer spoof *Dance of the Vampires* (1967), while Mel Brooks paid tribute to Universal Studios and James Whale with *Young Frankenstein* (1974). The 1980s delivered the most successful comedy horrors, with films blending classic horror themes (including excessive gore) with humour and camp theatricality. These included *Ghostbusters* (1984), which pitted comedians Bill Murray, Dan Aykroyd, and Harold Ramis against (then) cutting-edge special effects, and Joe Dante's darkly funny *Gremlins* (1984). Slasher films inspired their own slew of parodies, including *Saturday the 14th* (1981).

A special combination

Many comedy horrors play horror tropes for laughs, but a handful of films are both scary and funny. In John Landis's acclaimed *An American Werewolf in London* (1981), special effects creator Rick Baker delivered one of the greatest werewolf transformations in cinema.

In the 1990s, Wes Craven's *Scream* (1996) wittily deconstructed the slasher genre. It manages to be both darkly funny and genuinely shocking – particularly with its opening sequence, in which high schooler Casey Becker, played by Drew Barrymore, is terrorized by an anonymous caller who quizzes her on horror movie trivia before brutally dispatching her.

THE ROCKY HORROR PICTURE SHOW

A blend of horror, science fiction, and musical comedy, the 1975 film *The Rocky Horror Picture Show* began life as a successful stage musical, which premiered in London in 1973. Written by Richard O'Brien and directed by Jim Sharman, the film adaptation retained key cast members from the stage production, including Tim Curry as the cross-dressing, Frankenstein-like alien Dr Frank-N-Furter.

The plot follows a newly engaged couple, Janet and Brad, forced to seek refuge in an eerie castle after their car breaks down. During the night, their host, Dr Frank-N-Furter, seduces them both, and involves them in a series of riotous events along with his latest creation – a blond, muscular man named Rocky.

The film received negative reviews on its release, but quickly gained a cult following when US cinemas began screening it at midnight. At these late-night showings, audiences dressed as their favourite characters, recited lines, sang along to the songs, and threw items at the screen – traditions that remain popular for audiences today.

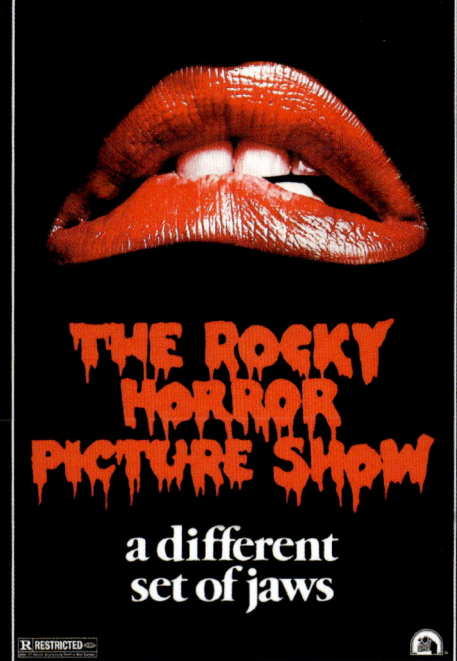

HAMMER HORROR

FOUNDED IN 1934 BY BRITISH COMEDIAN WILLIAM HINDS, HAMMER FILM PRODUCTIONS CREATED A DISTINCTIVE SUBGENRE THAT DOMINATED HORROR CINEMA THROUGH THE 1950S, 60S, AND 70S.

Hammer Film Productions's early features included dramas, comedies, shorts, and thrillers. In 1955, the company moved into horror, releasing *The Quatermass Xperiment* – thus spelled to highlight its adults-only X-certificate. A major success, the film introduced audiences to body horror in a tale about an alien-infected astronaut. A follow-up, *Quatermass 2* (1957), was filmed in black and

The horror of Christopher Lee
Hammer's *Dracula*, starring Christopher Lee as the Count, was renamed *Horror of Dracula* in the US to distinguish it from Universal Pictures's 1931 version of the story.

white, like its predecessor. In the same year, however, *The Curse of Frankenstein* (1957) gave viewers their first glimpse of blood and guts in colour.

Like Universal Pictures's change to sound, which added a new dimension to Gothic cinema, the introduction of colour thrilled audiences, as did the casting of Peter Cushing as Victor Frankenstein and Christopher Lee as the monster. Next came *Dracula* (1958), which immortalized

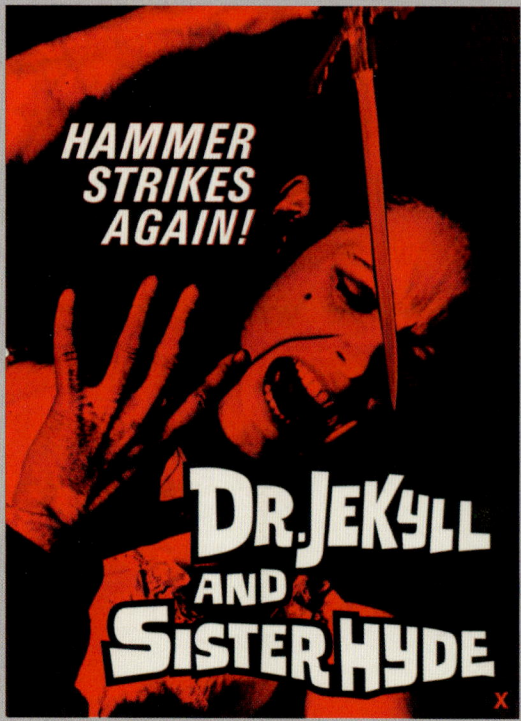

Sister Hyde
In 1971, Hammer reimagined Robert Louis Stevenson's *Strange Case of Dr Jekyll and Mr Hyde* by turning Dr Jekyll into a woman, Sister Hyde.

The Dawn of Modern Horror

Lee as the vampire and Cushing as his nemesis, Dr Van Helsing. *The Mummy* (1959) and *The Phantom of the Opera* (1962) swiftly followed, as did numerous sequels, including six Frankenstein films with Cushing as the baron.

Life after death

For audiences accustomed to films such as Universal's last classic monster movie, *Creature from the Black Lagoon* (1954), *Dracula*'s use of colour was mesmerizing. However, its content was also racy in a way that transgressed the boundaries of what was considered acceptable sexual content. Although tame by today's standards, sequels such as *The Satanic Rites of Dracula* (1973) continued to push limits, but by then Hollywood was making films that delivered documentary-style realism in a way that countered the fairy-tale nature of Hammer horror. In 1968, Hollywood had lifted its Hays Code, which had moderated content since 1934, opening the floodgates to a new kind of big-budget horror film, such as *The Exorcist* (1973), that was outside Hammer's range.

As well as its iconic Dracula and Frankenstein series, Hammer produced many horror films between 1957 and 1973. These included Oliver Reed's debut film, *The Curse of the Werewolf* (1961), and *The Witches* (1966), starring Joan Fontaine. Its film-making days seemingly over, Hammer made the TV series *Hammer House of Horror* in 1980, but financing dried up after 13 episodes. The company returned to making films in the new millennium, striking gold with *Let Me In* (2010) and *The Woman in Black* (2012). After another period of dormancy, British theatre producer John Gore acquired Hammer in 2023, giving the studio a new lease of life.

> "... there are dark corners; horrors almost impossible to imagine..."
>
> DR VAN HELSING, *DRACULA A.D. 1972*

Let Me In
Kodi Smit-McPhee and Chloë Grace Moretz star in Hammer's adaptation of John Ajvide Lindqvist's vampire novel *Let the Right One In*.

GODZILLA, KAIJU, AND NUCLEAR FEARS

FEW MONSTERS ARE MORE BELOVED THAN JAPAN'S *KAIJU* (STRANGE BEASTS). THEIR KING IS GODZILLA, WHOSE FILMS WERE BORN OF THE FEARS PLAGUING JAPAN AFTER WORLD WAR II.

Godzilla crashed onto Japanese screens in 1954, only nine years after the bombings of Hiroshima and Nagasaki and the same year as the Lucky Dragon No 5 incident, in which Japanese fishermen were contaminated by nuclear fallout following a US weapons test at Bikini Atoll. After two atomic bombs and a nuclear incident, Japanese nuclear fears were at an all-time high. *Godzilla*, directed by Ishirō Honda, was the manifestation of those fears – the story of a radioactive monster emerging from the sea. Honda also took inspiration from Eugène Lourié's *The Beast from 20,000 Fathoms* (1953), itself a nuclear commentary.

Unchecked destruction

Godzilla is a dinosaur that has mutated as a result of atomic tests. The monster rampages through Tokyo – with visuals of destroyed buildings and panicked civilians referencing the destruction of Hiroshima and Nagasaki – while the government stands by helplessly. Only a weapon called an Oxygen Destroyer, which eliminates oxygen molecules in living tissue, can hurt the monster.

Godzilla expresses deep anxiety over the arms race between global powers. The monster's sheer size and strength are a metaphor for the destructive power of nuclear weaponry, while the inventor's moral fears over his Oxygen Destroyer convey a hard reality: the only answer to a nuclear weapon is another nuclear weapon. His inner conflict mirrors that of the scientists who developed the atom bomb, highlighting ethical dilemmas around scientific advancement during wartime.

A world of monsters

Godzilla is the best-known Japanese *kaiju*, a word once used in literature and folklore to describe strange or mysterious creatures and now used specifically for giant monsters. In the film's marketing materials, Godzilla was described as a *daikaiju*, "giant monster", kicking off a genre that came to be called *kaiju*. Godzilla's sequels include *Godzilla Raids Again* (1955), *King Kong vs. Godzilla* (1962), and *Godzilla vs. Mechagodzilla* (1974), all more light-hearted than the original. Recent Godzilla films have been more serious. *Godzilla Minus One* (2023), the highest-grossing Japanese *kaiju* film, goes back to the franchise's roots, exploring the despair and trauma felt in Japan after World War II.

A recurring theme in these sequels is Godzilla's encounters with other *kaiju*. These include the three-headed King Ghidorah, the giant moth Mothra, and the pterodactyl-like Rodan, all of whom reappear in the recent *Godzilla: King of the Monsters* (2019). Perhaps most popular of all is Mothra, who had her own film in 1961 and made *Godzilla vs. Mothra* (1992) a roaring success.

> "Godzilla was baptized in the fire of the H-bomb and survived. What could kill it now?"
>
> DR KYOHEI YAMANE, *GODZILLA*

King of the Monsters
This poster advertises *Godzilla, King of the Monsters!* (1956), an English-dubbed version of the original film tailored for American viewers.

On the rampage
A composite image from the heyday of *kaiju* films shows Godzilla (right), Rodan (top), and King Ghidorah (left) fighting on the streets of Tokyo.

MANUFACTURED HORRORS

Although rooted in the horrors of war, *Godzilla* belongs to a tradition of stories about "science gone wrong" – or rather, of people misusing technology. Mary Shelley's *Frankenstein* is a template for these tales, which include David Cronenberg's *The Fly* (1986) and Michael Crichton's *Jurassic Park* (1990). However, they go back to the ancient Greeks, whose stories of Prometheus, who stole fire from the gods, and Icarus, who flew too close to the Sun, contain similar warnings.

THE HAUNTING OF HILL HOUSE

EXPLORING A HAUNTED HOUSE AND AN EQUALLY HAUNTED MIND, THIS POWERFUL NOVEL MARKS A BRIDGE BETWEEN M.R. JAMES AND STEPHEN KING.

Often voted one of the scariest novels ever written, Shirley Jackson's *The Haunting of Hill House* (1959) is in many ways the quintessential horror story. Featuring a haunted house, a young woman in psychological distress, supernatural happenings, and an unreliable narrator, it is a chilling Gothic tale that continues to unsettle readers.

The story revolves around four protagonists, who are introduced by an omniscient narrator. The first is Dr John Montague, an anthropologist who discovers Hill House in his search for a genuine haunting and rents it for the summer. Invited to join him are Eleanor Vance, a young woman who until recently has been her mother's carer, and an artist named Theodora. Rounding off the group is Luke Sanderson, the heir to the estate.

The haunted self

On their first evening together, Dr Montague reveals the tragic history of the house, which includes two violent deaths and a suicide. From this point onwards, the story begins to focus on Eleanor, revealing her inner thoughts and fears, and allowing readers to experience the house from her perspective. Paranormal events, including strange noises and mysterious sightings, begin to occur – many witnessed by Eleanor alone. These echo strange events from her childhood, and it is left unclear whether the disturbances are hallucinations or stem from supernatural abilities. Worried about her worsening mental state, Eleanor's companions urge her to leave Hill House, despite her strong compulsion to stay. However, the house exerts an irresistible pull on her and, unable to leave, she drives her car into a tree, dying by suicide.

In portraying Hill House as a psychological manifestation of its occupants' fears and desires, Jackson reinvented the trope of the haunted house, making it more than just a setting for supernatural events. The house plays an active role in Eleanor's mental deterioration, interrogating the concept of the home as a refuge from outside threats.

Shifting the focus of horror from external forces to Eleanor's internal struggles also allowed Jackson to explore female experiences and anxieties in a new way. An isolated figure – unmarried, without children, and unsure about her future now that her mother has died – Eleanor endures the pressures that many young women felt after World War II. When these stresses manifest in supernatural events with her at the centre, she gains a sense of importance, making psychological horror a form of female agency. This intense and terrifying form of psychic power is also expressed by the protagonist in Stephen's King's debut novel *Carrie*, which was inspired by Jackson's book.

Gothic reimagined

The Haunting of Hill House fed into the growing interest in psychological horror that emerged during the 1960s, with Robert Wise directing a faithful film adaptation – *The Haunting* – in 1963. In 2018, Netflix produced a limited series loosely based on the novel. While critical readings of the original story often note Eleanor's repressed desire for Theodora and its role in her mental breakdown, the series cast Eleanor, Luke, and Theodora as siblings, and made Theodora's lesbian identity explicit. In the show, Eleanor also experiences visions of a "Bent Neck Lady" – who turns out to be her future self, having died by suicide by hanging.

Who's there?
Claire Bloom plays the tragic Eleanor Vance in Robert Wise's *The Haunting* – still celebrated for retaining the suspense of Jackson's novel.

Losing touch with reality
A young girl, played by Violet McGraw, finds herself unexpectedly alone in the Netflix series *The Haunting of Hill House*. She had thought she was holding her sister's hand.

HORROR ON TELEVISION

TELEVISION BRINGS HORROR INTO WHAT IS SUPPOSED TO BE OUR SAFEST PLACE, TURNING A COSY EVENING AT HOME INTO A TENSE AND UNSETTLING EXPERIENCE. SINCE THE 1950S, HORROR HAS APPEARED IN VARIOUS GUISES ON THE SMALL SCREEN.

In the UK, TV horror began in 1953 when the *Quatermass* series introduced audiences to the terrors of outer space. It was the brainchild of Nigel Kneale, who went on to write *The Stone Tape* (1972), a drama exploring the notion that ghosts are memories stored in stone by electromagnetic waves. *Quatermass*'s fusion of science and horror set the stage for *Doctor Who*, which first aired in 1963. The show's sci-fi storylines owed a debt to many of the horror films that came before it, especially in the 1970s.

Highlights included "The Green Death", about giant white maggots in a Welsh mine; "The Brain of Morbius", about a scientist assembling a body for a renegade Time Lord, and "The Ark in Space", in which alien insects are intent on invading the bodies of the last human beings. While *Doctor Who* explored sci-fi horror, many British horror anthology series – including *Late Night Horror* (1968), *Dead of Night* (1972), and *A Ghost Story for Christmas* (1971–78) – kept to traditional supernatural fare such as vampires and zombies.

American anthologies

In the US, horror reached the small screen with the mystery anthology *Climax!* (1954), which included an adaptation of Robert Louis Stevenson's *The Strange Case of Dr Jekyll and Mr Hyde*, and *Alfred Hitchcock Presents*, which ran from 1955–62, and from 1962–65 as the *Alfred Hitchcock Hour*. Hitchcock hosted these eponymous series himself, already an established director by the time they premiered. The decade also saw the first episodes of *The Twilight Zone* (1959–64), many of which crossed over into the horror genre.

Horror TV took inspiration from literature. *Night Gallery*, which premiered in 1970, specialized in light-hearted stories with eerie premises. "The Cemetery", inspired by M.R. James's tale "The Mezzotint", features a murderer

Master of suspense
British film director Alfred Hitchcock plays with a magnifying glass on the set of his TV show *Alfred Hitchcock Presents*.

tormented by a painting of his victim's grave. R.L. Stine's *Goosebumps* series was also made into a TV show that ran from 1995–98.

Real terrors
In 1992, the BBC aired *Ghostwatch*, a fictional show masquerading as a live haunted house investigation. A decade later, TV turned its attention to reported hauntings in the real world. The UK show *Most Haunted* (2002–10), investigating paranormal activity, and MTV's *Fear* (2000–02), which put contestants in a supposedly haunted house, would be instrumental in shaping the appetite for horror and the supernatural in reality TV.

Grim inheritance
In "The Masks", episode 145 of *The Twilight Zone*, a man forces his family to wear masks on the day he dies. They duly inherit his estate, but find that their faces have changed to resemble their hideous masks.

Exterminate!
Popular villains from the *Doctor Who* series, the Daleks first appeared in 1963 and were based on the Nazis. Their goal is to conquer the Universe and exterminate all other lifeforms.

> "You are about to enter another dimension… Next stop, The Twilight Zone!"
>
> OPENING NARRATION, *THE TWILIGHT ZONE*

Quid pro quo
Hannibal Lecter (played by Anthony Hopkins) and Clarice Starling (Jodie Foster) exchange tales in *The Silence of the Lambs*.

PSYCHOLOGICAL HORROR

IN THE 1960S, A NEW SUBGENRE OF HORROR ARRIVED IN WHICH CHARACTERS CAME FACE TO FACE WITH THE DARK WORKINGS OF THEIR OWN MINDS RATHER THAN SUPERNATURAL ACTIVITY.

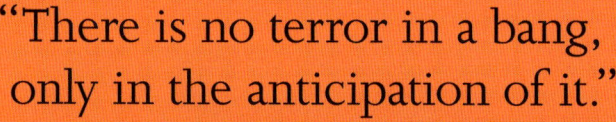

"There is no terror in a bang, only in the anticipation of it."

ALFRED HITCHCOCK, QUOTED IN
HALLIWELL'S FILMGOER'S COMPANION, 1984

Psychological horror plumbs the depths of the human mind, conceiving horrors that are all the more terrifying because of their plausibility. It often revolves around characters with psychological disorders rooted in repressed traumas, experiencing delusions, hallucinations, and what are believed to be paranormal events. In cinema, Robert Wiene's *The Cabinet of Dr Caligari* (1920) is often cited as the first example of the genre, which came of age in the 1960s with Alfred Hitchcock's *Psycho* (1960) and Roman Polanski's *Rosemary's Baby* (1968).

In *The Cabinet of Dr Caligari*, the world is that of a man trapped in his own delusions. In *Psycho*, the real world is the setting for the twisted actions of Norman Bates, a psychopath who has killed his mother and believes she is

"Here's Johnny!"
Deranged Jack Torrance (Jack Nicholson), stalks his family through the hotel in this iconic still from Kubrick's *The Shining*.

The Dawn of Modern Horror

Isolation is also a prominent theme in Darren Aronofsky's *Black Swan* (2010), which explores the mental breakdown of a prima ballerina. Urged by her overbearing mother and bullied by her teacher, she splits into two personalities – the ambitious "black swan" she needs to be and her "white-swan" innocent self. Her reflections in the ballet studio's mirrors symbolize her fractured mental state.

Psychological struggles

Many psychological films explore a protagonist's struggle to remain sane in response to trauma or manipulation. In *The Silence of the Lambs* (1991), audiences sympathize with FBI agent Clarice Starling when she is left alone with killer Hannibal Lecter, who torments her in exchange for information that will help her capture another serial killer. Clarice's mental battle against Lecter's psychological manipulation creates the film's tension.

In Jordan Peele's *Get Out* (2017), a Black man, Chris, visits his white girlfriend's parents and experiences mounting dread as they edge closer to their sinister goal: stealing his body to host a white person's brain. Chris is hypnotized into the Sunken Place, a kind of psychological imprisonment in which he loses control of his body while fully conscious. Chris's isolation, manipulation, and dehumanization all represent the real psychological effects of racism.

instructing him to commit further murders. *Rosemary's Baby* can be understood in two ways: it is both the tale of a couple being destroyed by a coven of witches and the story of a woman going insane, unable to accept that her husband has turned against her.

Isolation and breakdown

A key trait of psychological horror stories is the protagonist's drift into a state of extreme alienation, often reflected in the use of remote or abandoned settings. In Stanley Kubrick's *The Shining* (1980), the secluded Overlook Hotel provides the space for writer and alcoholic Jack Torrance to descend into madness. Likewise, it is while investigating a remote psychiatric hospital that US Marshal Teddy Daniels becomes isolated in Martin Scorsese's *Shutter Island* (2010). In both films, the focus on the protagonists' perspectives magnifies the audience's shock at discovering how distorted they are – the audience's sense of disorientation reflecting the characters' own.

Seeing double
Ballerina Nina Sayers, played by Natalie Portman, begins to doubt who she is in Darren Aronofsky's *Black Swan*.

AN ITALIAN FILM GENRE DEVOTED TO PSYCHOLOGICAL HORROR, GRAPHIC VIOLENCE, AND GRATUITOUS SEX, GIALLO FLOURISHED IN THE 1960S AND 70S.

The giallo genre took its name from the Italian *libri gialli* (yellow books) series published by Mondadori, which originally showcased the work of Agatha Christie, Edgar Wallace, Raymond Chandler, and Edgar Allan Poe. Its major influences were the films of Alfred Hitchcock, the German *krimi* (criminal) films, and *Blood Feast* (1963) – the original "splatter" film from "godfather of gore" Herschell Gordon Lewis. It also borrowed from Hollywood's noir tradition, which has roots in German Expressionism. The result was a series of stylized, non-supernatural crime dramas that prefigured the American slasher movie by nearly a decade.

Mario Bava established key giallo motifs in *The Girl Who Knew Too Much* (1963), about a young woman visiting Rome, witnessing a murder, and then tracking the killer herself, and *Blood and Black Lace* (1964), about a black-gloved killer who stalks fashion models. These included glamorous female protagonists, lavish sets, graphic violence, mysterious killers, and twist-filled narratives. However, it was Dario Argento who set the template for the genre in *The Bird with the Crystal Plumage* (1970). Featuring highly stylized and sexually provocative violence, the film prioritized theatricality over realism, and made bold use of

Proto-slasher
Mario Bava's *A Bay of Blood* (1971) influenced later slasher films with its high body count, graphic violence, innovative camera angles, and use of inventive murder set pieces, such as this scene of lovers impaled by a spear.

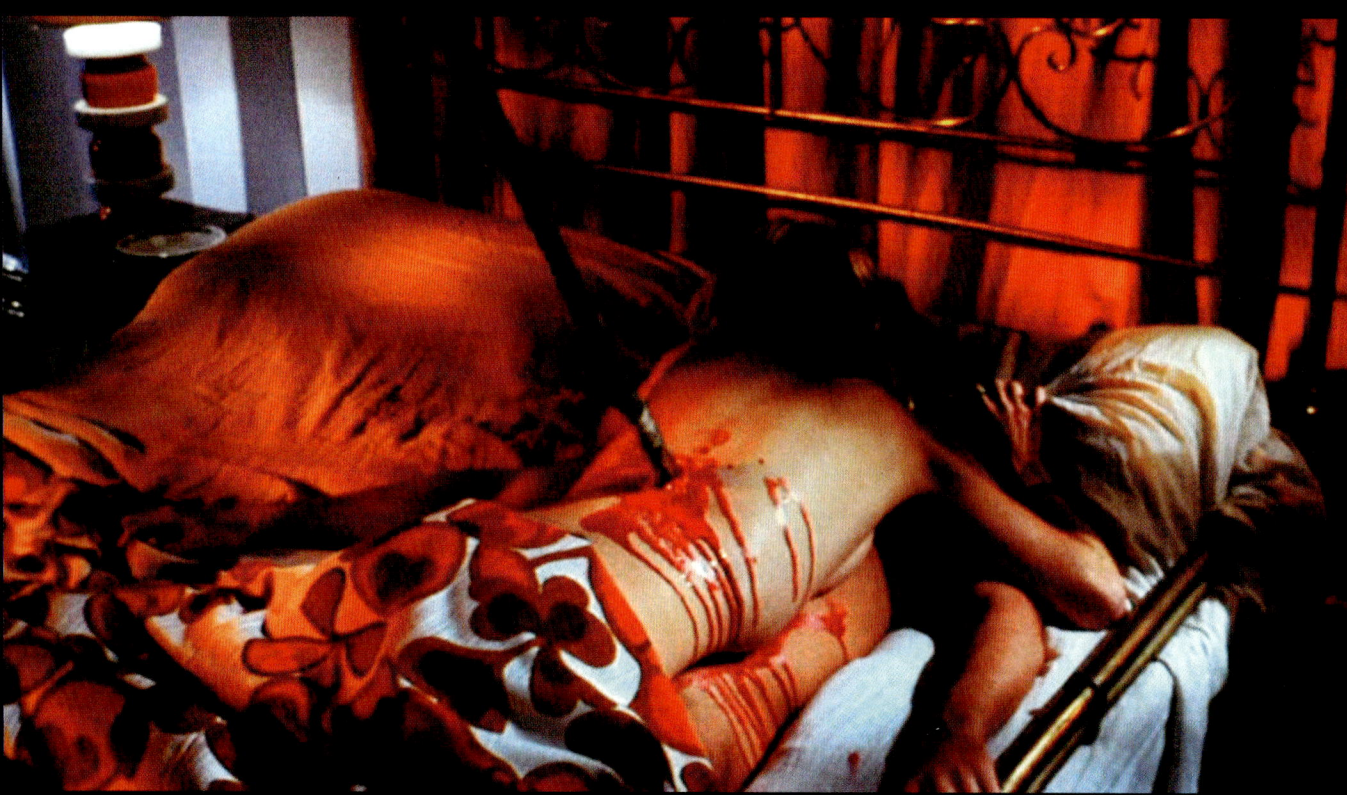

The Dawn of Modern Horror

Trademark yellow
A poster for the original Italian release of Dario Argento's *The Cat o' Nine Tales* (1971) features giallo's defining colour and captures the genre's stylized violence.

> "Horror is like a serpent: always shedding its skin, always changing."
> — DARIO ARGENTO

colour – a style that became Argento's signature. Over the next five years more than a hundred giallo movies were made, with many finding international success beyond Italy through foreign language releases. Popular productions included Bava's *A Bay of Blood* (1971), Lucio Fulci's *A Lizard in a Woman's Skin* (1971), Sergio Martino's *Your Vice Is a Locked Room and Only I Have the Key* (1972), Argento's *The Cat o' Nine Tails* (1971), and his masterpiece *Deep Red* (1975). These films assaulted audiences with vibrant colours, creative camerawork – including close-ups of eyeballs and long tracking shots – and complex stories about murder and paranoia.

Twisted legacy

After the mid-70s, the production of giallo slowed. Argento moved on to more supernatural fare, including the intensely colourful *Suspiria* (1977), before returning to the genre with *Tenebrae* (1982), as did Fulci with *The New York Ripper* (1982). However, the genre had already changed mainstream cinema, with Brian De Palma's *Dressed to Kill* (1980) and *Body Double* (1984) embodying the essence of giallo. Likewise, William Friedkin's *Cruising* (1980) and Sean S. Cunningham's *Friday the 13th* (1980) owed much to the genre, as did David Fincher's serial killer crime thriller *Se7en* (1995).

Over the years, giallo has had its share of criticism, frequently for being irredeemably of its time – misogynistic, gore-obsessed, and essentially designed for adolescent boys. However, at its heart, it expressed genuine fears about changes that were taking place in society in the 1960s, including the shifting roles of men and women. Like *Godzilla* (1954), which symbolizes nuclear catastrophe, giallo presented a world of social upheaval – one that had been thrown into the air and had yet to find its feet.

A study in red
David Hemmings and Macha Méril star in Dario Argento's blood-soaked *Deep Red*. The film was lauded for its camera work and distinctive visual style.

NEO-GIALLO

Modern takes on giallo embrace the genre's bold visual style, mystery plots, and fashionable settings. However, they also tend to employ more diverse casts and plotlines and reject the genre's misogynistic tropes. Yann Gonzalez's *Knife + Heart* (2018), for example, replaces giallo's archetypal protagonists – wide-eyed girls and hapless men – with queer characters working in the pornography industry. Neo-giallos often use irony to tackle giallo's legacy, providing the same voyeuristic lens but also commenting on the audience's taste for voyeurism.

Neo-giallo films have moved beyond the genre's Italian origins. Belgian film-makers Hélène Cottet and Bruno Forzani described their colour-saturated film *Amer* (2009) as a postmodern take on giallo, focusing on atmosphere and aesthetic over melodramatic plot. *Red Nights* (2010) is a collaboration between French, Belgian, and Hong Kong film-makers, and dubbed a "Hong Kong giallo". It takes the genre's psychosexual obsession to new heights as characters fight over an elixir that promises incomparable pleasures – and death.

The genre has also influenced arthouse films. Nicolas Winding Refn's *The Neon Demon* (2016) follows a teenage ingenue as she enters the Los Angeles fashion world, where her fresh-faced appeal provokes jealousy among a group of older models. This develops into erotic obsession, rivalry, and murder. Refn's neon colour palettes, fetishistic close-ups, and synth-heavy music score are all familiar for fans of Italian giallo, but the film is also a self-aware critique of beauty culture, as its models literally eat each other and suffer the consequences.

The burden of beauty
Elle Fanning plays an up-and-coming model terrorized by rivals in *The Neon Demon*. Refn's film eschews the classic giallo mystery element but, true to the form, does retain its shocking elements: extreme violence, cannibalism, and necrophilia.

ZOMBIES ON FILM

UP UNTIL 1968, ZOMBIES WERE PEOPLE IN HAITIAN FOLKLORE ENSLAVED BY VODOU MAGIC. THEN CAME GEORGE A. ROMERO'S *NIGHT OF THE LIVING DEAD*.

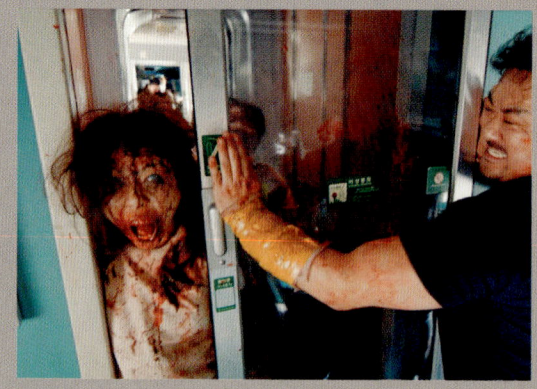

Speeding to Hell
Passengers attempt to contain a zombie outbreak caused by a virus on a high-speed train in *Train to Busan* (2016).

George A. Romero's *Night of the Living Dead* describes a day on which the dead rise from their graves to feed on the flesh of the living. It begins auspiciously, with siblings Barbra and Johnny visiting their father's grave. "They're coming to get you, Barbra", teases Johnny, as a man in a tattered suit appears in the background. The man – an animated corpse – kills Johnny as Barbra runs for her life. She escapes to a farmhouse and is soon joined by Ben, also fleeing from an attack. They board up the house and discover five people hiding in the cellar – a couple (Tom and Judy) and the Coopers (Harry, Helen, and their daughter, Karen, who has been bitten). As corpses besiege the farmhouse, one by one the survivors are killed; Helen is gutted by her own daughter, who has become a ghoul – the name given to the undead. After making it through the night, Ben is shot by a gun-wielding posse of locals who mistake him for a ghoul – a shocking finale to a gory, nihilistic tale.

Broken society

Unlike previous horror films, which tended to focus on external threats, *Night of the Living Dead* was about neighbours turning on neighbours. It is a film about societal breakdown, reflecting social, political, and cultural anxieties at the end of the 1960s when protests raged against the Vietnam War and race riots erupted in many US cities. While not intended as a commentary on racial issues, the film's ending, when Ben, played by Black actor Duane Jones, is shot by a mob, mirrored real-life violence against participants in the Civil Rights movement. As one of the first Black protagonists in horror, the casting of Jones also proved influential.

Zombie child
Actor Kyra Schon plays Karen Cooper in *Night of the Living Dead*. Bitten by a ghoul (zombie), she dies and reanimates before killing her mother.

Undead mob
Zombies attack a social housing complex in *The Horde* (2009), a French take on the genre.

That humans could be reduced to gorging on themselves – even after death – was a comment on consumerism. The critique was more explicit in *Dawn of the Dead* (1978), Romero's sequel, in which the dead gather in the only significant place they can remember – the shopping mall. Even those appalled by the film's gore acknowledged the social commentary: the American film critic Roger Ebert noted, "Nobody ever said art had to be in good taste".

Zombies, as they began to be called, were now synonymous with lumbering, reanimated corpses, featuring in films such as *Children Shouldn't Play with Dead Things* (1972) and *Zombie Flesh Eaters* (1979). Their character remained unchanged until Danny Boyle's critically acclaimed *28 Days Later* (2002) popularized a new type of zombie – living humans transformed into flesh-eaters after a viral infection. A remake of *Dawn of the Dead* (2004) inspired Romero's return with the post-apocalyptic *Land of the Dead* (2005) and found-footage horror *Diary of the Dead* (2007). Zombies as comedy were explored in *Shaun of the Dead* (2004) and *Zombieland* (2009) – the highest-grossing zombie film of all time. Then came *The Walking Dead* (2010–22), an 11-series television show, proving that zombies today are as lively as ever.

YOUTH HORROR

SOME PEOPLE THINK HORROR IS NOT FOR YOUNGSTERS, BUT EVEN FAIRY TALES AND CARTOON SHOWS ARE FULL OF THREAT, DREAD, AND VIVID HORROR.

> "We would have gotten away with it, if it hadn't been for you meddling kids!"
>
> THE SCOOBY-DOO SHOW, "WATT A SHOCKING GHOST", 1976

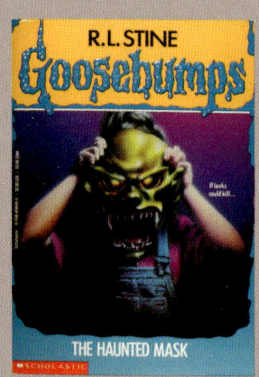

Best of the 'bumps
Praised for its suspenseful plot and memorable villain, *The Haunted Mask* is widely considered one of the best *Goosebumps* books.

Children's culture has always been full of monsters. Historic examples include the nursery rhyme "Ring a Ring o' Roses", about catching the bubonic plague; terrifying fairy tales such as the Brothers Grimm's "Hansel and Gretel", about children captured by a cannibal witch; and Heinrich Hoffmann's *Slovenly Peter* (1845). This illustrated book of rhymes about horrible events that befall disobedient children features one memorable tale about a tailor who cuts off thumbs.

Early exposure to horror also came from the screen. As times and attitudes changed, Universal Pictures's classic 1930s movies such as *The Mummy* and *Frankenstein* came to be reclassified as PG material and were many children's introduction to the genre when shown on TV. The cartoon series *Scooby-Doo, Where Are You!* (1969–78) was also a gateway to terror, following teenagers solving supernatural mysteries, usually to reveal their source as a man in a mask. Monsters have also frequently featured in comics and games; even adult films such as *Alien* and *Jaws* spawned official toys for children in the 1970s.

Hitting the right tone

Horror aimed at younger audiences was especially popular in the US during the 1980s and 90s. Disney released *The Watcher in the Woods* (1980) for youths, and *The Black Cauldron* (1985) for younger children. Although these films performed poorly at the box office, Warner Bros' *Gremlins* (1984) was a huge success. Its popularity sparked public debate about the level of violence that was acceptable in films targeted at children and led to

Nostalgia-fest
This pivotal scene from *Stranger Things* Season Four triggered nostalgia by using Kate Bush's 1985 hit song "Running Up That Hill".

Not just for kids
Prom Queen (2025) is one of several graphic slashers made for young adults that can also be enjoyed by an older audience.

the introduction of the PG-13 rating in the US. After this, children's horror tended towards stylized visuals, humour, or ambiguity in the storytelling, as in *The Nightmare Before Christmas* (1993), which includes spooky themes but no graphic violence or explicit fear.

On TV, children's horror thrived with the spooky anthology *Are You Afraid of the Dark?* (1991–2000) and quirky comedy *Aaahh!!! Real Monsters* (1994–97). Meanwhile, Disney mixed fright and fun in TV movies such as *Tower of Terror* (1997) and *Halloweentown* (1998).

Crossing the age barrier

Horror fiction was also growing as a genre in children's publishing. Examples include now-classic titles such as Alvin Schwartz's *Scary Stories to Tell in the Dark* (1981) and the multi-author teen series *Point Horror*, which included contributions from Christopher Pike, Diane Hoh, and early work by R.L. Stine.

For many, children's horror is synonymous with Stine's *Goosebumps* books (launched in 1992) and their TV adaptations. Stine defined children's horror for a generation. The Goosebumps franchise has continued uninterrupted since the end of the original book series in 1997 through various spin-offs and movie adaptations. He also turned his pen to books for older children and teens, such as anthology *The Haunting Hour* (2001) and the *Fear Street* series (beginning in 1989) respectively. Many of those books have also been adapted for the screen, with Netflix's *Fear Street* films (three in 2021, and one in 2025) proving to be big hits for the streaming platform.

Youth horror shows no sign of going away. Passed from parent to child, books and films such as *Coraline* and *The Addams Family* find new audiences year after year. Nostalgia plays a big role in horror plots aimed at teens, too. The *Fear Street* films and the horror/sci-fi crossover *Stranger Things* (2016–25) draw on memories of childhood and a child's first exposure to horror. This subgenre is exciting precisely because of its contradictions: simultaneously contemporary and nostalgic, foreign to children's cultures and yet entirely at home within them.

> "I don't [put] messages in these books: the only lesson is to run."
>
> R.L. STINE, INTERVIEWED IN UK NEWSPAPER *THE GUARDIAN*, 2021

1969–

PRESENT HORRORS

STEPHEN KING

POPULARLY KNOWN AS "THE KING OF HORROR", STEPHEN KING HAS PUBLISHED MORE THAN 65 NOVELS AND 200 SHORT STORIES. MANY HAVE BEEN ADAPTED AS EQUALLY SUCCESSFUL FILMS AND TV SERIES.

The 1970s were a golden age for horror novels, starting in 1971 with Richard Matheson's *Hell House* and William Peter Blatty's *The Exorcist*. The latter gained huge public attention when it was filmed in 1973, which proved that horror could work in a domestic setting. Enter *Carrie*, Stephen King's debut novel, in 1974.

Famously, the manuscript of *Carrie* was rescued from the bin by the author's wife, Tabitha. It went on to become a best-selling novel, which was filmed by Brian De Palma in 1976. The story is tragic, about a girl kept in such ignorance by her mother – a

Seeing red
Carrie White, played by Sissy Spacek, is pushed to the limit at her school prom in Brian De Palma's film version of *Carrie* (1976).

STANLEY KUBRICK'S THE SHINING

In 1980, *The Shining* was made into a feature film by director Stanley Kubrick. Starring Jack Nicholson, Shelley Duval, and Danny Lloyd, it is considered one of the scariest films ever made. However, Stephen King was unhappy with it and later collaborated with director Mick Garris to produce a TV adaptation, *Stephen King's The Shining* (1997), starring Steven Weber.

Danny Torrance, played by Danny Lloyd, sees ghosts in Kubrick's *The Shining*.

religious fanatic who despises everything to do with the body, especially sex – that she does not understand what is happening when she has her first period. This occurs at school, in the shower, in front of her classmates, who use it as an excuse to bully her. After a lifetime of such treatment, both at home and at school, Carrie develops telekinesis – the power to move objects with the mind – as if the stress she has endured has given her supernatural powers. At the novel's conclusion, these powers erupt when a prank leaves her drenched in pig's blood at her school prom. Her revenge leads to hundreds of casualties and the deaths of both herself and her mother.

Broken lives

As director Mick Garris has often said, King's stories are not just about the monster in the closet, but about the people living in the house that has the closet. *Carrie* succeeds because of Carrie herself, whom King describes both sympathetically and realistically. She endures most children's greatest fear – rejection – and her powers derive from that fear. In the novel *'Salem's Lot* (1975), the sheer pettiness of small-town life fosters isolation and moral decay, making it fertile ground for vampires. Jack Torrance, in *The Shining* (1977), is an alcoholic who makes the disastrous decision to stay in a remote hotel with his family over the winter so that he can write a book. What he does not know is that the hotel is haunted, and that his son, damaged by his alcoholism, is clairvoyant. Published nearly a decade later, and widely considered his masterpiece, *It* (1986) is a compendium of virtually everything that can go wrong in childhood, but also a story about children defeating an embodiment of evil – Pennywise the Dancing Clown.

Although famous for his horror stories, King describes himself as a suspense writer, having often stated that the most frightening thing of all is human nature. The government experiments in *Firestarter* (1980) and the mood changes of Annie Wilkes in *Misery* (1987) are as troubling as any demon. In *Danse Macabre* (1981), his analysis of horror fiction, King distinguishes between terror (fear of the monster), horror (seeing the monster), and revulsion (for what the monster does). He admits that while terror has the greatest impact, he often goes straight for revulsion, or the "gross-out".

Blazing talent
Drew Barrymore stars as Charlie McGee, a child who can create and control fire with her mind, in Mark L. Lester's film adaptation of King's *Firestarter* (1984).

"We make up horrors to help us cope with the real ones."

STEPHEN KING, *DANSE MACABRE*

BODY HORROR

THE HUMAN BODY BECAME A PLAYGROUND FOR FILM-MAKERS AS THE GROWING GENRE OF "BODY HORROR" EXPLORED GROTESQUE BIOLOGICAL TRANSFORMATIONS AND POSSESSION.

The term "body horror" was first coined by Australian film-maker and critic Philip Brophy in his 1983 essay "Horrality – The Textuality of the Contemporary Horror Film", where he describes a new wave of horror centred on the fear of one's own body and its destruction. Brophy introduced the term to capture the shift in horror cinema from exploring external threats to the fear of transformation, mutation, and decay from within – something going (supernaturally) wrong with one's own body.

Body horror had roots in literary works such as Mary Shelley's *Frankenstein* (1818), with its vivid details of a creature made of corpse parts, and

Less than human
Astronaut Victor Carroon (actor Richard Wordsworth) begins to mutate soon after returning from space in *The Quatermass Xperiment*.

> "I'm saying I – I'm an insect who dreamt he was a man and loved it."
>
> SETH BRUNDLE, THE FLY

The facehugger
To implant an embryo and reproduce, the creature in Ridley Scott's *Alien* must attach to a host, here officer Kane, played by John Hurt.

Franz Kafka's *The Metamorphosis* (1915), in which the protagonist wakes up one day as "horrible vermin" (usually imagined to be a giant beetle). In film, an early precedent was *The Quatermass Xperiment* (1955), a movie based on a British TV series about an astronaut infected by an alien organism.

Strange flesh

Aliens often serve as a catalyst for the grotesque transformations or invasions of the human body that define body horror. Ridley Scott's *Alien* (1979) is a classic example of parasitic, invasive horror centred on bodily violation, while in John Carpenter's *The Thing* (1982), an alien entity assimilates and mutates human bodies in horrific, unpredictable ways. Other alien possession stories include *Invasion of the Body Snatchers* (remade in 1978), about alien spores that produce undead doubles of humans, and films such as *Xtro* (1982) and *Lifeforce* (1985).

From the 1970s onwards, Canadian director David Cronenberg made key contributions to the body horror genre with what has been dubbed "visceral cinema". His films captured flesh and sinew in grisly detail, from *Shivers* (1975), *Rabid* (1977), and *The Brood* (1979), about body-altering parasites and infections, to *The Fly* (1986), in which a scientist's experiment with teleportation goes horribly wrong, merging his DNA with a fly's and triggering a grotesque physical transformation. Other directors in the genre include Brian Yuzna, whose *Society* (1989) features one of the most disturbing body-melding sequences in horror cinema. Japanese director Shin'ya Tsukamoto had a unique take on the genre with *Tetsuo: The Iron Man* (1989), a cyberpunk body horror fusing flesh and metal in an industrial, experimental style.

Recent growths

In the 1990s and 2000s, body horror became more psychological, surreal, and often metaphorical. Cronenberg's *Crash* (1996) was less about grotesque mutation and more about bodily obsession. In *Dans Ma Peau* (2002), a French extremity film directed by Marina de Van, the protagonist's arm detaches during dinner, representing the next stage in the character's tragic dissociation from herself. The 21st century has also seen a spate of films from female directors exploring body horror from a feminist perspective.

Brundlefly
In *The Fly*, Dr Seth Brundle (Jeff Goldblum) tests a teleportation device, unaware a fly has slipped in too. The experiment joins their cells.

FEMINIST BODY HORROR

In the 21st century, many directors have contributed to the body horror genre with films that explore the real terrors and transformations experienced by women. They use body horror as social commentary – often as a metaphor for gender politics, sexual agency, and bodily autonomy.

A number of these films explore the pain and transformations inherent to womanhood. Julia Ducournau's *Raw* (2016) uses a young woman's descent into cannibalism to explore sexual awakening and sexual repression, while in *Tiger Stripes* (2023), by Amanda Nell Eu, a Malaysian girl undergoes tiger-like changes as she hits puberty. Alice Lowe's *Prevenge* (2016) centres on a woman who believes her unborn child is commanding her to kill, portraying pregnancy as grotesque. In *Titane* (2021), also by Ducournau, pregnancy follows a bizarre sexual encounter with a car, leading to a monstrous transformation.

Sex and sexual violence are also common in feminist body horror. In Mitchell Lichtenstein's *Teeth* (2007), a teenager discovers she has sharp teeth in her vagina when she is sexually assaulted. Jen and Sylvia Soska's *American Mary* (2012) focuses on a medical student who becomes involved in underground body modification in response to her own sexual assault.

Body horror has even tackled the concept of the perfect body. Rachel Maclean's *Make Me Up* (2018) is a critique of cosmetic surgery and female body-image, while Coralie Fargeat's *The Substance* (2024) is a black satire on the beauty industry.

Emerging from within
In *The Substance*, an ageing former Hollywood star turns to a mysterious serum to regain her youth, only to physically split into a younger double. The two bodies mutate and decay as they battle for dominance.

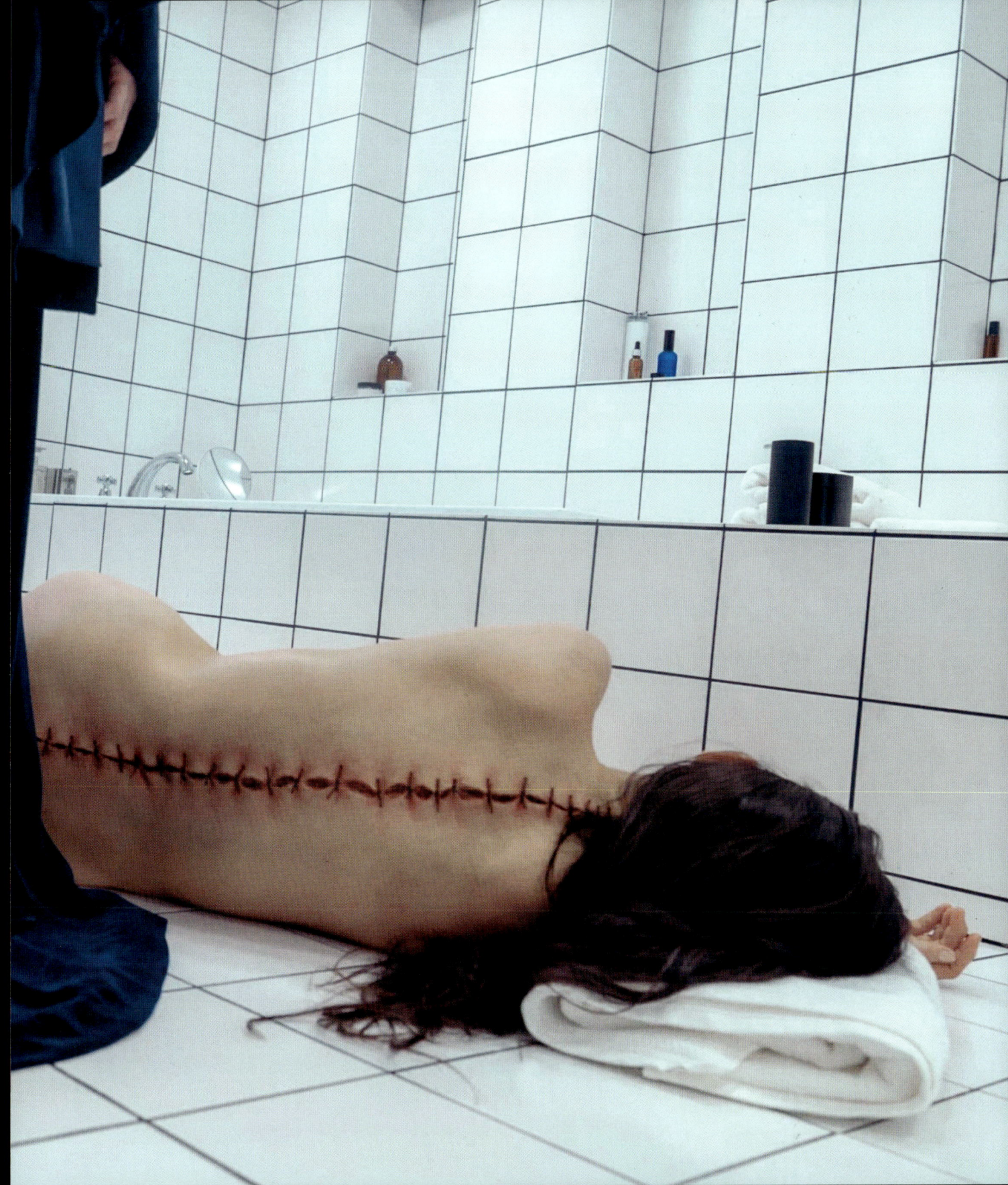

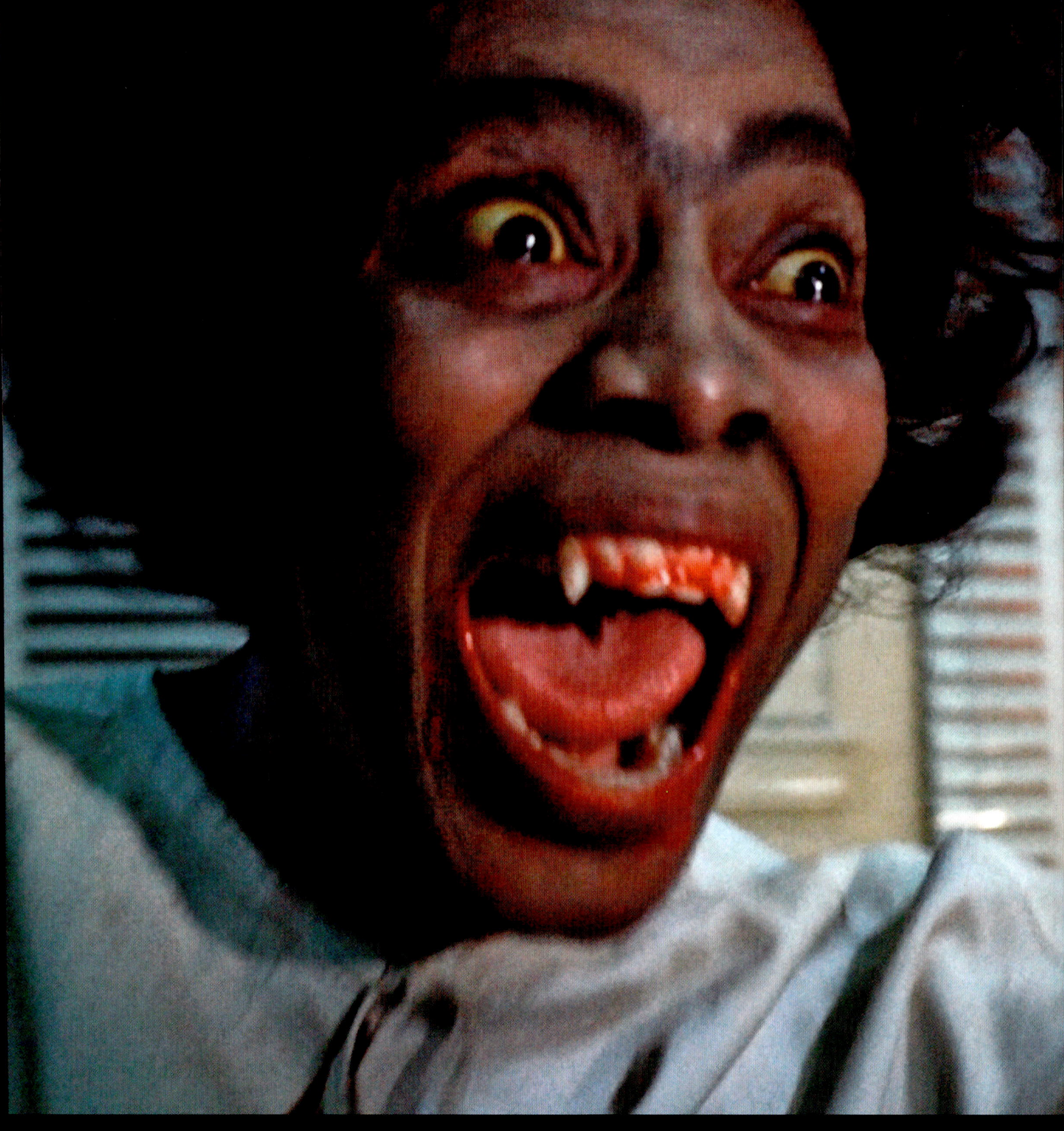

BLACULA, BLAXPLOITATION, AND BEYOND

BLAXPLOITATION CINEMA EMERGED IN THE EARLY 1970S, OFFERING POPULAR GENRES WITH NARRATIVES GROUNDED IN BLACK CULTURAL IDENTITY.

The monster inside
In a film based on *The Strange Case of Dr Jekyll and Mr Hyde*, a black doctor turns into a white monster after a medical experiment goes wrong.

Screaming back to life
Photographer Nancy (actor Emily Yancy) returns to life after being bitten by Blacula. He attacked her after she tried to photograph him.

Black Civil Rights activist Junius Griffin coined the term "blaxploitation" in 1972 to denounce films he felt perpetuated negative racial stereotypes. Although these films have been criticized for depicting characters involved in drugs, violence, or highly sexualized roles, they also represented a significant cultural shift. For the first time, Black characters were routinely placed at the centre of genre cinema, displaying agency, charisma, and complexity. They carved out a crucial space for Black representation and creative expression in a Hollywood industry long dominated by white perspectives. The films resonated with Black audiences, who were rarely reflected on screen, and laid the groundwork for more diverse storytelling in mainstream cinema. They also enjoyed wide popularity and have since acquired cult status.

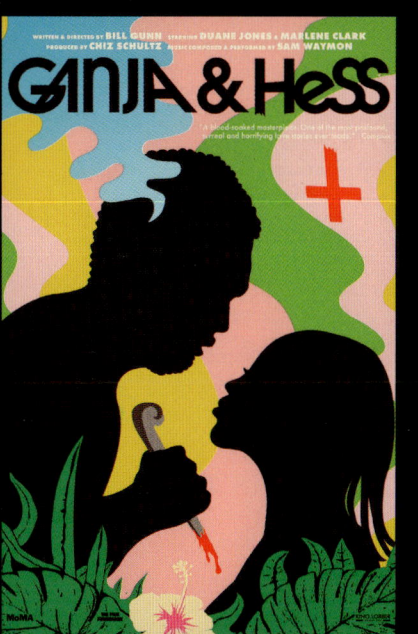

Reshaping horror
Pioneering Black film-maker William Crain directed *Blacula* in 1972, a landmark film that introduced Blaxploitation to the horror genre. The film tells the story of Mamuwalde (actor William Marshall), an African prince who travels to 18th-century Transylvania to seek support in ending the slave trade. Instead, he is betrayed and turned into a vampire by Count Dracula, imprisoned in a coffin, and awakens two centuries later in 1970s Los Angeles. The film incorporates many familiar tropes of Gothic vampirism, which clash to comic effect with the aesthetics and energy of the 1970s setting. More significantly, it uses the figure of the vampire to explore racial oppression, cultural displacement, colonial violence, and the haunting legacy of enslavement.

Despite its modest production values, *Blacula* creates a compelling atmosphere, with scenes such as those in the morgue and Blacula's gruesome, maggot-ridden death, offering moments of genuinely unsettling horror. Its success led to an equally interesting sequel, *Scream Blacula Scream* (1973), and inspired a wave of Blaxploitation horror films such as *Blackenstein* (1973), *Dr. Black, Mr. Hyde* (1976), and *Abby* (1974), the latter an appropriation of *The Exorcist*, released the preceding year.

In retrospect, *Blacula* is both a product of its time – exploiting pervasive stereotypes – and a bold reimagining of horror through a Black political lens. Its influence can be discerned in later Black horror, such as *Tales from the Hood* (1995) and *Nope* (2022), which also explore themes of race, identity, and exploitation.

Vampire romance
In *Ganja & Hess* (1973), Duane Jones plays an anthropologist who becomes a vampire after his assistant stabs him with a cursed knife. He then falls in love with his assistant's wife, played by Marlene Clark.

THE RISE OF FEMINIST HORROR

SINCE THE 1970S, FEMINIST HORROR FILMS HAVE CHALLENGED GENDERED TROPES AND EXPLORED THE TORMENTS OF WOMANHOOD, FROM SEXUAL VIOLENCE TO THE STRUGGLE FOR BODILY AUTONOMY.

Terror of change
The physical and emotional changes that come with puberty are explored through the metaphor of werewolf transformation in Canadian film *Ginger Snaps* (2000).

In 1972, American writer Ira Levin – author of the 1967 novel *Rosemary's Baby* – published a story about a woman named Joanna Eberhart, who moves to the (fictional) town of Stepford with her husband and children. As the family settle in, Joanna is surprised by the submissive nature of her female neighbours, who come across as subservient to their husbands and obsessed with housework. The wives' strange behaviour convinces Joanna that the men of the town are responsible, leading her on a quest for the truth that ends with a horrifying discovery.

The novel had a dramatic cultural impact. At the time, the so-called Second Wave feminist movement was challenging the gendered status quo, raising issues around sexuality, equal pay, birth control, abortion, and gender violence. *The Stepford Wives'* representation of women's desire for autonomy and the theme of consent resonated with feminists' desire to achieve equality in and outside the home.

The novel's commercial success led to a film adaptation in 1975, and a later remake in 2004, spawning a new cinematic genre. The term

Something wrong in Stepford
Tension mounts between Joanna (actor Katharine Ross) and her husband Walter (Peter Masterson) as she begins to realize the sinister nature of Stepford in *The Stepford Wives* (1975).

> "I won't be here when you get back… There'll be somebody with my name, and she'll cook and clean like crazy… but it won't be me!"
>
> JOANNA IN *THE STEPFORD WIVES*, 1975

"Stepford wife" also entered the vernacular, becoming a derogatory way to refer to a submissive married woman preoccupied with domestic matters.

On-screen battle

Feminist horror has continued to explore the societal expectations placed on women, patriarchal desires to control them and their bodies, and the everyday violence they endure. While director Bob Clark did not intend to make a feminist film, many consider his slasher *Black Christmas* (1974) an early example of feminist horror. Now regarded as a cult classic, the film depicts a sorority house attacked by a serial killer. Running parallel to this plot is the protagonist Jess's discovery that she is pregnant, and her subsequent decision to have an abortion – an acknowledgement of female agency in a film released only a year after the landmark Supreme Court ruling *Roe v. Wade* established (for a time) women's constitutional right to an abortion.

The 1980s were a rich period for feminist cinema. *The Mark of Lilith* (1986), a short film produced by students of feminist scholar Laura Mulvey, features an academic who catches the attention of a vampire while lecturing on women in the horror genre. Feminist writer Rita Mae Brown also wrote the script for a slasher movie – *The Slumber Party Massacre* (1982), which satirized the genre's misogynistic tropes.

The monstrous-feminine

While responding to the socio-political climate around feminism and its concerns, feminist horror also interrogates the representation of women within the horror genre. In 1993, cinema scholar Barbara Creed coined the term "monstrous-feminine" to describe female figures whose ability to arouse fear is intrinsically linked to their femininity and bodies. Within film, this concept has been imagined in various ways.

Sorority scares
In Sophia Takal's 2019 feminist remake of *Black Christmas*, the female characters band together to fight institutional patriarchy and rape culture as well as a killer.

Some female characters have been portrayed as supernatural creatures – such as Ginger in *Ginger Snaps* (2000), who is bitten by a werewolf when her first menstrual period attracts its attention – or as superhuman, like Carrie White in *Carrie* (1976), whose telekinetic powers emerge during puberty.

Feminist film-makers have also claimed and celebrated the monstrous-feminine as a source of female power, often manifesting as women who destroy men, through or with their bodies.

> "... the twist of the movie is that it's her brazen sexuality that keeps her alive."
>
> KARYN KUSAMA ON *JENNIFER'S BODY*, 2009

Lust for blood
Megan Fox's Jennifer becomes a succubus in *Jennifer's Body*, but cannot bring herself to eat her best female friend, Needy. Needy kills Jennifer, then goes after the men who hurt her.

In Karyn Kusama's *Jennifer's Body* (2009), teenager Jennifer is murdered as part of a rock band's ritual sacrifice of a virgin to Satan in return for fame. However, the band have made a mistake – Jennifer is not a virgin and she is reincarnated as a succubus who begins seducing and devouring boys.

In 2007, Mitchell Lichtenstein's *Teeth* brought to life the myth of *vagina dentata* – teeth inside a woman's vagina. *Teeth* can be seen as part of a tradition of feminist body horror films, which explore the female body as a site of pain, violence, and fear. It is also part of a genre of films about punishing this violence. Another example is Ana

Lily Amirpour's *A Girl Walks Home Alone at Night* (2014), which centres on a female vampire who patrols an Iranian town at night to protect women and punish men who seek to hurt them.

Since 2017, the increased attention paid to sexual violence against women in the wake of the #MeToo Movement has led to more films about sexual violence. Films that feature rape-revenge narratives, such as Coralie Fargeat's *Revenge* (2017) and Emerald Fennell's *Promising Young Woman* (2020), are unflinching in showing the brutality inflicted upon the female characters. These films also depict the power of female rage against male violence.

Meanwhile, Olivia Wilde's 2022 film *Don't Worry Darling* revisits themes first explored by *The Stepford Wives*, and is similarly set in an idyllic small town. It, too, ends in a shocking twist: the town turns out to be a computer simulation in which the women are drugged, brainwashed, and assaulted by men who want to live in an era when women had less power.

Imperfect portrayals

Feminist horror has recently turned on the film industry itself, criticizing the impossible beauty standards and ageism that female actors face. In 2024, Fargeat's *The Substance* received critical acclaim for its grotesque portrayal of vanity and society's obsession with youth. Nevertheless, even feminist horror can be guilty of perpetuating a gendered gaze. *The Substance*, for example, has been accused of falling into the "hag-horror" trope, in which ageing women are presented as mentally unstable or dangerous.

Girl's revenge
In *A Girl Walks Home Alone at Night*, Sheila Vand plays a vampire vigilante enforcing her own justice in Bad City, a fictional ghost-town.

LGBTQ+ HORROR

Queer women frequently feature in the horror genre. In early films, female same-sex desire was often equated with madness, as in Lambert Hillyer's *Dracula's Daughter* (1936). Vampirism and sapphic lust were intertwined in a number of films, including *Blood of Dracula* (1957), adaptations of *Carmilla*, and *Lesbian Vampire Killers* (2009). Queerness was often aligned with the "Other".

In the 21st century, queer female directors have explored LGBTQ+ issues through the horror genre in more complex ways. Stewart Thorndike's *Lyle* (2014) has been described as the "lesbian *Rosemary's Baby*", while Michelle Garza Cervera's *Huesera: The Bone Woman* (2022) sees a queer expectant mother haunted by a faceless woman with cracking bones.

Valeria in *Huesera* faces occult forces as her pregnancy becomes a curse.

The Rise of Feminist Horror

The Devil's child
Played by Mia Farrow, the protagonist of *Rosemary's Baby* sees her child for the first time.

OCCULT CINEMA

IN THE 1970S, CINEMA BECAME PREOCCUPIED WITH THE OCCULT, PARTICULARLY STORIES CONCERNING OUIJA BOARDS, THE ANTICHRIST, AND DEMONIC POSSESSIONS.

Occult cinema came of age in the late 1960s and early 70s, with a wave of films that tapped into anxieties about Satanism and the supernatural. Roman Polanski's *Rosemary's Baby* (1968) ushered in the era, its success inspiring a fascination with occult themes. The film follows a couple, Rosemary and Guy, who move into an old but sought-after apartment block in New York City. Little do they know that their neighbours are Satanists who will drug Rosemary, invite a demon to impregnate her, and gather to watch her give birth to the Antichrist. Although disturbing, it was not a film that gave people nightmares, unlike one released five years later – William Friedkin's *The Exorcist* (1973).

Devilish power

The Exorcist begins on an archaeological dig in Iraq, where Catholic priest Father Lankester Merrin disturbs a site associated with the Assyrian demon Pazuzu. Meanwhile, in Washington, D.C., a girl named Regan MacNeil plays with a Ouija board and befriends a spirit called Captain Howdy, whose name recalls her absent father, Howard. However, the spirit is not what it seems. What follows is the transformation of an all-American girl into the Devil himself – creating a hell for the child and her terrorized mother, Chris. After a horrific scene in which Regan stabs herself with a crucifix, assaults her mother, twists her head around 180 degrees, and rages in the voice of a man she recently killed, Chris seeks the help of a priest named Damien Karras. An exorcism ensues, which is aided by Karras but performed by Father Merrin. They save the girl, but the ordeal kills them both.

In terms of delivering terror, *The Exorcist* raised the bar so high that horror cinema struggled in its wake. A string of copycat films ensued, including *Beyond the Door* (1974), *The Antichrist* (1974), and *Exorcist II: The Heretic* (1977). However, *The Wicker Man* (1973) sparked a new interest in realism and showed that occult horror could have serious themes. Exploring a clash between different belief systems, and the potential for violence and fanaticism in religion, the film follows a devout Christian detective as he investigates a missing child in a remote community steeped in paganism. Grounding the supernatural in the everyday, its believable characters and settings set the tone for films such as *The Omen* (1976), *The Amityville Horror* (1979), and more recently, Robert Eggers's *The VVitch* (2015), which explores 17th-century fears of Satan seducing women into witchcraft.

The only hope
In a composition inspired by a Magritte painting, Father Merrin looks up at Regan's room, bathed in ethereal light.

The Antichrist
In *The Omen*, directed by Richard Donner, the child Damien Thorn is born of Satan and a female jackal. His identity as the Antichrist is revealed after a series of violent deaths.

JAWS AND NATURAL HORROR

IN 1975, STEVEN SPIELBERG REINVENTED THE "REVENGE OF NATURE" TALE WITH *JAWS*. A HUGE BOX-OFFICE SUCCESS, IT HERALDED A NEW ERA OF BLOCKBUSTER FILM-MAKING IN HOLLYWOOD.

Deadly waters
Roger Kastel's iconic illustration of the first scene of *Jaws* was used as both the cover of the novel and the poster for the film.

Based on a best-selling novel by Peter Benchley, *Jaws* redefined the thriller and became one of the highest-grossing films of all time. It was the first summer blockbuster, and won three Academy Awards, including one for John Williams's musical score, with its iconic two-note "shark theme".

However, the film's success was partly due to a failure of special effects – the animatronic shark that played the key role rarely worked, forcing Steven Spielberg to focus more on his characters' reactions than graphic action. This technique has since become standard for building suspense.

Nature gone bad

The premise was simple. A great white shark picks off tourists on a beach, starting with the women and children. Police Chief Brody wants to shut the beach, but the mayor objects, not wanting to damage the local economy. Finally, oceanographer Hooper convinces the mayor, so Brody, Hooper, and shark-hunter Quint set off to kill the creature. A tense search ensues, in which the trio throw meat into the ocean to entice the predator – ending with the shocking moment when Brody sees it surface nearby.

Unlike *King Kong* (1933) or even *Godzilla* (1954), *Jaws* does not evoke sympathy for the creature. If anything, it seems psychotic – nature gone mad as well as bad. For this reason, audiences cheer when the shark finally explodes, taking both an oxygen tank and a bullet to its mouth.

Like *Psycho* (1960), *The Exorcist* (1973), and later *Alien* (1979), *Jaws* plays on our fears of the unknown – of entering seemingly innocuous that is actually dangerous territory – in this case, on a sunny afternoon at the beach.

Biting back

The success of *Jaws* spawned a raft of nature horrors, a form of eco-horror in which vengeful animals (or plants) attack humans. Tapping into fears about the potential for nature to turn against humanity, films included *Day of the Animals* (1977), in which animals experience psychosis because of the depletion of the Earth's ozone layer, *The Swarm* (1978), *Piranha* (1978), and *Jurassic Park* (1993), in which reanimated dinosaurs run amok on an island near Costa Rica. With growing fears about animal extinctions and the consequences of human destruction of the natural world, the appetite for natural horror films remains undiminished. Recent films in the genre include *Exists* (2014), about an endangered bigfoot, and *Crawl* (2019), which uses floodwaters to stage the first ever alligator home-invasion movie.

Attack from the air
In *The Swarm*, fears about the introduction of killer bees to the US manifest in a natural horror about venomous bees that attack Texas, causing widespread destruction.

> "What we are dealing with here is a perfect engine, an eating machine. It's really a miracle of evolution."
>
> OCEANOGRAPHER MATT HOOPER, *JAWS*

SUSPIRIA

"Suzy Bannion decided to perfect her ballet studies in the most famous school of dance in Europe", intones a nameless, sleepy-sounding narrator at the beginning of Dario Argento's *Suspiria* (1977). "She chose the celebrated academy of Freeborge. One day, at nine in the morning, she left Kennedy airport, New York, and arrived in Germany at 10.40pm local time."

So begins what sounds like an optimistic fairy tale, but the music – a homage to *The Exorcist* – tells viewers otherwise. As Suzy reaches her destination, she sees a girl fleeing the academy and plunging into a forest. Thunder and lightning rend the air as the girl tears through the rain, shrieking for help. The audience follow her to her lodgings – a complex of buildings in which a murderer is on the loose. In a scene illuminated by lightning and drenched in neon-bright colours, she and her friend are killed. She is smashed through a window, stabbed multiple times, and dropped through a glass ceiling with a noose around her neck; her friend is merely impaled to the floor with a shard of glass through her head.

This was Argento's first foray into pure horror, after making three *gialli* – *The Bird with the Crystal Plumage* (1970), *The Cat o' Nine Tails* (1971), and *Four Flies on Grey Velvet* (1971). Relating Suzy's discovery that the school is run by witches, the film is based on a story by actress Daria Nicolodi, who co-wrote the script, and Disney's *Snow White and the Seven Dwarfs* (1937), a story about a princess being tormented by her stepmother. *Snow White* also provided inspiration for *Suspiria*'s saturated colour palette, which inverted the traditional association of horror with darkness. Argento drenched his film with vivid green, red, and blue tones, using a dye transfer printing method that replicated the three-strip Technicolor process used for animated films in the 1930s, '40s and '50s.

Intensely evil
The colourful interiors of the dance school reflect the powers of the witches who control it – the outside world is bland in comparison.

SLASHER FILMS

IN THE 1980s, TEENAGERS CAME TO THE FORE — TO KILL AND BE KILLED IN INCREASINGLY INGENIOUS WAYS. THE NEW GENRE WAS BORN OF JOHN CARPENTER'S *HALLOWEEN*.

> "Monsters in movies are us, always us, one way or the other."
>
> — JOHN CARPENTER

Few images sum up a genre so completely as that of Norman Bates tearing open the shower curtain, knife raised for slashing. Such was the horror of *Psycho* (1960), Alfred Hitchcock's shocking study of psychosis, a film so influential it drew a line in cinema history.

It took nearly 15 years for the slasher genre to be revived. In the 1970s, serial killings were on the rise, particularly in the US, and it was natural for films to address that fear. *The Texas Chain Saw Massacre* (1974), *Black Christmas* (1974) and *The Town That Dreaded Sundown* (1976) paved the way for a new era of slasher movies, with the latter based on the real-life "Phantom Killer", who murdered five people in Texarkana in 1946.

The boogeyman

In 1978, John Carpenter's surprise box office hit *Halloween* popularized and redefined the slasher genre. The film did away with explaining the motives of a killer. Norman Bates kills out of a twisted sense of guilt, but the psychology of Michael Myers, *Halloween*'s infamous villain, is never explored. Wearing a mechanic's overalls and a white, expressionless mask, Myers stalks Laurie Strode, a teenager whose father is trying to sell the Myers family home. It is 31 October, and rumours are spreading that the "boogeyman" is coming. Myers fulfils that role, killing three of Laurie's friends. He is shot, stabbed, and knocked off a balcony, at which point his body disappears.

Myers is not a man but a monster, called only "The Shape" in the film's closing credits. However, he is also ordinary enough to enable viewers –

The Shape
With its trademark knife, mask, and boiler suit, The Shape – the monster formerly known as Michael Myers – stalks a victim in John Carpenter's *Halloween*.

Leatherface
Clad in a rotten suit and a skin mask, the antagonist of Tobe Hooper's *The Texas Chain Saw Massacre* was a prototype for the villains of the slasher genre.

Dream demon
A Nightmare on Elm Street's demonic villain Freddy Krueger is recognizable by his distinctive fedora, striped sweater, and clawed glove. His face is disfigured – a result of being burned alive by vengeful parents.

at a time now dubbed "the golden age of serial murder" – to imagine being a victim. Across *Halloween*'s many sequels (with varying timelines), Myers kills more than 120 people.

The last one standing

Halloween set the template for what became known as a "slasher" film. These typically feature a group of sexually active teenagers being hunted by a serial killer, who is finally defeated by a virginal, watchful, and resourceful character – a female survivor termed the "Final Girl" by scholar Carol J. Clover in her 1987 study of horror.

Sean S. Cunningham's *Friday the 13th* (1980) follows this pattern. It begins with a group of young camp counsellors reopening an abandoned summer camp 21 years after its closure due to the drowning of a young boy, Jason Voorhees, and two murders. History appears to repeat itself when the teenage counsellors are murdered one-by-one, leaving a Final Girl, Alice. In a twist on what would become the typical formula, the killer is not Jason's ghost seeking revenge but Mrs Voorhees – his mother. Like Myers's "Shape" in *Halloween*, *Friday the 13th* introduces Jason as an iconic, vaguely supernatural figure. His corpse rises from the lake and continues his mother's murder spree in the film's sequels. Killing teens in creative ways became a feature of the series, which saw the liberal use of machetes, ice-picks, arrows, and outboard motors.

The slasher craze

By the mid-1980s, around 100 more slasher films had been made, a number of which vanished without a trace. Many, however, stood the test of

> ## "Whatever you do, don't fall asleep."
> NANCY THOMPSON IN *A NIGHTMARE ON ELM STREET*

THE FINAL GIRL

A recurring trope in the slasher genre is that of the Final Girl – a female who survives to the end and defeats the monster. In *Psycho*, it is Lila Crane, the sister of Norman Bates's first victim, who brings justice. Typically, the killer's perspective is slowly replaced by that of the Final Girl. While the original Final Girls were often "good girls" – morally pure, clever, and sexually innocent – modern slashers have subverted the trope, allowing these characters to be flawed, morally complex, and to fight back proactively, rather than merely survive.

time, including *My Bloody Valentine* (1981) and *The Prowler* (1981), the latter featuring prosthetic effects by gore maestro Tom Savini. Other hits included *Prom Night* (1980), *Maniac* (1980), and *Halloween II* (1981).

In 1984, the first film in the Elm Street franchise was released. Considered one of the greatest horror films of all time, Wes Craven's *A Nightmare on Elm Street* featured the villain Freddy Krueger, the ghost of a child-killer, who has turned to murdering teens in their dreams. The film proved that slashers could be fun and scary at the same time. *Child's Play* (1988), which introduced the murderous doll Chucky, maintained the same light-hearted approach.

A self-conscious turn

In the 1990s, the appetite for straightforward slashers declined, giving way to parodic films such as *Scream* (1996). *Scream* satirized the genre while still delivering terror through its iconic killer, Ghostface. Amidst the thrills, one character spells out how to survive in a slasher movie: never have sex, never drink alcohol, and never promise to be right back. *Scream* breathed new life into the genre, bringing in popular TV actors and music to appeal to young – especially female – viewers. It influenced other self-referential slashers including *I Know What You Did Last Summer* (1997), written by *Scream*'s Kevin Williamson, and Jamie Blanks's *Urban Legend* (1998).

The so-called neo-slasher films of the 2010s were also inspired by *Scream*'s approach. These often subvert or comment on slasher tropes and some give their Final Girls more agency. In *The Final Girls* (2015), characters are trapped inside a slasher movie but use their knowledge of horror tropes to survive, while the protagonist in *Happy Death Day* (2017) changes her fate by repeatedly reliving the day she dies. Two films, *Totally Killer* (2023) and *Time Cut* (2024), feature female characters who travel back in time to stop a serial killer. Other films play with point of view or pace, such as Chris Nash's *In a Violent Nature* (2024), which takes cues from slow cinema with its long, ambient shots.

Modern slashers tend to reflect contemporary culture: *They/Them* (2022), for example, is set at an LGBTQ+ conversion camp, and its Final Girl is a non-binary character, Jordan. The black horror comedy *Bodies Bodies Bodies* (2022) is a satire on Gen Z, commenting on both societal privilege and young people's dependence on technology. Among these new tales, nostalgia for original slasher franchises has led to a number of reboots, sequels, and retellings – such as *Halloween* (2018), *Scream* (2022) and *I Know What You Did Last Summer* (2025) – which revisit the franchise's characters along with a new generation of protagonists in more modern settings.

Stubborn survivor
After avoiding his attempts to kill her, Final Girl Ginny Field (Amy Steel) wields a pitchfork against Jason in *Friday the 13th Part 2* (1981).

His 2020 novel *The Only Good Indians*, in which an elk spirit seeks revenge against a group of male hunters who shot a herd, won several horror prizes. The novel's title references a provocative comment by General Philip Sheridan in the 1860s when US troops drove Indigenous nations from their homelands: "The only good Indian is a dead Indian".

Other influential Indigenous writers include Waubgeshig Rice, whose post-apocalyptic novel *Moon of the Crusted Snow* (2018) is about an Arctic Anishinaabe community cut off from the rest of Canada due to a power failure. A white man in the community turns to cannibalism, eating an Anishinaabe man in a metaphor for the historical genocide of Indigenous peoples. The far north is also the setting for *Taaqtumi: An Anthology of Arctic Horror Stories* (2019), which showcases Indigenous writers such as Sean and Rachel Qitsualik-Tinsley, Thomas Anguti Johnston, and Gayle Kabloona.

Queer fears

While queer horror's origins can be found as early as J. Sheridan Le Fanu's *Carmilla* (1872), the genre has gained considerable traction in the 21st century. Eric LaRocca won the Splatterpunk Award for Best Novella for *Things Have Gotten Worse Since We Last Spoke* (2022), about a toxic online relationship between two women, while Julia Armfield's debut novel *Our Wives Under the Sea* (2022) added to the lesbian horror canon with a story about a woman whose wife comes back horribly changed after a deep-sea expedition. Horror, feminism, and queerness intersect in the fiction of Carmen Maria Machado — who won the Shirley Jackson Award for her short-story collection *Her Body and Other Parties* (2017) — and Scottish writer Kirsty Logan. In Logan's collection *Things We Say in the Dark* (2019), a series of unsettling stories is interspersed with non-fiction vignettes about the author's past, writing process, and isolation.

In the 21st century, several horror directors have explored LGBTQ+ topics on screen. Carter Smith's feature *Into the Dark: Midnight Kiss* (2019) is a slasher film that critiques gay male hookup culture, while Jane Schoenbrun's *I Saw the TV Glow* (2024) is an allegory for the "egg crack" — when a person realizes that they are transgender.

Queer horror has also reached the music scene. In 2022, transgender artist Ethel Cain released *Preacher's Daughter*, a concept album inspired by her religious upbringing. The songs are written from the perspective of a teenager who, trying to

> "Authentic, sincere diversity is the solution to almost all problems of race in storytelling."
>
> NNEDI OKORAFOR, INTERVIEW, 2013

Exploring gender
The haunting *I Saw the TV Glow* blends queer identity and media obsession in an innovative exploration of fear and belonging.

A haunting tale of loss
The Orphanage delivers a distinctly Spanish take on maternal grief and psychological dread.

Fairy tale for adults
In *Pan's Labyrinth*, childhood innocence meets the terrors of war with horrifying effect.

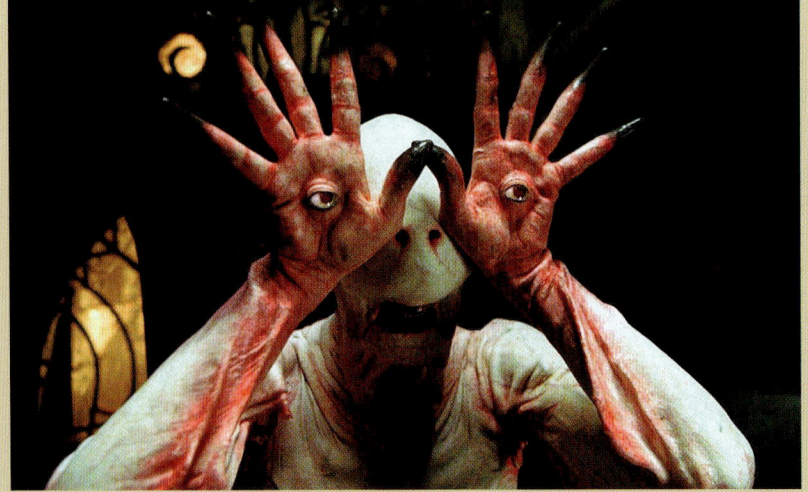

escape the grip of her family, falls in love with a cannibal. With grotesque, vivid details of her death and consumption, Cain's lyrics and haunting vocals make for a truly horrifying listen.

Global success

International horror is increasingly popular, with many literary works being translated for a wider audience. Among these, Spanish-language horror has been particularly successful. Argentinian author Agustina Bazterrica's novel *Tender Is the Flesh* (2017), for example, was published in English in 2020. Although written in English, Mexican-Canadian author Silvia Moreno-Garcia's novels *Mexican Gothic* (2020) and *The Daughter of Doctor Moreau* (2022) have also received international acclaim for blending science fiction, horror, and commentary on colonialism.

Similarly, many international films have had an English adaptation. These include the 2008 Swedish movie *Låt Den Rätte Komma In* (*Let the Right One In*), the 2014 Austrian film *Ich Seh, Ich Seh* (*Goodnight Mommy*), the 2007 Spanish film *Rec* (*Quarantine*), and Michael Haneke's 2007 remake of his own 1997 Austrian film *Funny Games*.

The interest in Spanish-language horror can also be seen in film-making through the success of Mexican director Guillermo del Toro. His Spanish Civil War horror *The Devil's Backbone* (2001) was followed in 2006 by the dark fantasy *Pan's Labyrinth*, set during Spain's Francoist dictatorship. Del Toro also co-produced *The Orphanage* (2007) by Spanish film-maker J.A. Bayona, which was well received internationally.

Combining horror tropes
The US remake of *Goodnight Mommy* blends psychological tension, thriller pacing, and jump scares, as twin boys begin to doubt their mother's identity.

New perspectives
In *Resident Evil Survivor* (2000), players see the game world from the perspective of the character they are controlling, simulating real life.

HORROR GAMES AND ENTERTAINMENT

PROVIDING THRILLS, SCARES, TENSION, AND ENTERTAINMENT, HORROR GAMES HAVE BECOME ONE OF THE MOST POPULAR WAYS TO EXPERIENCE HORROR FIRST-HAND.

The earliest horror video games were innovative and fun, but rarely actually scary. *Haunted House*, released in 1972 alongside the Magnavox Odyssey console (the first commercial home video gaming system), established key elements of the genre, including puzzle solving, exploration, and the evasion of dangerous enemies. However, the game's basic graphics required players to stick an overlay over their television screen to create the game world. Tackling graphic limitations in a different way, *Hunt The Wumpus* (1973) relied on text rather than animation to drive the action, with players navigating a network of caves by typing commands or selecting options from a list of written prompts.

Graphic evolution

Improvements in technology during the 1980s changed the gaming experience, launching horror games with more sophisticated graphics and sound that could generate atmosphere and evoke fear. An updated version of *Haunted House*, for example, released in 1981 for the Atari 2600 console, allowed players to scroll through rooms and had a new "darkness mechanic" that let them illuminate hidden items by lighting a match.

Capitalizing on improved graphics capabilities, a number of games attempted to translate popular films into a gaming experience. These included *Halloween* and *The Texas Chain Saw Massacre*, both released as games in 1983, which were deemed so terrifying that some retailers refused to stock them. Later in the decade, the arcade game *Splatterhouse* (1988) also shocked with its graphic violence. Drawing on horror films such as *Friday the 13th*, this "beat-'em-up" game featured brutal acts, including grisly decapitations and gore.

Reinforcing these ties between gaming and cinema, Japanese game company Capcom released *Sweet Home* in 1989, alongside a horror film of the same name. The game follows a team of five film-makers who enter an old mansion to recover some famous frescoes. They quickly discover that the mansion is haunted and must work together to defeat a series of terrifying attackers to escape alive. The game pioneered many of the themes that would characterize the genre later termed "survival horror", including vulnerable characters with limited resources at their disposal, puzzle-solving, and dangerous combat in eerie, isolated settings.

Arrival of evil

Originally intended as a remake of *Sweet Home*, Capcom's *Resident Evil* (1996) revolutionized gaming history and was marketed as the first survival horror. Set in a mysterious mansion inhabited by humans and animals mutated by a secret bioweapon, players had to escape by evading these zombies and monsters and solving a series of fiendish puzzles.

> "That was too close. You were almost a Jill sandwich!"
>
> BARRY BURTON IN *RESIDENT EVIL*, 1996

Scary navigation
In the video game *Silent Hill* (1999), players must guide the main character Harry Mason through an eerie town filled with monsters.

Immersive horror
An actor brings horror to life at the Ministry of Peculiarities, an escape room experience that blends theatrical performance with game-playing to create a fully immersive event.

Unlike previous games that focused on action, *Resident Evil* built tension through the possibility of sudden death around every corner. Avoidance rather than confrontation was usually the best strategy, as the enemies were powerful and players had little ammunition and limited healing powers. The game generated feelings of fear and suspense not just through jump scares and an engaging horror narrative, but from the ongoing experience of trying to stay alive.

The success of *Resident Evil* inspired a series of survival horror games over the next decade. One of the most influential, *Silent Hill* (1999), shifted the focus towards psychological horror. Set in a dark, fog-shrouded town, the game features a man searching for his daughter while being menaced by supernatural beings. The fog limits visibility, increasing tension, while the deliberately mysterious plot has five possible endings.

Survival legacy

Resident Evil and *Silent Hill* spawned multiple sequels, as well as clones of varying quality, such as *Nocturne* (1999) and *Countdown Vampires* (1999). However, by the 2000s, the formula was growing stale. Advances in computing power meant that open-world games (where players roam freely in large, interconnected environments rather than progressing through levels) and multiplayer combat

Under fungal attack
A mutant fungus infects humans in *The Last of Us* (2013), which was made into a successful television show (2023–).

games were gaining popularity. Some games still used elements of survival horror, but most were more action-oriented, focusing on combat. These games included *BioShock* (2007), featuring a man trapped in a dystopian underwater city who must battle mutated humans, and *Dead Space* (2008), set in a science fiction universe in which a stranded astronaut boards a spaceship overrun with monsters.

The close relationship between horror games and other visual media has continued. Alex Garland, writer of the 2002 film *28 Days Later*, has cited *Resident Evil* as his source for the idea of fast-moving zombies, and the cinematic fascination with zombies in gaming persists. *The Last Of Us* (2013), a game about a father escorting a girl through a post-apocalyptic American wasteland, inspired another highly successful crossover when it was adapted into a critically lauded TV series in 2023.

Other ways to play horror

Horror trends have also influenced other forms of gaming. *Haunted House* (1962), one of the first horror-themed board games (not related to the computer game), involved navigating a ghostly mansion full of traps. Moving away from simple roll-and-move play, more modern board games, such as *Mansion of Madness* (2011) and *Dead of Winter* (2014), use complex narratives and cooperative, strategic gameplay to create a more immersive experience.

Role-playing games (RPGs) have proven to be one of the most engaging forms of horror play. *Dungeons & Dragons* (*D&D*), launched in 1974, established the genre in which storytelling and imagination are as important as the basic mechanics of dice rolls. Players craft characters with unique traits and backstories, steering them through campaigns guided by a storyteller – the Dungeon Master – who orchestrates the world, its lore, and dangers. While its first modules were rooted in fantasy rather than horror, *D&D* soon inspired the production of horror-specific RPGs, such as *Call of Cthulhu* (1981), which adapted H.P. Lovecraft's horror story of the same name. In 1983, *D&D* produced its own Gothic horror adventure module, *Ravenloft*, which incorporated classic tropes such as haunted castles, vampires, and eerie landscapes.

RPGs expanded the concept of horror games by blurring the line between fiction and reality. This more immersive type of play has been taken to new levels by games played in real time, such as horror-themed escape rooms. These combine complex narratives with tactile problem solving – players must decode puzzles under time pressure to prevent events such as a zombie apocalypse or to escape a serial killer's trap. These experiences reflect the evolution of horror gaming into a dynamic, multi-sensory genre. It is one thing to read or watch horror: playing horror games can be powerfully visceral in agency and urgency.

Horror fantasy
In role-playing games, players engage in imaginary quests or battles using miniature figures. Many of the characters, like these undead skeleton warriors, draw on the horror genre.

FOUND FOOTAGE

IN RECENT YEARS, HAND-HELD CAMERAS AND SMARTPHONES HAVE ENABLED DIRECTORS TO EXPLORE A NEW GENRE OF HYPER-REALISTIC, LOW-BUDGET HORROR FILMS.

> ### SCREENLIFE HORROR
> Born of the pseudo-documentary, the action in screenlife films unfolds on smartphones or computer screens. Examples include *Unfriended* (2014), about a dead girl disturbing a Skype meeting, *Searching* (2018), about a father exploring his missing daughter's online activity, and *Host* (2020), about an internet chat that goes diabolically wrong. The horror is heightened by the restricted view of events, and the intimate connection that the audience makes with the characters.

In the autumn of 1994, three students, Heather, Mike, and Josh, go missing in the Black Hills Forest near Burkittsville, Maryland, having entered the area to film a documentary about the legendary Blair Witch. The area is searched, but no bodies are found. Then, a year later, some hikers find a duffel bag in a disused cabin. The bag contains two film cameras, various tapes, and the journal of one of the missing students, Heather Donahue. Can the tapes explain what happened? Did the students film their killer? Such is the premise of *The Blair Witch Project* (1999), which purports to be that footage, spliced together and left to speak for itself.

With its jarring camerawork, the film conveys the anxiety of the students with striking immediacy. As they explore the forest, they get lost and are attacked by something at night. Whatever it is, it does not like being seen — like the local child-killer who, we learn, got his victims to face the wall while killing them one by one. Mike and Josh similarly become angry at being watched — by Heather — and regularly tell her to stop filming. In the final sequence — after Josh has gone missing, followed by Mike — Heather looks for them in the wrecked shell of a house. In the basement, she is attacked and the camera falls to the ground. However, we have seen her final shot — of Mike in the corner with his back to the room, unable to turn around. Whatever it is, we are in the room with it now.

Documentary realism

The Blair Witch Project spawned a family of pseudo-documentary horror films, including *Rec* (2007), *Paranormal Activity* (2007), and *Cloverfield* (2008), but it was not the first film to use the found-footage technique. Only the year before, *The Last Broadcast* (1998) focused on tapes made by a group of friends who are killed while filming a documentary about the Jersey Devil in the Pine Barrens. *Cannibal Holocaust* (1980) also served as an important predecessor. Many of these films, with their discovered footage, serve to update the "found manuscript" trope, a well-worn literary device used by horror writers.

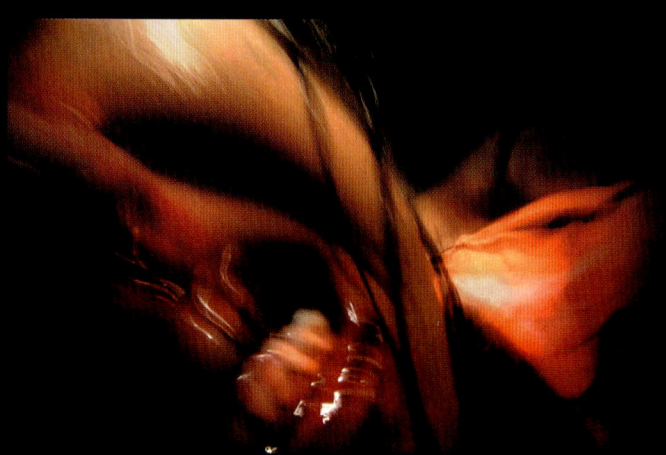

Demonic plague
In the found-footage film *Rec*, a journalist investigates mysterious disturbances in a plague-infected apartment block in Barcelona.

"I'm so sorry..."
Heather Donahue records a final message towards the end of *The Blair Witch Project*. She apologizes to her mother, and to the families of Mike and Josh, for having pursued her project so recklessly.

"TORTURE PORN"

The term "torture porn" was first coined in a 2006 article by critic David Edelstein in *New York Magazine*. He called the genre "so viciously nihilistic that the only point seems to be to force you to suspend moral judgements altogether". Despite his criticism, the inventiveness of the atrocities inflicted on screen and the unremitting violence made for surprising box-office success.

The genre emerged in response to the real violence of the early 21st century: 9/11, the War on Terror, the Iraq War, and the Abu Ghraib scandal involving the torture of Iraqi prisoners. The first major film was James Wan's *Saw* (2004), centring on two strangers shackled in a bathroom and forced to endure grisly games. Shot for just $1.2 million, it grossed more than $100 million on its US release. Eli Roth's *Hostel* (2005), in which backpackers are tormented by wealthy businessmen, made $80 million on a budget of just over $4.5 million.

These films were commentaries on modern violence, power, and morality, not just spectacles of gore. *Saw*'s villain, John Kramer, or Jigsaw, does not torture victims for pleasure – he makes them hurt themselves in order to teach them to value their own lives, just as he learned to do after losing his child. *Hostel* uses a "murder-for-profit" business as a metaphor for unchecked capitalism and imperialism. It is a commentary on American exploitation and violence towards other nations in the context of the Iraq War.

The popularity of torture porn in pop-horror was mirrored in the arthouse world, with the rise of New French Extremity and the work of Danish director Lars von Trier. By the 2010s, however, interest began to wane. The *Saw* franchise was shelved (until its 2017 revival) in 2010, while *Hostel Part III* (2011) went straight to DVD.

Gruesome games
This still from *Saw X* (2023) shows a torture device imagined by John Kramer (Jigsaw). The device is a vacuum to suck out the victim's eyes.

NEW FRENCH EXTREMITY

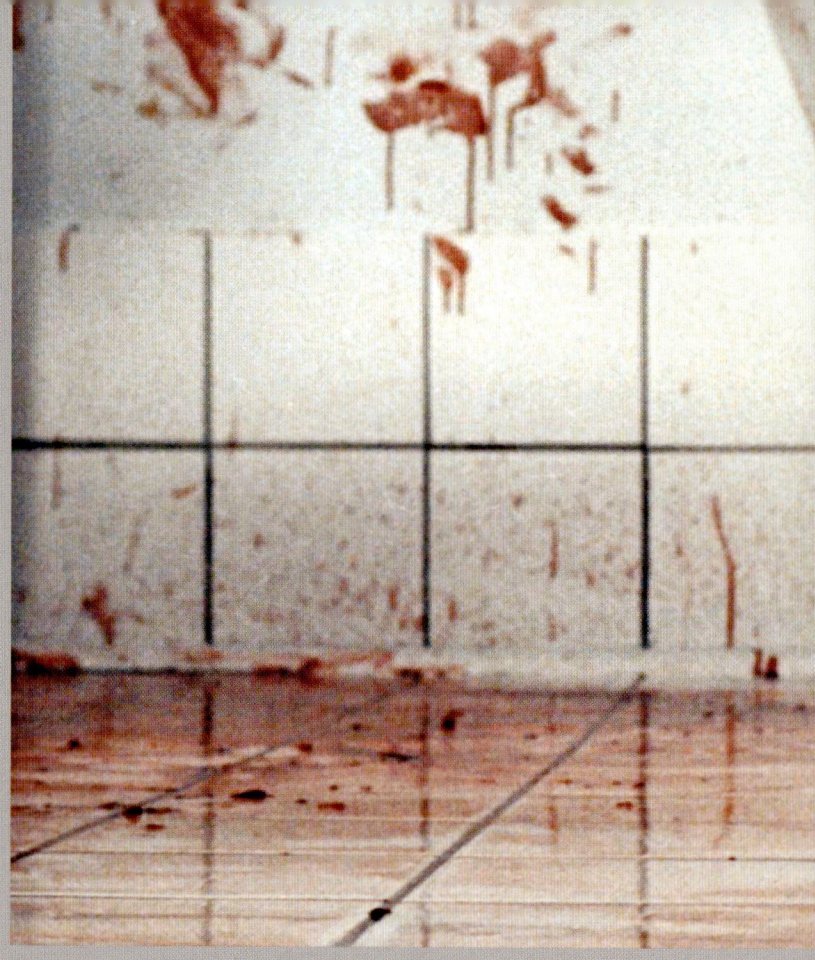

IN FRENCH CINEMA, THE TURN OF THE 21st CENTURY WAS MARKED BY AN ERUPTION OF BLOOD, GUTS, AND BODY HORROR; THE TREND WAS DUBBED "NEW FRENCH EXTREMITY".

From 1897–1962, the Théâtre du Grand-Guignol in Paris specialized in deliberately provocative plays featuring acts of extreme violence and copious amounts of fake blood. A year after the Grand-Guignol closed, the American splatter film *Blood Feast* (1963) was released and Italian giallo cinema was born – a film genre filled with shocking, stylized sex and violence. It was as if graphic horror had to go somewhere.

Transgressive content

At the turn of the millennium, graphic horror returned to favour in France, where various film directors took sledgehammers to the boundaries of acceptability. The term "New French Extremity" was coined by Canadian film historian James Quandt in 2004. He was denouncing films such as Virginie Despentes and Coralie Trinh Thi's *Baise-Moi* (2000; released in the US as *Rape Me*), which contains unsimulated sex, and Gaspar Noé's *Irréversible* (2002), which includes a ten-minute rape scene. However, both films had their defenders: *Baise-Moi* was lauded for its honest depiction of its female leads seeking justice, and *Irréversible* for its cinematography and backwards-running narrative, and for making a rape scene play as uncomfortably as possible. Detractors rejoined that the films were merely money-making machines that pandered to their audience's lowest instincts.

Meanwhile, the genre blossomed, with director Michael Haneke providing two of its most critically acclaimed titles: *Le Temps du Loup* (2003), released in English as *Time of the Wolf*, a post-apocalyptic film which explores the worst of humanity; and *Caché* (2005), also released as *Hidden*. *Caché* follows a couple terrorized by someone who films them and leaves the evidence on their porch; the identity of the antagonist is never revealed.

At its best, French extremity forces audiences to confront traumas that are otherwise ignored or downplayed by mainstream cinema. It also

End of the road
In *Martyrs*, two women seeking revenge for being tortured as children find themselves in a nightmare of physical and psychological abuse.

explores the limits of human experience. Many of its exemplars, such as Marina de Van's *Dans Ma Peau* (2002; released in English as *In My Skin*), about an injured woman who becomes obsessed with self-mutilation, and whose arm becomes independent, are nightmarishly graphic examples of body horror. Other films in the genre, such as Julien Maury and Alexandre Bustillo's *À l'intérieur* (2007; released in English as *Inside*), about a woman being butchered for her unborn child, or Pascal Laugier's *Martyrs* (2008), about women seeking revenge on their kidnappers, are not only gruesome but masterclasses in suspense.

Although the initial wave of New French Extremity had passed by 2010, there is no sign that the genre has yet exhausted itself. Julia Ducournau's *Raw* (2016) follows a young vegetarian at veterinary school as she discovers a taste for meat, while Gaspar Noé's *Climax* (2018) watches a dance rehearsal disintegrate into drug-fuelled carnage. More recently, Ducournau's critically acclaimed *Titane* (2021) charts the life of a girl who, after a car accident, grows up to be a serial killer with a sexual passion for cars.

Inconvenient desire
Garance Marillier stars in *Raw*, a coming-of-age drama about a vegetarian who develops a craving for meat. This quickly turns into an insatiable desire for human flesh.

HORROR ON STAGE

AS THE 21ST CENTURY DREW NEAR, THEATRE AUDIENCES BECAME EVER HUNGRIER FOR TALES OF GRISLY MURDER, GHOSTLY GOINGS-ON, AND MAGIC.

A filmic show
Ghost Stories uses live illusions, psychological twists, and horror film techniques to explore fear and memory.

From Renaissance revenge tragedies and Victorian spectral melodramas to the blood-soaked Grand Guignol, horror has long been a staple of live theatre. When *The Woman in Black* ended its West End run in 2023, it had haunted London for 33 years. During that time, horror theatre had re-emerged in a range of forms and venues. Adaptations of Gothic and horror classics had gained fresh prominence, culminating in Nick Dear's *Frankenstein*, staged at the National Theatre in London in 2011. In this acclaimed production, Benedict Cumberbatch and Jonny Lee Miller alternated the roles of Victor Frankenstein and the Creature, earning them joint Laurence Olivier Awards for Best Actor. The National Theatre returned to Gothic horror in 2018, with Anthony Neilson's all-female reimagining of Edgar Allan Poe's *The Tell-Tale Heart*.

Original horror narratives have also thrived on the British stage. Notable examples include Martin McDonagh's *The Pillowman* (2003), Jeremy Dyson and Andy Nyman's *Ghost Stories* (2010), Danny Robins's *2:22 – A Ghost Story* (2021), and John Donnelly's *Apex Predator* (2025).

Some theatres have made horror their speciality. In the US, dedicated horror companies have emerged, including San Francisco's Thrillpeddlers (founded in 1991), the Molotov Theatre Group in Washington, DC (2007), and Chicago's WildClaw Theatre (2008). These and other cult companies rediscovered the horror ensemble in the Grand Guignol tradition. Other traditional genres were also reinvented: off Broadway, illusionist Teller and magician Todd Robbins co-created *Play Dead* (2010), an homage to the traditional spook show, complete with astounding grisly illusions.

Adapting and responding

Horror performance culture has never been so ambitious or popular, with "haunted" attractions for Halloween and "edutainment" experiences such as the London Dungeon thrilling mass audiences. Stage adaptations of popular screen material has also widened audiences for horror in the theatre.

Disturbing brutality
One of the stories told in Martin McDonagh's darkly comic play *The Pillowman* mixes fairy-tale logic and brutal violence as a six-year-old girl is crucified by her parents.

The full picture
Audience members in white masks had to visit multiple floors for the full experience of Punchdrunk's *The Masque of the Red Death*.

Inside No. 9: Stage/Fright (2025), based on the BBC television series *Inside No. 9*, successfully exploited the eerie possibilities of live performance.

Several horror films have been adapted for the stage, including John Pielmeier's *The Exorcist* (2012), Imitating the Dog's *Night of the Living Dead – Remix* (2020), Jessica Andrews's *Saint Maud* (2024), and Levi Holloway's *Paranormal Activity* (2024), directed by Felix Barrett, best known for his work with immersive specialists Punchdrunk.

Immersive experiences

Punchdrunk's *The Masque of the Red Death* premiered in London in 2007, offering a dreamlike journey through Poe's Gothic universe by adapting and intertwining multiple tales across several floors of the venue. In *It Felt Like a Kiss* (Manchester, 2009), the company presented a stylized vision of mid-century America that gradually descended into a nightmare, paying tribute to horror cinema. The company again used elements of scare attractions, including claustrophobic spaces and a chainsaw-wielding actor who chased audience members. Similarly, Marisa Carnesky's *Ghost Train* (2004) and Dries Verhoeven's *Phobiarama* (2017) combined traditional fairground rides, live theatre, and illusions to thrilling effect.

Theatre has always been uniquely responsive to the moment – as an experience and as a genre. Horror on stage is more than fright for fright's sake: it can be deliriously escapist while also probing contemporary anxieties and deep-seated phobias. Additionally, it can reflect broader societal debates around truth, belief, and uncertainty, while using modern technology to fulfil an enduring desire for tales of terror.

> "... God is thrown away and humankind takes control."
>
> NICK DEAR, DIRECTOR OF *FRANKENSTEIN*, 2011

THE FOLK HORROR REVIVAL

FROM BRITISH ROOTS, THE FOLK HORROR GENRE HAS SPREAD AROUND THE WORLD, INSPIRED BY STRANGE MYTHS AND SINISTER ANCIENT TRADITIONS.

The term "folk horror" was first used by British director Piers Haggard to describe his 1971 film *The Blood on Satan's Claw*. Soon after, the name was applied to other British films with plots rooted in folkloric myths and history, such as Michael Reeves's *Witchfinder General* (1968) and Robin Hardy's *The Wicker Man* (1973). These films were later popularized by British writer and film-maker Adam Scovell as the "unholy trinity" of folk horror.

Critical and popular interest in these classics precipitated a new wave of folk horror films, beginning in 2009 with David Keating's *Wake Wood* and Ben Wheatley's *Kill List* (2011). In 2013, Wheatley's *A Field in England* broadened the scope of the genre by blending historical drama and occult themes with psychedelia, including

Pursuing purity
In *Midsommar*, a group of friends unwittingly join a pagan cult during the Swedish festival of Midsummer. The film includes rituals, human sacrifice, and Old Norse practices.

disorientating scenes that explored the effects of hallucinogens. In the late 2010s, further British efforts contributed to the revival, including *The Ritual* (David Bruckner, 2017), situated in a sinister Swedish wilderness, and Welsh director Gareth Evans's *Apostle* (2018), which follows a man attempting to rescue his sister from a cult on an idyllic island. The rural landscapes of the first wave of folk horror films remain important, with remote settings distancing the protagonists from the modern world and its moral codes. This fits with Adam Scovell's definition of the folk horror formula: isolation leads to alienation, leaving characters vulnerable to supernatural influences that culminate in a ritualistic summoning or event.

New takes on old tales
While traditional folk horror themes remain integral to the genre, film-makers have begun to interpret them in different ways. Some international films have moved away from isolated backdrops, instead exploring folkloric myths in contemporary urban landscapes. Jerome Pikwane's film *The Tokoloshe* (2018), for example, portrays a young hospital worker in Johannesburg pursued by the titular evil spirit, a figure in the folklore of the Zulu and Xhosa peoples. Guatemalan director Jayro Bustamante reinterprets a Latin American myth, the ancient legend of the weeping woman, in his critically acclaimed film *La Llorona* (2019).

Ritual burning
In the shocking finale of *The Wicker Man*, Sergeant Neil Howie is sacrificially burned inside a giant wicker statue by the residents of the fictitious Scottish island of Summerisle. He had been investigating the disappearance of a young girl.

Meanwhile, Robert Eggers's *The VVitch* (2015) and Ari Aster's *Midsommar* (2019) are both folk and "elevated" horror. Similarities between them and early iterations, such as *Witchfinder General* and *The Wicker Man*, show that the folk horror genre has come full circle.

> "It is the evil under the soil… the ghosts that haunt stones and patches of dark, lonely water."
>
> ADAM SCOVELL WRITING FOR THE BFI, 2016

Alone and afraid
Robert Eggers's period film *The VVitch* has many of the hallmarks of folk horror: a family living on the edge of civilization, fear of an unknown evil, and a final summoning.

Alien predator
Exploring themes of identity and humanity, A24's sci-fi horror *Under the Skin* (2013) depicts an alien disguised as a woman who preys on men.

A light in the dark
The psychological horror *The Lighthouse* (2019) is one of several critically acclaimed elevated horror films directed by Robert Eggers.

A24 AND "ELEVATED HORROR"

THE TERM "ELEVATED HORROR" GAINED TRACTION IN THE EARLY 21ST CENTURY, BUT SOME CONSIDER IT A SLUR — USED BY THOSE WHO THINK THE GENRE IS BENEATH THEM TO DESCRIBE THE HORROR FILMS THEY LIKE.

The notion of elevated horror is relatively new. With various alternative names, including post-horror, smart horror, and slow horror, the label emerged in the 2010s following the critical and commercial success of films such as David Robert Mitchell's *It Follows* (2014), Robert Eggers's *The VVitch* (2015), Jordan Peele's *Get Out* (2017), and Ari Aster's films *Hereditary* and *Midsommar*, released in 2018 and 2019, respectively. Produced by independent companies, these films were celebrated as marking a new age in horror cinema.

For those who see these films as taking horror cinema in a new direction, elevated horror is credited with shunning conventional tropes such as jump-scares and the shock value of gratuitous gore, instead evoking unease and an agonizing sense of dread in viewers through gradually intensifying suspense. The subgenre aligns itself with the art-horror tradition, where the cinematography, sound, and visuals are more sophisticated. It also tends to avoid archetypal horror figures, such as possessed individuals, serial killers, and supernatural entities and is more plot-driven than its predecessors, favouring morally ambiguous characters and complex narratives that may also offer critical commentary about social issues.

New approach

While not responsible for all of the films that have signalled this new era of horror, A24 has established itself as the go-to production and distribution company for elevated horror cinema. Founded in 2012, it has continuously promoted independent, alternative narrative-driven films and has become known for giving a platform to debut directors. Based in New York, it initially grabbed attention with 2015's *The VVitch*, Eggers's first feature film. Considered a linchpin of the folk horror revival and subtitled *A New-England Folktale*, the film transports viewers to 1630s New England, where an ostracized Puritan family finds itself plagued by signs of witchcraft.

Creeping paranoia
Released by A24 in 2017, *It Comes at Night* charts a family's survival amid a mysterious outbreak. This psychological horror film covers themes of paranoia and the fear of the unknown.

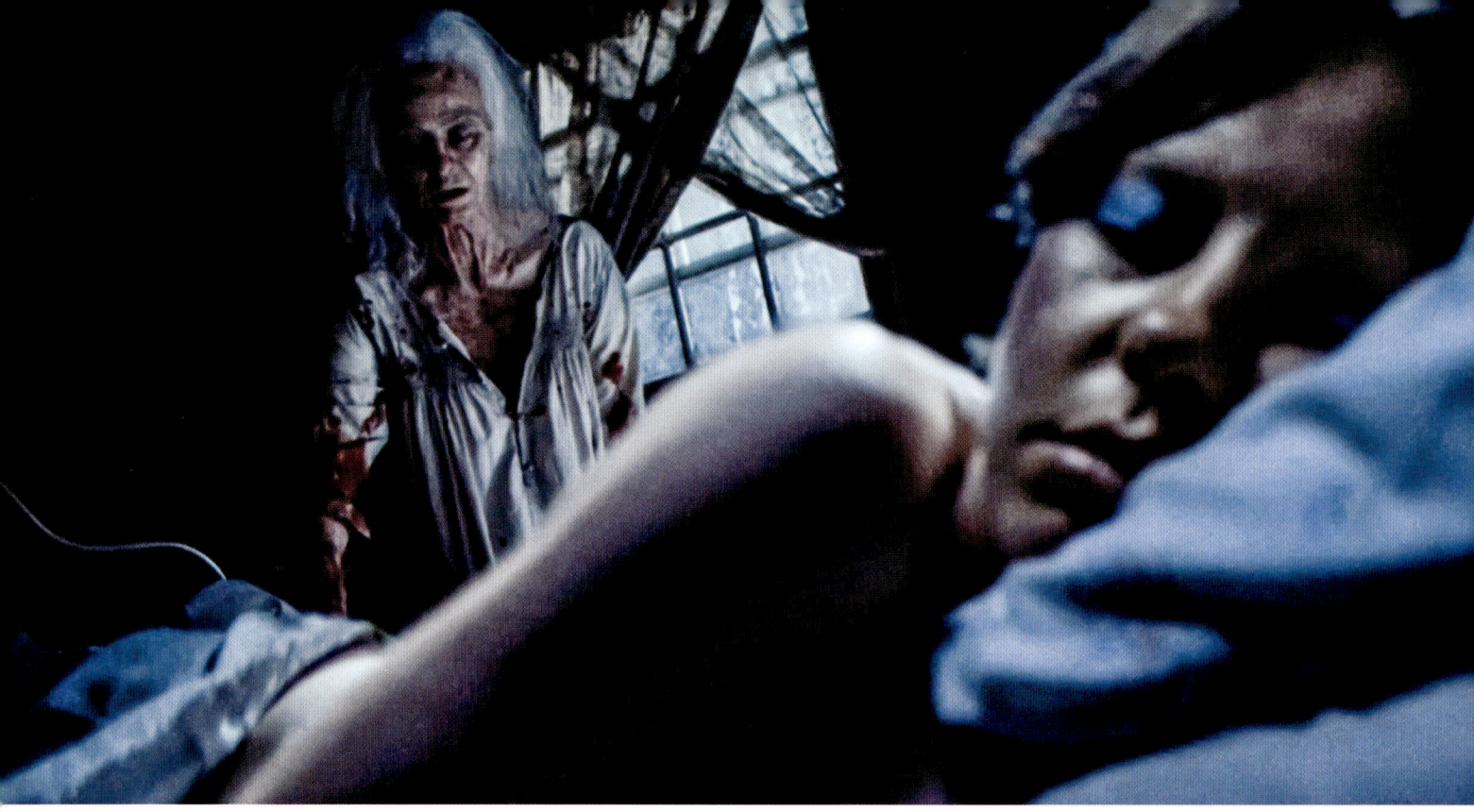

The X factor
In *X*, Mia Goth plays both Maxine Minx (foreground) and Pearl (behind) – roles she reprised in the next two films in Ti West's trilogy.

A24 later consolidated its image as a trusted source of high-quality horror through its consecutive collaborations with Aster, also a new director. While his films feature their fair share of violence, *Hereditary* and *Midsommar* both stand out for their slow pace and exploration of grief. In *Hereditary*, when a tragedy-stricken family endures another sudden loss, their struggles begin to manifest as supernatural and sinister events. In *Midsommar*, a grieving young woman joins her partner and his friends on a visit to a Swedish commune to celebrate the summer solstice, but they soon become embroiled in the villagers' disturbing practices. *Midsommar* is unusual in that most of the horrors take place in broad daylight. This subversion of the typical horror setting, paired with the cultish practices of the commune, make for a compelling and unsettling watch.

While not all of A24's releases fall into the elevated horror category, the arthouse has consistently sought out films that experiment with horror, including those combining typical horror tropes with other genres. Examples include Yorgos Lanthimos's absurdist psychological horror *The Killing of a Sacred Deer* (2017); Gaspar Noé's psychedelic horror *Climax* (2018); and Halina Reijn's *Bodies Bodies Bodies* (2022), which was marketed as a black comedy horror. Its list of films also includes Ti West's slasher horror series starring Mia Goth: *X* (2022), *Pearl* (2022), and *Maxxxine* (2024).

Other "elevated" producers

In addition to A24, other independent production houses have made a name for themselves as authorities in contemporary horror. Blumhouse Productions had long been a promoter of horror before it released *Get Out*, with franchises such as *Paranormal Activity* (from 2007), *Insidious*

> "It's a shame that the genre has such a bad reputation among the 'elite' [that] you need to distinguish whether a film is… an elevation of the genre."
>
> ARI ASTER, INTERVIEWED FOR *CULT MTL*, 2018

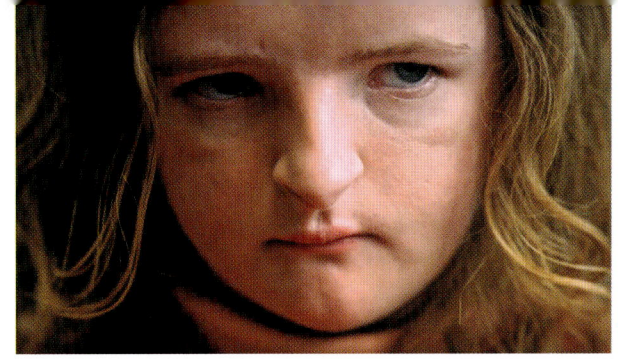

An unforgettable child
The quiet and haunting character of Charlie plays a pivotal and unforgettable part in Ari Aster's chilling 2018 film *Hereditary*.

(from 2010), and the latest *Halloween* films (2018–22). Another company that has gained a reputation for producing quality horror is Neon, which has been behind films such as Julia Ducournau's *Titane* (2021), and *Longlegs*, directed by Osgood Perkins (2024).

Produced by his own company Proximity Media, Ryan Coogler's 2025 film *Sinners* has also been tagged as elevated-horror, and received both critical acclaim and box-office success. Set in the Mississippi Delta in 1932 – deep into the Jim Crow era of racial segregation – the film follows a Black American community that is targeted by a small clan of vampires. Blending traditional vampire folklore with African traditions, *Sinners* was celebrated for its rich storytelling, social and historical commentary on cultural resistance (particularly in the face of racism), and slow-building tension – while still delivering the bloody elements expected in a horror film.

A divisive name

The rise of elevated horror has brought a new audience to the horror genre, but not everyone is in favour of this name. Critics of the label claim that its trademark qualities were already present in horror before the arrival of Eggers and Aster and the term dismisses the quality of the films that came before. They argue that "elevated horror" is a marketing tool that film companies use to attract a wider audience and increase their chances during the movie awards season – a strategy inspired by the success of *Get Out* at the 90th Academy Awards in 2018, where it won the Oscar for Best Original Screenplay.

Since *Get Out*, any horror films recognized by the Academy and other award bodies have automatically been labelled "elevated", as was the case with Coralie Fargeat's 2024 body horror film *The Substance*. The praise heaped on modern horror often overshadows the plaudits that classic horror films have received for direction, production, script, and performances. Many psychological horrors have won Academy Awards, including *Rosemary's Baby* (1968), *Misery* (1990), and *Black Swan* (2010; arguably one of the first of the modern elevated horror films), as did the supernatural horror classic *The Exorcist* (1973).

While elevated horror may not truly offer anything new to the genre in terms of style or content, it has brought greater recognition and respect to horror films. Better reviews lead to more viewers, which in turn means more artists have the opportunity to terrify audiences.

Bloodsucker blues
Ryan Coogler's genre-defying *Sinners* blends horror with Black history and blues music to create a unique vampire tale.

CONTEMPORARY BLACK HORROR

THIS SOCIALLY CONSCIOUS GENRE SHOWS THAT THE DEEPEST FEARS AND MOST THRILLING NARRATIVES CAN BE ROOTED IN THE REALITIES OF POWER, HISTORY, AND RACE.

Referencing trauma
In a nod to Black history, *Get Out*'s Chris picks the cotton stuffing out of his chair to distract himself from attempts to hypnotize him.

> "We've always loved horror, it's just that horror, unfortunately, hasn't always loved us."
>
> DOCUMENTARY FILM *HORROR NOIRE: A HISTORY OF BLACK HORROR*, 2019

Contemporary Black Horror

Inescapable suffering
In Nikyatu Jusu's psychological horror *Nanny*, Anna Diop plays a Senegalese immigrant haunted by a watery spirit, foreshadowing her son's drowning.

George A. Romero's *Night of the Living Dead* (1968) revolutionized horror cinema in more ways than one, though its impact was not immediately recognized. The film follows Ben (Duane Jones), a Black man fighting to survive the onslaught of all-white flesh-eating ghouls. In the end, Ben is mistaken for a ghoul and shot by a white posse, concluding a violent depiction of a fractured nation. It was a particularly apt story in the context of both the Civil Rights Movement of the 1950s and 60s and the Vietnam War (1955–75), and Jones's casting became a powerful racial symbol.

Reflecting on race

Nearly half a century later, Jordan Peele's *Get Out* (2017) reconfigured horror for a new era. Peele defines his film, like Romero's masterpiece, as a "social thriller" in which the divisions and injustices of society are the real antagonist. Chris (Daniel Kaluuya) visits the home of his white girlfriend Rose (Allison Williams), only to discover he is the target of a sinister plot. The liberal facade of her family masks a grotesque scheme: they abduct Black people to steal their bodies and exploit them as vessels for white consciousness.

Peele imagined audiences yelling the title at the screen, urging Chris to flee – an encapsulation of both horror's adrenaline-fuelled urgency and the film's complex social commentary. Chris's hypnosis-induced plunge into the "Sunken Place" – a dreamlike void where he remains aware but can only scream in silence – is a harrowing metaphor for Black marginalization. Race and racism underpin Peele's subsequent films: the doppelgänger movie *Us* (2019) and UFO thriller *Nope* (2022).

Peele's films are part of a broader wave of Black horror, or *horror noire* – a term coined by scholar and critic Robin Means Coleman in 2011 and popularized in the 2019 documentary *Horror Noire: A History of Black Horror*. Since *Get Out*, other films have developed the genre: *Nanny* (2022) includes supernatural elements in a tale of domestic servitude; *Candyman* (2021) reinvigorated a 1990s franchise; *Sinners* (2025) is a spooky portrayal of 1930s Mississippi; and *The Blackening* (2022) is a horror-comedy satirizing the genre's tropes. Meanwhile, films such as *His House* (2020), about refugees in the UK who fled the Sudanese Civil War, show that Black horror's resonance goes beyond its US origins.

A haunting home
Traumatized Sudanese refugees meet evil in an English town in Remi Weekes's widely acclaimed *His House*.

AFRO-GOTHIC

Black horror on film has a literary counterpart in Black Gothic and "Afro-Gothic", a term coined by British art historian Kobena Mercer. Such works, which include Toni Morrison's *Beloved* (1987), explore Gothic tropes – hauntings, the uncanny, trauma, monstrosity – in narratives shaped by the histories of the African diaspora. They interrogate Black displacement, colonial violence, and racial terror, using the Gothic to reclaim cultural memory, agency, and identity.

Nature fights back
Winston (actor Anthony Oseyemi) is overtaken by an ancient fungus in *Gaia* and decides to impale himself and die by suicide.

ECO-HORROR

CLIMATE CHANGE IS ONE OF THE MOST URGENT CONCERNS OF THE 21ST CENTURY. A NUMBER OF HORROR FILMS GRAPPLE WITH HUMANITY'S ROLE IN THIS CRISIS.

Since the mid-20th century, anxieties about the natural world have inspired a rich subgenre of horror cinema about real-world ecological crises. Termed eco-horror, it explores the devastating impact of climate change, industrial pollution, biodiversity loss, and genetic modification, as well as human arrogance in dismissing these problems.

The 1970s was a particularly fruitful decade for eco-horror, reflecting rising public awareness of environmental issues, such as oil spill pollution and the harmful effects of toxic chemicals. In George McCowan's *Frogs* (1972), for example, a wealthy family is attacked by frogs, snakes, and lizards during a party at their mansion — located in a swamp they have polluted with toxic pesticides. Richard Fleischer's *Soylent Green* (1973) also

Present Horrors

"Why do we despise the world that gave us life?"

THE LAST WINTER, 2006

warned against environmental degradation. Set in New York City in the future, it portrays a world in which overpopulation, climate change, pollution, and food shortages have led to dystopia.

Earth fights back

The 21st century (especially the 2020s) has seen a new rise in eco-horror. The exploitation of Earth's natural resources is a common theme, with several films focusing on oil drilling and fracking. In *The Feast* (2021), a Welsh folk horror film directed by Lee Haven Jones, an ancient earth spirit posing as a waitress at the dinner party of a wealthy oil family enacts nature's revenge in increasingly bloody ways. Other films in this vein include Larry Fessenden's *The Last Winter* (2006), about drilling at the Arctic National Wildlife Refuge, and John C. Lyons's *Unearth* (2020), in which fracking releases a toxic substance that causes horrifying physical and psychological transformations.

Natural evil
More than a scary setting, the forest is an active, hostile force that conjures physical and psychological horror in Ben Wheatley's *In the Earth*.

Films about ecological disasters often involve viruses or infections that humans are unable to cure. Ben Wheatley's *In the Earth* (2021), made during the Covid-19 outbreak, is set in a world suffering from an unspecified viral pandemic. Similarly, in Jaco Bouwer's *Gaia* (2021) an ancient fungus is infecting humans and reclaiming Earth. This South African horror film portrays nature not just as hostile, but as a superior force reasserting control over an exploitative species.

The same eco-horror trend has spawned television series such as *Fortitude* (UK; 2015), *The Rig* (UK; 2023), *The Rain* (Denmark; 2018), and *Snowpiercer* (US; 2020), based on the 2013 South Korean film about survival in a frozen world, the result of a failed geoengineering experiment intended to stop global warming.

Taking responsibility

Modern eco-horror films increasingly grapple with questions of blame. In Camille Griffin's *Silent Night* (2021), a terrifying portrayal of climate fatalism, friends gather for one last Christmas as a toxic cloud approaches Britain, with state-issued euthanasia pills at the ready. The film shows the characters enjoying their last moments while ignoring their impending fate. Meanwhile, Barry Levinson's found-footage eco-horror *The Bay* (2012) explores the disastrous consequences of environmental pollution in a small American town. In these films, nature's revenge is shown to be an inevitable consequence of humanity's treatment of Earth.

Facing catastrophe
At the end of *Silent Night*, Art (actor Roman Griffin Davis) wakes up beside his dead parents, who have taken euthanasia pills.

ONES TO READ

WHILE EVERY HORROR FAN HAS THEIR OWN LIST OF THE BEST BOOKS IN THE GENRE, THE TITLES HERE REPRESENT KEY MILESTONES IN HORROR FICTION, CHOSEN BECAUSE THEY INTRODUCED TERRIFYING TROPES, CREATED CHARACTER ARCHETYPES, OR RAISED IMPORTANT PHILOSOPHICAL QUESTIONS.

Frankenstein, Mary Shelley, 1818
Shelley's Gothic masterpiece was a trailblazer in science fiction. Victor Frankenstein creates life from death, unleashing a "Creature" who vows revenge against him and raising philosophical questions about man's right to play God in a major age of scientific progress.

Dracula, Bram Stoker, 1897
The seminal vampire novel, *Dracula* has influenced horror for over a century with adaptations across many mediums. This Victorian story captured fears around sexuality and modernity.

1984, George Orwell, 1949
Orwell's grim vision of control and surveillance in a totalitarian state – where even truth itself is manufactured – is a foundational work of political horror and dystopian fiction.

Lord of the Flies, William Golding, 1954
Golding's castaway tale sees a group of stranded schoolboys descend into savagery. A novel exploring humanity's inherent brutality, *Lord of the Flies* has influenced numerous survival horror and isolation narratives and other dystopian fiction.

The Midwich Cuckoos, John Wyndham, 1957
In this alien horror tale, the women of Midwich become pregnant after a blackout and bear strange children with psychic powers. Wyndham's novel has inspired other horror depictions of creepy, telepathic, and otherworldly children.

The Haunting of Hill House, Shirley Jackson, 1959
Jackson's atmospheric novel fuses ghost story and psychological breakdown, redefining haunted-house fiction with its deep character analysis and ambiguity as to whether its ghosts are real.

The Exorcist, William Peter Blatty, 1971
Blatty's tale of a young girl's possession elevated supernatural horror into mainstream respectability and was adapted into a horror blockbuster in 1973.

The Amityville Horror, Jay Anson, 1977
This recounts the supposedly true experiences of a family living in an infamous house where six people were murdered in 1974. The story's mix of horror and alleged fact ignited a wave of "based on real events" haunting tales.

Domain, James Herbert, 1984
In Herbert's grim, fast-paced story, survivors of nuclear devastation face swarms of mutant rats. The novel combines post-apocalyptic dread with creature terror.

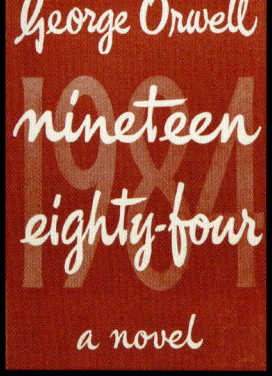
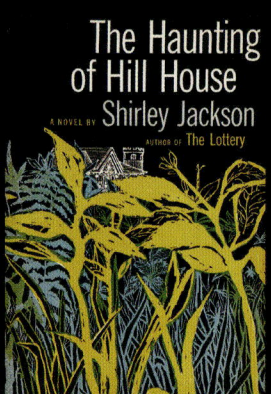

The Wasp Factory, Iain Banks, 1984
A teenager recounts bizarre rituals and past killings in Banks's darkly comic, grotesque novel. It pushed psychological horror to extremes, gaining cult status for its willingness to break taboos.

Blood Meridian, Cormac McCarthy, 1985
Known for its brutality, McCarthy's epic tale depicts a boy who joins scalp hunters in the 19th-century American West. It influenced popular horror novels with its relentless depictions of violence.

It, Stephen King, 1986
Many of Stephen King's novels have had a lasting influence on the horror genre – but this is especially true of *It*, in which childhood friends reunite against a shape-shifting evil. King's novel redefined the scope of small-town terror.

The Hellbound Heart, Clive Barker, 1986
Seeking forbidden pleasures, a man summons the Cenobites: beings who merge pain and ecstasy. Barker's novella inspired the film *Hellraiser* (1987) and presented a transgressive vision of desire and damnation.

The Silence of the Lambs, Thomas Harris, 1988
The novel that inspired the wildly popular film blends psychological horror and procedural suspense. It reshaped the portrayal of serial killers as charismatic, terrifying intellects.

Ring, Koji Suzuki, 1991
The influential *Ring* is a technological ghost story: a cursed videotape kills its viewers in seven days unless the mystery is solved. Suzuki's novel mixed urban legend with modern technological fears.

House of Leaves, Mark Z. Danielewski, 2000
A house impossibly larger on the inside than outside becomes an obsession documented in fragmented narratives. Danielewski's experimental novel blurred the lines between reality and fiction by using a "story within a story" structure. It gained cult status for its unsettling, disorienting form.

Let The Right One In, John Ajvide Lindqvist, 2004
This Swedish novel blends a tender coming-of-age story with brutal horror as a lonely boy befriends a centuries-old vampire. It subverts vampire myths and explores love, abuse, and alienation.

A Head Full of Ghosts, Paul Tremblay, 2015
Tremblay's novel revitalizes the exorcism trope for modern audiences, with a reality TV show capturing a teenage girl's supposed possession. This meta-horror critiques media exploitation, mental illness stigma, and our continuing hunger for the supernatural.

Mexican Gothic, Silvia Moreno-Garcia, 2020
A young woman investigates claims that her husband is trying to murder her in this modern Gothic tale set in 1950s Mexico. Praised for its critique of colonialism, racism, and eugenics, the novel weaves horror themes into Mexican history.

The Reformatory, Tananarive Due, 2023
Blending historical fiction and supernatural horror, Due's novel explores racial injustice in the 1950s US. Inspired by real events, it follows a young Black boy sent to a segregated reform school in Florida known for abusing and killing the children sent there.

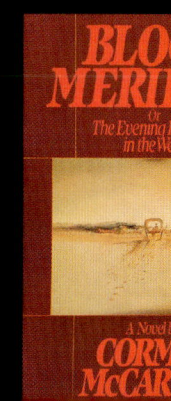
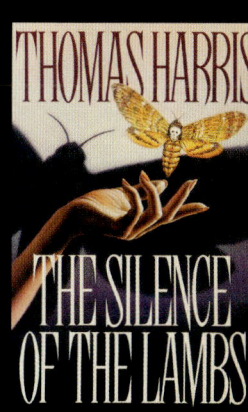
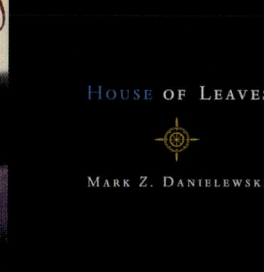

ONES TO WATCH

GRISLY MURDERS, FRIGHTFUL APPARITIONS, AND TORTURED SOULS ABOUND IN THESE HIGHLIGHTS OF THE HORROR GENRE. WHILE SUBJECTIVE, THIS IS A MUST-WATCH BUCKET LIST FOR ANY FAN INTERESTED IN THE HISTORY OF FEAR ON FILM.

Psycho (1960)
Alfred Hitchcock's film is memorable for more than its shower murder scene; its shocking twist redefined horror, introducing psychological terror and breaking taboos around violence and sexuality.

The Exorcist (1973)
In William Friedkin's X-rated horror film, a young girl is possessed by the Mesopotamian demon Pazuzu, prompting a battle between faith and evil. *The Exorcist* terrified global audiences, with people reportedly fainting in cinemas.

Don't Look Now (1973)
Nicolas Roeg's *Don't Look Now* is a chilling tale of grieving parents haunted by visions. Its disorientating editing techniques, reflecting their fractured mental state, helped elevate horror into arthouse territory.

The Texas Chain Saw Massacre (1974)
In an age when serial killer fears were high, Tobe Hooper's story of teens encountering a family of cannibals became a horror landmark. Its raw, documentary feel and nihilistic approach shaped slasher conventions and rural horror to come.

Jaws (1975)
A shark stalks a beach town in Steven Spielberg's horror hit known for its iconic score. *Jaws* was a major cultural moment, sometimes considered the first summer blockbuster.

The Hills Have Eyes (1977)
Wes Craven's savage survival tale, in which a suburban family encounters desert cannibals, is an allegory for the experience of American soldiers in the Vietnam War. His critique of civilization's thin veneer stands out as a highly influential backwoods horror film.

Dawn of the Dead (1978)
The second film in what was an influential trilogy, *Dawn of the Dead* traps survivors in a mall during a zombie outbreak. George A. Romero combined gore with anti-consumerist satire, establishing the zombie as a vehicle for social commentary.

Halloween (1978)
John Carpenter's film introduces masked killer Michael Myers, stalking babysitters on Halloween. Its suspenseful direction, music, and Final Girl archetype shaped modern slasher horror and inspired countless imitations.

The Exorcist

The Texas Chain Saw Massacre

Jaws

Alien (1979)
A spaceship's crew is hunted by an alien parasite in Ridley Scott's first film in this successful franchise. It fuses both sci-fi with body horror and creature horror with claustrophobic dread.

The Shining (1980)
Stanley Kubrick adapted Stephen King's novel into this landmark psychological horror film, known for its eerie and surreal depiction of one man's descent into madness at a haunted hotel. King himself was reportedly unhappy with Kubrick's adaptation.

Evil Dead (1981)
This cult classic by director Sam Raimi traps friends in a cabin besieged by demonic forces. Its fast-paced, brutal violence and extreme gore led to it being banned in several countries, but it eventually became a successful film franchise and television show.

The Thing (1982)
With groundbreaking special effects and a strong sense of paranoia, John Carpenter's depiction of Antarctic scientists facing a shape-shifting alien became a body horror classic. Many consider it an allegory for the Cold War.

Ring (1998)
Based on the 1991 novel, *Ring*'s haunting tale follows a cursed videotape that kills viewers in seven days. Hideo Nakata's film launched J-horror globally, emphasizing atmosphere, folklore, and psychological terror over gore. It was remade in the US in 2002 by Gore Verbinski.

Audition (1999)
Takashi Miike lures viewers into a slow-burn romance that spirals into horror as a lonely man stages fake film auditions to find a partner. Its shocking twist and gender commentary made it a milestone in psychological and body horror.

The Blair Witch Project (1999)
Daniel Myrick and Eduardo Sánchez used supposed "found footage" to tell a story of students lost in haunted woods. Its low-budget realism, viral marketing, and intoxicating sense of mystery initiated a new wave of found-footage horror.

American Psycho (2000)
An adaptation of Brett Easton Ellis's controversial novel (1991), Mary Harron's film is a satirical critique of 20th-century consumerism and the emptiness of Wall Street culture. Exposing a world of toxic masculinity, the film follows an investment banker who leads a double life as a serial killer.

The Grudge (2004)
This iconic film brought J-horror aesthetics and storytelling into the Western mainstream. Takashi Shimizu's American remake of his Japanese hit *Ju-On: The Grudge* (2002) features a curse spreading from a haunted house.

Sinister (2012)
Scott Derrickson's film follows a writer who uncovers cursed home videos tied to a pagan entity. Blending supernatural horror with true-crime dread, Sinister reinvigorated modern jump-scare horror.

Raw (2016)
Julia Ducournau sets women's experience centre stage in this body horror exploring themes of female sexuality and identity. A coming-of-age story, it follows a vegetarian veterinary student who develops an insatiable appetite for human flesh.

Us (2019)
In this critically acclaimed psychological horror, Jordan Peele explores societal divisions and challenges horror tropes with the story of a Black family haunted by their murderous doppelgängers.

The Shining   *The Blair Witch Project*   *Sinister*

GLOSSARY

Afterlife A place or realm where a person's spirit or soul is sometimes said to go after death; or what the spirit is thought to experience after death – often some kind of journey that culminates in a final judgement.

Apparition A ghost or similar supernatural phenomenon that appears, seemingly from nowhere. *See also* Ghost.

Archetype A pattern or model. In fiction, this could describe a recurring character type, such as a Final Girl, or trope. *See also* Final Girl and Trope.

Bestiary A work describing different creatures, whether natural or supernatural. Medieval bestiaries often contained both real and mythical creatures.

Bicephalic A term used to describe a person or animal with two heads. Similarly, tricephalic means having three heads, and polycephalic describes something with many heads.

Black horror; horror noir A genre of horror created by Black film-makers or for Black audiences, often including social commentary on Black experiences, Black history, and racism.

Blaxploitation A genre of low-budget independent films made in the 1970s, placing Black characters in familiar genres for the first time. The term "Blaxploitation" was coined by activist Junius Griffin to denounce these films, which perpetuated stereotypes about drugs, violence, and overt sexualization.

Body count The number of people killed in a film or by a particular villain.

Body horror A genre of horror that focuses on a mutation or transformation within the human body – often something biologically impossible. Plotlines commonly include grotesque mutilations, metamorphoses, or parasitic infestation.

Book of the Dead A book or roll of papyrus found in ancient Egyptian tombs that contains spells to guide the deceased in the afterlife. No two copies are the same.

Cannibalism The act of one creature eating other creatures of the same species. Horror often involves stories of human cannibalism: people eating other people.

Changeling A creature left behind as a replacement by supernatural beings, such as fairies or trolls, after they have stolen a human child.

Cosmic horror A horror genre that focuses on the fear of the vast and incomprehensible nature of the Universe, as well as humanity's insignificance within it. It is also known as Lovecraftian horror after writer H.P. Lovecraft, who explored this fear and referred to it as "cosmicism".

Cosmos A society's or religion's worldview; its conception of the Universe, its realms, deities, beginning, and end.

Coven A group or meeting of witches, who have joined together to perform rituals.

Cthulhu An ancient, cosmic entity created by H.P. Lovecraft, this octopus-headed, winged monster lies in a slumber, waiting to return and rule over Earth. He is part of a race of Great Old Ones within Lovecraft's universe.

Cult In religion, a group dedicated to the worship of one particular deity, person, or object. The term can also describe a film or other piece of fiction that has achieved unusual levels of devotion among fans. Cult horror films are those that are not well received initially but later develop small but passionate fanbases.

Curse A solemn utterance that is intended to invoke a supernatural power to inflict harm or punishment on someone or something else.

Dark fantasy A genre that combines elements of fantasy fiction with horror. It includes supernatural elements, such as magic and mythical creatures, but in disturbing, morally ambiguous, or twisted ways, often with unhappy endings.

Demon A wicked spirit able to access occult powers; demonology is the study of demons. In Judaism, Christianity, and Islam, the Devil is the most powerful demon.

Demoniac In early modern Europe, this term referred to a person possessed by a demon. *See also* Possession.

Demonology The study of demons and the branch of magic related to them; also a type of manual produced between the late 15th and late 18th centuries that classified and described demons or matters relating to witchcraft.

The Devil The most powerful demon in the Abrahamic religions (Judaism, Christianity, and Islam). He is variously known as Satan, Lucifer, and Iblis (in Islam). The Devil is believed to have dominion over other demons and evil spirits.

Disembodiment Separation from the body. It could describe a spirit leaving the physical body, or an unattached (living) body part, such as a disembodied hand.

Dismemberment The removal of a limb from a human or animal. Graphic depictions of dismemberment are portrayed in a number of horror films.

Doom painting A genre of medieval English wall painting depicting the Last Judgement.

Doppelgänger A double or exact duplicate of a person, but not simply a twin. In Gothic and horror fiction, a doppelgänger is often a ghostly or malevolent being, or a harbinger of doom.

Eco-horror A genre of horror focusing on fears of the natural world and emphasizing the need for humans to respect nature. It often serves as commentary on the ecological damage that humanity has done and presents nature as fighting back or seeking revenge against humankind.

Evocation The calling or summoning of a spirit, demon, or other supernatural entity to a location. Often used interchangeably with the term "invocation". *See also* Invocation.

Existentialism A philosophy centred on the belief that humans must take responsibility for creating a meaningful life through their own actions and choices. Many horror films tackle some form of existential dread – a deep sense of fear or anxiety over the meaning and purpose of life, death, and one's place in the Universe.

Exorcism The process of forcing a spirit to leave a person or place by using prayers or magic. Exorcism rituals are used to drive out demons or spirits. *See also* Possession.

Faustian Relating to the story of Faust, who made a deal with the Devil to sell his soul in exchange for knowledge. The term "Faustian bargain" describes any similar arrangement whereby something morally valuable is sacrificed as a result of greed or ambition.

Feminist horror A genre that gives voice to female experience by subverting traditional horror tropes. It often features women in positions of power and agency.

Final Girl A female archetype in slasher films. The Final Girl is a teenager who is usually cleverer and less promiscuous than her peers, allowing her to survive the killer. Modern slasher films often subvert this trope or comment on its misogynistic implications. *See also* Slasher.

Folk horror A subgenre of horror based on folklore, often including rural isolation and pagan or traditional rituals. First used by British director Piers Haggard in the 1970s, the term was applied to films about British mythology and occult history, including historical witch trials. New interest in folk horror in the 21st century has generated films exploring the folklore of other parts of the world.

Found-footage horror A film genre that appears to contain real events, from home videos, CCTV, or documentary footage. *The Blair Witch Project* (1999), which claims to be documentary footage captured by some missing college students, is a pioneering example of the genre.

Friday the 13th A date combination associated with bad luck, likely stemming from a mixture of ancient mythology and pagan and Christian ideas. Its association with horror was cemented by Sean S. Cunningham's 1980 slasher film *Friday the 13th* and its sequels.

Ghost Also known as a spectre, phantom, or apparition; the spirit of a dead person (or animal); often bodiless, with varying ability to be seen or heard by the living or to manipulate objects. Ghosts are often thought to be the spirits of those unable to reach the afterlife due to unfinished business, punishment for misdeeds in life, or other reasons, and may be tied to a person, object, or place.

Ghoul Originally from Arabic mythology, a shape-shifting spirit that lingers in graveyards and eats human flesh.

Giallo An Italian thriller/horror genre that emerged in the 1960s, featuring stylized violence, psychological tension, murder investigations, and gratuitous sex scenes.

Golem A creature from Jewish folklore; typically a clay figure that has been brought to life by a ritual.

Gore In horror, this term applies to scenes with copious amounts of blood as a result of violence or injury.

Gothic A genre of art and literature that flourished from the 1790s onwards, blending supernatural and romantic elements. Typical Gothic themes include damsels in distress, vengeful ghosts, and grand, imposing settings, such as castles and abbeys, often situated in remote or exotic locations.

Grimoire A term used from the 18th century onwards to refer to a handbook of magic, often dating from the medieval period. Also used by Wiccans to refer to the books used by individual practitioners to record their spells and rituals.

Gui Ghosts in the Chinese tradition. Usually translated as "ghost", the term can include all supernatural beings.

Halloween A festival on 31 October, the eve of All Saints' Day, when the divide between the human and spirit worlds is believed to be thinnest, allowing ghosts to roam freely. *See also* Samhain.

Haunting The appearance of a ghost, usually in such a way that causes harm or disturbance to the living.

Hedonistic reversal A psychological phenomenon in which pleasure is derived from experiences that inspire feelings of pain, fear, or suffering.

Hell A realm of the afterlife designated for the punishment of wicked souls.

Home invasion In horror, a narrative in which intruders enter the protagonists' home, violating their sense of security and often tormenting or trapping them. Such stories play on the fear of a safe space becoming compromised.

Hungry ghost In Buddhism and Chinese folk religion, a spirit damned to an eternity of insatiable hunger, due either to their actions in life or their families' failure to perform the correct funeral rites.

Incantation Words that are believed to have a magical effect when spoken or sung.

Incubus A type of male demon believed to have sexual intercourse with sleeping women. *See also* Succubus.

Invocation Technically, drawing a spirit into one's body. Often used interchangeably with "evocation". *See also* Evocation.

J-horror Japanese horror films. The term refers to movies from the 1980s onwards, which tend to focus on psychological horror, hauntings, and atmosphere over gore. *See also* K-horror.

Jinn In Arabic mythology, invisible beings that are thought to be able to grant wishes. In the Islamic faith, *jinn* are believed to be capable of evil, just as humans are, because they have free will. The Arabic *jinni* (the singular form of *jinn*) became the English term "genie".

Jump scare A sudden appearance in a film – often of a killer or creature – that makes the audience literally jump in fright.

Kabbalah The ancient Jewish practice of the mystical interpretation of the Tanakh (Hebrew Bible), first by word of mouth and then by secret codes. Kabbalah includes beliefs in the possibility of being possessed by evil spirits such as *dybbuks* and *ibburs*.

Kabuki A classic form of Japanese theatre dating from the 17th century, known for its flamboyant make-up and costumes and dramatic stories.

Kaidan A genre of Japanese ghost stories, based on ancient Buddhist tales, which evolved during Japan's Edo period.

Kaiju Large monsters in Japanese fiction. The term originally described strange mythical creatures in folklore and literature but now more commonly refers to gigantic beasts such as Godzilla.

K-horror The South Korean equivalent of the label J-horror. *See also* J-horror.

Liminal In-between. A liminal space, for example, is transient – a threshold between one place and another.

Mantra A repeated statement, sound, or word, often used in Hindu and Buddhist meditation practice to help people to focus.

Mesopotamia The ancient West Asian region between the rivers Tigris and Euphrates, mostly within the present-day borders of Iraq. Known as the cradle of civilization, Mesopotamia is where ancient societies such as the Akkadians, Babylonians, and Sumerians flourished.

Monster A strange or terrifying creature; also used to describe humans who act in cruel or inhumane ways. Monster films usually pit a protagonist or group of humans against a being that wants to attack or exterminate them. The term "monster of the week", coined by writers on *The Outer Limits* (1963), describes a TV show that introduces a new monster story in each episode, such as *The X-Files* or *Doctor Who*.

Mummification The process of preparing a corpse to prevent it from decomposing. Ancient Egyptians famously mummified the dead by removing their organs, drying the body, and wrapping it in linen to preserve it for the afterlife. The mummy sometimes appears as an undead monster in horror.

Mysticism The belief that life has a hidden meaning or that each person can unite with a deity or absolute truth through deep contemplation of spiritual knowledge. Also used in a more general sense to mean belief in religion, spirituality, or the occult.

Necromancy The branch of magic that concerns communication with people who have died, originally as a way of acquiring knowledge from them. In the late medieval era, it came to mean the conjuring of demons to harness their magical powers.

Netherworld The realm of the dead. *See also* Underworld.

Nihilism A philosophy that life is inherently meaningless. Nihilistic horror explores the deep fear and hopelessness in the belief that existence is pointless and human life has no purpose.

Noir; film noir A black-and-white cinematic style of the 1940s and 50s. Usually intricate crime stories that feature cynical anti-heroes and femmes fatales.

Obsession An external attack on a person by an aggressive spirit, or when a demon takes over a person's senses through dreams or apparitions. *See also* Possession.

Occult Secret mystical, supernatural, or magical powers, practices, or phenomena.

Omen An event regarded as a portent, or sign, of good or evil.

Otherworld Another realm of existence, often an afterlife – as in the Hindu faith. In Celtic mythology, the otherworld is the domain of spirits, gods, and other supernatural beings.

Paganism Polytheistic religious beliefs and practices with origins in the ancient world. The term "pagan" has sometimes been used as a pejorative or to describe any belief system outside the major world religions.

Paranormal Something that cannot be explained by our existing knowledge of science and the natural world.

Penny dreadful; penny blood A cheap 19th-century British publication that featured sensational stories, often of a violent or supernatural nature.

Poltergeist A "noisy ghost", a type of spirit that can manipulate objects.

Possession The invasion of a person's consciousness by a spirit or demon that may control their movements, speech, and actions. The human body serves as a host, or vessel. In some cultures, possession is an honour that people actively seek to achieve.

Post-apocalyptic horror A genre that depicts the horrors of life after the collapse of civilization, whether due to war, disaster, or environmental catastrophe. Common tropes in this genre include the arrival of terrifying monsters and the spread of fatal or zombifying viruses. *See also* Zombie.

Primordial Something that has existed since the earliest stages of time or creation.

Pulp (fiction) A literary genre of fast-paced, sensational stories published cheaply, in either magazines or books. The name derives from the low-quality paper on which they were printed.

Purgatory In the Catholic faith, a place between Heaven and Hell where sinners atone for their sins. Souls in Purgatory must undergo purification to enter Heaven.

Reanimation Reviving the dead or restoring life through supernatural or scientific means. Often, "reanimation" is used rather than "resurrection" to denote that the being lacks self-determination. *See also* Resurrection.

Recreational fear A term used to describe the pursuit of frightening experiences in safe, controlled settings – such as horror films, theme parks, or haunted houses – for the purpose of enjoyment.

Reincarnation The rebirth of a soul in another body or life form after death. Buddhism and Hinduism include the concept of continual reincarnation, based on a person's actions in each life, until they earn liberation from the cycle.

Resurrection When a person (or creature) comes back from the dead. In Christianity, the Resurrection is the return of Jesus Christ to the living, which is said to have occurred three days after his Crucifixion.

Revenant A corpse that comes back from the dead, from the French word *revenir* ("to return"). See also Zombie.

Ritual A set of fixed actions and sometimes words performed regularly, especially as part of a ceremony.

Romantic movement An art movement that flourished towards the end of the 18th century, emphasizing emotion, nature, and individual expression over the rationalism and order that characterized the preceding Enlightenment era. The Romantics explored folk traditions and mythology and revisited ancient stories, often with dark or disturbing themes. Nature was depicted as sublime: beautiful, but vast and awe-inspiring.

Samhain; also called Samhuinn (Scots) or Sauin (Manx) The ancient Celtic festival of the dead, celebrated halfway between the autumn equinox and winter solstice with bonfires and animal sacrifices. Its traditions influenced Halloween.

Seer A person who claims to be able to predict what will happen in the future.

Shaman Someone believed to have special powers to communicate with good and evil spirits. They may use this ability to gain insight into past and future events.

Shape-shifter A person or thing with the apparent ability to change from one form into another. See also Were-creature.

Slasher A genre of horror film in which a killer (usually masked) stalks and murders a group of teenagers. These victims are often portrayed as sexually promiscuous, while the killer is survived by one virtuous female. See also Final Girl.

Solstice Marking the longest and shortest days of the year (the summer and winter solstices, respectively) this is the time when the Sun is directly above the furthest point north or the furthest point south of the equator.

Soul A person's innermost essence or "spirit", often associated with morality or purity. Selling the soul, or destroying it in some way, is a common horror trope.

Spirit A non-physical entity, sometimes called a soul or spark. Many cultures believe that the spirit is the psychic form of a person that lives on after the body dies.

Splatter A genre of horror film that features extreme gore and violence (its literary equivalent is splatterpunk). See also Gore.

Subconscious The level of human thought that is not conscious or deliberate but still influences thought and feelings. The term is sometimes used interchangeably with what Sigmund Freud called the unconscious mind. See also Unconscious.

Succubus A female demon believed to have sexual intercourse with men while they are sleeping. See also Incubus.

Summoning Calling something forth from one place into another; often the calling of a spirit to aid a magical practitioner.

Supernatural A phenomenon that cannot be explained by science or nature; attributed to forces such as gods, spirits, or magic.

Surrealism An art movement that emerged in the 1920s, in the aftermath of World War I. Surrealist art represents the unconscious mind, often manifested in unsettling or frightening images.

Therianthrope An animal/human hybrid. The term is used to describe figures in Neolithic art – possibly representations of shamans – that have both human and animal features. It also describes supernatural creatures with both human and animal forms. See also Were-creature.

Torture porn A genre of 21st-century horror films featuring extreme violence, such as the *Saw* and *Hostel* franchises, often commenting on issues such as American imperialism and capitalism. The term was coined by David Edelstein in his 2006 criticism of the genre in *New York* magazine.

Trope A recurring theme, idea, storyline, or character type within a specific genre.

Uncanny Something that has the qualities of being both familiar and unfamiliar, causing a sense of unease.

Unconscious Described by Sigmund Freud as the part of the human psyche that contains memories, suppressed feelings, conflicts, and desires. It affects conscious thoughts and behaviour. See also Subconscious.

Undead Deceased but animated and able to mimic some functions of life. Creatures such as vampires and zombies fall into this category.

Underworld The mythical realm of the dead; in many cultures, it is often imagined as being underground.

Vampire A type of undead mythological creature believed to drink the blood of the living. Between the 18th and early 19th centuries, vampire scares (linked to outbreaks of tuberculosis) in Eastern Europe and some northeastern American states resulted in people digging up the graves of the dead to identify potential vampires.

Weird fiction A genre that blends horror, fantasy, and the supernatural. The work of H.P. Lovecraft falls into this category. Since the 1990s, another genre called new weird has emerged. This subverts weird fiction tropes to address contemporary issues such as race, gender, and class.

Were-creature These are supernatural creatures that can shift between human and animal form, such as a werewolf. See also Shape-shifter.

Wild Hunt A horde of ghosts and other terrifying spirits that in some cultures are said to ride on horseback across the skies, often during midwinter.

Witch Someone believed to have or harness malign magical powers. Witches are often thought to have made a pact with the Devil and to have a "familiar" – a spirit helper in the form of a small, domestic animal.

Yūrei Japanese ghosts, unable to pass from the world of the living to the afterlife. The term literally means "dark soul".

Zombie A reanimated corpse. The modern idea of the zombie derives from the Haitian *zonbi* – a mindless corpse that must do the bidding of its maker. See also Revenant.

INDEX

Page numbers in **bold** refer to main entries.

9/11 284
28 Days Later 237, 281
1984 (Orwell) 300
2001: A Space Odyssey 119

A

À l'intérieur 287
A24 **292–5**
Aaahh!!! Real Monster (TV show) 239
Abbott and Costello Meet Dr Jekyll and Mr Hyde 221
Abbott and Costello Meet Frankenstein 209, 220
Abbott and Costello Meet The Invisible Man 221
Abbott and Costello Meet The Killer, Boris Karloff 220–21
Abbott and Costello Meet The Mummy 221
Abby 249
abiku 56, 57
abortion 250, 251
Abu Ghraib scandal 284
Academy Awards 256, 271, 295
Adam and Eve 69, 93, 114
Addams Family, The 239
adrenaline/adrenaline junkies 185, 186
Adventures Into The Unknown (comic book) 214, 215
adze 56
Aeacus 23
Aeneid (Virgil) 44
Aerial demons 121
Aeschylus 35
Africa
  Afro-Gothic **297**
  mythology **56–7**
afterlife
  Aztec and Inca view 102, 103
  Celtic view 42
  Chinese view 55
  Daoist view 65
  Egyptian view **22–3**, 25
  Greek view **23**, 60
  Maya view 53
  medieval European view 98
  Mesopotamian view **20–21**
  prehistoric view 14, 15
  Roman view 44, 60
Agamemnon (Aeschylus) 35
Agrippa, Heinrich Cornelius 121
aitu 39
Akkadians 18
Albertus Magnus 93, 135
alchemy 192
Alcott, Louisa May 154
Alecto 33
Alfred Hitchcock Presents (TV series) 228
Algonquian-speaking peoples 82
Alhazred, Ahmed 207
Alien 206, 238, 245, 257, **264–5**, 303
alien possession 245
All Hallows' Eve 175
All Saints' Day 175
All Souls' Day 175
allegories 28, 90, 93, 96, 271, 275
Allen, Grant 139

Amazon River 83
Amer 234
America, colonial **126–9**
American Civil War 153, 154, 155
American Gothic **152–5**
American Horror Story (TV show) 213
American Mary 246
American Psycho 303
American Sign Language 213
American Werewolf in London, An 221
Amicus 215
Amirpour, Ana Lily 252–3
Amityville Horror, The (Anson/film) 255, 300
Ammit (Ammut) 23, 24, 25
amulets 19, 24, 26, 56
amygdala 184, 185
ancestor spirits 15, 39
ancestor worship 44, 54, 57
Andean Gothic 181
Andrews, Jessica 289
Angel Heart 123
animals
  fear of 183
  hunter-gatherers and 17
Ankou 42
Annihilation (VanderMeer/film) 206, 274
Anson, Jay 300
Antichrist, The 255
Anubis 23
Anzû 18–19
apocalypse 60, 75, 146, 218, 281
Apocalypse of Peter 60
Apophis (Apep) 24
Apostle 291
Appointment with Fear (radio show) 211
Aqueous demons 121
Aquinas, Thomas 135
Arapaho people 83
Arbo, Peter Nicolai 78–9
Arbuda (hell of blisters) 41
Are You Afraid of the Dark? (TV show) 239
Argento, Dario 232–3, 258, 268
Arkham House 194, 195
Armfield, Julia 275
arms race 224
Aronofsky, Darren 160, 231
art
  Bosch **114–15**
  Edo ghost art **172–3**
  European Romantic movement **146–7**
  horror in modern **216–17**
  horror in Surrealist **218–19**
  Japanese Edo period 170, 172–3
  medieval church 61
  prehistoric 14, 16–17
Arthur, King/Arthurian legends **88–9**
artificial intelligence 119
Asbjørnsen, Peter Christen 78
asfodius 93
Asgard, ride of (*Asgardsreien*) 78–9
Asian horror renaissance **268–71**
ašipu 19
Asmodeus 121
association, fear and 183, 185
Assyrians 18
Astaroth 135

Aster, Ari 291, 292, 294, 295
asuras 26, 27
Athena 31, 36
Atreus 47
audio horror 211
Audition 269, 303
Austen, Jane 151
Australian horror **176–7**
Austronesian expansion 38
Avici (uninterrupted hell) 41
Awar 69
Aykroyd, Dan 221
Aztecs **102–3**, 110

B

Ba'al Shem, Rabbi Elijah 118
Baba Yaga 50
babies, changelings **48–9**
Babylonians 18
Bacchae, The (Euripides) 33
Bacon, Francis 216–17
Bag an Noz 42
Baise-Moi 286
Baker, Rick 221
bakwas 83
Balagueró, Jaume 268
Baldr 75
Balor 43
Banks, Iain 301
banquets, Roman 44
Bantu people 57
Bar Yochnei 95
barbarism 81
Bardugo, Leigh 198
Barker, Clive 123, 198, 266, 267, 301
Baron Samedi 138
Barrett, Felix 289
Barron, Laird 274
Barrow, Gertrude *see* Stevens, Francis
Barrymore, Drew 221
basilisks 92
Basotho people 57
Báthory, Elizabeth 142
Battle Royale 269
Bava, Lamberto 268
Bava, Mario 232, 233, 268
Bay of Blood, A 232, 233
Bay, The 299
Baynton, Barbara 176
Bayona, J.A. 276
Bazterrica, Agustina 276
Bean, Sawney **163**
bears 75
Beast from 20,000 Fathoms, The (Lourie) 224
Beelzebub 121
Before I Wake 125
Behemoth 94–5
Bekker, Balthasar 113
Belial 121
Bellmer, Hans 201
Beloved (Morrison) 154, 297
Belphegor 121
Benchley, Peter 256
Benét, Stephen Vincent 123
Beowulf **80–81**
"Berenice" (Poe) 154
Bergerac, Cyrano de **158**
Berlioz, Hector 123
bestiaries, medieval **90–93**

Beyond the Door 255
bhutas 27
Bible
  on demons 121
  on exorcism 85
Bidhukh 69
Bierce, Ambrose 154
bies 50
Binsfield, Peter 121
biology of fear 183, 185
BioShock (game) 281
Bird with the Crystal Plumage, The 232–3, 258
birth defects 49
"Black Cat, The" (Poe) 156
Black Cauldron, The 238
Black Christmas (1974/2019) 251, 260
Black Death 100, **101**
Black Gothic 154–5, 297
Black horror 249, 263, 274, **296–7**
Black Sunday 11
Black Swan 160, 231, 295
Blackening, The 297
Blackenstein 249
Blacula **248–9**
Blagojević, Petar 142
Blair Witch Project 282–3, 303
Blake, William 98–9, 124, 146
Blank, Jamie 263
Blatty, William Peter 242, 300
blaxploitation cinema 249
Bleak House (Dickens) 164
Bloch, Robert 195
Blood and Black Lace 232
Blood Feast 232, 286
Blood Meridian (McCarthy) 301
Blood of Dracula 253
Blood on Satan's Claw, The 290
bloodletting 102
Blumhouse Productions 294–5
board games 281
Boccacio, Giovanni 191
Bodies Bodies Bodies 263, 294
Bodin, Jean 116
Body Double 233
body horror 9, 213, **244–5**, 264, 272, 287
  feminist **246–7**, 252
  new wave 267
Boguet, Henri 117
Bolon Ti' K'uh 53
Bombal, María Luisa 181
Bong, Joon-ho 270, 271
bonnacon 91
Books of Blood (Barker) 267
Books of Chilam Balam 53
boruta 50
Bosch, Hieronymus **114–15**
Bouwer, Jaco 299
Boyle, Danny 237
Bradbury, Ray 198, 199
brain, and fear 184, 185
Bram Stoker's Dracula 205
Branagh, Kenneth 159
Bride of Frankenstein 11
Britain
  birth of Gothic literature **148–51**
  horror in Arthurian legends **88–9**
  new wave horror **266–7**
  penny dreadfuls **162–3**
  revenge tragedies **130–31**
  terrors of the night **124–5**
  Victorian Gothic **164–7**

Index

British Board of Film Censors 212
Brontë, Charlotte 166
Brood, The 160, 245
Brooks, Mel 221
Brophy, Philip 244
Brown, Charles Brockden 153, 154
Brown, Mercy 143
Brown, Rita Mae 251
Browning, Tod 208, 212
Bruckner, David 291
Brueghel, Peter the Younger 86
Buddhism
    and Chinese traditional beliefs 55
    ghosts 27, 64–5
    influence via Silk Road 64–5, 67
    painted temples 64, 65–6
    realms of hell **40–41**
Buffalo Evening News, The 214
Bundle, Seth 245
Buñuel, Luis 218
Bunyip 176
Burgot, Pierre 116
burial practices
    burial alive 49
    Daoist 65
    prehistoric **14–15**
    Roman 44
Bush Studies (Baynton) 176
Bustamante, Jayro 291
Bustillo, Alexandre 287
Butler, Octavia E. 155, 179
Byron, Lord 158

C

Cabin in the Woods 10
Cabinet of Dr Caligari, The 10, **202–3**, 208, 230
Caché 286
Cain 80, 81
Cain, Ethel 275–6
Call of Cthulhu (RPG) 281
"Call of Cthulhu, The" (Lovecraft) 206–7, 281
Calmet, Augustin 143
cameras, hand-held 282
Campbell, Ramsey 207, 267
Candomblé 84
Candyman 267, 297
Cannibal Holocaust 282
cannibalism 14, 27, 47, 81, 82, 130, 138, 153, 246
Carmilla (Le Fanu) 166, 179, 253, 275
Carnesky, Marisa 289
Carpenter, John 206, 245, 260, 302, 303
Carrie 11, 227, 242–3, 252
Carroll, Lewis 267
cartoons 238
"Casting the Runes" (James) 192
Castle of Otranto, The (Walpole) 148–50
castles, in Gothic literature 145, 150
Cat o' Nine Tails, The 233, 258
Çatalhöyük 15
cathedrals, in Gothic literature 144–5
Catholicism
    exorcist ritual 85
    Protestant view of 145
cauac 53
Caucasian Eagle 33
cautionary tales 10, 73, 82, 83, 176, 238
Cave of the Hands (Argentina) 17
cefusas 92–3
celestial dog 72
celestial fox 72
Celts
    death omens **42–3**
    folklore 174–5
    mythology 42–3, 49
censorship 85, 212, 239, 266
Cerberus 32, 33
čert 50

Certain Dark Things (Moreno-Garcia) 198
Cervera, Garza 253
Ceto 31
Chambers, Robert W. 195
Chandler, Raymond 232
change, horror as a catalyst for 28
changelings **48–9**
Chanthaly 271
chaos
    Egyptian fear of 24
    golems 118
    in Hinduism 26
    in Kabbalah 94
Chapman Brothers 217
Charles Island (Connecticut) 126
Charles V, Emperor 106
Charybdis 30
Chestnutt, Charles W. 154–5
Cheyenne people 83
children
    changelings **48–9**
    child development 183
    childhood fears 200
    infant deaths 56
    moral and spiritual decay 166
    unbaptized 77
Children Shouldn't Play with Dead Things 237
Child's Play 263
Chimaera 32
chimidoro-e (bloody pictures) 172
China
    evil beings in Chinese tradition **54–5**
    ghostly texts 67
Choephori, The (Aeschylus) 35
chort (czort) 50
Chrétien de Troyes 89
Christianity
    and traditional African beliefs 57
    bestiaries 90
    concepts of hell 9
    Day of Judgement 60
    demonic possession and exorcism **84–5**
    last judgement 62–3, 114–15
    monsters with positive associations 93
    witchcraft 104–5, 106
Christie, Agatha 232
Chrstensen. Benjamin 105
churel 67
Cihuacoatl 110
Circe 30
Circles of Hell, Dante's 60, 96
Citadel of Fear, The (Stevens) 198
Civil Rights movement 236, 249, 297
Clark, Bob 251
Clark, P. Djèlí 274
Clarke, Marcus 176
Clasen, Mathias 186
climate change 10, 298, 299
Climax 287, 294
Climax! (TV series) 228
Clover, Carol J. 262
Cloverfield 282
Clytemnestra 33, 35
Coen, Joel 132
Colchian dragon 32
Coleman, Robin Means 297
Collin de Plancy, Jacques 121
Collins, Wilkie 164–5, 166
Colombiers, Sister de 135
colonialism 126–9, 180
Colored Sculpture (Wolfson) 217
comedy horror 10, 209, **220–21**, 237
comic books, horror 89, **214–15**
Comics Code 214–15
Compendium Maleficarum 107
confessions, false 129
Confucius/Confucianism 55, 65
Conjure Woman, The (Chestnutt) 155
Conjuring, The 271

consecrated host 86
consumerism 237
Coogler, Ryan 295
Coppola, Francis Ford 205
Coraline 239
corpses
    reanimation of 25
    restless 75
Cortés, Hernán 110
cortisol 185
cosmic horror **194–5**, 206
Cottet, Hélène 234
Countdown Vampires (game) 280
Crafts, Hannah 154
Craigie, Sir William Alexander 78
Crain, William 249
Crash 245
Craven, Wes 221, 263, 302
Crawls 257
creation myths 18, 53, 102
Creature from the Black Lagoon 209, 223
Creature Walks Amongst Us, The 209
Creed, Barbara 251
Creepshow 215
creepypasta 271
Crew, The (comic book) 215
Crichton, Michael 225
crocodilians 53
Cronenberg, David 160, 225, 245, 287
Crucible, The (Miller) 129
Cruising 233
Cthulhu 194, 206–7
Cú Chulainn 42
Cumberbatch, Benedict 288
Cunningham, Sean S. 233, 262
Curry, Tim 221
Curse of Frankenstein, The 222
Curse of the Werewolf, The 223
curses 56
Cushing, Peter 222–3
cyclopes 31

D

Daddy Longlegs Of The Evening – Hope! (Dalí) 218–19
Daemonologie (James I) 107, 128, 132
Dafoe, William 205
Dahl, Johan Christian 146
Daleks 229
Dalí, Salvador 200, 218–19
damnation, eternal **60–61**
Dance of Death (*Danse Macabre*) **100–101**
Dance of Death (Holbein) 101
Dance of the Vampires 221
Dancing Plague 87
Danielewski, Mark 145, 301
Dans Ma Peau 245, 287
Danse Macabre (King) 243
Dante Alighieri 60, **96–9**
Dante, Joe 221
Daoism 64, 65
Dark Carnival (Bradbury) 199
dark fantasy **198–9**, 267
Dark Tower, The (King) 198
Dark Water (Suzuki/film) 269
Darwin, Charles 17, 183
Daughter of Doctor Moreau, The (Moreno-Garcia) 276
Dawn of the Dead 237, 302
Day of Judgement 60
Day of the Animals 257
De Nugis Curialium (Map) 87
De Palma, Brian 233, 242
Dead of Night (TV series) 228
Dead of Winter (board game) 281
Dead Space (game) 281
Deafula 213
Dear, Nick 288, 289
Dearest Sister 271

death
    Aztec and Inca gods **102–3**
    Celtic death omens **42–3**
    fear of 44
    in modern art 217, 218
    medieval anxieties about 86
    monsters linked with 93
    prehistoric rituals **14–15**
    skeletons as reminders of 100
Decameron (Boccaccio) 101
Deep Red 233
Deep, The 274
del Toro, Guillermo 159, 268, 276
Deliverance 155
Demon, The (Rubinstein) 169
demoniacs **84–5**
demonologies 104, 121
Demons 268
demons
    African 57
    and changelings 49
    demonic hierarchies **120–21**
    Egyptian **24–5**
    Elizabethan nightmares 124
    Heian Japan **70–73**
    in Judaism 94
    in Kabbalah 94
    Islamic 69
    Loudun possession **134–5**
    medieval European 62, 86
    Mesopotamian **18–19**
    possession and exorcism **84–5**
    sexual encounters with witches 107
Der Berggeist (Spohr) 168
Der Fliegende Holländer (Wagner) 168
Der Freischütz (Weber) 168
Der Vampyr (Marschner) 168, 169
Derleth, August 194, 195, 207
Derrickson, Scott 303
desaparecidos (disappeared) 110, 180
Despentes, Virginie 286
devil
    and werewolves 116, 117
    and witchcraft 105, 106, 107, 112, 113, 124, 128–9, 137
    Faustian pacts with **122–3**, 168
    in colonial America 128
    in Kabbalah 94
    infant abductions 49
    powers at night 125
    worship 153
Devil's Backbone, The 276
Devils, The 134–5
Diana 77, 105
Diary of the Dead 237
Dickens, Charles 164
dictatorships, Latin America **180**
Dime Mystery Magazine 214
Dionysus 33
Dirks, Folkert 116
disability
    ancient anxieties about 49
    in horror **212–13**
disease
    monsters linked with 93
    vampires and 143
disfigurement 205
Disney 238, 239
divination 84, 174
Divine Comedy (Dante) 60, **96–9**
Do, Mattie 271
Doctor Who (TV series) 228, 229
Domain (Herbert) 300
Donnelly, John 288
Don't Breathe 213
Don't Look Now 302
Don't Worry Darling 253
doppelgängers 167, 297
Doré, Gustave 98
Douglass, Frederick 154
Doyle, Arthur Conan 139

Dr. Black, Mr. Hyde 249
Dr Faustus (Marlowe) 122, 123
Dr Jekyll and Mr Hyde 208
Dr Jekyll and Sister Hyde 222
Dracula (film) 11, 205, 208, 222–3
Dracula (*Horror of Dracula*) 222–3
Dracula (Stoker) 145, 150, 158–9, 166, 204, 205, 300
Dracula's Daughter 205, 253
dragons 32, 90, 93
    in *Beowulf* 81
Drakensberg Caves (South Africa) 17
drama *see* literature
dramatic realism 98
draugar 75
Dreaming, The 176
Dresden Romantic circle 146
Dressed to Kill 233
Drover's Wife, The (Drysdale) 176
Drysdale, Russell 176
Du Bo 54–5
du Maurier, Daphne 200
Duchess of Malfi, The (Webster) 130
Ducournau, Julia 246, 287, 295, 303
Due, Tananarive 155, 274, 301
Dungeons & Dragons (RPG) 281
Durga 26, 28
Duvalier, Baby Doc 139
Duvalier, Papa Doc 139
Duyvis, Corinne 274
Dyson, Jeremy 288
dystopia 299
Dystopia Horror Run – Zombie Massacre (horror experience) 186–7

E

Earthly demons 121
Ebert, Robert 237
EC Comics 214, 215
Echidna 32
eco-horror 209, **298–9**
Edelstein, David 284
Edgar Huntly (Brown) 153
Eggers, Robert 129, 205, 255, 291, 292, 295
Eggleston, Colin 177
Egypt, ancient
    ghosts and demons **24–5**
    judgement of souls **22–3**, 25
Ekkehard of Aura 86
"elevated horror" **292–5**
Ellis, Brett Easton 303
elves 49
Enikdu 20, 21
Enlightenment 9, 113, 125, 137, 146
Enríquez, Mariana 110, 180, 181
enslavement 139, 154, 249, 274
Enuma Elish 18
Epic of Gilgamesh **20–21**
Epicureanism 44
Episcopi 104–5
Ereshkigal 21
Ermine de Rheims 86
Eu, Amanda Nell 246
Eumenides (Aeschylus) 35
Euripides 33, 35
Europe
    changelings in folklore **48–9**
    Dance of Death **100–101**
    Golem of Prague **118–19**
    hell and damnation **60–63**
    Malleus Maleficarum and witchcraft **104–7**
    medieval bestiaries **90–93**
    medieval mysteries **86–7**
    possession and exorcism **84–5**
    Renaissance scepticism **112–13**
    vampire panics **142–3**
    werewolf trials **116–17**
    witch trials **136–7**

Euryale 36
euthanasia 299
Evans, Gareth 291
Evil Dead 303
evolution, fear and 183, 185
excarnation 14
exhumation 15
existential dread 194, 267
Exists 257
exorcism 19, 135
    Christian **84–5**
    jinn 68
Exorcist II: The Heretic 255
Exorcist, The (Blatty) 300
Exorcist, The (film) 19, 85, 223, 242, 249, 255, 257, 258, 264, 295, 302
Exorcist, The (stage) 288
Expressionism, German 119, 122, 203, 209, 232

F

fairies
    changelings and evil **48–9**
    fairy horde 77
    fairy tales 238
"Fall of the House of Usher, The" (Poe) 156
familiars 56
famine 9, 100
fantasy horror 10, **198–9**
Fargeat, Coralie 246, 253, 295
fate
    in Greek drama **34–5**
    Norse belief in 74
Faulkner, William 154, 155
Faust (Goethe) 122–3
Faust, Johann Georg 122
Faustian bargains **122–3**, 168
fear
    allure of horror **186–7**
    evolutionary advantage of 17
    facing 186
    fear junkies **184**
    in hunter-gatherer societies **16–17**
    science of **182–5**
Fear Street (Stine/TV series) 129, 239
Fear (TV series) 229
Feast, The 299
female protagonists, Gothic novels 150, 164–6
feminism 245
    feminist body horror **246–7**, 252
    feminist horror **250–53**
Fennell, Emerald 253
Fenrir 75
Fessenden, Larry 299
Fever Dream (Schweblin) 181
Field in England, A 290
film 10–11
    A24 and "elevated horror" **292–5**
    Alien **264–5**
    Asian horror renaissance **268–71**
    blaxploitation cinema **248–9**
    body horror **244–7**
    The Cabinet of Dr Caligari **202–3**
    comedic horror **220–21**
    contemporary black horror **298–9**
    disability on film **212–13**
    diversification **274–7**
    eco-horror **298–9**
    feminist horror **250–53**
    folk horror revival **290–91**
    found footage **282–3**
    giallo **232–5**
    Godzilla **224–5**
    Hammer Horror **222–3**
    highlights **302–3**
    Jaws and natural horror **256–7**
    New French Extremity **286–7**
    new wave horror **266–7**

Nosferatu and Dracula films **204–5**
    occult cinema **254–5**
    psychological horror **230–31**
    slasher films **260–63**
    Suspiria **258–9**
    "torture porn" **284–5**
    Universal monsters **208–9**
    youth horror **238–9**
    zombies on film **236–7**
Final Girl trope 262, **263**
Final Girls, The 263
Fincher, David 233
Firestarter 243
First Australians 15, 176
Flanagan, Mike 213
Fledgling (Butler) 179
Fleischer, Richard 298
flesh-eaters 71, 176
Florentine Codex 110
flu pandemic 1918-20 205
Fly, The 160, 225, 245
Flying Dutchman 168
folk horror 10, 192, 290
    revival **290–91**
folklore
    African **56–7**, 291
    Australian 176
    British 267
    colonial American 126
    European **48–9**, **76–7**, 168
    Germanic 77, 86
    Haitian 138–9, 236
    indigenous American **82–3**
    Irish 49, 77, 174, 175
    Japanese 70, 269
    Latin American 180
    Scandinavian 49, 77, **78–9**
    Scottish 174
    Slavic **50–51**, 143
    Welsh 87
    see also myths and legends
Fontaine, Joan 223
For the Term of His Natural Life (Clarke) 176
"Forbidden, The" (Barker) 267
forests, fear of 50
Formicarius (Nider) 106
Forzani, Bruno 234
Fortitude 299
found footage 237, **282–3**
found manuscript trope 282
Four Flies on Grey Velvet 258
foxes 72, 73, 90
Fra Angelico 62–3
France
    Grand Guignol Theatre **188–9**, 286
    new French extremity **286–7**
Frankenstein (film) 159, 208, 209, 238
Frankenstein Meets the Wolf Man 209
Frankenstein (Shelley) 9, 118, 151, **158–61**, 167, 179, 212, 225, 244, 300
Frankenstein (stage) 159, 288
Freaks 212
freeze-dried body parts 217
French Revolution 148, 151
Freud, Sigmund 183–4, **200–201**, 218
Freund, Karl 209
Friday the 13th (film) 233, 262
Friday the 13th (game) 279
Friday the 13th Part 2 263
Friedkin, William 233, 255, 302
Friedrich, Caspar David 146
Frogs 298
Frombald, Ernst 142
Fukasaku, Kinji 269
Fulci, Lucio 233, 268
funerals, Roman 44
Funny Games 276
furies 33
Fuseli, Henry 146

G

Gaia 31, 33
Gaia 298, 299
gallu 18
Game of Thones, A (Martin) 198
games, horror **278–81**
Gandillon, Perrenette 117
Ganja & Hess 249
Garden of Earthly Delights, The (Bosch) 114
Garden of Eden 93
Garland, Alex 281
Garris, Mick 242
Gawain, Sir 89
gender politics 246
genetic modification 298
genetics, and fears 183
genocide 110, 275
Geoffrey of Burton 86
Geoffrey of Monmouth 89
Germany
    Germanic folklore 77, 86
    Gothic opera 168–9
    krimi films 232
    "terror novels" 153
Get Out 220, 231, 249, 292, 294, 295, **296–7**
Ghost Stories (stage) 288
Ghost Story, A (stage) 288
Ghost Story for Christmas, A (TV series) 228
Ghost Train (stage) 289
Ghostbusters 221
ghosts
    Asian 67
    Australian ghost hoaxers **176**
    Buddhist 27, 64–5
    Chinese 67
    Daoist 65
    Egyptian **24–5**
    Elizabethan 124
    ghost food 83
    ghost ships 42
    hungry 55
    Japanese Edo period **170–71**
    Latin American **110–111**
    medieval European 86
    Phantom of the Opera **196–7**
    Roman 44
    vengeful 67
Ghostwatch (TV series) 229
ghouls 27
ghul 69
giallo **232–3**, 234, 286
giants, Norse 74–5
Gibson, Rick 217
Giger, H.R. 206
Gilbert, Sandra M. 166
Gilda Stories, The (Gomez) 179
Gilgamesh **20–21**
Gilman, Charlotte Perkins 10, 154, 166
Ginger Snaps 250, 252
Girl Walks Home Alone at Night, A 253
Girl Who Knew Too Much, The 232
gods
    Aztec and Inca death gods **102–3**
    belief in 16
    Greek mythology **30–33**
    Hindu **28–9**
    Norse 74–5, 78
    Polynesian 38–9
Godzilla **224–5**, 233, 256
Godzilla: King of the Monsters 224
Godzilla Minus One 224
Godzilla Raids Again 224
Godzilla vs. Mechagodzilla 224
Godzilla vs. Mothra 224
Goethe, Johann Wolfgang von 119
    Faust 122–3
Golding, William 300

Golem, The: How He Came into the World 118, 119
Golem, The (Meyrink) 119
golems **118–19**
  Golem of Chelm 118
  Golem of Prague 118
Gómez de Avellaneda, Gertrudis 180
Gomez, Jewelle 179
Gonzalez, Yann 234
Goodnight Mommy 276–7
Goosebumps (Stine) 229, 238, 239
Gore, John 223
Gorgons 31, 36
Gorriti, Juana Manuela 181
Goth, Mia 294
Gothic architecture **144–5**, 150, 164
Gothic horror 9, 167, 227, 249
Gothic literature 146
  Afro-Gothic **297**
  American Gothic **152–7**
  Australian Gothic **176–7**
  birth of British **148–51**
  Frankenstein and **158–61**
  Latin American **180–1**
  setting of early novels 145
  Victorian Gothic **164–7**
Gothic opera **168–9**
Gothic paintings **146–7**
Gothic Revival 144
Gothic terror 153–5
Goya, Francisco 146
Grand Guignol Theatre **188–9**, 286, 288
Grandier, Urbain 135
Grau, Albin 204, 250
grave goods 15, 17
Gray, Alasdair 160
Great God Pan, The (Machen) 167
Great Red Dragon and the Woman Clothed with the Sun (Blake) 146
Great Vampire Epidemic 142
Greece, ancient
  fate and revenge in Greek drama **34–5**
  judgement of souls **22–3**
  Medusa **36–7**
  mythology **30–3**, 34, 225
Green children of Woolpit 87
Green Knight 89
Green Knight, The 89
Gremlins 221, 238
Grendel **80–1**
Griffin, Camille 299
Griffin, Junius 249
griffins 93
Grim Reaper 42
Grimm, Jacob and Wilhelm 77, 78, 238
Grudge, The 303
guardian spirits 45
Gubar, Susan 166
Guinevere 89

H

Haborym 121
Hades 33
hag-horror trope 253
Haggard, Piers 290
Haitian folklore 138–9, 236
Hall, G. Stanley 183
Hall of Maat 23
Halloween **174–5**, 288
Halloween (film) 260, 262, 295, 302
Halloween (game) 279
Halloween II 263
Halloweentown (TV movie) 239
hallucinogens 103, 291
Hamlet (Shakespeare) 130, 131
Hammer Horror 10, 205, **222–3**
Hammer House of Horror (TV series) 223
Han dynasty 54, 55
Hand of Merlin, The (video game) 89
Haneke, Michael 276, 286

"Hansel and Gretel" (Brothers Grimm) 238
Happy Death Day 263
Hardy, Robin 290
harpies 32
Harris, Charlaine 179
Harris, Thomas 301
Harron, Mary 303
Haunt of Fear, The (comic book) 214
"haunted" attractions 186, 288
Haunted House (game) 278, 279, 281
haunted house trope 227
Haunted Palace 11
Haunting Hour, The (TV series) 239
Haunting of Hill House, The (Jackson) 145, **226–7**, 300
Haunting, The 226–7
Haus u r (Schneider) 217
Hawthorne, Nathaniel 153–4
Häxan 105
Hays Code 223
Head Full of Ghosts, A (Tremblay) 301
heart, ritual sacrifices 102, 103
heaven 62
heavy metal bands 215
Hecate 47
hecatoncheires 31
hedonistic reversal 186
Hel 75
Helena 33
Helheim 75
hell
  Bosch's vision of **114–15**
  concepts of 9
  Dante's vision of **96–9**
  in Buddhism **40–1**
  in Hinduism 40
  medieval notions of **60–1**, 62–3, 98
Hell (Chapman Brothers) 217
Hell House 242
Hellbound Heart, The (Barker) 267, 301
Hellboy (comic book) 215
Hellraiser 266, 267
Hepburn, Audrey 213
Her Body and Other Parties (Machado) 275
Heracles 33
Herbert, James 267, 300
Hereditary 294, 295
heresy, witchcraft as 105, 106
Hermit's Cave, The (radio show) 211
Herodias 77
Hesiod 31
Hidden 286
Hills Have Eyes, The 302
Hillyer, Lambert 253
Hinds, William 222
Hinduism
  evil beings **26–7**, 67
  hell 40
  Kali **28–9**
Hiroshima 224
His House 297
Historia Regum Britanniae (Geoffrey of Monmouth) 89
Hitchcock, Alfred 228, 230, 232, 260
Ho-Chunk people 83
Hodgson, William Hope 194, 195
Hoffmann, E.T.A. 169, 200, 201
Hoffmann, Heinrich 238
Hofstadter, Richard 155
Hoh, Diane 239
Hokusai 172
Holbein, Hans the Younger 101
Höllenzwang grimoires 122
Holloway, Levi 289
Hollywood
  lifts Hays Code 223
  noir tradition 232
  revitalised by Asian horror renaissance 271

Holy Grail 89
Holy Innocents Cemetery (Paris) 100–101
Homer 23
homes, burial under 15
Honda, Ishirō 224
Hong Kong giallo 234
Hooper, Tobe 261, 302
Horde, The 237
"Horror at Red Hook, The" (Lovecraft) 154
horror fiction
  definition of 9
  diversification of **274–7**
  for children 239
horror noire 297
Horror Noire: A History of Black Horror (documentary) 297
Host, The 270–71
Hostel 284
Hostel Part III 284
hounds of God 117
House of Leaves, The (Danielewski) 145, 301
House of Seven Gables, The (Hawthorne) 153, 154
House on the Borderland, The (Hodgson) 195
Howard, Robert E. 195, 207
huacas 103
Huesera: The Bone Woman 253
Hugo, Victor 145
human activity, and natural world 257
Human Earrings (Gibson) 217
human flesh, appetite for 103
human-made entities 118–19
Hunchback of Notre Dame, The (Hugo/film) 145, 208, 209
Hundred Years' War 100
hungry ghosts 55, 64–5
Hunt The Wumpus (game) 278–9
hunter-gatherers **16–17**
hunters, demonic **76–7**
Hurston, Zora Neale 139, 155
Hush 213
Hyakumonogatari Kaidankai (party game) 170–71
hybrid beasts 32, 53, 91–3, 114
Hydra of Lerna 30, 32, 33
hypothalamus 185

I

I Am Legend (Matheson) 179
I Know What You Did Last Summer 263
I Saw the TV Glow 275
Iblis 69
Icarus 225
Ich Seh, Ich Seh 276
Igneous demons 121
illusionists 288
Imitating the Dog 289
imix monster 53
impunduku 56
In a Violent Nature 263
In the Earth 299
Inca **103**
incendiarism 121
inclusivity 213
incubi 105, 125
Indigenous Americans **82–3**, 126–7, 153, 274–5
Indigenous Australians 15, 176
industrialization 159
infanticide 49
inferno, vision of hell as 98
Inner Sanctum Mystery (radio show) 211
Innocent VIII, Pope 105
Inside No. 9: Stage/Fright 289
Insidious 271, 294
Interview with the Vampire (Rice) 179

Into the Dark: Midnight Kiss 275
Invasion of the Body Snatchers 245
Invisible Man, The (Wells/film) 160, 208
Iraq War 284
Irish folklore 49, 77, 174, 175
Iron Maiden 215
Irréversible 286
Irving, Washington 152–4
Ishtar (Inanna) 21
Islam
  and traditional African beliefs 57
  jinn and *shayatin* **68–9**
Island of Doctor Moreau, The (Wells) 160
It Comes at Night 292
It Felt Like a Kiss (stage) 289
It Follows 292
It (King/film) 198, 243, 271, 301
Italian, The (Radcliffe) 151
Italy, *giallo* **232–3**, 234, 268, 286
Itzam Kab' Ayin 53
Ixion 23

J

J-horror **268–9**, 271
"jack-o'-lanterns" 174, 175
Jackson, Shirley 145, 193, **226–7**, 300
Jacobs, Harriet 154
James, Henry 166
James VI of Scotland (James I of England), King 107, 126, 128, 132
James, M.R. **192–3**, 225, 228
Jamestown settlement 153
Jane Eyre (Brontë) 166
Japan
  Edo ghost art **172–3**
  Edo period ghost stories **170–71**
  Godzilla, *kaiju*, and nuclear fears 224
  horror renaissance **268–9**, 271
  monsters and demons of Heian **70–73**
Jason 35, 47
Jawbone (Ojeda) 180
Jaws 209, 238, 256–7, 302
Jeanne des Anges, Prioress 135
Jennifer's Body 252
Jentsch, Ernst 200
jiangshi (stiff corpse) 55
jinn 68–9
John of Salisbury 106
Johnston, Thomas Anguti 275
Jones, Duane 236, 249, 297
Jones, Lee Haven 299
Jones, Mary Cover 185
Jones, Stephen Graham 155, 274
Jörmungandr 75
Jotunheim 75
Ju-On: The Grudge 269
Judaism
  chaos and evil in Kabbalah **94–5**
  golems **118–19**
judgement
  Christian view 60
  of souls **22–3**
Jurassic Park 225, 257
Jusu, Nikyatu 297

K

K-horror 268, **269–71**
Kabbalah **94–5**
Kabloona, Gayle 275
kabuki theatre 172
Kafka, Franz 200, 245
kaidan eiga 268, 269
kaiju 224
Kala Sutra (black thread hell) 40
Kali **28–9**
kami 72, 73
kappa 72, 73
Karloff, Boris 11, 159, 160–61, 208, 209
karma 40, 64, 67

Keating, David 290
Ketchum, Jack 267
Khonsuemheb 25
Kidd, Captain William 126
Kiernan, Caitlín 274
Kill List 290
Killing of a Sacred Deer, A 294
King Ghidorah 224, 225
King in Yellow, The (Chambers) 195
King Kong 256
King Kong vs. Godzilla 224
King, Stephen 10, 123, 145, 179, 193, 198, 206, 211, 227, **242–3**, 271, 274, 301
Kinski, Klaus 205
kitsune 73
Kneale, Nigel 228
Knife + Heart 234
Kobayashi, Masaki 268
Konjaku Monogatarishū 72
Kracauer, Siegfried 203
Kramer, Heinrich 104, 105–6, 128
Krasinski, John 213
krimi films 232
Kubrick, Stanley 119, 200, 230, 231, 242, 303
Kunisada Utagawa 172
Kuniyoshi Utagawa 172
kuntilanak 67
Kusama, Karyn 252
Kwaidan 268
Kwakwaka'wakw people 83
Kyd, Thomas 124, 131

L

La Amortajada (Bombal) 181
La Llorona (Weeping Woman) 110–111, 291
La Malinche 110
La Muelona 110
"La Ondina del Lago Azul" (Gómez de Avellaneda) 180
La Siguanaba 110
La Sucia (Dirty Woman) 110
La Valle, Victor 155
Labours of Heracles 33
Lamashtu 18, 19
Lancelot 88
Land of Reeds 23
Land of the Dead 237
Landis, John 221
Lang, Fritz 119, 203
Langella, Frank 205
Langsuyar 69
Lanthimos, Yorgos 294
Laos, horror films 271
LaRocca, Eric 275
larvae 44–5
Las Voladoras (Ojeda) 181
Lascaux Cave (France) 17
Last Broadcast, The 282
Last Judgement, The (Bosch) **114–15**
Last Judgement, The (Fra Angelico) **62–3**
Last Judgement, The (Van Eyck) 8
Last Night in Soho 233
Last of Us, The (game/TV show) 280, 281
Låt Den Rätte Komme In 276
Late Night Horror (TV series) 228
Latin America
　death gods **102–3**
　ghosts **110–111**
　Latin American Gothic **180–81**
Laugier, Pascal 287
L'Autre Monde (de Bergerac) 158
laws, witchcraft 106–7
Lawson, Henry 176
Laymon, Richard 267
Le Cegua 110
Le Fantôme de l'Opéra (Leroux) 196

Le Fanu, J. Sheridan 166, 179, 275
le Fèvre, Jean 100
Le Morte d'Arthur (Mallory) 89
Le Respit de la Mort (le Fèvre) 100
Le Temps du Loup 286
learning disabilities 212
Lecter, Hannibal 230, 231
Leda 33
Lee, Christopher 193, 205, 222–3
"Legend of Sleepy Hollow, The" (Irving) 152–3
lemures 44–5
Lermontov, Mikhail 169
Leroux, Gaston 196, 212
Les Contes d'Hoffmann (Offenbach) 168–9
Lesbian Vampire Killers 253
leshy 50
Lester, Mark L. 243
Let Me In 223
Let the Right One In (Lindqvist/film) 223, 276, 301
leucrota 92
Leviathan 94, 95, 121, 135
Levin, Ira 250
Levinson, Barry 299
Lewin, Albert 167
Lewis, Herschell Gordon 232
Lewis, Matthew 145, 148, 151
LGBTQ+ horror **253**, 263, 275–6
L'Homme Qui a Tué la Mort 180–81
Liber Monstrorum 81
Lichtenstein, Mitchell 246, 252
Life and Miracles of St Modwenna (Geoffrey of Burton) 86
Lifeforce 245
Light in August (Faulkner) 155
Lighthouse, The 292–3
Lights Out (radio show) 211
Likho 51
liminal spaces 82
Lindqvist, John Ajvide 223, 301
literature
　American Gothic **152–7**
　Australian Gothic **176–7**
　Beowulf **80–81**
　birth of British Gothic **148–51**
　Dante's Divine Comedy **96–9**
　diversification **274–7**
　fate and revenge in Greek drama **34–5**
　Frankenstein and science fiction **158–61**
　The Haunting of Hill House **226–7**
　highlights **300–301**
　horror comics **214–15**
　H.P. Lovecraft **206–7**
　Latin American Gothic **180–81**
　M.R. James **192–3**
　new wave horror **266–7**
　penny dreadfuls **162–3**
　revenge tragedies **130–31**
　Senecan tragedy **46–7**
　Stephen King **242–3**
　vampire fiction **178–9**
　Victorian Gothic **164–7**
　youth horror **238–9**
Lives of the Most Notorious Highwaymen, Footpads, &c. 162
Lizard in a Woman's Skin, A 233
Loew, Rabbi Judah 118
Logan, Kirsty 275
Loki 75
London Dungeon 288
Long, Frank Belknap 195
Long Weekend (Eggleston) 177
Longlegs 287
Lorde, André de 181
Lords of Salem, The 129
Loudun possessions **134–5**
Lourie, Eugène 224
Lovecraft Circle 195

Lovecraft, H.P. 9, 154, 194–5, 198, **206–7**, 267, 274, 281
Lovecraft Investigations, The (podcast) 211
Lowe, Alice 246
Lucifer 121
Lucifugi demons 121
Lugosi, Bela 11, 205, 208
Luke, Gospel of 121
Lumley, Brian 207
Luttrell Psalter 92
lycanthropy see werewolves
Lyle 253
Lynch, David 218, 272
Lyons, John C. 299

M

M 203
ma'at 24
Macbeth (Shakespeare) 132, 171
McCarthy, Cormac 301
McCowan, George 298
McCullers, Carson 154
McDonagh, Maitland 288
Machado, Carmen Maria 275
Machen, Arthur 167
MacLean, Rachel 246
Mademoiselle Fifi 189
Madrid Codex 53
maenads 33
magic
　and demonic possession 84
　indigenous traditions 105
　magicians 288
　vodou 138
magic lantern shows **164**
magical realism 180
Mahabharata 26, 27
Mahapadma (great crimson lotus hell) 41
Make Me Up 246
Malleus Maleficarum (Kramer) **104–7**, 128
Malory, Sir Thomas 89
Maman Brigitte 138
Mammon 121
Maniac 263
Manicheaism 65–7
Manitou, The 267
Mansion of Madness (board games) 281
manticore 90, 93
mantras 26
Māori 38, 39
Map, Walter 87
Marchant, Guyot 101
Margolles, Teresa 217
Mark of Lilith, The 251
Marlowe, Christopher 122, 123, 130
Marschner, Heinrich 168, 169
Marthe de Saint-Monique, Sister 135
Martin, George R.R. 198
Martin, John 146
Martino, Sergio 233
Martu people 176
Martyrs 286
Mary Shelley's Frankenstein 159
Masque of the Red Death (stage) 289
"Masque of the Red Death, The" (Poe) 156
mass hysteria 87, 267
Masterton, Graham 267
matchmaking 175
Mather, Cotton 128
Matheson, Richard 179, 242
Matthew, Gospel of 121
Maury, Julien 287
Maxa, Paula 181
Maxxxine 294
Maya **52–3**, 103
#MeToo Movement 253

Medea (Euripides) 34, 35
Medea (Seneca) 47
medieval period
　bestiaries **90–93**
　Dance of Death (Danse Macabre) **100–101**
　Dante's journey through hell **96–7**
　Hell and eternal damnation **60–61**
　horror in Arthurian legends **88–9**
　Malleus Maleficarum and fear of witchcraft **104–7**
　medieval mysteries **86–7**
　monsters in medieval bestiaries **90–93**
Medium, The (mockumentary) 271
Medusa 31, 32, 33, **36–7**
Megaera 33
memento mori 44
mental divergence 212
mental illness 10, 166
Mephistopheles 122
Mercer, Kobena 297
Mercury Theatre on the Air 210
Mesopotamia
　demons **18–19**
　Epic of Gilgamesh **20–21**
Metamorphosis, The (Kafka) 245
Metropolis 119
Mexica people 110
Mexican Gothic (Moreno-Garcia) 276, 301
Meyer, Stephenie 179
Meyrink, Gustav 119
"Mezzotint, The" (James) 228
Michelangelo 62
Mictlān 102–3
Mictlāntēcutli 102, 103
Middleton, Thomas 130
Midgard 75
Midgard serpent 74, 75
Midsommar 290–91, 294
Midwich Cuckoos, The (Wyndham) 300
Miéville, China 160, 274
Miike, Takashi 269, 303
Miller, Arthur 129
Miller, Jonathan 193
Miller, Jonny Lee 288
Minos, King 23, 31
Minotaur 31, 32
mirrors, Halloween 175
Misery 295
misogyny 106, 233, 234, 251
Mist, The (King) 206
Mitchell, David Robert 292
Mjölnir 74
Modernism 216
Molotov Theatre Group (Washington, DC) 288
Monk, The (Lewis) 145, 148, 151
monsters
　African mythology 56, 57
　Arthurian legends 88, 89
　Frankenstein **158–61**
　Greek mythology **30–33**
　Heian Japan **70–73**
　in Beowulf **80–81**
　in children's culture 238
　in films 10, 270
　indigenous American **82–3**
　Maya **52–3**
　medieval bestiaries **90–93**
　Pacific Islands 39
　Universal **208–9**
Moon of the Crusted Snow (Rice) 275
Moreno-Garcia, Silvia 198, 276, 301
Moritz, Edvard 215
Morrígan **42–3**
Morrison, Toni 154, 297
Most Haunted (TV series) 229
Mother Joan of the Angels 135
Mothra 224
Mulcahy, Russell 177

Mulvey, Laura 251
mummies/mummification 23, 24
   in horror films **25**
   Inca 102, 103
Mummy, The 25, 208, 209, 223, 238
Munch, Edvard 216
Murders in the Rue Morgue, The (Poe) 156, 157
Murnau, F.W. 203, 204
Murphy, Ryan 213
Murray, Bill 221
Muschietti, Andy 271
music
   Gothic opera **168–9**
   queer horror 275–6
My Bloody Valentine 263
Myrick, Daniel 303
Mysteries of London, The (Reynolds) 162
Mysteries of Udolpho, The (Radcliffe) 145, 150, 151
Mysterious Traveller, The (radio show) 211
Mystery of Marie Rogêt, The (Poe) 156
myths and legends
   African **56–7**
   ancient Chinese 54, 55
   ancient fears 17
   ancient Greek **30–33**, 34, 225
   Arthurian legends **88–9**
   Celtic **42–3**
   German 169
   Norse **74–5**
   Pacific Islands **38–9**
   Roman 44
   Silk Road **64–7**
   see also folklore

N

Na, Hong-jin 271
Nagasaki 224
Nakata, Hideo 268, 303
Nakurulk, Balang 177
nanabolele 57
Nanboku, Tsuruya IV 171
Nangananga 39
Nanny 297
naraka 40–41
Narakasura 27
Nash, Chris 263
Nashe, Thomas 124–5
National Theatre (London) 288
Native Americans, Gothic genre 155
natural horror **256–7**
nature, worship of 57
Nazi regime 203
Nebusemekh 25
necromancy 104, 112
Necronomicron 207
Neilson, Anthony 288
Nemean Lion 32, 33
neo-giallo **234–5**
neo-slasher films 263
Neon 295
Neon Demon, The 233, **234–5**
neopaganism 78
Nero, Emperor 46, 47
Nestorian Christians 65
New England Folk Tale, A 292
new French extremity **286–7**
New Newgate Calendar, The 163
new wave horror **266–7**
new weird fiction 160, **274**
New York Ripper, The 233
ngayurnangalku 176
Nicolodi, Daria 258
Nider, Johannes 106
Night Gallery (TV series) 228
Night of the Demon 193
Night of the Living Dead 236, 297

Night of the Living Dead – Remix (stage) 289
night rides, witches 106
Nightmare and Other Tales of Dark Fantasy, The (Stevens) 198
Nightmare Before Christmas, The 239
Nightmare on Elm Street, A 125, 262, 263
Nightmare, The (Fuseli) 146
nightmares **124–5**, 218
Nihon san dai kaidan 171
Nihon Shoki 70, 72
ninki i nanka 57
Ninth House (Bardugo) 198
Nirabuda (hell of bursting blisters) 41
Nishi Dak 69
Nocturn (game) 280
Noé, Gaspar 286, 287, 294
Nope 297
Norse mythology **74–5**, 78
North America
   American Gothic **152–7**
   supernatural fears in colonial **126–9**
Northanger Abbey (Austen) 151
Nosferatu 10, 205
Nosferatu: A Symphony of Horror **204–5**, 208
Nosferatu the Vampyre 205
nostalgia, in horror plots 239
nuclear fears 224
Nuestra Parte de Noche (Enriquez) 180
Nyman, Andy 288

O

O'Brien, Fitz-James 154
O'Brien, Richard 221
occult 84
   Halloween **174–5**
   occult cinema **254–5**
O'Connor, Flannery 154
Odin 74, 75, 77, 78
Odysseus 30
Oedipus 32
Oedipus Rex (Sophocles) 34–5
Oedipus (Seneca) 47
Oehme, Ernst Ferdinand 146
Offenbach, Jacques 168–9
"Oh, Whistle, and I'll Come to You, My Lad" (James) 193
Ojeda, Mónica 180, 181
Okorafor, Nnedi 274
Old Ones 194, 206
Old-New Synagogue (Prague) 118, 119
Oldboy 270
Oldman, Gary 205
Omen, The 255
On Dreams (Freud) 200
Once & Future (comic book series) 89
One Hundred Ghost Stories 172
oni 70–72
Onibaba 268
Only Good Indians, The (Jones) 155, 274, 275
onryō 171
opera, Gothic **168–9**
Oresteia trilogy (Aeschylus) 35
Orphanage, The 276
Orthus 32
Orwell, George 300
Osiris 23, 24, 25
Oskoreia 77
others, fear of 17
Otherworld, Celtic 42
Ötzi the Iceman 205
Ouija boards 255
Ouranos 33
Our Wives Under the Sea (Armfield) 275
Out There Screaming: An Anthology of New Black Horror 274
Ovid 36
Own Voices hashtag 274

P

Pacific Island mythologies **38–9**
pagan rituals 78, 105, 192
pain, fear in anticipation of 183
Pa'itele 39
Palais Garnier (Paris) 196
Pall Mall Gazette 163
pandemics 299
Pan's Labyrinth 268, 276
Paradise (Suzuki) 269
paranoid style 155
Paranormal Activity (film/stage) 282, 289, 294
paranormal, investigating the 229
Parasite 271
parasites 245
Parentalia 44
Park, Chan-wook 270
Park, Ki-hyeong 270
Pasiphaë 31
Pauguset Nation 126
Pavlov, Ivan 183, 184
Pazuzu **19**, 255
Pedro Páramo (Rulfo) 181
Peele, Jordan 220, 231, 274, 292, 297, 303
Pele 38
pelicans 90
penny dreadfuls **162–3**, 164
Pentheus 33
Perchta 77
Perkins, Osgood 295
Perseus 36
Peterborough Chronicle 77
Phantasmagorie (magic lantern show) 164
Phantom of the Opera (Leroux/film) 11, **196–7**, 208, 209, 223
Phips, William 129
Phobiarama (stage) 289
phobias 183–5, 289
Phorcys 31
physical disabilities 212
physiological response to fear 183, 185
Physoplogus 90
Picnic at Hanging Rock 177
Picture of Dorian Gray, The (Wilde/film) 166–7
Pielmeier, John 289
Pike, Christopher 239
Pikwane, Jerome 291
Pillowman, The (stage) 288
Pinhead 266
Pinochet, Augusto 180
Piranha 257
pishachas 27, 67
plague 9, 100, 101, 205
Plato 44
Play Dead (stage) 288
Plaza, Paco 268
Pliny the Younger 45
podcasts 211
Poe, Edgar Allan 154, **156–7**, 192, 200, 232, 288, 289
poetry *see* literature
poison, vodou 133
Polanski, Roman 221, 230, 255
Polidori, John William 142, 158, 168, 179
political oppression 180
pollution 298–9
Polydectes 36
Polynesians 38–9
Polyphemus 31
polytheism 57
pontianak 67
Poor Things (Gray) 160
pop-horror 284
Popol Vuh 53
Poseidon 31, 36

possession, demonic **84–5**, 128, **134–5**, 255
post-apocalyptic 237, 275, 281, 286
post-horror 292
poverty 180
Preacher's Daughter (Cain) 275–6
predictions 132
pregnancy 246
prehistoric peoples
   death rituals and burial practices **14–15**
   role of fear in hunter-gatherer societies **16–17**
Prevenge 246
priests, teachings on hell 61
printing, advances in 162
Prom Night 263
Prometheus 33, 225
Promising Young Woman 253
Protestant Church 85
Prowler, The 263
Proximity Media 295
Prozession im Nebel (Oehme) 146–7
Psellos, Michael 121
pseudodocumentary horror films 282
psychedelia 290
Psycho (Bloch/film) 11, 195, 230, 257, 260, 263, 302
psychoanalysis 195
psychological dread 267
psychological horror 9, 213, 227, **230–31**
psychology 192, 218
   in Gothic fiction 151, 154, 166
   of fear **183–5**
psychosis 260
PTSD (post-traumatic stress disorder) 184
pumpkins 174, 175
Punchdrunk 289
punishments
   after death 9, 23, 40–41
   and social cohesion 16
   Day of Judgement 60, 62, 114
   in hell 60, 96–7
   oblivion as 44
pupils, dilated 182–3
Puritans 128, 129
Putus 97
pythons 92

Q

qalupaliks 83
Qasavara 39
Qitsualik-Tinsley, Sean and Rachel 275
Quandt, James 286
Quatermass 2 222
Quatermass Xperiment, The 222, 228, 244, 245
Quechua people 83, 103
queer horror **275–6**
Questing Beast 88, 89
Quiet Place, A 213
Quiet, Please! (radio show) 211
Quinn, Marc 216, 217
Qur'an 68, 69

R

Ra 24, 25
Rabid 245
race riots 236
racism 231, 249, 297
   horror genre 274
   in American Gothic 154
Radcliffe, Ann 145, 150, 151
radio, horror on **210–211**
Ragnarök 75
Raikō 70
Raimi, Sam 303
Rain, The 299

rakshasas/rakshasis 26
Ramayana 26
Ramis, Harold 221
Ramses II, Pharaoh 22
rape 286
rape-revenge 253
rationalism 159
Rats, The (Herbert) 267
Ravenloft (RPG) 281
Raw 246, 287, 303
Ray, Man 200
Rayner, Rosalie 184
Razorback (Mulcahy) 177
Ready or Not 123
realism, documentary-style 264, **282**
reality TV 229
rebirth and regeneration 15, 28, 40, 53, 64
Rec 268, 276, 282
recreational fear 184, 185
Recreational Fear Lab (Aarhus University) 186
Red Lady of Paviland 14–15
Red Nights 234
Reed, Oliver 223
Reeves, Michael 290
Refn, Nicolas Winding 233, 234
Reformatory, The (Due) 274, 301
Regino of Prüm, Abbot 104
Reijn, Halina 294
reincarnation 40
religious fanaticism 9, 255
Resident Evil (game) 279–80, 281
Resident Evil Survivor (game) 278
restless dead, appeasing 54
revenants 86
Revenge 253
revenge
 in Greek drama **34–5**
 murder victims 16
 revenge tragedies/dramas 124, **130–31**, 288
Revenge of the Creature 209
revulsion 243
Reynolds, George W.M. 162
Rhadamanthus 23
Rice, Anne 179
Rice, Waubgeshig 275
Richelieu, Cardinal 135
Rickman, Thomas 144
Rig, The 299
Ring (Suzuki/film) 268–9, 271, 301, 303
Ritual, The 291
rituals, uniting human groups 17
Roanoke Island (Virginia) 126–7
Robbins, Todd 288
Robert, Étienne-Gaspard 164
Robins, Danny 288
rock art 14, 15
Rocky Horror Picture Show, The 221
Rodan 224, 225
Roeg, Nicolas 302
role-playing games (RPGs) 281
Romans
 lemures or *larvae* **44–5**
 Senecan tragedy **46–7**
Romantic movement 98, **146–7**, 148
Romero, George A. 215, 236, 237, 297, 302
Rose and the Key, The (Le Fanu) 166
Rosemary's Baby (Levin/film) 230, 231, 250, 253, 255, 295
Rossetti, Christina 151
Roth, Eli 284
Rowley, William 130
Rubens, Peter Paul 36–7
Rubinstein, Anton 169
Rulfo, Juan 181
runes 192
Ruskin, John 144–5
Russel, Ken 135

S

sabbaths, witches' 107, 129, 137
sacrifices, human 102, 103, 138
Sahagún, Bernardino de 110
Saint Maud (stage) 289
Salem Witch Trials **128–9**, 153, 255
Salem's Lot (King/film) 179, 243
Samagatha (crushing hell) 40–41
Samhain 42, 174–5
Sami people 105
Samuel 104
San people 17
Sánchez, Eduardo 303
Sandman (comic book) 215
"Sandman, The" (Hoffman) 169, 200, 201
Sanjiva (reviving hell) 40, 41
Santa Claus 78
Satan 9, 57, 60, 96, 97, 135
 and Behemoth 94
 and demons 121
 and dragons 81
 and witches 105, 107, 136
Satanic Rights of Dracula, The 223
Saturday the 14th 221
Saul, King 104
Savini, Tom 263
Saw 10, 284
Saw X 284–5
Scandinavian folktales 49, 77, 78–9
Scarlet Letter, The (Hawthorne) 153
Scary Stories to Tell in the Dark (Schwartz) 239
scepticism, Renaissance **112–13**, 124–5
Scheuberin, Helena 105
Schneider, Gregor 217
Schoenbrun, Jane 275
Schreck, Max 204, 205
Schwartz, Alvin 239
Schweblin, Samanta 181
science
 and horror 228
 gone wrong **225**
 of fear **182–5**
science fiction 267
 Frankenstein and **158–61**, 167
 sci-fi horror 10, 228, 268
Scientific Revolution 159, 183
Scooby-Doo, Where Are You! 238
Scorsese, Martin 231
Scot, Reginald 112
Scott, Ridley 245, 264, 303
Scottish folklore 174
Scovell, Adam 290, 291
Scream 221, 263, 268
Scream Blacula Scream 249
Scream, The (Munch) 216
scrying 174
Scylla 30, 32
Se7en 233
sea monsters
 Greek 30
 Pacific Islands 39
Seabrook, William 139
Seduction of the Innocent (Wertham) 214
Sekhmet 24
Self (Quinn) 216
self-censorship 214
self-mutilation 287
Seneca, tragedies **46–7**
serial killings 260, 262
serpents
 African 57
 Kabbalah 94
 Māori 38, 39
 Maya 53
 medieval monsters 92, 93
 Medusa **36–7**
 Norse mythology 74, 75

Set (Seth) 24
seta 91
Seven Deadly Sins 120–21
Seven Years' War 148
sexual content
 feminist body horror 246
 Hammer Horror 223
 sexual violence 250, 253
Shadow of the Vampire 205
Shakespeare, William 124
 Macbeth 132, 171
 revenge tragedies 130, 131
 Seneca's influence on 47
shamans
 and possession 84
 burials 14, 15
 grave goods 17
 in film 271
shape-shifters 27, 38, 43, 50, 71, 73, 75, 176
sharks 53
Sharman, Jim 221
Shaun of the Dead 237
shayatin 68, **69**
shell shock 197
Shelley, Mary 9, 118, 151, 167, 179, 209, 212, 225, 244, 300
shem 118
Shen Yi Jing 55
Sherwood, Grace 128
Shimizu, Takashi 269, 303
Shindō, Kaneto 268
Shining, The (King/film) 145, 200, 230, 231, **242**, 243, 303
shirikodama 73
Shiva 28
Shivers 245
Shrine (Herbert) 267
shudder pulps **214**
Shuten-dōji 71
Shutter Island 231
Silence of the Lambs, The (Harris/film) 11, 230–31, 301
Silent Hill (game) 279, 280
Silent Night 299
Silk Road **64–7**
sin, medieval idea of 60
Sinister 303
Sinners 295, 297
Sinnett, Frederick 176
Sir Gawain and the Green Knight 89
sirens 30
Sisyphus 23
Skarsgård, Bill 205
skeletons
 Dance of Death **100–101**
 Roman images 44
slasher films 221, 232, 251, **260–63**
Slavic folklore **50–51**
Slender Man meme 271
Slovenly Peter (Hoffmann) 238
slow horror 292
Sluagh Sidhe 77
Slugh, the 43
Slumber Party Massacre, The 251
smart horror 292
smartphones 282
Smile 200
Smith, Carter 275
Smith, Clark Ashton 194, 195, 198, 207
Smith, L.J. 179
snakes 36–7, 38, 39, 57, 74, 75, 92, 93, 94
Snow White and the Seven Dwarfs 258
Snowpiercer 299
social control 39
social injustice 10
social unease 164, 267
societal breakdown 236
Society 245
Solomon, Rivers 274

Something Wicked This Way Comes (Bradbury) 198
Son of Dracula 205
Song of Ice and Fire, A (Martin) 198
Sophocles 34–5
"Sorcerer's Apprentice, The" (Goethe) 119
Soska, Jen and Sylvia 246
"soul cakes" 175
souls
 judgement of **22–3**, 25
 of the dead 71
South Korea, horror renaissance 268, **269–71**
Southern Gothic subgenre 154–5
Southern Vampire Mysteries, The (Harris) 179
Soylent Green 298–9
space, horror in 264
Spanish Inquisition 145
Spanish Tragedy, The (Kyd) 131
special effects
 film 256
 theatre 181
spectral melodramas 288
Spee, Friedrich 113
spells, conjuring/commanding spirits 25, 122
Sphinx 32, 33
Spielberg, Steven 256, 302
spirits
 appeasing 175
 avenging 124
 belief in 16
 conjuring 25, 122
 flesh-eating 176
 spirit children 56
 spirit communication 84
 spirit mediators 15
 worship 57
splatter films 286
Splatterhouse (game) 279
splatterpunk 267, 275
Spohr, Louis 168
Sprenger, Jacob 105
statuettes, ritual 56
Stepford Wives, The (Levin) 250–51, 253
Stephen King's The Shining 242
Stevens, Francis 198
Stevenson, Robert Louis 160, 164, 166, 222, 228
Stheno 36
stimuli, and association 183, 185
Stine, R.L. 129, 229, 239
Stingy Jack 175
Stoic philosophy 44, 46
stoker, Bram 145, 150, 166, 178–9, 204, 205, 300
storytelling 17
Stow, Randolph 177
Strange Case of Dr Jekyll and Mr Hyde (Stevenson) 160, 164, 166, 222, 228
Stranger Things (TV series) 239
String of Pearls, The 163
Strzyga 143
Stubbe, Peter 116, 117
Study after Velázquez's Portrait of Pope Innocent X (Bacon) 217
Stymphalian birds 33
subconscious mind 218
sublime, the 150, 151
Substance, The 246–7, 253, 295
substitution stories 49
Subterranean demons 121
succubi 105
Sudanese Civil War 297
Sueños y Realidades (Gorriti) 181
suicide 97
Sulay 103
Sumerians 18
Summis desiderantes affectibus (papal bull) 105

supernatural, belief in 16, 54, 55
  colonial America 126, 129
  Elizabethan age 124
  Japan 70
  medieval fears 86–7
  Silk Road 64
superstition 124, 126
Surapadma 26
Surrealism 200, 201, **218–19**, 267
Suspiria 233, **258–9**, 268
Sutoku, Emperor 73
Suzuki, Kojo 268, **269**, 301
Svartalfheim 75
Swarm, The 257
Sweeney Todd: The Demon Barber of Fleet Street 163
Sweet Home (film/game) 279
syncretism, religious 67

T

Taaqtumi: An Anthology of Arctic Horror Stories 275
taboos 39, 56, 81
Táin Bó Cúailinge 42
Taiping Guanbgji 67
Takal, Sophia 251
Tales From the Crypt (film/comic book) 214, 215
Tales from the Hood 249
Talmud 94
Tang dynasty 67
Tangaroa 38–9
taniwha 38, 39
Tantalus, King 23
Tapana (heating hell) 41
tapu 39
Tartarus 23, 33
Taylor, Terence 274
teenagers, slasher films 260, 262, 263
Teeth 246, 252
television
  horror on **228–9**, 239
  Twin Peaks **272–3**
"Tell-Tale Heart, The" (Poe) 156
Tell-Tale Heart, The (stage) 288
Teller 288
Tender Is the Flesh (Bazterrica) 276
Tenebrae 233
tengu 72–3
Terrors of the Night, The (Nashe) 124–5
Tetsuo: The Iron Man 245, 268
Tetsuo II: Body Hammer 268
Texas Chain Saw Massacre, The (film/game) 260, 261, 279, 302
Thailand, horror films 271
theatre
  Grand Guignol Theatre (Paris) **188–9**, 286, 288
  horror on stage **288–9**
  revenge in Greek drama **34–5**
  revenge tragedies **130–31**, 288
therianthropic art 16, 17
They/Them 263
Thiess of Kaltenbrun 117
Thing, The 206, 245, 303
Things Have Gotten Worse Since We Last Spoke (LaRocca) 275
Things We Say in the Dark (Logan) 275
Thirst 270
Thirty Years' War 136–7
Thomasius, Christian 113
Thorndike, Stewart 253
Three Studies for Figures at the Base of a Crucifixion (Bacon) 216–17
Thrillpeddlers (San Francisco) 288
thunderbirds 82–3
Thyestes (Seneca) 47
Tiger Stripes 246
Time Cut 263
Tisiphone 33

Titane 246, 285, 287
Titans 33
Tituba 128
Titus Andronicus (Shakespeare) 130
Tlingit people 83
To the Islands (Stow) 177
Todd, Sweeney 162–3
Tokoloshe, The 57, 291
tombs
  Chinese 54
  Egyptian 23
  Roman 44
torment, cycles of 60
torture
  after death 23, 40–41, 98
  "torture porn" **284–5**
Totally Killer 263
totemic figures 83
Tourneur, Jacques 193
Tower of Terror (TV movie) 239
Town That Dreaded Sundown, The 260
Tragedy of Macbeth, The 132–3
Train to Busan 236, 271
transvection 106
traumas, confrontation of 286
Tremblay, Paul 301
"trick-or-treating" 175
tricksters 50
Trier, Lars von 284
Trinh Thi, Coralie 286
trolls 49
True Blood (TV show) 179
Tsukamoto, Shin'ya 245, 268
Tuatha Dé Danann 42
Turn of the Screw, The (James) 166
Twilight 179
Twilight Zone, The (TV series) 228, 229
Twin Peaks (TV series) **272–3**
Typhon 32, 33

U

ubume 67
ukiyo-e 170, 172–3
Un Chien Andalou 218
uncanny, the **200–201**
Uncanny, The (Freud) 200
undead creatures 75, 77, 142, 204
Under the Skin 292
underworld
  Egyptian view **22–3**
  Mesopotamian view **20–21**
  Roman view 44
Unearth 299
United States
  American Gothic **152–5**
  Halloween celebrations **174–5**
  Hammer Horror **222–3**
  Universal monsters **208–9**
Universal Pictures 10, 159, 205, **208–9**, 222–3, 238
unknown, fears of the 194
upiór 143
Urban Legend 263
Uridimmu 18
Us 11, 297, 303
Ushumgallu 18
Utagawa school 172

V

Valhalla 75
valkyries 78
Vampire Diaries, The (Smith) 179
vampires 27, 69, 86, 223, 228, 249, 253
  adze 56
  in films 204–5, 208, 270, 295
  vampire fiction **178–9**
  vampire panics **142–3**
"Vampyre, The" (Polidori) 142, 158, 168, 179

Van Eyck, Jan 8–9
Van, Marina de 245, 287
VanderMeer, Jeff 160, 206, 274
Vault of Horror, The (comic book) 214
vengeance, revenge tragedies **130–31**
Verdun, Michel 116
Verhoeven, Dries 289
vetalas 27
Video Nasties 214, 266
Video Recordings Act (UK, 1984) 266
Vietnam War 236, 297
Vikings 74, 75
Virgil 44
visceral cinema 245
Visions of Tundale 60, 61
Vitalis, Oderic 86
Vlad the Impaler 142
vodou/voodoo 84, **138–9**, 236
volcanic activity 38

W

Wagner, Richard 148
Wailing, The 271
Wait Until Dark 213
Wake Wood 290
Walking Dead, The (TV series) 237
Wallace, Edgar 232
Walpole, Horace 145, 148–50
Wan, James 271, 284
Wandrei, Donald 195
War of the Worlds, The (Wells) 160, 210
War on Terror 284
Warm, Hermann 203
Warner Bros 238
"Warning to the Curious, The" (James) 192–3
Wasp Factory, The (Banks) 301
Watcher in the Woods, The 238
waterlily serpent 53
Watson, John B. 184
wayinyantanka 83
Weaveworld (Barker) 198
Weber, Carl Maria von 168
Webster, John 130
Weekes, Remi 297
Wegener, Paul 118, 119
weeping woman 291
Weir, Peter 177
weird fiction 194
Weird Tales (magazine) 195
Welhaven, Johan Sebastian 78
Welles, Orson 210
Wells, H.G. 160, 210
Welsh folklore 89
wendigos 82–3
We're Alive (podcast) 211
werewolves 86
  European trials **116–17**
Wertham, Fredric 214
West, Ti 294
Wewe Gombel 69
Weyer, Johann 112, 113
whale, James 159, 221
Wheatley, Ben 290, 299
Whispering Corridors 270
Whistle and I'll Come to You 193
White Devil, The (Webster) 130
white knucklers 186
White, Patrick 177
White Zombie 139
Whitehead, Henry 139
Wicker Man, The 255, 290, 291
Wieland (Brown) 153, 154
Wiene, Robert 203, 230
Wild Hunt 43, **76–7**, 78, 86
WildClaw Theatre (Chicago) 288
Wilde, Olivia 253
Wilde, Oscar 123, 166–7
William of Newburgh 86
Williams, John 256

Williamson, Kevin 263
Wilson, Harriet 154
Winthrop, John 128
Wise, Robert 227
Witch of Endor 104
Witch, The 255, 291
VVitch, The 129, 292
witchcraft
  African 56
  colonial America 126, **128–9**
  Elizabethan England 124
  European witch hysteria **136–7**
  hunts/trials 104, 105, 106–7, **128–9**, 132, **136–7**, 153
  medieval Europe **104–7**
  scepticism about 112–13, 121, 129
Witchcraft Through the Ages 105
Witches Tale, The (radio show) 210–211
Witches, The 223
Witchfinder General 290, 291
Witkin, Joel-Peter 217
Wolf Man, The 209
Wolfson, Jordan 217
wolves 75
Woman in Black, The 223, 288
Woman in White (Collins) 164–5, 166
women
  as monsters in Greek mythology 30
  gender violence and rights 181
  see also feminism; misogyny
Wood of the Suicides 97
woodblock prints 172–3
World War I 184, 195, 198, 204–5, 208
World War II 216, 218
worms 91
Wright, Edgar 233
Würzburg witch trials **136–7**
Wyndham, John 300

X

X 294 Pearl 294
Xhosa folklore 291
Xiao 55
Xolotl 103
xook 53
Xtro 245
Xuan of Zhou, King 54–5

Y

Yacumama 83
Yawkyawk (Nakurulk) 177
Yellow Wallpaper, The (Gilman) 10, 166
Yeon, Sang-ho 271
Yggdrasil (world tree) 74, 75
yōkai 70, 72, 73, 172
Yoruba people 56
Yoshiiku, Utagawa 170
Yoshitoshi, Tsukioka 170, 172
Young, Alse 128
Young Frankenstein 159, 221
Your Vice Is a Locked Room and Only I Have the Key 233
youth horror **238–9**
Yule 78
yūrei 171, 172
Yuzna, Brian 245

Z

zhiguai xiaoshuo 67
Ziz 94, 95
Zohar 94
Zombie Flesh Eaters 237
Zombie, Rob 129
Zombieland 237
zombies **138–9**, 228, **236–7**, 271, 279, 281
Zues 33
Zulu people 56, 291

ACKNOWLEDGMENTS

Dorling Kindersley would like to thank Justin Kamerer, Angryblue, for the cover illustration and printed edges; Steve Crozier, Butterfly Creative Services Ltd for image retouching; Oliver Drake for proofreading; Helen Peters for indexing.

PICTURE CREDITS

The publisher would like to thank the following for their kind permission to reproduce their photographs:

(Key: a-above; b-below/bottom; c-centre; f-far; l-left; r-right; t-top)

2 Bridgeman Images. 4-5 Freepik: kues1 (t/background). **6 Freepik:** kues1 (t/background). **8 Photo Scala, Florence:** Image copyright The Metropolitan Museum of Art / Art Resource. **11 Alamy Stock Photo:** Album (br); Pictorial Press Ltd (cr); Photo 12 (bc). **Bridgeman Images:** © Universal Pictures / Diltz (tl); Everett Collection (tc, tr); J. T. Vintage (cl); © Galatea Film / Jolly Film / Diltz (c); Diltz / © Red Bank Films / United Artists (bl). **12-13 Freepik:** kues1 (background). **14 Zdenek Kratochvil / CC BY-SA 4.0. 15 Alamy Stock Photo:** Image Source Limited / Jeff Mauritzen. **16 Dagmar Hollmann / CC BY-SA 4.0. 17 Alamy Stock Photo:** Thom Lang (b). **Kenneth Garrett:** (t). **18-19 Alamy Stock Photo:** CPA Media Pte Ltd (t). **18 Alamy Stock Photo:** Zev Radovan (bl). **19 Shutterstock.com:** Kobal / Hoya Prods / Warner Bros (br). **20 Getty Images:** DEA / G. Dagli Orti. **21 Getty Images:** DEA / G. Dagli Orti. **22 Getty Images:** DEA Picture Library / De Agostini. **23 Alamy Stock Photo:** BasPhoto (t). **Photo Scala, Florence:** (b). **24 The Walters Art Museum, Baltimore:** Henry Walters, Baltimore, 1929, by purchase; Walters Art Museum, 1931, by bequest. **25 Alamy Stock Photo:** Archive PL (b). **Bridgeman Images:** © Mary Jelliffe. All rights reserved 2025 (t). **26 Alamy Stock Photo:** Dinodia Photos. **27 Bridgeman Images:** San Diego Museum of Art / Edwin Binney 3rd Collection. **28-29 Los Angeles County Museum of Art:** Purchased with funds provided by Dorothy and Richard Sherwood and Indian Art Special Purpose Fund (M.80.101). **30 Alamy Stock Photo:** Donald Cooper (t). **© The Trustees of the British Museum. All rights reserved. 31 Bridgeman Images:** G. Dagli Orti / © NPL - DeA Picture Library. **32 Alamy Stock Photo:** Artefact. **33 Alamy Stock Photo:** Donald Cooper. **34 Getty Images:** Erwin Blumenfeld / Condé Nast via Getty Images. **35 Alamy Stock Photo:** Donald Cooper (b). **Bridgeman Images:** Mondadori Portfolio / Archivio Dell'arte Luciano Pedicini / Luciano Pedicini (t). **36-37 Bridgeman Images:** Luisa Ricciarini. **38 Getty Images:** Werner Forman / Universal Images Group (l). **Wikimedia:** Kahuroa (r). **39 Alamy Stock Photo:** Cheryl Forbes. **40 Alamy Stock Photo:** Charles Walker Collection (t); LGASIASTOCK (b). **41 Alamy Stock Photo:** Gibson Green. **42 Alamy Stock Photo:** Chronicle. **43 Lucy Purrington. 44 Bridgeman Images:** Raffaello Bencini (b). **The J. Paul Getty Museum, Villa Collection, Malibu, California, 78.AB.307** (t). **45 Alamy Stock Photo:** Classic Image. **46 Photo Scala, Florence:** Courtesy of the Ministero Beni e Att. Culturali e del Turismo. **47 Alamy Stock Photo:** Heritage Image Partnership Ltd (t). **ArenaPAL:** Mark Douet (b). **48 Städel Museum, Frankfurt am Main. 49 Bridgeman Images:** Chris Beetles Ltd, London. **50 Bridgeman Images:** Giancarlo Costa. **51 Alamy Stock Photo:** Daniel Eskridge. **52 Los Angeles County Museum of Art:** Purchased with funds provided by Camilla Chandler Frost (M.2010.115.625). **53 Alamy Stock Photo:** Album. **54 Getty Images:** Heritage Art / Heritage Images (t). **The Metropolitan Museum of Art:** Purchase, Ann Eden Woodward Foundation Gift, 1979 (b). **55 Alamy Stock Photo:** Sarwono Edi Subarkah (b). **Getty Images:** Manan Vatsyayana / AFP (t). **56 Bridgeman Images:** Patrice Cartier. All rights reserved 2025 (l). **56-57 Bridgeman Images:** © Twins Seven Seven / Photo: Indianapolis Museum of Art / Gift of Mr and Mrs Harrison Eiteljorg. **58-59 Freepik:** kues1 (background). **60 Alamy Stock Photo:** Charles Walker Collection. **61 Bridgeman Images. 62-63 Bridgeman Images. 64 Getty Images:** DEA / G. Dagli Orti (t); Mondadori Portfolio (b). **65 Getty Images:** Pictures from History. **66 Getty Images:** Photo12 / Universal Images Group. **67 Alamy Stock Photo:** Historic Collection. **68 Alamy Stock Photo:** Danvis Collection. **69 Bridgeman Images:** Bodleian Libraries, University of Oxford (t); Luisa Ricciarini (b). **70-71 © Trustees of the Chester Beatty Library, Dublin:** (b). **71 Alamy Stock Photo:** Chronicle of World History / National Diet Library (t). **72 Alamy**

Stock Photo: The Picture Art Collection. **73 Harold B. Lee Library, Brigham Young University. 74 Bridgeman Images. 75 Alamy Stock Photo:** Ivy Close Images (t). **Bridgeman Images:** Arni Magnusson Institute (b). **76 Lenbachhaus.** Städtische Galerie im Lenbachhaus und Kunstbau, München. **77 Alamy Stock Photo:** Vintage Archives (t). **78-79 Bridgeman Images. 80 Bridgeman Images:** Look and Learn. **81 Ryan Driscoll. 82 Photo Scala, Florence:** Digital Image Museum Associates / LACMA / Art Resource NY. **83 Getty Images:** Buyenlarge (cr). **The Estate of Norval Morrisseau:** (tl). **84-85 Alamy Stock Photo:** Album (c). **85 Getty Images:** Silver Screen Collection (r). **86 Alamy Stock Photo:** piemags. **87 Alamy Stock Photo:** Peregrine (t). **Harry Bell:** (b). **88 Bridgeman Images:** Photo Josse. **89 Bridgeman Images:** From the British Library archive. **90 The J. Paul Getty Museum, Los Angeles,** Ms. Ludwig XV 3, fol. 89, 83. MR.173.89. **91 Bridgeman Images:** From the British Library archive. **92 Bridgeman Images:** Fine Art Images (l); From the British Library archive (r). **93 Manuel Cohen. 94 Bridgeman Images:** Prismatic Pictures. **95 Bridgeman Images:** From the British Library archive. **96 The J. Paul Getty Museum, Los Angeles,** Ms. 30, fol. 17, 87.MN.141.17.17. **97 Bridgeman Images:** Mondadori Portfolio / Electa / Marta Carenzi (l); Mondadori Portfolio / Electa / Marta Carenzi (r). **98-99 Getty Images:** Sepia Times / Universal Images Group. **100 Alamy Stock Photo:** CPA Media Pte Ltd. **101 Photo Scala, Florence:** bpk, Bildagentur für Kunst, Kultur und Geschichte, Berlin (b). **Wellcome Collection:** (t). **102 Alamy Stock Photo:** Hemis (r); Luiz Souza (l). **103 Science Photo Library:** Library of Congress. **104 Alamy Stock Photo:** Penta Springs Limited / Artokoloro. **105 Alamy Stock Photo:** Charles Walker Collection. **106 Bridgeman Images:** Royal Collection Trust / © His Majesty King Charles III, 2025. **107 Getty Images:** PHAS / Universal Images Group. **108-109 Freepik:** kues1 (background). **110 Ivan Palma. 111 Alamy Stock Photo:** NurPhoto SRL. **112-113 Bridgeman Images:** From the British Library archive (t). **112 Shutterstock.com:** Alfredo Dagli Orti (b). **113 Alamy Stock Photo:** The Picture Art Collection (b). **114-115 Bridgeman Images:** Luisa Ricciarini. **116 Science Photo Library:** SwissCollections (t). **117 The Metropolitan Museum of Art:** Harris Brisbane Dick Fund, 1942. **118 Bridgeman Images:** SZ Photo. **119 Dreamstime.com:** Jewish History Center. **120 Alamy Stock Photo:** Charles Walker Collection. **121 Alamy Stock Photo:** Charles Walker Collection. **122 Alamy Stock Photo:** Photo 12 (t). **Getty Images:** ullstein bild (b). **123 Bridgeman Images:** NPL - DeA Picture Library / © Estate of Ernest Klausz. **124 Alamy Stock Photo:** Historic Collection. **125 Alamy Stock Photo:** Allstar Picture Library Ltd (b). **The Detroit Institute Of Arts:** (t). **126 Alamy Stock Photo:** The Granger Collection. **127 President and Fellows of Harvard College. 128 Bridgeman Images:** Peter Newark American Pictures. **129 Alamy Stock Photo:** AJ Pics. **130 Bridgeman Images:** Look and Learn. **131 Alamy Stock Photo:** Science History Images. **132-133 Alamy Stock Photo:** Album. **134 Alamy Stock Photo:** Cinematic. **135 Getty Images:** Bildagentur-online / Universal Images Group. **136 Alamy Stock Photo:** Heritage Image Partnership Ltd. **137 Alamy Stock Photo:** Chronicle (tr). **Bridgeman Images:** From the British Library archive (bl). **138 Photo Scala, Florence:** RMN-Grand Palais / Photo Patrick Gries / Maxène Dorcéan. **139 Alamy Stock Photo:** Everett Collection Inc (b). **State Library of Pennsylvania:** The Magic Island by W. B. Seabrook; illustrated with drawings by Alexander King.. Literary Guild of America, 1929 (t). **140-141 Freepik:** kues1 (background). **142 Alamy Stock Photo:** WENN Rights Ltd (b). **Dreamstime.com:** Cindy Goff (t). **143 Alamy Stock Photo:** Chronicle. **144 Magnum Photos:** Ian Berry. **145 Getty Images:** Heritage Art / Heritage Images (t); Sanja Baljkas (b). **146-147 Photo Scala, Florence:** bpk, Bildagentur für Kunst, Kultur und Geschichte, Berlin. **148 Forum Auctions. 149 Yale University Library:** The Lewis Walpole Library. **150 Alamy Stock Photo:** CPA Media Pte Ltd (b). **© National Gallery of Ireland:** (t). **151 Bridgeman Images:** From the British Library archive (tr). **152 Getty Images:** Historica Graphica Collection / Heritage Images. **153 Alamy Stock Photo:** Chronicle (tr); piemags / CMB (bl). **154 Alamy Stock Photo:** Chronicle. **155 Heritage Auctions:** Penguin Random House LLC (b). **Shutterstock.com:** Films Du Centaure / Kobal (t). **156 Bridgeman**

Images: From the British Library archive. **157 Complete Works of Edgar Allan Poe** 10 Vol. Limited Ed. 1902 Fred De Fau & Co., NY, 1902. **158 Bridgeman Images:** Leonard de Selva. **159 John Coulthart. 160 Alamy Stock Photo:** Element Pictures / Album (b); The Picture Art Collection (tl). **161 Bridgeman Images:** Everett Collection. **162 Alamy Stock Photo:** Chronicle (bc); Science History Images (t); Classic Collection (bl); The History Collection (fbl). **163 Bridgeman Images:** © DreamWorks / Everett Collection (b); From the British Library archive (t). **164 Bridgeman Images:** Archives Charmet. **165 The Metropolitan Museum of Art:** Harris Brisbane Dick Fund, 1928. **166 Bridgeman Images:** AF Fotografie. **167 Alamy Stock Photo:** Allstar Picture Library Ltd (bl). **Bridgeman Images:** Art Institute of Chicago / Gift of Ivan Albright (r). **168 Alamy Stock Photo:** Lebrecht Music & Arts (b). **Bridgeman Images:** Giovanni Coruzzi (t). **169 Getty Images:** Xavi Torrent. **170 The Art Institute of Chicago:** Clarence Buckingham Collection (br). **Bridgeman Images:** Pictures from History (l). **171 ©The Trustees of the British Museum. All rights reserved**. **172-173 Bridgeman Images:** National Museum of Asian Art, Smithsonian Institution, The Pearl and Seymour Moskowitz Collection. **174 Alamy Stock Photo:** Artepics (b). **© National Museum of Ireland** (t). **175 Getty Images:** Kirn Vintage Stock. **176 National Gallery Of Australia, Canberra:** Gift of American Friends of the National Gallery of Australia, Inc., New York, NY, USA, made possible with the generous support of Mr and Mrs Benno Schmidt of New York and Esperance, Western Australia, 1987 / © Russell Drysdale / Copyright Agency. Licensed by DACS 2026. **177 Alamy Stock Photo:** Album (b). **Queensland Art Gallery, Gallery of Modern Art (QAGOMA):** Purchased 1998 with funds raised through The Conrad Martens Queensland Art Gallery Foundation Appeal and with the assistance of the Queensland Government's special Centenary Fund (t). **178 John Coulthart. 179 Bridgeman Images:** © Jonathan Barry. All Rights Reserved 2025 / Bridgeman Images (b); Fototeca Gilardi (t). **180 Alamy Stock Photo:** Andrew Hasson (b). **Coffee House Press:** Design by Zoe Norvell (t). **181 Alamy Stock Photo:** Album. **182 Alamy Stock Photo:** Diana J. / Stockimo. **183 Alamy Stock Photo:** Science History Images (b). **Wellcome Collection:** (t). **184 Science Photo Library:** Kateryna Kon. **185 Alamy Stock Photo:** Trinity Mirror / Mirrorpix (t). **Archives of the History of American Psychology, The University of Akron:** (b). **186-187 Andrés Baldursson:** Dystopia Haunted House, Denmark. **188-189 Bibliothèque nationale de France, Paris. 190-191 Freepik:** kues1 (background). **192 Alamy Stock Photo:** sjbooks / Cover from The Penguin Complete Ghost Stories of M.R. James published by Penguin General. Reprinted by permission of Penguin Books Limited (t). **192-193 Alamy Stock Photo:** Claudia Gannon (b). **193 Alamy Stock Photo:** TCD / Prod.DB (t). **194 The Mask of Cthulhu by August Derleth**. Published by Arkham House, 1958 © Arkham House (tr). **Dave McKean:** Image first published in House on the Borderland edition published by Conversation Tree Press (b). **Out of Space and Time by Clark Ashton Smith.** Published by Arkham House, 1942 © Arkham House. Photo Nate D Saunders (tc). **195 Alamy Stock Photo:** Collection Christophel. **196-197 Alamy Stock Photo:** Album. **198 Richard A. Kirk. 199 Heritage Auctions:** © Estate of Michael Ayrton. **200 Alamy Stock Photo:** FlixPix. **201 Bridgeman Images/**© ADAGP, Paris and DACS, London 2026. **202 Getty Images:** John Kobal Foundation / Decla-Film. **203 Alamy Stock Photo:** BFA / Nero-Film AG. **204 Bridgeman Images:** Diltz. **205 Alamy Stock Photo:** Allstar Picture Library Limited (bc). **Getty Images:** Fabian Cevallos / Sygma (r). **206 Brown University Library:** Howard P. Lovecraft collection / Brown Digital Repository (bc). **207 Getty Images / iStock:** Wachirawit Thongrong. **208 Alamy Stock Photo:** Allstar Picture Library Limited (l). **Shutterstock.com:** Universal / Kobal (t). **209 Alamy Stock Photo:** Album (b); photo-fox (t). **210 Alamy Stock Photo:** Archive PL (l). **Getty Images:** Photo12 / Universal Images Group (r). **211 Getty Images:** Bettmann (t); CBS (b). **212 Shutterstock.com:** THA. **213 Alamy Stock Photo:** Moviestore Collection Ltd. **214 Alamy Stock Photo:** Associated Press (t). **Getty Images:** Buyenlarge (b). **215 Alamy Stock Photo:** Retro AdArchives (r). **American Comics Group, Fall 1948** (l). **216 Photography by Marc Quinn Studio. Courtesy the artist. 217 Alamy Stock Photo:** Associated Press / © Jake and Dinos Chapman. All Rights Reserved, DACS 2026 (b). **Bridgeman Images:** © The Estate of Francis

Bacon. All rights reserved. DACS 2026 (t). **218-219 Alamy Stock Photo:** Album / © Salvador Dali, Fundació Gala-Salvador Dalí, DACS 2026. **220 Alamy Stock Photo:** Everett Collection Inc. **221 Alamy Stock Photo:** AJ Pics (t); Everett Collection Inc (b). **222 Alamy Stock Photo:** Studiocanal Films Ltd (l). **222-223 Alamy Stock Photo:** RGR Collection (c). **223 Alamy Stock Photo:** RGR Collection (br). **225 Alamy Stock Photo:** Moviestore Collection Ltd (r); Bill Waterson (l). **226 Alamy Stock Photo:** TCD / Prod.DB. **227 Alamy Stock Photo:** Everett Collection Inc. **228 Getty Images:** Bettmann. **229 Alamy Stock Photo:** Peggy Baker (b). **Getty Images:** CBS Photo Archive (t). **230 Alamy Stock Photo:** BFA (bl). **230-231 Alamy Stock Photo:** AJ Pics (t). **231 Shutterstock.com:** FoxSearch / Everett (br). **232 Alamy Stock Photo:** The Picture Art Collection. **233 Alamy Stock Photo:** AJ Pics (b); Album (t). **234-235 Alamy Stock Photo:** Atlaspix. **236 Alamy Stock Photo:** PictureLux / The Hollywood Archive (b); TCD / Prod.DB (t). **237 Alamy Stock Photo:** AJ Pics. **238 Alamy Stock Photo:** Photo 12 (b). **© Scholastic Inc.:** (cl). **239 Alamy Stock Photo:** FlixPix. **240-241 Freepik:** kues1 (background). **242 Alamy Stock Photo:** Album (t); Landmark Media (b). **243 Alamy Stock Photo:** Album. **244 Alamy Stock Photo:** RGR Collection. **245 Alamy Stock Photo:** Maximum Film (b); TCD / Prod.DB (t). **246-247 Alamy Stock Photo:** Album. **248 Alamy Stock Photo:** TCD / Prod.DB. **249 Alamy Stock Photo:** Everett Collection Inc (r, l). **250 BFA Imaging:** Artisan Entertainment (t). **Bridgeman Images:** Everett Collection (b). **251 Alamy Stock Photo:** TCD / Prod.DB. **252 Alamy Stock Photo:** Maximum Film. **253 Alamy Stock Photo:** Pictorial Press Ltd (b); XYZ Films / Courtesy Everett Collection (c). **254 Alamy Stock Photo:** Allstar Picture Library Limited. **255 Alamy Stock Photo:** Moviestore Collection Ltd (b); Pictorial Press Ltd (t). **256-257 Alamy Stock Photo:** Allstar Picture Library Limited (b). **257 Alamy Stock Photo:** Everett Collection Inc (t). **258-259 Alamy Stock Photo:** TCD / Prod.DB. **260 Alamy Stock Photo:** PictureLux / The Hollywood Archive. **261 Alamy Stock Photo:** FlixPix. **262 Shutterstock.com:** New Line / Kobal. **263 Alamy Stock Photo:** AJ Pics. **264-265 Alamy Stock Photo:** TCD / Prod.DB. **266 Alamy Stock Photo:** Entertainment Pictures. **267 Alamy Stock Photo:** TCD / Prod.DB (t). **New English Library:** James Herbert, The Rats, 1974 (b). **268 Shutterstock.com:** Omega / Kadokawa / Kobal. **269 Alamy Stock Photo:** AJ Pics. **270 Shutterstock.com:** Focus / Kobal (t). **270-271 Alamy Stock Photo:** TCD / Prod.DB (b). **272-273 Getty Images:** CBS Photo Archive. **274 Alamy Stock Photo:** TCD / Prod.DB (b). **Titan Publishing Group Limited:** Cover design by Julia Lloyd. Images © Shutterstock (t). **275 Alamy Stock Photo:** Everett Collection Inc. **276 Alamy Stock Photo:** AJ Pics (t); Cinematic (b). **277 Alamy Stock Photo:** Landmark Media. **278 Alamy Stock Photo:** ArcadeImages. **279 Alamy Stock Photo:** ArcadeImages. **280 Getty Images:** Allen J. Schaben (tl). **280-281 Alamy Stock Photo:** Album (c). **281 Shutterstock.com:** Cafera13 (r). **282 Alamy Stock Photo:** Photo 12. **283 Shutterstock.com:** Moviestore. **284-285 Visual Icon:** Saw X courtesy of Lions Gate Films Inc. **286-287 Alamy Stock Photo:** Moviestore Collection Ltd (tc). **287 Alamy Stock Photo:** Moviestore Collection Ltd (b). **288 Alamy Stock Photo:** ZUMA Press, Inc. (b). **Nick Hern Books:** (t). **289 Steve Forrest/Workers Photos**. **290 Alamy Stock Photo:** Pictorial Press Ltd. **291 Alamy Stock Photo:** BFA (tr); Cinematic (b). **292 Alamy Stock Photo:** Lifestyle pictures (b). **Shutterstock.com:** Film4 / Filmnation / Jw / Kobal (t). **293 Alamy Stock Photo:** TCD / Prod. DB. **294 Alamy Stock Photo:** Landmark Media. **295 Alamy Stock Photo:** Album (b); Collection Christophel (t). **296 Alamy Stock Photo:** Album. **297 Alamy Stock Photo:** Album (t); Moviestore Collection Ltd (b). **298 BFA Imaging:** Altitude Film Distribution. **299 Alamy Stock Photo:** TCD / Prod.DB (t). **BFA Imaging:** RLJE Films (b). **300 AF Fotografie:** Blond & Briggs, London, 1971 (fbr); Secker & Warburg, 1949 (fbl); Coward-McCann, New York, 1955 (bl); Viking Press, 1959 (br). **301 AF Fotografie:** Pantheon, 2000 (fbr); Viking, 1986 (fbl); Random House, New York, 1985 (bl); St. Martin's, New York, 1988 (br). **302 Alamy Stock Photo:** Blue Robin Collectables (bc); TCD / Prod.DB (bl); TCD / Prod.DB (br). **303 Alamy Stock Photo:** Landmark Media (bl); TCD / Prod.DB (bc); TCD / Prod.DB (br)

Cover illustration and printed edges: Dorling Kindersley: Justin Kamerer, Angryblue

DK LONDON

Senior art editor Jane Ewart
Designers Judy Caley, James Pople
Senior editor Victoria Heyworth-Dunne
Editors Anna Cheifetz, Abigail Mitchell,
Dorothy Stannard, Andy Szudek
Picture researchers Sarah Smithies, Jo Walton
Picture research manager Martin Copeland
Production editor Robert Dunn
Senior production controller Laura Andrews
Managing editor Gareth Jones
Managing art editor Luke Griffin
Art director Maxine Pedliham
Design director Phil Ormerod
Publishing director Georgina Dee

DK DELHI

Pre-production image manager Pankaj Sharma
Pre-production image coordinator Neeraj Bhatia
Project jacket designer Juhi Sheth
Senior jacket designer Suhita Dharamjit
Senior DTP designer Harish Aggarwal
Senior jackets coordinator Priyanka Sharma Saddi

Cover illustration and printed edges by
Justin Kamerer, Angryblue

SANDS PUBLISHING SOLUTIONS LLP
Design partner Simon Murrell
Editorial partners David & Sylvia Tombesi-Walton

First published in Great Britain in 2026 by
Dorling Kindersley Limited
20 Vauxhall Bridge Road, London SW1V 2SA

The authorized representative in the EEA is
Dorling Kindersley Verlag GmbH
Arnulfstr. 124, 80636 Munich, Germany

Copyright © 2026 Dorling Kindersley Limited
A Penguin Random House Company
10 9 8 7 6 5 4 3 2 1
001–354885–April/2026

All rights reserved.
No part of this publication may be reproduced, stored in or introduced into a retrieval system, or transmitted, in any form, or by any means (electronic, mechanical, photocopying, recording, or otherwise), without the prior written permission of the copyright owner. DK values and supports copyright. Thank you for respecting intellectual property laws by not reproducing, scanning or distributing any part of this publication by any means without permission. By purchasing an authorised edition, you are supporting writers and artists and enabling DK to continue to publish books that inform and inspire readers. No part of this publication may be used or reproduced in any manner for the purpose of training artificial intelligence technologies or systems. In accordance with Article 4(3) of the DSM Directive 2019/790, DK expressly reserves this work from the text and data mining exception.

A CIP catalogue record for this book is available from the British Library.
ISBN: 978-0-2417-7744-2
Printed and bound in China
www.dk.com